Religion and the Environment

How does religion relate to our global environment? *Religion and the Environment* provides a comprehensive and accessible introduction to this controversial question by covering the following important themes:

- the religion–environment interface
- pre- and post-industrial religious practices related to resource extraction and the rise of the Anthropocene
- an analysis of religious response to the impacts of contemporary industrialization, globalization, and urbanization
- religious thought, leadership, policy formation, and grassroots activism relative to the environment.

Religion and the Environment will offer students and general readers a sophisticated yet accessible exploration of the relationship between religion and the environment, through case studies ranging from climate change to the impacts of warfare. This engaging book will be an excellent addition to introductory courses and those approaching the topic for the first time.

Susan Power Bratton is Professor and former chair of the Department of Environmental Science at Baylor University, USA.

D1599898

Engaging with Religion

Religion, the Body, and Sexuality
An Introduction
Nina Hoel, Melissa M. Wilcox, and Liz Wilson

Religion and the Environment
An Introduction
Susan Power Bratton

For more information about this series, please visit: https://www.routledge.com/religion/series/EWR

Religion and the Environment

An Introduction

Susan Power Bratton

Routledge
Taylor & Francis Group

LONDON AND NEW YORK

First published 2021
by Routledge
2 Park Square, Milton Park, Abingdon, Oxon OX14 4RN

and by Routledge
52 Vanderbilt Avenue, New York, NY 10017

Routledge is an imprint of the Taylor & Francis Group, an informa business

British Library Cataloguing-in-Publication Data
A catalogue record for this book is available from the British Library

Library of Congress Cataloging-in-Publication Data
Names: Bratton, Susan, author.
Title: Religion and the environment: an introduction / Susan Power Bratton.
Description: Abingdon, Oxon; New York: Routledge, 2021. |
Includes bibliographical references and index. |
Identifiers: LCCN 2020033005 | ISBN 9781138569775 (hardback) |
ISBN 9781138569782 (paperback) | ISBN 9780203702765 (ebook)
Subjects: LCSH: Human ecology—Religious aspects.
Classification: LCC GF80 .B69 2021 | DDC 201/.77—dc23
LC record available at https://lccn.loc.gov/2020033005

ISBN: 978-1-138-56977-5 (hbk)
ISBN: 978-1-138-56978-2 (pbk)
ISBN: 978-0-203-70276-5 (ebk)

Typeset in Bembo
by KnowledgeWorks Global Ltd.

Contents

Figures

Boxes

Abbreviations

4-H	agricultural youth organization, 4H stands for head, heart, hand, and health
AAAS	American Association for the Advancement of Science
AAEC	Association of African Earthkeeping Churches
AIRFA	US American Indian Religious Freedom Act
AME	African Methodist Episcopal Church
BCE	before common era or number of years before the year 1 in the current annual calendar
BINGO	a big international non-governmental organization
BP	years before the present date
C°	centigrade degrees (temperature)
ca	circa (around the date)
CE	common era or since year 1 in the current annual dating system
CFC	chloro-fluoro-carbon
CFFO	Christian Farmers Federation of Ontario Canada
CITES	Convention on Trade in Endangered Species of Wild Flora and Fauna
CREMA	Community Resource Environmental Management Area
DAPL	Dakota Access (petroleum) Pipeline
DDT	the insecticide, dichloro-diphenyl-trichloro-ethylene
DoSER	Dialog on Science, Ethics, and Religion, sponsored by AAAS
EBM	ecosystem-based management
EEN	Evangelical Environmental Network
ENGO	an environmental, non-government organization
EPA	US Environmental Protection Agency
ESA	US Endangered Species Act
FIP	Faith in Place, a Chicago multifaith environmental organization
Four Cs	creed, code, cult, and community
GMO	genetically modified organism
ha	hectares, a metric unit of area
HYV	high yield variety of a cultivated species
IPCC	International Panel on Climate Change
ISIS	(DESH) the Islamic State of Iraq and Syria (or the Levant)
IUCN	International Union for Conservation of Nature
IWC	International Whaling Commission
kg	kilogram
kw	kilowatt

LBGTQ	lesbian, bisexual, gay, transgender, queer
LED	light emitting diode, an energy saving form of electric light
LEED	Leadership in Energy and Environmental Design certification, sponsored by the Green Building Council
m	meter (unit of length)
MMPA	US Marine Mammal Protection Act
MOOC	massive open online course
MOSE	Sperimentale Electromechanico, the mobile floodgates protecting Venice, Italy
MTM	mountain top mining, where removal of the over-burden alters landscapes
NEPA	U.S. National Environmental Protection Act
NOAA	US National Oceanic and Atmospheric Administration, an agency under the U Department of Commerce
OSHA	US Occupational, Health and Safety Administration
PCB	poly-chlorinated-biphenyl, a carcinogenic industrial waste
pH	a measure of alkalinity (high) and acidity (low)
REDD	Reducing Emissions from Deforestation and Forest Degradation
RENGO	a religious, environmental non-governmental organization
TVA	Tennessee Valley Authority, US water and energy management agency
UN	United Nations
UNEP	United Nations Environmental Program
UNESCO	United Nations Educational, Scientific, and Cultural Organization
USFS	United States Forest Service under the US Department of Agriculture
WCC	World Council of Churches

Acknowledgments

Many people deserve my gratitude for their assistance in bringing this endeavor to fruition. I am especially thankful for the support of Virginia Humanities and Jeanne Siler during a fellowship in Charlottesville, Virginia (with the primary project on the Appalachians), and the College of Arts and Sciences of Baylor University, who funded a research leave. Both institutions encourage bridging the sciences and the humanities. Colleen Peters, Lynne Baker, and Mypower UK graciously provided photographs of sites I could not reach. Julie King and Rita Cantú read early drafts and along with anonymous reviewers contributed helpful comments. Multiple religious communities extended a welcome when I undertook short visits. The insightful and pragmatic research conducted by the current generation of scholars made my task far more fulfilling. The editors from Routledge, Amy Doffegnies and Rebecca Shillabeer, have speedily addressed my inquiries and offered timely advice.

1 Introduction

Religion, social action, and the environment

Key concepts

1 The controversy at Standing Rock concerned Native American concepts of sacred ground, Native American water rights, and protection of water quality.
2 Religion has four interactive components or the four Cs: Creed, code, cult, and community. Religion may be ordinary, setting the norms for daily life, or extraordinary, exploring human existence transcending the constraints of the material.
3 Religious engagement with the environment locates religion in the public sphere and generates dialog among faith, science, and public policy.
4 Religions are addressing environmental issues and incorporating environmental concepts, such as sustainability, into their values. Conversely, environmental change is affecting the four Cs.
5 Marginalized, minority, and indigenous groups often actualize environmental leadership through grassroots activism. They utilize religious symbols and concepts to build solidarity and to focus public attention on specific issues.
6 Contemporary environmental issues are often national or global in scale, prompting multireligious engagement.

An environmental scenario: Blocking a pipeline

In December 2016, as winter storms blew into North Dakota, the US federal government ordered hundreds of people living in tepees and temporary shelters in the Oceti Sakowin (Seven Council Fires) Camp to leave in the face of plummeting temperatures. A few days prior, the state governor had declared the portable housing unsuitable for winter habitation and in violation of building safety codes. Occupying several makeshift villages on the Standing Rock Reservation and US Army Corps of Engineers land, a mix of Standing Rock Sioux, Native American rights advocates, and environmental activists were blocking the proposed easement for the Dakota Access Pipeline (DAPL). Funded by Energy Transfer Partners, the $3.7 billion project would transport crude petroleum interstate from North Dakota's Bakken field oil wells to Illinois refineries. The months-long resistance movement had stoically reiterated concerns that a future pipeline rupture, at the confluence of Missouri and Cannonball Rivers, would threaten the water resources of the Sioux. Digging through the prairies and bluffs disturbed sacred sites and burial grounds dating back to 15,000 years (Medina 2016 a,b; Erbentraut 2016; Estes and Dhillon 2019).

The self-identified water protectors of the #NoDAPL movement had garnered national and international support. The "Front Line" village displayed more than 350 flags of Native American Nations above the accumulating snow. Members of such far-flung tribes as the Tlingit of the Pacific Northwest coast had brought sleeping bags and portable heaters to help them survive the rugged conditions. As a symbol of shared community, a sacred fire burned day and night in Oceti Sakowin. Signs hung at the entrance proclaimed *Mni Wiconi*—"Water is Life." In addition to the two to three thousand water protectors at the confluence, *The Huffington Post* reported 1.6 million Facebook supporters "checking-in" in solidarity. Smaller groups had been holding demonstrations in other regions. At a four-mile march in downtown Phoenix, Arizona, a Navajo participant reiterated the "need to protect water for the children and for the future" (Erbentraut 2016; Mitchell 2016; Estes and Dhillon 2019).

Aside from the on-going faceoffs with regulatory authorities and law enforcement resulting in more than 400 arrests, the Standing Rock Sioux filed a motion for an injunction against the Corps of Engineers permit, allowing the pipeline to cross federally regulated waters along its 1172-mile length. Meanwhile, not all North Dakota voters concurred with the Sioux over the disruption of DAPL completion. A recent fall in petroleum prices had caused job lay-offs in the oil fields. The information website posted by Energy Transfer Partners (2016) stated that aside from providing a cost-effective means of domestic energy production, pipeline construction would generate 8,000 to 12,000 local jobs.

Shortly after they ordered the December 2016 eviction, the Army Corps changed their minds. The Corps temporarily denied the permit necessary to excavate the pipeline's subsurface path under Lake Oaha, to allow evaluation of a proposed reroute. Energy Transfer Partners, in turn, called the decision "purely political." They released a statement accusing the Obama administration of abandoning "the rule of law" and of "currying favor with a narrow and extreme political constituency" (Medina and Sottile 2016).

In many ways, the DAPL standoff was a microcosm of contemporary environmental controversies. Although DAPL is a regional development project pitting corporate planning against local landholders, DAPL has global implications. Extending into Canada, North Dakota's Bakken oil field utilizes **hydraulic fracking**, or the injection of water into active wells to extract petroleum. Via seepage and spills, the wastewater from fracking transports contaminants into groundwater and streams. Inventorying over 3,900 fracking-related spills by 2015, scientific investigations documented soil contamination by radioactive selenium and high levels of salts, ammonium, and other toxins in Bakken wastewater. One massive fracking-based pipeline leak allowed over a million gallons of brine to flow into Lake Sakakawea, just upstream from a drinking water intake (Duke University 2016; Lauer et al. 2016).

Recent geological research has verified the connection between injecting fracking wastewater into disposal wells and an increased frequency of earthquakes. By 2016, the US Geological Survey had measured fracking-generated quakes in Oklahoma at magnitudes as high 5.8 on the Richter scale, which is more than enough to close businesses, shift residences on their foundations, and destabilize roads and bridges (Wethe and Sachetta 2016). From a global perspective, the crowning concern is that fossil fuel combustion contributes to air pollution, global climate change, and ocean acidification. DAPL supports energy consumption strategies tapping nonrenewable sources, thereby stoking the US contribution to rising levels of **greenhouse gases**—the greatest of any nation.

Religion and DAPL

Religion played a prominent role at the interface of the scientific and policy issues emerging at Standing Rock. Although the original route for the DAPL did not cross the Standing Rock Reservation, sacred stones and other unexcavated religious artifacts stood in the path of DAPL construction crews. The Lakota Sioux had once counted adjoining properties now supervised by the Army Corps of Engineers within their territory. The Crops had evicted the Sioux in order to construct the Oahe Dam and flood Sioux land (Estes and Dhillon 2019). In September 2016, DAPL pipeline crews used bulldozers to clear a two-mile swath and disturbed or unearthed 82 cultural sites and 27 Native American burials in the process. In October, a crew uncovered a cultural site, then delayed for 10 days before reporting it to the North Dakota Public Service Commission as the permitting agency (Gilio-Whitaker 2019: 131). The Standing Rock Sioux Tribe's (2016) motion for a preliminary injunction claimed the Sioux nation would be irreparably harmed, as DAPL "crosses the Tribe's ancestral lands, and traverses landscapes that are sacred to the Tribe and carry great historical significance." The Sioux invoked the National Historic Preservation Act, which requires federal agencies to consult with affected tribes before authorizing projects that would disturb sites of "religious and cultural significance" even if the sites are on ceded ancestral lands.

As plaintiffs, the Sioux (2016) also invoked The Clean Water Act and The Rivers and Harbors Act. Their motion expressed concerns for the:

> …risk of harm to the Missouri River, which is central to the culture, religion, and economy of Tribe, and because of the sacredness of the landscapes across which DAPL would traverse…In particular, the confluence of the Cannonball and Missouri Rivers, the site chosen by DAPL for the pipeline's crossing of the Missouri at Lake Oaha, is sacred ground to the Standing Rock Sioux.

Their filing went a step further in stating: "Water is sacred to the Standing Rock people, as is the Missouri River itself." Crude oil spills pose "an **existential threat** to the Tribe." A federal judge did not accept the arguments and denied the injunction in September 2016, resulting in renewed action on the part of the protesters. In response, the Army Corps and Department of Interior temporarily halted DAPL construction 20 miles short of Lake Oaha, pending further federal review (Erbentraut 2016).

Participants in the DAPL controversy appealed to three oft conflicted strategies for environmental planning: Optimal economic growth, conservation, and preservation. Planning for economic growth focuses on goals incorporating job creation, raising corporate incomes, growing new businesses, and making raw materials less expensive and more accessible. **Conservation** balances financial income with ensuring the productivity of farms, forests, and rivers for future generations. This environmental philosophy plans to prevent erosion, pollution, and unnecessary loss or degradation of natural resources. Conservation seeks the common good or the optimal benefit for the greatest number of people. **Preservation** holds that selected areas and resources should remain relatively undisturbed or undeveloped, including exemplars of undeveloped **natural ecosystems** and habitats supporting exceptional **species diversity**. Preservation also applies to cultural structures or landscapes of outstanding value. As later chapters will outline, all three strategies have religious roots or associations.

The DAPL controversy as religiously diverse

The Standing Rock Sioux's insistence that corporate developers honor their religious beliefs may superficially appear provincial and anti-scientific, yet their concern about spills has scientific support. Most North Dakota voters welcoming DAPL are of European heritage, and if they have a religious preference, it is likely to be Christian. Treating the role of religion at Standing Rock as indigenous religions versus the Christian mainstream is, however, as unjustified as considering the controversy to be a battle between religion and science. Many members of the Native American Nations supporting the water protectors self-identify as Christian. The Standing Rock Reservation has Christian congregations within its boundaries.

On November 3, 2016, over 500 clergy and laity from 20 faiths walked together to form a circle around the sacred fire in the Oceti Sakowin Camp. Episcopal, Presbyterian, Lutheran, and Baptist ministers publicly testified that their denominations had officially repudiated the 15th-century Doctrine of Discovery, awarding Christian explorers the right to claim the lands they entered in the Americas. The ministers asked the Sioux elders to burn a copy of the Doctrine—a form of ritual cleansing. The elders ignited fragments of the Doctrine in pots near the sacred fire rather than by placing the disruptive document in the sacred fire itself (Wilson 2016). Fueled by wood, sage, tobacco, and other natural combustibles, sacred fires are a key ritual element in indigenous American religions. Throwing paper or other manufactured materials, like cigarette butts into a sacred fire, violates its purity.

In encouraging his fellow Episcopalians to support the Sioux, Rev. John Floberg called solidarity as a "powerful opportunity to exercise our shared baptismal ministry." Floberg identified the passing of the peace around the sacred fire as a Niobrara Circle—a combination of Christian and Sioux symbolism (Wilson 2016) (Box 1.1). To add to the diversity of perspectives at Standing Rock, the environmental advocates and Facebook followers who joined forces with the Sioux originated from a variety of faith backgrounds, including east Asian religions and the **new or alternative religions**. The belief systems categorized as New Age or metaphysical, for example, have spread in industrialized countries as alternatives to both Christianity and the flaws of technology-driven culture.

Although diverse, Standing Rock was not a religious free-for-all. Conflicts did sometimes arise when non-Native Americans refused to camp where they were assigned, avoided chores, or interfered with the daily water ceremony. The Lakota staff insisted that non-Native Americans residing in one of the encampments respect Sioux religious practice

---

Box 1.1 Niobrara Circle origins

The first Christian missionaries forced Sioux converts to give up all symbols and objects associated with their Plains religious heritage. A more recently instituted annual gathering, the Niobrara Convention, conducts Christian services using Sioux language, dress, symbols, and drumming, thereby acting as a ritual recovery of Sioux culture and ancestry. During noon prayers with sage burning, clergy unroll a buffalo robe painted with 72 pictographs depicting the life of Jesus as recounted in the Gospel of Luke. The robe is in the tradition of the Winter Count, a ceremony honoring important events and people in the history of the Tribe. The Niobrara Circle combines Christian and Sioux ritual and symbols. Not all Native Americans, however, condone synthesizing their traditions with Christian ritual.

Source: Schjonberg (2012)

by not taking over ceremonial spaces, not attempting to lead rituals, and not taking photos as souvenirs. Organizers conducted orientation sessions emphasizing **decolonization** for new arrivals. For Native Americans, outsiders appropriating or exploiting their rites and spiritual experiences violate their sovereignty. The corporation building DAPL was similarly extracting resources and damaging sacred spaces without permission (Oster 2017).

Religion and environment in the public sphere

A quick, news bite view of Standing Rock can lead to a false conclusion—that religion inherently promotes division at the interface of politics and science. Media reporting favors religion's immediate consequences and most dramatic expressions, rather than pervasive day-to-day activities and the beliefs of ordinary people. Repeated front-page coverage of religious extremism reinforces the notion that highly-committed religious groups are disruptive of societal progress and economic health. Aside from playing a role in controversies, the interface of religion with the environment incorporates a range of strategies from individual ethical commitments and environmentally conscious lifestyles, to programs advocating global change. Much of the environmental activity of the Native American Nations, for instance, concerns planning for tribal lands and improvements in economically critical natural resource management. Ordinarily, Sioux initiatives for protecting water quality would not draw camera crews and reporters.

Participants in the DAPL protests have not been the only people to connect their faith with the environmental future of the American Midwest. Religious institutions around the Great Plains invest in environmentally conscious infrastructure and plan for **sustainability** (Box 1.2). When the Jewish Reconstructionist Synagogue in Evanston, Illinois, renovated their building complex, they decided to add water and energy-saving features and to participate in **LEED certification** (Leadership in Energy and Environmental Design), supervised by the US Green Building Council. They became

---

Box 1.2 Defining environmental sustainability

The practice of sustainability is based on the concept that humanity should not deplete or unnecessarily damage the natural resources on which we depend. Logging operations, for example, should not degrade forest soils or inhibit reproduction of tree seedlings. Manufacturing processes should not generate toxic pollution of air or waters or excessive waste. The products should be fully useable or **recyclable**, and not end up as mountains of garbage. Contemporary sustainability emphasizes **product life cycle**, where the negative impacts of manufacturing processes are minimal. When an item finally wears out, it can either be **reused, restored, or recycled**.

Mining fossil fuels like coal to produce electricity is considered unsustainable as coal beds were deposited in ancient swamps, and reserves are currently being depleted. Coal-fired power plants produce carbon dioxide, a greenhouse gas accelerating global climate change, and release **contaminants** such as sulfur and mercury into the atmosphere. Energy generated by wind turbines is sustainable, as the source is not depleted, and does not generate chemical pollution. The sustainability movement recognizes that technology and industrialization have steep environmental and societal costs. One of their mottos is "There is no such thing as a free lunch."

Source: Caradonna (2014)

the first US Jewish congregation to achieve a Platinum Certification, the highest level, in 2008. According to Carole Caplan, a past president of the Reconstructionist board: "We studied what our values are [concerning] environmentalism and the earth, and we were able to decide how to put that into action." The synagogue board did struggle with the additional initial costs, and then voted "to build as green as feasible." The congregation has initiated a lay-led task force to "work with the membership on living sustainably," and offered tours of their LEED building to guide other property owners in adopting environmentally friendly practices (Spiro 2011). Across the same region fermenting the DAPL controversy, municipalities have welcomed these practical and community-conscious sustainability projects—often with only passing recognition.

Defining religion

In analyzing the role of religion in environmental decision making, questions arise about exactly what religion is and how it functions. While religion does encompass what people believe about deities, it is notoriously difficult to characterize. The word "sacred," for example, has multiple meanings, including its definition relative to the US federal courts. Religion has **ordinary** aspects, setting the norms for daily life and providing a matrix of symbols pointing to the keystones of existence. Ordinary religion is often **implicit religion**, embedded within material and social culture. People experience ordinary religion when they pass crosses marking graves, celebrate seasonal holidays, or say a prayer before a soccer match. The environmental values of ordinary religion are often overlooked. An unassuming Islamic cemetery protecting older trees in a densely populated city is an excellent urban wildlife habitat (Fig. 1.1).

Figure 1.1 A historic Islamic cemetery in Kampong Glam, Singapore, as an example of ordinary religion. Unlike the mosques nearby, this unassuming religioscape is not a major stop for tourists. The **aniconic** markers (no representational images) and lack of formal landscaping encourage the retention of clusters of native trees, enhancing urban wildlife habitat in a densely developed neighborhood.

Engaging the supernatural, **extraordinary religion** utilizes specialized language and narratives to reach beyond the usual boundaries of human society and to explore human existence transcending the constraints of the material. Religious mystical and prophetic experiences, as well as beliefs concerning the afterlife and spiritual beings, actualize extraordinary religion (Albanese 2013: 5–6). Rather than being too ethereal to be environmentally relevant, extraordinary religion invokes natural imagery or offers explanations for the organization of the cosmos. The concept of Paradise as a lush and well-watered garden, for example, promises a diverse and beautiful living landscape as the outcome of a righteous life.

American religious historian Catherine Albanese (2013: 7–9) has defined religion as comprised of four interactive components or **the four Cs: Creed, code, cult, and community**. **Creeds** are the core or central beliefs about human meaning and role in the universe. From an environmental perspective, creeds include cosmologies and origin stories, which in turn convey environmental values and model human relationships to the nonhuman. **Codes** are the rules for behavior, including norms for such environmentally important matters as treatment of animals, disposal of human waste, care of rivers, and the management of material wealth. Codes are embedded in ethical systems, customs, taboos, or shared social norms. **Cult** emerges through rituals and ceremonies, as well as sacred spaces and objects. This aesthetically rich aspect of religion provides a symbolic bridge to landscapes, seascapes, and natural processes. The Sioux conduct rituals and deem certain behaviors appropriate or inappropriate relative to the sacred fire and sacred sites, thereby linking cult with code. Religious buildings and monuments are common cult features and can be vulnerable to environmental changes like sea-level rise (Fig. 1.2). **Communities** share the symbol systems formed by creed, code, and cult.

Figure 1.2 An historic Hawaiian heiau (temple) on Kona, Hawai'i, is very vulnerable to climate change and sea level rise. The thatched building and wood carvings are reconstructions and can be moved; the stone wall on the left is historic and cannot be easily relocated nor can the sacred fishponds nearby.

Proponents of field study examine how religion operates in everyday circumstances. Robert Orsi's (1997) investigation of **lived religion** focuses on what people do and how they act, rather than undertaking an abstract analysis of creeds alone. The Evanston Reconstructionist Synagogue reported that they had studied Jewish values concerning the earth (theory), and then came up with a plan for community action (practice). The terms spiritual and spirituality frequently arise relative to human–earth relationships. Spirituality may imply a search for personal meaning and connection with a greater-other outside the self. For world religions, spirituality concerns the pursuit of practices and disciplines such as prayer or contemplation. Buddhists achieve enlightenment following the Eight-Fold Path. For Christians, the goal of spiritual formation is to become more like Christ in their thoughts and actions.

Religious pluralism

The sociological aspects of faith demonstrate its indefinite boundaries. The religious and the secular are, as is the case with DAPL, often intertwined and indistinct from each other. Introductory textbooks covering world religions usually divide faiths into clear categories defined by geography and ethnic composition. The Niobrara Circle, however, intentionally synthesizes or **syncretizes** two traditions. Religion is dynamic and responds to cultural trends, including the contemporary environmental movement.

From an environmental perspective, regional or indigenous religions have evolved in concert with the natural processes and biota dominant within a geographic area. They thus reflect bioregional economies, like the migratory hunting of the Sioux. The world religions are more populous and geographically dispersed. Hinduism first emerged on the Indian subcontinent, yet trading, conquest, and migration transported it first into Southeast Asia, and then worldwide. Festivals originating in south Asia now thrive in Europe and the Americas (Figs. 4.1 and 5.1). The creeds of Christianity, Islam, and Buddhism encourage cross-cultural recruitment. Missionaries, monastics, and other religious professionals have introduced these faiths into new regions in efforts to glean more followers.

When aligned with political and military authority, world religions often displace or disempower indigenous religions. World religions, however, have many denominations and sects and absorb elements from regional religions. While rooted in Hellenistic Judaism, Christianity's history verifies other influences, including Greco-Roman philosophy, popular cults of the Roman Empire, and Buddhism traveling ancient Asian trade routes. Islam has universally shared theories, such as the centrality of the *Qur'an* and its teachings. Islam also incorporates two major sectarian divisions in Sunni and Shia and numerous regional variants. Some regions of the world have a dominant religion, while others, such as Syria or Kerala State in India, have been home to two or more faiths for many centuries. Today, in global cities such as London and Singapore, **religious pluralism** has become the norm. Post-pluralism, these faiths interact and influence each other, producing new religious movements and ideas (Albanese 2013: 11). The cultural diversity within a world religion makes it difficult to generalize how a global religious tradition values or protects the physical and biotic environment. As has been case concerning DAPL, members of the same faith, denomination, or congregation may take different sides in environmental controversies.

In the academic study of religion and the environment, the religious background and point of view of an author are essential considerations, especially when validating claims of expertise or association with a constituency. Academics who study world religions are not necessarily adherents of the faiths they investigate. While this can lead to greater objectivity, the scholar is also an outsider who might not have access to all ceremonies, councils, and sacred spaces. The personal history of an observer influences his or her interpretation of religious theory and practice. As the modern academic study of world religions arose in the 19th and 20th centuries, many of the field's founding scholars were Christians. They often interpreted other religions relative to Christian creeds and norms, resulting in bias and oversights in their analyses. Different **discourses** about a faith have different emphases and degrees of accuracy. In weighing sources, it is prudent to ask: What is the role of the individual or group cited, what are their presuppositions and perspective, and what stake do they have in the environmental case under consideration?

As Standing Rock demonstrated, global environmental change is precipitating religious change. The primary purpose of this book is to ask why and how religion influences environmental attitudes and the adoption of green practices, like LEED. It conversely asks how the environment affects the four Cs, and how contemporary environmentalism interacts with religious foci, such as cosmology and spirituality. Rather than comparing the environmental philosophies of different religions, this book begins with an overview of how faiths retain information about the natural environment and how they value natural objects and processes. The text then delves into the foundations of human-caused or **anthropogenic** environmental change—via harvest of natural resources, agriculture, and industrialization. The later chapters cover "big picture" global issues, including urbanization, the effects of pollution on human health, and global climate change. This structure accentuates commonalities among religions, and consilience between faith and science. Throughout, religion engages modernity's advances, costs, and stresses. In historic study the modern era emerges at the end of the Middle Ages; in this volume the focus is on the late modern cultural changes beginning circa 1800.

This text seeks out examples of successful faith-based environmental engagement from a variety of traditions, and also examines misguided and flawed responses—often linked to rapid cultural change, intransigent ideologies, or dissonance with a scientific epistemology. Religion and science share the roles of villains, by-standers, and thoughtful reformers. Despite their variety, the case histories explore eight core concepts, all of which were evident at Standing Rock:

1 All religions are inextricably embedded in interdependent ecological networks and human interactions with the environment.
2 For the world's faiths, addressing contemporary environmental issues is inherently an encounter with modernity.
3 Actualizing environmental values draws faith communities into the public sphere and conversations with science.
4 Religions respond to environmental issues within a hierarchy of scales from local, to regional, national, and global.
5 Colonialism, industrialization, and economic globalization have suppressed or undermined religiously based sustainable environmental management in multiple cultural contexts.
6 Minorities, marginalized cultural groups, and the economically disadvantaged bear more of a burden from environmental mismanagement than societal majorities and

the economically advantaged. Contributing to solidarity, religion can provide a platform for pursuing **eco-justice** and resisting the negative impacts of environmental hazards and degradation.

7 Any religion, from indigenous, to world, to alternative, can contribute to environmental care. Different types of religion, however, face different barriers and challenges in environmental problem-solving. Some religious approaches are more effective than others, relative to the socio-political context of a specific issue.

8 Contemporary religiously informed environmental accountability and care require cooperation among people of different faiths and cultural heritages.

The legacy of the water protectors

A week after his inauguration in January 2017, President Donald Trump instructed the US Army Corps of Engineers to release the permits allowing the completion of the DAPL. In June 2017, Trump issued an executive order withdrawing US participation in the 2015 Paris Climate Accord. The story of the DAPL protests, however, does not end with the victory for Energy Transfer Partners. Participants have joined sacred circles and developed new networks. The concept of Native American Nations as water protectors has spread far outside the Dakotas. The Canadian Coastal Salish Water Protectors, for example, protested the expansion of the Kinder-Morgan Trans Mountain Pipeline through British Columbia in 2018. Today's dialogs between religions and the environment are on-going and continually reconstructing their responses to environmental needs.

Suggested readings

Albanese, Catherine. *America: Religion and Religions*. Belmont, CA: Wadsworth Publishing, 2013.

Bohannon, Richard, ed. *Religion and Environments: A Reader in Religion, Nature, and Ecology*. London, U.K.: Bloomsbury Academic, 2014.

Estes, Nick, and Jaskiran Dhillon, eds. *Standing with Standing Rock: Voices from the #NoDAPL Movement*. Minneapolis: University of Minnesota Press, 2019.

Gilio-Whitaker, Dina. *As Long and Grass Grows: The Indigenous Fight for Environmental Justice from Colonization to Standing Rock*. Boston, MA: Beacon Press, 2019.

Gottlieb, Roger. *A Greener Faith: Religious Environmentalism and Our Planet's Future*. Oxford: Oxford University Press, 2009.

Grim, John, and Mary Evelyn Tucker. *Ecology and Religion*. Washington, DC: Island Press, 2014.

Jenkins, Willis, Mary Evelyn Tucker, and John Grim, eds. *The Routledge Handbook of Religion and Ecology*. New York: Routledge, 2016.

Kinsley, David. *Ecology and Religion: Ecological Spirituality in Cross-Cultural Perspective*. New York: Pearson, 1994.

2 Connections

Sacred stories, sacred springs

Key concepts

1 Cosmologies and creation stories describing the origins of humans, life, and the universe reflect regional environmental and cultural contexts.
2 Informed by an array of experiences, religious myth is neither pure invention nor untrue and retains information about human interactions with environmental processes. Myths arise via a process of bricolage, where a society combines available materials or information to solve new problems.
3 Both indigenous and world religions sacralize natural objects, landscapes, and hydroscapes, cultivating greater human respect and facilitating rituals, focused on living organisms and natural features.
4 Colonial depictions of indigenous religions as more primitive than the world religions diminish the humanity and political authority of indigenous communities.
5 Concurrent with the emerging environmental movement in the 1960s, Lynn White Jr. and other historians and philosophers identified the Abrahamic faiths as more anthropocentric than other religions. Critics argued monotheism and the concept of a transcendent god encourage human exceptionalism.
6 The recent academic study of religion and the environment has become more global and multi-religious in focus. Disciplined scholarly analysis considers myths, art, and sacred locales within their historic and bioregional contexts.

Communication and memory

Religion plays diverse and complex roles in human relationships to the planet's ecosystems. In opening an investigation of these interactions, the first step is to examine how religion accomplishes two of its fundamental environmental functions: retaining information about natural processes and valuing the non-human portion of the cosmos. The various aspects of religion contribute to cultural memory and distinguish connections to the landscapes and **hydroscapes** on which humans depend. In cultures where regional religions evolved without writing, the young learn chants and dances depicting natural phenomena. Entire families join planting ceremonies held in conjunction with the onset of seasonal rains. From information-infused pictographs on rocks to magnificent murals and mosaics, religious visual art depicts relationships between the deities, humans, and the biophysical realm. World religions assemble consolidated volumes of wisdom, such as the *Qur'an* and the *Bible*, and amass scholarly libraries. Rabbis, monastics, imams, and other religious professionals elucidate and interpret these documents, as well as translating them into additional languages. As their economic, technological, and political contexts change, religions evolve. Whether embedded in oral or written traditions, religious memory is both a stable anchor and a dynamic point of exchange—subject to revision, synthesis, and adaptation to new social and ecological settings.

This chapter investigates how religious **cosmologies** or stories about the origins and structure of the universe describe natural processes and the relationships of deities to physical reality and humanity. It briefly compares the orally transmitted origin stories of indigenous Polynesian religions to those found in the scriptures of the Abrahamic faiths. After describing the sacralization of natural features and their roles in generating religious experience, it reviews criticisms of religion arising with the environmental movement beginning in the 1960s.

Cosmologies

Religions accumulate a corpus of sacred stories or cosmologies concerning human origins and our role within the universe. For Jews, Christians, and Muslims, the universe originates with a generative act by a creator god. Not all religious cosmologies incorporate a definite beginning and end to time or physical reality. For many traditions, all life emerges from a sexual or unifying act, representing the ecological and geophysical realms. The Hawaiian chant, the *Kumulipo*, for example, describes a pre-existing god and goddess who give birth to each of the islands. They produce one tiny offspring, the coral polyp—the foundation for life. Reef forming corals do biologically begin as a single polyp, which divides into many connected individuals building the branching colonies and coral heads. The corals, in turn, form complex habitats for hundreds of other species. The *Kumulipo* depicts an ascendant order of beings from invertebrates, like starfish, to the upper levels of island food webs, including fish, birds, mammals, and sea turtles. Oceanic and terrestrial ecosystems are not separate but are linked by the crawlers and nibblers, sharing both realms (Beckwith 1970: 57–88). For the Hawaiians, creation is not abstract or distant. Beginning in ankle-deep water and spreading out into the depths, the productive reef is both the source and the ultimate expression of the **biosphere**—the entire living fabric of the earth.

Informed by an array of experiences, myth is neither pure invention nor untrue. Anthropologist Claude Levi-Strauss described the generation of myth as **bricolage**, where a society combines available materials or information to solve new problems. Religious narratives personify or deify natural processes, creating complex characterizations, such as families or hierarchies of gods playing various biophysical roles. Creation accounts merge insights into human relationships with narratives about natural processes. The Hawaiians describe the capricious aspects of volcanism via myths about the goddess Pele. Pele has a lover, Kamapua'a, who can change from a human form to that of a wild boar and other animals and plants. The shape-shifter roots through the forests as a pig, yet he also dictates the protocols for sacrificing hogs and other edible offerings. Initially rejecting this canny suitor, irritated Pele and her family responded to his advances with awing fountains of flame. Kamapua'a sent an army of pigs to invade and conquer Pele's domain, and with the assistance of his oceanic sister, Keliiomakahanaloa, who sent fog and rain, filled Pele's magnificent flaming crater with water (Beckwith 1970: 201–206).

Just as the rainforest ultimately covers cooled magma, Kamapua'a had his way with Pele, and they divided the islands in two. The windward sides receive more seasonal precipitation, and the leeward sides with their local rain-shadow are much drier.

Kamapua'a rules the lush rainforests with their ample food for hogs, and Pele rules the sunny leeward slopes and beaches. The ecologically insightful storyline recognizes the importance of the trade winds and the ability of plants to form a thick forest on what had been barren basalt, producing what scientists term vegetation succession. In parallel with many other creation myths, an embattled courtship symbolizes interactions among opposing natural forces, which are simultaneously destructive and creative.

Religious cosmologies adapt to local environments. In contrast to the tropical Hawaiian archipelago, the islands of New Zealand settled by the Polynesian Māori are temperate and covered with thousands of hectares of forest growing massive trees, like the kauri. The Māori creation story turns inland and features Tāne, the god of the forest. Tāne's parents, Ranginui, the Sky Father, and, Papatūānuka, the Earth Mother, gave birth to multiple deities who became trapped in the narrow space between them. Tāne-Muahuta, Father of the Forest and living creatures, stood up and with immeasurable strength forcibly separated the primordial parents. The divided spouses grieved for each other, and Rangi's tears became the rains feeding the lakes and rivers. In his enthusiasm for growing woodlands, Tāne planted the first trees upside down, with the bare roots in the air. He then pulled up a stout kauri and set the straight trunk upright with the leaves toward the heavens welcoming the birds and insects he had formed. The Māori **pantheon** each maintain a portion of the universal order, thus act as caretakers. Rango-mā-tāne attends to the earth's fertility, while Tangaroa rules the seas and other waters (Reed 2011: 9–12).

In its original cultural settings, religious memory is seldom expressed through words alone but coordinates ritual, performance, costuming, and architecture to create perceptually rich experiences. The Hawaiians performed chants accompanied by sacred *hula* dances at *heiau*, or temples, with views of the sea or volcanic summits (Fig. 1.2). Religions recognize seasonal and celestial changes with extended ritual events. *The Mountain Chant* of the Navahos is the centerpiece of a multi-night ceremony that concludes outdoors within a circular fence of piñon pine branches, erected after sunset. Comprised of over a hundred stanzas, *The Mountain Chant* describes the noisy entre of the downpours as the Thunders singing to regenerate the living vegetation, beautifying the arid southwestern landscape, and sustaining agriculture (Matthews 1884: 459) (Box 2.1).

Box 2.1 *The Navaho Mountain Chant*—Twelfth Song of the Thunder

I   The voice that beautifies the land!
    The voice above,
    The voice of the thunder,
    Within the dark cloud,
    Again and again it sounds,
    The voice that beautifies the land.

II   The voice that beautifies the land!
    The voice below;
    The voice of the grasshopper,
    Among the plants,
    Again and, again it sounds,
    The voice that beautifies the land.

Source: (Matthews 1884: 459)

A unified creator

The Abrahamic faiths, Judaism, Christianity, and Islam, all share narratives from the ancient Hebrew scriptures relating the histories of Abraham, Moses, and other religious founders. All three religions hold God sends angels or divine messengers and calls prophets who convey divine truth. The three faiths differ, however, in their concept of the person or being of God. In the creation account in Genesis, the Spirit moved over the waters in response to God's Word. God saw that the creation was "good," or in Hebrew *tob*, which also means "beautiful." Most Christians believe Jesus Christ was the Son of God and present at the original creation. God is triune, consisting of the Father, the Son, and the Holy Spirit—the Trinity. For Muslims, Allah alone is God.

Many Jews and Christians interpret the creation in Genesis to be *ex nihilo*—from nothing. An unseen God acts to generate matter, energy, and time. Islamic scholar Seyyed Hossein Nasr (1996: 63) nuances the sense of *ex nihilo* and applies it to "the primal archetypal reality before it existentiated through the *fiat lux* [God commanding let there be light] or the Quranic Be! (*kun*)." Kaltner (2011: 48–49) concurs, "there is already some 'thing' or matter to which God is speaking, so it is better to think of this as a transformation or reordering rather than calling something into being out of nothing." In the *Qur'an*, "it is stated that God simply has to speak in order to create something."

A **construct** of Eden or paradise as an environmental ideal is common to all three faiths. Genesis presents God as establishing Adam and Eve in Eden as an earthly locale. While locating God in Heaven, the earliest Hebrew texts provide few descriptive details concerning an afterlife and do not mention a heavenly paradise. Originating within the Roman Empire, early Christianity focused on eternal salvation. The first western churches appropriated pastoral landscape imagery from Roman art to depict the peaceful and virtuous Christian life and afterlife. In a detailed portrait, the *Qur'an* describes paradise as two fruiting gardens where springs flow, associating the Eden with the celestial realms (Suras 11, 37, 55).

The earliest Hebrew texts do not mention Satan or clearly describe hell. Influenced by Babylonian and Greco-Roman religions, Hellenistic Judaism acquired a more embattled view of the interface between the supernatural and earthly realms, where demons could possess animals, spread disease, and cause high winds. Religious historian Elaine Pagels (1995) aligns the increasing importance of fallen angels and cosmic dualism in Jewish literature with the struggles of Jews deciding whether to rebel against the foreign authorities, first under Greek and then under Roman rule. At odds with Roman governance, early Christians enhanced the theme of cosmic warfare with prophecies of an **apocalyptic** series of disasters followed by God's creation of a new earth. The evolving roles of supernatural beings demonstrate that monotheistic cosmologies absorb concepts from polytheistic religions. Beliefs concerning supernatural activity in nature can mirror human political and social structures.

Sacred natural features and living creatures

In addition to explanations of physical existence, honoring or venerating distinctive natural objects, living organisms, and locales is widespread among the world's religions. Among the most common natural features credited with exceptional religious meaning or power are waterfalls, rivers, caves, and exposed mountain peaks. **Animism** is the belief that natural objects have souls or are imbued with supernatural entities or spirits.

Animal spirit guides, sacred groves with resident deities, and healing stones or minerals are thus components of animist rituals. Sacred natural features are not confined to indigenous or ancient religions and assume similar roles for world religions.

The anthropologist Mircea Eliade has highlighted the widespread image of the world trees, representing the productivity of the generative cosmic event. Honored by Māori chants, large kauris still symbolize Tāne's creation of the earth's biota. In China, where potent forest spirits originally inhabited sacred trees, the trees have relocated from the countryside to temple gardens. Devotees circumambulate their stout trunks while saying prayers—a practice connecting them to the life-giving sun. Practitioners of a wide array of faiths, including Shinto, Daoism, Hinduism, and Roman Catholicism, attach **votive offerings** like prayer plaques and pieces of cloth to exceptional trees. Votive offerings are petitions for favors, such as good harvests or healing from an illness, and **ex-votos** symbolize thanks for a petition fulfilled (Fig. 2.1). Hundreds of years old, the massive trees serve as evocative metaphors for longevity and as intermediaries between humans and beneficent natural processes (Altman 1994: 1–70).

Sacred trees and landscape features also originate from historical associations with spiritual leaders. When **Gautama Buddha** left his life as a prince and sought deeper insight into the reasons wrong action and sorrow so infused in human existence, he entered a contemplative phase. Remaining immobile under a canopy of heart-shaped leaves of the **bodhi** or bo tree, the Buddha received enlightenment. According to tradition, a bodhi still stands at a temple in Bodh Gaya, India, at the original spot occupied by the Buddha. More than one antagonist of the Buddha's teachings has destroyed historic trees at Bodh Gaya. Resisting sacrilege and natural stresses, Buddhists continue to replant and regrow fallen bodhi. In warmer climates, Buddhist temples and monasteries plant bodhi in their gardens, where they continue to succor meditation. Devotees

Figure 2.1 Aside from being ritual foci, sacred trees add to the beauty of Asian temple landscapes and perform a practical function by shading buildings and courtyards. An image of Buddha underneath a bodhi wrapped in a red cloth and surrounded by offerings, Thailand.

Figure 2.2 The monkey army battles demons in Hindu cravings from a sacred monkey forest, Indonesia.

Photo: Colleen Peters

pour water at the base, tie strips of cloth on its branches or around the bole, leave votive offerings, or smear ochre (red or orange clay) on the trunk (Fig. 2.1). A frequent subject in Buddhist art, the bodhi symbolizes right practice, right relationship, and acquisition of wisdom (Altman 1994: 11–12, 39–40, 161–199).

Religions award animals a special status, as "ancestors" of human clans, **avatars** of deities, or beings with empowered spirits. Monkeys, for example, are prominent characters in Hindu and Buddhist mythology, where they move easily between the natural and supernatural realms. The Hindu god Hanuman is **therianthropic**, having a monkey's face and a human body. In the *Ramayana,* the king of demons Rawana kidnaps Rama's wife Sita, and it is heroic Hanuman as an incarnation of Shiva who finds her. Hanuman leads a monkey army to victory over treacherous Rawana (Schillaci et al. 2010). In the Chinese Buddhist classic, *Journey to the West*, a monkey becomes a pilgrim. Temple art incorporates monkeys as actors in religious history (Fig. 2.2).

Sacred natural features and religious change

Not all sacred natural features are exclusive to a single faith. Hindus, Buddhists, and Bons all undertake pilgrimages across high-elevation passes to circumambulate Mt. Kailas in Tibet. Hindus approach Kailas not as the mere home of a local deity, but as a manifestation of the great Vishnu. (Johnson and Moran 1989) Migrating peoples and colonizing cultures overlay their religious symbols on a landscape. At Bath, England, the ancient Romans displaced the Celts depositing offerings to the solar goddess Sulis in the thermal springs. Inserting a goddess of their own, the Romans built a temple to syncretized Sulis-Minerva. They transplanted other deities, like Asclepius, Greek demi-god of medicine, who welcomed pilgrims seeking healing at his shrine.

Imperial soldiers from the forts along Hadrian's Wall, separating the Britons from the unruly Picts to the north, placed coins, jewelry, and small altars in Coventina's spring. A Roman water nymph and the concept of ***genius loci*** or the spiritual empowerment of a locale thus moved with the troops to the dangerous frontier. Devotion to the *genius loci* did not, however, slow the Roman establishment of cities, clearing of forests, or conquest of indigenous clans (Rotherham 2012; Bird and Cunliffe 2012).

The meaning and religious practices associated with sacred natural features evolve with cultural change. After Rome abandoned the conquest of Britain, Christians adopted Celtic and Roman sacred waterscapes. The new faith sacralized additional monastery and church wells. Christians named their holy fonts for saints—either those who had personally drawn water from the springs or those, like the Biblical apostles, serving as spiritual patrons. Fearing the wells encouraged devotion to the saints instead of to Christ, leaders of the Protestant Reformation identified the springs as pagan retentions. The iconoclasts banned ritual practices such as well dressing—bringing green branches to the wells on holy days. Attempting to erase and reconstruct religious memory, Puritans were particularly avid in **desacralizing** the countryside. In demolishing sculptures and shrines, Protestant zealots also removed the religious symbols of the old royalist hierarchy (Walsham 2011).

The cultural memory of the wells was deep-rooted, however, and devotions at wells quietly continued in off-the-beaten-track villages. As battling among Christian factions ceased, parishes returned to maintaining these sacred waterscapes. Entrepreneurs commercialized the most prominent healing springs and piped them into enclosed baths. St. Ronan's Well in the Scottish borders acquired a building, a spa clientele, and an appearance in a novel by Sir Walter Scott. In this case, the association with medieval St. Ronan was a 19th-century literary invention. In Victorian Britain, the rise of suburban angst, folklorists, and antiquarians fueled a U.K.-wide search for neglected wells and lost ceremonies, resulting in a wave of historic conservation and recovery of folk religious practices (Cope 2015: 36; Rattue 1995: 132–147).

Lady's Well in Holystone, Northumberland, England, began as a Roman watering tank, acquired associations with Christian saints, and recovered its holy status in the wake of the Reformation. In recognition of its historical importance, Lady's Well is now under the care of the National Trust (2016) (Box 2.2). Another deep-rooted

---

Box 2.2 The History of Lady's Well, Holystone, U.K.

Originally a stone-rimmed watering tank along a Roman road, Lady's Well, Holystone, became associated with the Celtic saint Ninian, who carried the new faith to the Picts beginning in 500 CE. Legend holds that St. Paulinus, a missionary from Rome, used the well to baptize three thousand new converts at Easter 627 CE. No historic written or archeological records verify either saint visiting the well. Augustinians then constructed a nunnery near the site, and changed the name to Lady's Well, in honor of the Virgin Mary. Prior to the Reformation, the well likely had a cross or other sculpture, but no original medieval fixtures remain today. Residents of Holystone reconstructed the walls enclosing the pool in the late 18th century, and, as a snub on the Reformers, transported a 15th-century statue, supposed to be of St. Paulinus, from a church in a nearby town, and placed it in the center of the pool. In the 19th century, villagers moved the statue of St. Paulinus to the edge, replacing him with a concrete solar cross. Villagers still pipe their drinking water from the well.

Source: Durham and Northumberland Counties (2016)

system of belief, co-existing with the cult of the saints, was evident when the author visited Lady's Well in 2016. Someone had laid out a spiral of coins on a small rock table. Local folk ordinarily leave money for the fairies or "little people" who guard such glades, although they may also deposit it to draw the attention of a saint. One county away, visitors to The Cheese Well still leave pieces of cheese to appease the fairies, and thereby ensure safe travel across the moors (Cope 2015: 24). Drawing on a resurgence in interest in Celtic and folk traditions, alternative religions in the British Isles incorporate supernatural **anthropomorphic** (human-form) beings as part of their beliefs, and reconstruct rituals centered on sacred natural features.

Semiotics, the study, and interpretation of a constellation of symbols can provide insights into the cultural meanings of sacred sites and natural objects. The Lady's Well weaves human history into the geology and flora of the aquifer. The aged trees forming a de facto **sacred grove** and water bubbling clear and pure from the earth are reminiscent of the original creative event and eternal replenishment of life. The untainted flow is a metaphor for Christ as living water and the authority of baptism as entry into the afterlife. The transport of the saint's statue and a solar cross to the spring reclaimed religious heritage. Leaving coins is a form of **gift exchange**, where humans return some token of their wealth to the non-human in recognition humanity is not in control of natural forces. The practices of constructing well boxes, fencing the pool, and allowing native vegetation to encircle the spring maintain water quality where livestock are present.

Sacred waters have **restorative** religious functions, "bringing back a sense of order and safety, of tranquility and peace." They are also **transformative**, defining human interactions with the non-human in a **constructive** or life-enhancing way (Albanese 2013:10). Beloved reminders of human dependence on water, the sacred springs of the British Isles have survived Roman imperialism, Puritan desacralization, industrialization, Victorian dramatization, and the advent of the automobile-based tourist trade.

Issue: Indigenous peoples as "children of the forest"

Just as the assumption that sacred natural objects are predominantly a feature of indigenous religions is incorrect, the concept that the so-called "primitive" religions encourage humans to live in harmony with nature has questionable origins. It emerged during the colonial era when European governments annexed much of the Americas, Africa, and Asia. Colonists treated the societies they encountered as part of the environment and thereby freely exploitable. Entrepreneurs attempting to recruit immigrants wrote glowing reports of the natural resources of the "New World" and depicted the stands of timber and fish-rich rivers as if they were the untainted, unoccupied original Eden. In the worst cases, the conquerors identified the inhabitants of their colonies as lacking "the same attributes as those in which the animals were deficient: technology, intelligible language, Christianity." The most arrogant of the invaders referred to non-Europeans as "brutish savages," "filthy animals," and as "having no better predecessors than monkeys" (Thomas 1983: 42). A more favorable, if patronizing stereotype identified the long-established peoples of the wet tropics or the vast American woodlands as "children of the forest." Animals and juveniles, of course, could not legitimately claim property or governance rights, justifying European displacement of indigenous cultures.

Issue: Environmental critique of Christianity

A variant of "primal natural harmony" is the thesis that animists do relatively little harm to forests and savannahs, and innately constrain their hunting and resource harvest, because they respect spirits in nature. The best-known advocate for this position was the historian Lynn White Jr., who proposed the Christian concept of a **transcendent** god, existing external to the natural world, was the root of the environmental crisis emerging in the 1960s. In a 1967 article in *Science*, White examined Christian cosmology and reasoned that Christianity was the most **anthropocentric** or human-focused of religions, as it eliminated guardian spirits resident in trees or springs, thereby reducing fear of initiating anthropogenic disturbance or harvest (Box 2.3). Christianity disregarded the ***genius loci*** and replaced the nymphs and dryads (tree spirits) with a divine-human figure. White's thesis holds that modern science had arisen in Europe and the Americas because Christians were not afraid to manipulate natural objects and were, therefore, free to conduct the experiments underpinning the scientific revolution. Christians had no qualms about damning rivers or loading logs on to railroad cars.

During the 1960s and 1970s, White was not alone in examining western Christian or philosophical culpability for modernity's failures. Historian Roderick Nash (1967) depicted colonial Puritans as fearing the New England wilds and disregarding the virtues of wilderness because they believed dense forests harbored the demonic. Ethicists were asking why Christian values had failed to stop the horrors of World War II, with its atrocities, massive civilian casualties, death camps, and atomic weapons? The soul-searching suggested the West might be entering a post-Christian phase. Environmental philosophers were beginning to dissect western cosmologies, including their pre-Christian foundations like **Platonism**. While not anti-religious per se, the **Deep Ecology movement** disparaged the "shallow ecology" supporting anthropocentric forms of environmentalism. Many scientifically oriented environmentalists avoided or ignored religion in general, in the belief

> **Box 2.3 Lynn White's hypothesis—a selection from "The historic roots of our ecological crisis," *Science* (1967) 1955: 1203–1207**
>
> "Especially in its Western form, Christianity is the most anthropocentric religion the world has seen. As early as the 2nd century both Tertullian and Saint Irenaeus of Lyons were insisting that when God shaped Adam he was foreshadowing the image of the incarnate Christ, the Second Adam. Man shares, in great measure, God's transcendence of nature. Christianity, in absolute contrast to ancient paganism and Asia's religions (except, perhaps, Zoroastrianism), not only established a dualism of man and nature but also insisted that it is God's will that man exploit nature for his proper ends.
>
> At the level of the common people this worked out in an interesting way. In Antiquity every tree, every spring, every stream, every hill had its own genius loci, its guardian spirit. These spirits were accessible to men, but were very unlike men; centaurs, fauns, and mermaids show their ambivalence. Before one cut a tree, mined a mountain, or dammed a brook, it was important to placate the spirit in charge of that particular situation, and to keep it placated. By destroying pagan animism, Christianity made it possible to exploit nature in a mood of indifference to the feelings of natural objects."

Box 2.4 Methodological questions concerning the Lynn White Jr. thesis

Five methodological questions concerning White's reasoning are as follows:

1   To what extent is it appropriate to generalize about a broad cosmological categorization, like animism, or a major branch of a world religion like Latin Christianity?
2   What kind of evidence, including scientific documentation, is necessary to prove a religion, and more specifically its cosmology, ritual, or codes have either released humans to degrade the environment or have provided a motive for environmental care?
3   How environmentally influential is the thought of religious leaders, like Tertullian and Irenaeus, as opposed to the beliefs and entrenched economic behaviors of the general populace?
4   Whose discourse is the most informative about a religion's influence on environmental management?
5   To what extent is **presentism**, an insertion of current values and concerns into interpretation of historic events or ideas, appropriate to scholarly analysis of historic religious interactions with the environment? Did the values of late antiquity ultimately undergird the industrial revolution?

it is ineffective or burdensome in correcting the most severe forms of environmental degradation.

In questioning the environmental legitimacy of Christian cosmology and values, White's article elicited a barrage of objections and counter-arguments—initially from Christians, followed by anthropologists, religious historians, and scholars of other faiths. Despite publication in a prestigious journal, White's analysis introduces the question of what constitutes a valid methodology for studying how religion generates and guides environmentally significant actions (Box 2.4). The essay invokes **presentism**—interpreting the past through the lens of today's cultural values. White assumed that animist religions were unilaterally protective of **keystone species** (those critical to the structure and function of natural ecosystems), and that respect for the *genius loci* of sacred natural features extended to the surrounding countryside. The prolific historian did not outline any concrete cases supporting pagan or animist forest protection, which suggests he depended on the pre-suppositions of his readers to support his logic.

In lauding the *genius loci*, White dismissed what he surely knew about the ancient Romans and the extent of their military and commercial ventures. By the 1960s, forest historians had documented the degree to which the classical civilizations had logged and overgrazed the lands encircling the Mediterranean Sea. Although the Greeks and Romans conserved sacred groves around their temples and shrines, the greater landscapes surrounding these sites lost their forest cover. Respect for romping fauns and satyrs did not counter the demand for oak for ship hulls and fuel for smelting metals. Nor did the *genius loci* slow goats browsing on tree seedlings (Thirgood 1981: 43; Harrison 1992: 52–58). Anthropologist Shepard Krech III (2017) has critiqued the Lynn White thesis for its simplistic and overly generalized representation of the conservation effectiveness of animism, which did not unilaterally constrain over-hunting by indigenous American cultures.

White's essay pictures the supernatural animist entities occupying trees and springs as if they are purely natural. As Polynesian religions demonstrate, deities associated with ecological or geophysical phenomena are frequently anthropomorphic. Pele appears as a beautiful young woman or as an unremarkable gray-haired elder. She addresses the people she encounters and corrects wrongdoing. Her lessons are both cultural and environmental (Pukui 2010). Roman devotional monuments at sacred springs depicted water nymphs as beautiful semi-nude young women, suggesting human fertility as well as the purity of water emerging from the earth. When Christians adopted holy wells, they sometimes revived the pre-Christian guardian such as the Celtic goddess Brigid and remythologized the ancient deity as a source of Christian miracles (Brenneman and Brenneman 1995: 96–99). Disciplined analysis avoids generating stark dichotomies between "nature spirits" and the anthropomorphic supernatural. It studies myths, art, and sacred locales within their historic and **bioregional** contexts. Religious environmental ethicist Whitney Bauman (2017) concludes White's arguments reflect the historian's social background and educational worldview. White, who held a degree from Union Theological Seminary in New York, was operating from the perspective of a US, Protestant, Caucasian male. White told just "one story," rather than summarizing diverse points of view.

Issue: The Abrahamic faiths as promoting human exceptionalism

Lynn White Jr.'s criticisms of monotheism also apply to Judaism and Islam. He found two themes in the creation narratives in the *Torah* problematic. First, the pre-existing God is the absolute regent and is transcendent and external to creation rather than embedded in it. Second, God establishes humanity as over-lords of the entire earth and all other living species. During the 1970s and 1980s, some environmental philosophers, such as Arne Naess of the Deep Ecology movement, joined White in concluding the Abrahamic faiths encourage **human exceptionalism**, or depict Adam's offspring as morally superior to the fallen creation. Deep Ecologists recognize the **intrinsic value** of all living creatures and the diversity of life, thus advocate a form of **biospheric egalitarianism** (equal rights for all forms of life).

For Muslims, however, the unity of God requires a deity who is close to the world (Box 2.5). Seyyed Hossein Nasr (1996: 63) observes: "On the level of theological and exoteric formulations, the three Abrahamic religions assert the fundamental truth of *creatio ex nihilo* as a means of negating all reality independent of God; additionally, the

---

Box 2.5 God's relationship with the creation

John Kaltner (2011: 47) summarizes the argument that divine unity requires a God who is not distant from the world. For Muslims:

"There is no division within God and no separation between God and what God creates. Everything is dependent upon God for its existence and so, in a certain sense, all of creation is imbued with God's presence. That may explain why, in a well-known *ḥadīth* attributed to him, the Prophet Muhammed said, 'The whole earth is a mosque that is a place to worship.' It is also why some scholars have that *tawḥīd*, or unity, is the starting point for Islamic understanding of the environment. If all is created by God, and God is one, it follows that there is a unity and connectedness within creation."

esotericism of these faiths speak not only of creation *by* God but also *in* God." The *Qur'an* depicts God as *muhit*, or "encompassing." God is everywhere, so there is no way to hide from God. "All that is in the heavens and on the earth belongs to God. God surrounds everything." (*Qur'an* 4:126) (Kaltner 2011: 47).

Christians describe the omnipresent God as both **transcendent**, as creator above and over the creation, and as **immanent**, or universally present and in interaction with the creation. For monotheists, the question arises as to whether the entire cosmos is equally sacred and whether that is possible if evil exists in the world. Most Jews, Christians, and Muslims reject **pantheism,** the belief the universe itself is God or is a manifestation of God. Some adherents of the Abrahamic faiths, though, pursue **panentheism** as a basis for environmental theology. For panentheists, God is infinite and greater than the universe, yet interpenetrates physical existence. God is thus always present and accessible within creation. Both the *Bible* and the *Qur'an* present a multi-faceted deity with many names and qualities.

White's argument that the God of Genesis gave Christians the authority to harvest creation at will, also applies to the *Qur'an* (2:29) which states: "It is he who created for you everything on the earth, and turned to the sky and fashioned the seven heavens. He knows all things." Environmental ethicists from the Abrahamic faiths have argued in response that the scriptures are not anthropocentric but **theocentric** (God–centered), as they concern divine regency and not the ultimate authority of humans. The *Qur'an* emphasizes the beauty and blessings provided by the natural world. It appeals to the consciences of its readers and elicits their gratitude toward God. Sura 55 reads (10–12): "And the earth; He set up for his creatures; In it are fruits and palms in cluster. And grains in blades, and fragrant plants." From the oceans (55:22), "emerge pearls and coral" (Itam 2018: 91). Islamic scholar Ibrahim Özdemir (2003) has proposed that from a Qur'anic perspective, humans are not masters, but viceregents entrusted with the care of the creation and "its rich resources," and with the creation are called to serve God. Humans should relate to the environment in ways advancing the welfare of other people, its creatures, and the earth itself (Box 2.6).

Box 2.6 Qur'anic perspectives on human care for the environment

Ibrahim Özdemir (2003: 27) has interpreted the Qur'an as holding humans accountable to God for their treatment of the environment and natural resources:

> "It should be apparent that nature has been entrusted to us, as we are God's vicegerents on Earth. We are not the lords of nature and the world, however; the world is not our property, at our disposal to be used haphazardly and irresponsibly. On the contrary, nature was created by God, and it belongs to Him. What is important in the Qur'anic context is that we are responsible and accountable for our actions here on Earth. This means we are answerable for all that we do, both the good and the evil. As God's vicegerents, at the Last Judgement we will be called to account for our actions in fulfilling this trust: 'Whoever does an atom's weight of good shall see it, And whoever does an atom's weight of evil, shall see it' (*Qur'an* 99:7–9). And again: 'So glory to Him in whose hands is the dominion of all things: And to Him will you be all brought back." (*Qur'an* 36:83)

Issue: Christianity and Islam as the most populous religions

The question of whether monotheistic cosmologies are environmentally flawed leads to a critical political reality. According to demographic data gathered by the Pew Research Center for Religion and Public Life (2015), Christianity is currently the world's most populous religion, followed by Islam, which is the fastest-growing. In 2010, 16% of the world's population had no religious affiliation, but this will decline to 13% by 2050, while the monotheistic faiths will continue to gain adherents. Indigenous and folk religions will continue to comprise 5 to 6% of the world's population and form an environmentally-significant minority resident in unique ecosystems, including oceanic islands. The support of people with religious affiliations is thus critical to resolving environmental dilemmas. Due to their numbers and dominance in many countries, the Abrahamic faiths must rise to the demands of ethical leadership to ensure global progress toward sound strategies for environmental sustainability.

Conclusion: Trends in the study of religion and the environment

Religious responses to contemporary environmental concerns have proliferated since Lynn White Jr.'s controversial essay. During the 1970s and 1980s, scholars grounded in the Abrahamic faiths opened a dialog with the emerging field of environmental ethics. In a 1983 article critiquing the US Secretary of the Interior, James Watt, for his Biblical justification of human-centered natural resource harvest, Susan Bratton introduced the term **eco-theology** as a subfield of Christian theology paralleling eco-philosophy. At the same time, religious thinkers were adopting the philosophic concept of **intrinsic or inherent value**. Resolving the problem of human exceptionalism, intrinsic value recognizes all living organisms as creations of God that have worth in themselves regardless of whether they are useful to people. (Bratton 1984). Beginning in 1996, Roman Catholic theologian Mary Grey led the editorial team for the academic journal *Ecotheology*, followed by Celia Deane- Drummond in 2002. In 2006, the publication assumed a more cross-cultural identity as *The Journal for Religion, Nature, and Culture*, with Bron Taylor as senior editor (Taylor 2007).

During the 1980s, academics began to take a less adversarial and more multicultural approach to faith-based, environmental dialog (Hargrove 1986). Recognizing that religious support was necessary to global-scale species conservation and preservation, in the early 1990s, the World Wildlife Fund sponsored a publication series positively explicating the environmental perspectives of five world religions. Comparative religious scholars, Mary Evelyn Tucker and John Grim organized a sequence of conferences held from 1996 to 1998 at Harvard University, each generating a volume centered on the environmental creeds, coda, and contributions of a major belief system. Tucker's and Grim's ambitious project accelerated a scholarly shift from a preoccupation with Christianity to a global perspective. Recent research trends in religion and the environment include an enhanced concern for policy and economics, expanded use of ethnographic study, more specific applications of science, an increasingly diverse international authorship, and a greater emphasis on praxis.

Suggested readings

Kaltner, John. *Introducing the Qur'an for Today's Reader.* Minneapolis, MN: Fortress Press, 2011, 42–74.

LeVasseur, Todd, and Anna Peterson, eds. *Religion and Ecological Crisis: The "Lynn White Thesis" at Fifty.* New York Routledge, 2017.

Özdemir, Ibrahim. "Toward an understanding of environmental ethics from a Qur'anic perspective." In *Islam and Ecology*, edited by Richard C. Folta, Frederick M. Denny, and Azizan Baharuddin, 3–37. Cambridge, MA: Harvard University Press, 2003.

Nasr, Seyyed Hossein. *Religion and the Order of Nature.* Oxford, U.K.: Oxford University Press, 1996.

Walsham, Alexandra. *The Reformation of the Landscape: Religion, Identity, & Memory in Early Modern Britain & Ireland.* Oxford, U.K.: Oxford University Press, 2011.

White, Lynn, Jr. "The historic roots of our ecological crisis." *Science* 155 (1967): 1203–1207.

3 Communities

Harvesting and respecting the wild

Key concepts

1 Since we emerged as a species, humans have modified the structure of the plant and animal communities on a landscape scale via tools such as fire.
2 Animism and shamanism deploy human models of self—including language and symbols—as the means for understanding other organisms and natural phenomena.
3 While religions do not unilaterally prevent species extinctions or degradation of consumptive resources, moral tales, shared rituals, and sacralization of species can guide sustainable harvest. Religions can legitimate other species as moral subjects worthy of ethical consideration.
4 Multiple religions codes, including those of world religions, identify excessive natural resource harvest, lack of shared distribution, and spoilage as wrong acts.
5 Indigenous religions serve as reservoirs for traditional knowledge. Treating space, time, and biodiversity as sacred dimensions, indigenous religions express complex and precise eco-dimensionality, integrating environmental values, caretaking norms, and sustainable practices.
6 Colonialism disrupted indigenous land tenure and displaced indigenous discourses concerning the value of living organisms, and natural ecosystems like rivers.
7 Environmental regulations and environmentalism may fail to recognize the religious significance of harvested ecosystems or species, such as rivers or marine mammals. Ontological dissonance can lead to misunderstandings between indigenous cultures or natural resource-dependent communities, government agencies, and environmentalists.
8 Scientifically informed environmental management is seeking new models incorporating the cultural and spiritual values of local communities in plans for natural resource conservation. Strategies include co-management, community management, and incorporating traditional ecological approaches.

The balance of nature and human hunting

The concept of animist and other indigenous religions promoting a non-destructive balance with nature reflects western cultural biases, thus is scientifically suspect. Nevertheless, cultures embedded in a bioregion for many centuries have evolved restraints on harvesting too much, too quickly. This chapter investigates several controversies concerning religion and human stresses on natural ecosystems and wild species, including the question of whether animism is universally protective of native biota and prevents species extinctions. The findings are not consistent. Case histories document both human-caused, pre-modern species extinctions, and religions guiding sustainable harvest of fisheries and forest products like bark and wood. Colonialism and industrialization have interfered with pre-modern or indigenous religious resources management, displacing models for right action and respect of other species. As the end of the chapter explicates, today's scientists, environmentalists, and indigenous or regional religious communities are testing improved methods for incorporating the spiritual and ritual values of wild species and uncultivated landscapes in natural resources planning and management.

Pleistocene over-hunting

Relative to the question of whether pre-modern cultures lived in balance with nature, archeological research has found that even humanities' ancestors were able to modify the structure of the plant and animal communities on a landscape scale. The tool of choice for removing or regenerating vegetation was not the stone axe but fire. The European colonists in regions like Australia greatly underestimated the degree to which aboriginal practices had already altered forests and grasslands. When humans first arrived in Australia, marsupial lions and giant kangaroos 3 meters (10 feet) tall were present. Although paleontologists are still arguing over the roots of their demise, current evidence supports the thesis that human-set fires reduced food availability for these marsupials and many other species, causing their extinction (Pyne 1995; Thomas and McAlpine 2010: 17; Prideaux et al. 2007).

In the late Pleistocene, North America had a diverse mammal fauna, including mastodons, mammoths, and giant ground sloths. Paleontologists initially thought these species disappeared due to changes in temperature and precipitation following the recession of the continental glaciers at the end of the last ice age. Many now favor the **Pleistocene overkill (over-hunting) hypothesis** proposed by Paul R. Martin. The paleo-hunters' tactics and stone spearheads were sufficient to bring down the most formidable game. In Eurasia, Neanderthals and their human cousins also became competitors with the **megafauna** and accelerated their demise by reducing available prey and modifying habitats (Martin 2005).

Anthropogenic charcoal and stone tools precede the appearance of possible ritual objects in the archeological record. Some of the oldest remains of symbolic expression are in subterranean refuges. Archeologists have dated stone circles constructed by Neanderthals deep inside inaccessible Bruniquel Cave in southwestern France, to approximately 176,000 years BP (before present). The circles are 336 meters (over 1000 feet) from the cave entrance. Neanderthals must have configured the rings via firelight (Jaubert et al. 2016). Symbolic behaviors emerged widely among paleo-humans about 50,000 BP. Ironically, ancient artists carved some of the oldest religious artifacts, including full-bodied female figurines and extinct animals from mammoth ivory (Guthrie 2005: 303–371).

Around 35,000 BP, Paleolithic artists began to design **therianthropic** statuettes and painted figures merging human and animal features. A mammoth ivory statuette from Germany (ca. 32,000 BP) depicts a man with a lion's head. A cave painting in southwest France known as "the Sorcerer" (15,000 BP) presents a stag's body and antlers, merged with the face, hands, and feet of a human. Some of these figures have bent knees or leaning postures, suggesting dance or ritual movement. The first grave goods were flowers, pieces of bone, or stone tools commonplace around a camp. During the Upper Paleolithic, embellished animal materials became more prevalent. In Sungir, Siberia, for example, thousands of mammoth ivory beads, polished mammoth-ivory bracelets and lances, a belt with 250 polar fox canine teeth, and two antler batons decorated three burials circa 28,000 BP (Sidky 2017: 53–115).

Animism and shamanism

Paleolithic **material culture** is consistent with **animism** and **shamanism**, a proto-form of religious professionalism, where exceptionally knowledgeable individuals communicate with the spirits of animals or the dead. As spirit masters, shamans enter transformed or trance states where they may become an animal, interact with para-normal entities, or journey to other geographic or supernatural realms. (Sidky 2017: 13–15) The fragmented evidence makes it difficult to determine if, as the megafauna populations declined, the paleo-hunters responded via religious or other means to con-strain their collapsing harvests. Intended to improve success in capturing and dispatch-ing game, craving talismans from ivory or bone continued as megafauna populations disappeared.

The emergence of animism was a cognitive change in the way humans perceived their environments. Animism attributes the goal-directedness and **sentience** of living animals to stones, springs, mountains, trees, and thunderstorms. The anthropomor-phism inherent in "the Sorcerer" deploys human **models of self**—including language and symbols—as the means for understanding other organisms and natural phenomena. Retaining cultural memories of past events, animism provides a theory of causation and a means of explaining the mysterious and unpredictable. Graham Harvey (2006) and other religious theorists have rescued animism from 19th-century identification as primitive, irrational, and unscientific. Current interpretation finds animism "is free of the mind–body, nature–culture, matter–spirit, science–religion dichotomies of western thought…" Its identification and empathy with other species inspire the animist to act respectfully toward "other-than-human-persons" (Sidky 2017: 135–138).

More recent evidence concerning species extinctions

A more recent wave of extinctions provides additional evidence for the environmental impacts of pre-industrial technologies. Approximately 3500 years ago, Polynesian navi-gators began to settle the western Pacific islands. They finally made landfall on the more distant chains, including Hawai'i and New Zealand, between 900 and 700 BP. The crews of out-rigger canoes brought sophisticated agricultural techniques, and domestic animals to previously uninhabited atolls and emergent volcanoes. The isolated islands support **endemic** biota (found only at one site or in a limited range). Archeologists have excavated early Polynesian camps, identified vertebrate bones present, and discovered many of these endemic species are now extinct. In combination with human hunting and the addition of new predators like pigs, clearing for agriculture disturbed island habitats and eliminated many vertebrate species (Steadman 2006).

The Polynesian islands lost nearly 1000 species of flightless or ground-dwelling birds alone, including the Hawaiian moa-nalo. Iguanas and other island reptile species simul-taneously disappeared. The arrival dates of colonists correspond with the decline of bird species, providing evidence for cause and effect. When the Māori reached New

Zealand about 800 BP, they found nine species of flightless moas. The largest moas were 3.6 m (12 feet) in height and weighed up to 250 kg (550 pounds). The Māori used fire to facilitate their moa hunts, and the moas vanished within approximately 150 years. The activities of the Māori indirectly resulted in the extinction of the Haast's eagle, which depended on moas for its prey (Duncan et al. 2013; Steadman 2006; Kirch 2012; Gemmell et al. 2004; Worthy and Holdaway 2002; Bunce et al. 2005).

Despite their sacralization of trees, the Māori's fires removed 3 million ha (7 million acres) of forest from South Island alone, disturbing the habitat for many additional endemic species (Thomas and McAlpine 2010: 17; Martin 2005: 41–43). Unlike the mammoth hunters, where our knowledge of their religions is restricted to remnants of material culture, Māori tradition retains stories of early human activities in the New Zealand landscape. According to orally transmitted sources, the Māori founders used fire and erection of worship sites called *tuaha* to establish their land claims. The narratives justify the clearing of native vegetation for agriculture and the displacement of the mysterious pre-Māori "little people" from their settlements (Shorthand 2015) (Box 3.1).

Following the megafaunal collapse in North American, human hunting continued to reduce and demographically modify game populations. As one example among many, in Puerto Marques, Mexico, ancient shell middens prove regular capture of sea turtles, followed by a decline beginning 5500 BP. The harvest pressure resulted in local **extirpation** (complete disappearance) of sea turtles around 2500 BP, just as Mayan culture was gaining momentum. Historic documentation of green and hawksbill turtle populations throughout the Caribbean suggests a significant loss of nesting populations preceding European arrival, followed by decimation of the remaining nesting populations since 1700. Today's western Atlantic green turtle population is an estimated 0.3% of its size preceding human advent. For each 1000 green sea turtles previously present before human harvest began, only three are present today (Lotze and Mcclenachan 2014).

Box 3.1 Māori founder myths and the use of fire for land clearing

Note: These narratives express the cultural values at the time they were recorded while often retaining information on former practices

A heroic Māori founder named Ihenga traveled with four companions across the unoccupied New Zealand landscape. Ihenga mistook the smoke from hot springs for anthropogenic fire and unnecessarily diverted his course as he mistakenly believed another Māori had already taken possession. Ihenga established a sacred place or *tuaha* for himself, by building an enclosure with fresh earth and newly cut wood poles. A *tuaha* is a religious structure where the Māori make offerings of foods and the first fruits of their agricultural fields. Ihenga later encountered a hilltop settlement belonging to little people, or fairies, who were singing about a blazing *kawa* tree. The band moved forward to capture Ihenga, who took a brand as he fled and torched the dry ferns, setting the entire area alight. The large fire routed the fairies who fled to the forests. Ihenga returned to examine the burned hill and found "the *kauae* or jawbone of a moa," so he named that site Kauae, and the hill itself Ngongotaha, or "flight of the fairies." Ihenga's *tuaha* symbolically replaced the sacred burning tree of the little people with a sacred space accommodating religious rituals based in land clearing and cultivation.

Source: Shorthand (2005: 68–72)

Box 3.2 Ecosystem services

Ecosystems provide services to humans that do not involve direct harvest of living organisms:

- Forests prevent landslides and flooding by stabilizing soils and absorbing water.
- Wetlands trap sediment and act as pollution filters.
- Mangroves and coral reefs buffer the effects of hurricanes and typhoons.
- Vegetation moderates climate via shading and reducing wind speed.
- Trees serve as air filters trapping particulates.
- Prairie grasses conserve soil moisture and contribute to soil organic matter.
- Microbial communities decompose organic matter including wastes.
- Marine grass beds and coral reefs serve as nurseries for multiple species, including those useful to humans.

Consumptive and productive resources

To return to current dilemmas, environmental economists identify foods, fuels, fibers, and pharmaceuticals collected from the wild and utilized locally without sale or trade as **consumptive resources** or **subsistence harvest**. Very few contemporary cultures maintain economies based on hunting and gathering wild species alone, yet many rural populaces supplement their diets with bushmeat or gather firewood for fuel. Not just a feature of pre-industrial societies, dependence on wild-caught fish for protein is still critical to coastal cultures worldwide. Overharvest of oceanic fisheries has, however, caused steep declines in stocks. Fish and timber sold at a market or loaded onto ships and exchanged internationally are **productive resources.** In today's global networks, the harvester, the trader, and the consumer are unlikely to know each other, and the person purchasing a natural product often has no idea if the extraction method was environmentally sustainable.

Today, our land clearing and economic development displace native species sensitive to disturbance and habitat modification. Anthropogenic disturbances interfere with **ecosystem services**—functions useful to humans provided by natural biotic systems (Box 3.2). Although some environmentalists and ethicists are concerned about the concept because it invites estimating the value of these services in monetary terms, many religions recognize their importance without commodifying their benefits. Life scientists have found the earth is losing species and their genetic information faster than at any time since the last **global mass extinction** event that eliminated the dinosaurs at the end of the Cretaceous period. Sometimes termed the sixth mass extinction, the accelerating depletion is anthropogenic and has precipitated a **biodiversity crisis,** far exceeding that of the late Pleistocene.

Religion as a vehicle for fisheries conservation

Although religious codes might appear to be the best means for countering over-harvest, depending on rules or taboos alone can promote individualism and cheating, especially when the harvester is out to sea or in a dense forest where no one else is watching. Determining how many organisms can be safely removed from a population without damaging the **reproductive potential** requires extensive observation. Effective religious means for moderating harvest are therefore holistic and promote communitarian behaviors in concert with technological restraint. Moral tales, shared rituals, and sacralization of consumptive species guide religiously informed **sustainable harvest**.

Indigenous cultures residing along the coasts and rivers of the northern Pacific caught salmon for many centuries without exterminating the diverse genetic stocks adapted to each local watershed. The available technologies of traps, weirs, and nets could easily have eliminated the salmon runs from the tributaries of the Yukon, Columbia, or Sacramento Rivers. Significant features of Pacific coast religions in the United States and Canada are shamanism, animism, and myths incorporating **transformers** or beings that can convert themselves into other living creatures or inanimate objects. The most prominent transformers, Raven and Coyote, are also **tricksters** who accomplish their goals through cleverness and deceit (Muckle 2014).

Creation myths relate how the salmon offered themselves to people for sustenance, or how Raven, the wisest of birds, brought salmon in from the sea to breed in the rivers. Among the Haida and Tlingit, Raven married the beautiful daughter of Chief Fog-Over-The-Salmon. When a time of food shortage arrived, his wife wove a giant basket that fills with water and with salmon each night—thus, a female anthropomorphic figure created the bounty of fish. Indeed, fog floats over the river mouths at the beginning of the summer, announcing the arrival of the salmon (Smelcer 2015: 7–8).

Multiple tribes conduct a **First Fish ceremony** as a salmon run begins. Rather than rushing to set a thicket of nets as salmon surge up-river, a village captures one salmon from the beginning of the run. All fishing stops for several days, as the community bakes the first fish and conveys it to the chief. The chief then returns the head, bones, and fins to the water while reciting prayers. As a sacred time, the delay in fishing allows escapement of salmon—thereby guaranteeing many breeders will reach their redds (nests). The ritual deposit of the bones in the stream imitates the natural cycle of nutrient replenishment via the bodies of the salmon, which die post-spawning. Salmon return to their natal streams to breed, thus removing most of the gravid females from one stream would destroy the future runs for that tributary (Taylor 1999: 1–78).

According to environmental historian Joseph E. Taylor III (1999), the division of the small watersheds and prime fishing sites on the major rivers into family territories discouraged overexploitation. The families would themselves suffer multi-year deficits if they caught too many breeding adults in one season. The tribes organize by "houses" or groups of relatives, identified by an animal totem. Holding rights to fishing and hunting territories, each house or clan has fish chiefs leading rituals and monitoring the harvest. Ignoring the chief, poaching on another's fishing site, or wasting fish could result in loss of fishing rights. Taylor concludes the combination of "aboriginal spiritual beliefs, ritual expression, social sanctions, and territorial claims effectively moderated salmon harvests."

Social values and fisheries

Religions have discourses or codes that counter avarice, theft, and coveting a neighbor's livelihood. Other widespread religious norms are avoidance of waste and unnecessary collateral damage to natural resources. Pacific coast legends of Coyote, Raven, and Salmon Boy serve as moral lessons depicting greed and disrespect of natural resources as likely to back-fire and ultimately harm the envious and careless (Box 3.3). When

---

Box 3.3 Salmon legends

Coyote and the salmon—the Klamath people

Coyote visited the Klamath River (Oregon) found the people were poor and lacked food. Three Skookums (monsters, bad people) had built a dam so they could capture salmon, but no fish could proceed upstream. Coyote decided to help the Klamath people and went sulking around the Skookum camp whining for fish. The Skookums would not share their food, but coyote saw where they kept the key to the dam. The next day, when a Skookum went to collect fish, Coyote tripped her, and she dropped the key. Coyote snatched it and opened the dam. The fish ran all the way upstream, thus all the Klamath had salmon to eat. Coyote broke down the dam and the salmon runs have continued ever since.

Salmon boy—the Haida people

In variants of the story of salmon boy, a child either disrespects salmon by refusing to eat salmon offered during a famine or by not returning all the uneaten salmon body parts to the creek. The salmon people capture him and transport him to their village in the sea. The boy's parents grieve for him. When he returns as a salmon, he swims in front of his mother, who catches him. She recognizes the necklace he was wearing when he disappeared, thus, his family do not eat him. He metamorphoses back to human form as a shaman. When the salmon return the next year, the people spear a salmon which is the boy's own soul. The tribe places his corpse on plank in deep pool with his drum, which then continues to sound from the depths, drawing plentiful salmon runs.

Sources: Judson 1910: 123–134; Swanton 1905: 7–13

Raven became abusive toward his spouse Fog Woman, she departed and took the basket generating the precious salmon with her. When Raven grew hungry and tried to bring her home, she slipped away as a nebulous mist. Without directly banning taking one fish too many, tales of tricksters trigger thoughtful decisions concerning how much is too much. They dissuade fishers from the destructive use of technologies like dams and traps. The narratives affirm respectful and cooperative family and societal interactions, which, in turn, maintain the harvest.

Due to the site fidelity of breeding salmon, a strategy of sacred space protecting one stream, while allowing intensive fishing at another would not be as effective for maintaining **population viability** and **genetic diversity** as allowing escapement for each run is. In other geographic settings where harvested species disperse widely, the establishment of sacred spaces where breeding individuals or **keystone resources,** like old-growth forests, are protected can maintain populations of consumptive biota. Subsisting on root crops and fish, the Tukanos of the upper Rio Negro, Brazil, weave the river into "all aspects of Tukanoan life, social, cosmological and technological." The river is integral to religious practice, beginning when a newborn's first rites take place at the river's edge. The Tukano's sacred trumpets, played during male initiation rituals, are stored in the water to maintain their bright sheen. Pan-Tukano myths relate how a great ancestral anaconda-fish exited the Primordial water door and swam upstream to the Uaupes River headwaters. The massive aquatic creature then turned back downstream, and segments of its body became the first ancestors of each local clan settled along the Uaupes. Amazonian narratives cast other riparian animal species as human relatives, including the aracu fish (*Leporinus* species) as a sib ancestor (sharing a common origin) from a time before patrilineal inheritance (Jackson 1983: 45; Reichel-Dolmatoff 1997: 306; Chernela 1999).

Tukano communities prohibit cutting riparian trees on the grounds the forests belong to the fish. They thus harvest less than 40% of the river margin, as well as closing fishing during prescribed seasons. Scientific investigation has confirmed the Tukano have sacralized the critical spawning areas and created **refugia** for the aracu that is a staple of their diet. Each patrilocal clan defends its boundaries, based on the concept of ancestral precedence. Members of another clan or language group violating these boundaries can precipitate violence or retaliation. Natural rock formations and human cravings within the river itself memorialize ancestral events and serve as the homes of each clan's spirit guardians, maintaining fishing territories and sacred spaces from year to year (Chernela 1999). Anthropologist Gerardo Reichel-Dolmatoff (1997: 19–20) observes that, aside from building social bonds, Tukano rituals address concerns that animal life is declining along the river, and the environment is becoming disordered. World-recreating ceremonies endorse "shared rules of conduct." They recognize the quality of human life can only be perpetuated "if all other life forms too are allowed to evolve according to their specific needs, as stated in cosmological myths and traditions."

The ecological sophistication of the Pacific coastal and Tukano religions in conserving fisheries brings up the question of why the Māori did not similarly protect the moas? Animism or "nature religion" does not by itself mitigate the introduction of spears, anthropogenic fire, and agricultural activity into ecosystems lacking prior human presence. Some species and ecological communities are far more sensitive than others to novel stressors. Moa had no mammalian predator before the arrival of the Māori. In contrast, salmon runs sustain predation from bears and otters, along with orcas, seals, and other marine carnivores. The salmon have evolved spawning patterns where runs are cyclical with high and low years—limiting the potential growth of predator populations, including humans. Like scientific management, religious oversight must acquire **bio-regional knowledge** and adapt to inherent environmental limits. Environmental manager Fikert Berkes (2018: 1–12) defines **traditional ecological knowledge** as "a cumulative body of knowledge practice and belief, evolving by adaptive processes and handed down through generations by cultural transmission, about the relationship of living beings (including humans) with one another and with their environment." While traditional knowledge shares some features with natural science, including its memory of trial and error and its biotic inventories, its religious dimensions and sacred ecology fall outside the boundaries of modern scientific research.

Māori watershed management

The first Polynesian arrivals in New Zealand between 1200 and 1400 CE initially concentrated in coastal settlements at rivers mouths and on bays. Archeologists have found a predominance of moa, and seal remains in the oldest layers of excavated sites. In more recent strata, fish, shellfish, and the bones of small birds dominate. The human population was not more than a few thousand at the point where depletion of the moa and more easily harvested marine species forced a move inland. After roughly three centuries, the Māori transitioned from a coastal to a river people and relocated their *pa* or fortified settlements to the interior (Knight 2016) (Fig. 3.1a).

Figure 3.1 A former Māori fishing locale, at rapids suitable for weirs. The remains of the abandoned
Ngapuhi Pa stand on the hill above (out of sight to the left). For the Māori, the river is
an ancestor with māna or spiritual authority. The buildings across the Kerikeri River are
the Church Missionary Society station (ca. 1822) and a general store, now preserved as a
historic site. A modern dam blocks passage for eels above this area. Although recreational
fishing, boating, and swimming have taken over, Kerikeri has a complex history as a
sacred landscape.

The Māori began to trace the genealogy of water and embedded the streams in creation traditions linking fluvial habitats to the gods. Religious narratives identify the
rivers as *tupuna awa*—"a river that is an ancestor itself or derives from ancestral title."
Environmental historian Catherine Knight (2016) concludes the Māori river is not dis-
tinct from land, rather encompasses "an indivisible whole" consisting of the bed, banks,
springs, and estuaries comprising the watershed. Rivers possess *mauri* or life force, combining natural and metaphysical aspects. The **māna** or spiritual power and authority
of the Māori protected and managed the waters, while rivers as ancestors have māna of
their own. As is typical of Polynesian marine fisheries, the Māori developed detailed
codes ensuring water purity and sharing of consumptive resources by prescribing correct behavior relative to fish capture and waste disposal in fluvial systems (Box 3.4).
Despite engineering sophisticated enough to build large weirs for capturing eels in the
middle of rapids, Māori fisheries management evolved toward intentional sustainability
(Fig. 3.1). Organic aquatic forms are common in Māori sacred art. They may be totems
of *iwi* or play mythic roles, such as acting as messengers between humans and the waters.

From thingness to respect

Common denominators in these geographically dispersed systems for maintaining
consumptive resources include a concept of shared ancestry with aquatic organisms
or legends of shape-shifting between human and fish forms. Fish have rights of their
own, including ancestral rights, or animal societies exist in parallel to human tribes

---

Box 3.4 Māori fishing codes

Pre-colonial Māori fishing codes incorporated:

- Avoiding any disrespect toward the river or gods
- Fishing only at times permissible for individual species
- Regulating bathing and assigning places for washing and for conducting river ceremonies
- Forbidding processing fish within the river and directing waste disposal to specific terrestrial sites
- Not discharging waste into the rivers but onto the land
- Preserving fish for latter consumption
- Sharing catches

Source: Knight 2016

---

or villages, giving keystone species like salmon worth in themselves. Tribes of the Columbia River valley self-identify as Salmon People, and the Tukano construct "houses" for their clan spirit-guardians descended from fish. The traditions maintain fish as legitimate **moral subjects** worthy of ethical consideration. Religion constrains human inclinations toward excess and conveys indigenous spatial–temporal knowledge concerning fish spawning. Sacralization of space and environmental processes protects ecosystem services. The emphasis on sharing, combined with sanctions imposed on violators, reduces motivation for individuals to act independently or selfishly.

These integrative approaches discourage human exceptionalism. Guardian spirits, family totems, ancestral myths, and armed retaliation reinforce the spatial boundaries protecting critical reproductive and feeding habitats for the fish. These religions are eco-spatial or, considering time and biodiversity as vital dimensions and express complex and precise **eco-dimensionality**. Eco-dimensionality is the integrative expression of environmental values, caretaking norms, and sustainable practices. It encompasses the symbolism, myth, art, ritual, and ethics, which recognize and specifically adapt to keystone environmental processes and ecosystemic diversity (Bratton 2018).

An inadequately explored question concerning cultures with sophisticated eco-dimensionality is how these religion-based conservation systems learn from their mistakes? A second question is whether sustainability concerning one consumptive resource promotes sustainable practices relative to others? Unlike whales and lizards, the moa never assumed a prominent role in Māori myth or art. When Europeans first arrived in New Zealand, the Māori did not mention moa. Unlike other birds, the avian giants lacked a mythic genealogy, perhaps because they had disappeared so speedily (Worthy and Holdaway 2002). The Māori continued to hold bird hunting and trapping in high regard and pursued sensitive taxa such as the endemic wood pigeon and kiwi species for their tasty meat and soft, decorative feathers. Even without the firearms introduced by Europeans, Māori tracking and snaring continued as a stressor on avian populations.

In contrast, the Māori did not harpoon whales at sea but opportunistically butchered stranded whales. (They may have beached whales by driving them toward shore, while numbers were likely low.) Whalebone and oil were highly valued, yet the Māori exerted only minor impacts on whale reproduction. As the pre-colonial Māori population grew, their occupation of more interior regions of New Zealand resulted in further burning and clearing, along with inter-tribal competition for land (Garlick et al. 2010: 81–83, 138–169). Māori practices formed a dynamic gradient from little impact on whales, to moderate stresses on freshwater fisheries, to continuing consequential effects on seals, birds, and forest cover. At the point they encountered Europeans, the Māori were still adjusting regulation and sacralization of hunting and fishing to the disturbance-sensitive New Zealand biota.

The Tukano, Pacific coastal, and Māori religions all reduce the "thingness" of fish and raise their status relative to humans. Without positive cultural interpretation, things and matter are mere stuff to manipulate and throw away. In an oft-cited essay on the **Land Ethic**, published with *A Sand County Almanac*, American wildlife ecologist Aldo Leopold (1949) pointed out that when Odysseus returned home from the Trojan war, he hanged his slave girls for misconduct. They were his property, and he had the authority to do dispose of them as he wished. Leopold argued that when we treat the land as a mere property that we are free to buy and sell, we tend to abuse it. If humans saw themselves as citizens of a land community, along with earthworms, oak trees, and deer, we would be less inclined to clear-cut forests, leave exposed soil to erode, and deplete wildlife. More than awarding fish and coyotes intrinsic worth, indigenous religions credit them with supernatural powers, ethical insights, and primordial authority. Coyotes speak as sages, and anacondas emerge as honored ancestral founders. Animism and shamanism impart a deep sense of value and personal identification with other species and ecosystem processes.

Animal societies, universal spirits, and codes

Treating animals and plants as if they have societies paralleling human tribes or awarding them protection as family members are widespread among indigenous religions. The Cherokees of the Eastern American woodlands establish their settlements in stream valleys with soils deep and fertile enough to farm. Each village has a town-house and dance ground for communal meetings and celebrations. The Cherokees identify distinctive mountain summits as sites of the subterranean town or council houses occupied by the various animal tribes, like the bears, mountain lions, and rabbits. The White Bear, chief of all the bears, oversees councils within *Kuwo-i* or Mulberry Place (Clingmans Dome), the second-highest pinnacle in the Appalachians. Before denning, the bears hold their seasonal dances inside the peaks (Mooney 1992: 250). The concept of animal societies does not eliminate hunting, any more than the recognition of other human tribes prevents warfare. It does demand respect for the slain bear, and for the bears' need to share food resources like chestnuts and mulberries with the Cherokees.

A related eastern woodland belief is that a universal, omnipresent spirit called **Manitou** animates the world and infuses both living creatures and inanimate objects. The term originates in the Algonquin language root for "to make." The Algonquian limited excessive harvest of natural resources, such as fur-bearing animals or medicinal plants, to prevent disturbing or disrespecting Manitou. Building **reciprocity**, the hunter gives offerings and prayers back to the animal society or Manitou in exchange for the animal offering itself to the hunter. Other religious beliefs reinforce the concept of moderating harvest. The Lenape (Delaware) honor a bear-like being, mounted on a deer. If Lenapes disrespect the wildlife or became greedy, this **keeper of the game** moves the wildlife far from Lenape towns. The eastern woodland nations, in general, avoid wanton harm to animals (Tooker 1979: 11–39; Grumet 2001).

Reducing waste and ensuring future productivity

Multiple religious codes identify excessive harvest, lack of shared distribution, and spoilage as wrong acts. The biblical concept of **baal tashit** or "do not destroy" (Deuteronomy 20: 19–20) originally prohibited Hebrew armies from cutting fruit trees when laying siege to a city. For contemporary Judaism, *baal tashit* mandates that harvest should not unnecessarily damage living creatures or potentially useful resources, either wild or cultivated. Religious laws and taboos prohibit interference with pregnant, breeding, suckling, or nesting animals. The Koyukon of Alaska, for example, do not disturb nesting waterfowl (Nelson 1985). The Hebrew Tanak prohibits removing a female wild bird from her nest or taking the unhatched eggs or young (Deuteronomy 22: 6).

Societies with dependence on hunting or fishing for protein and caloric intake often deify carnivores at the top of the food web, even if they are dangerous to humans. Hawaiians once protected and fed offerings to large sharks as ancestral deities and constructed an underwater *heiau* (temple) for the shark gods, aligned with a terrestrial *heiau* complex on Kona (James 1995: 140–144). Interestingly, modern ecological science has found that maintaining large predatory fish contributes to the health of coral reefs and leads to higher fish productivity as the top carnivores keep the lower levels of the food chains in check. Regional religions, however, rarely entirely exempt populous edible or useful species from consumptive harvest.

Issue: Colonial and corporate disruption

Aside from being historically inaccurate, the concept of primal cultural balance with nature underreports indigenous facility with navigation, tool manufacture, and agriculture. It forwards western ideologies concerning trading rights, territorial government, and proprietary ownership of technological expertise. When Westerners began to establish residence in the Hawaiian Islands, the Hawaiian kingship and *ali'i* (chiefs and ruling class) were still in place. Cultural historian Elizabeth Buck (1993: 57–77, 112–113) identifies the encounter as one of western penetration, structural transformation, and reordering of social relationships. The Hawaiian *ali'i* had managed land for agriculture and wood harvest as community property. Foreigner advisors encouraged the institution of policies like taxation and sale of land, which supported capitalism and turned the Hawaiians into proletariat labors for sugar plantations. New laws unraveled indigenous Hawaiian **land tenure** and **commodified** island ecosystems (allowed financial purchase).

In New Zealand, government based in English law similarly crippled the indigenous consumptive economy. Although Christian missionaries did not intentionally undermine Māori food gathering, their presence supported radical cultural change and adoption of English jurisprudence (Fig. 3.1). European colonists disregarded Māori traditions of keeping the rivers clean and initially did little to protect water quality. Aside from allowing gold miners to drain cyanide-laced waste into the fluvial ecosystems, fear of disease outbreaks caused 19th-century towns to construct sewers delivering untreated human waste to the rivers and estuaries with no consideration for people or fish living downstream. European-heritage residents introduced trout and salmon to New Zealand's rivers and lakes. As native eels consumed non-native trout, trout acclimatization societies attempted to exterminate the large eels that the Māori depended on for food. The trout preyed on the smaller whitebait or fish fry also harvested by the Māori. Hydroelectric projects flooded *pa* or settlements, along with burial caves and *wahi tapu* or spiritually significant sites (Knight 2016: 49–89, 141).

Similar changes occurred in the North American Pacific salmon fisheries, where state regulation dissolved indigenous fishing territories and, with them, motivation for fishers to maintain breeding stocks. The advent of new technologies, including hydroelectric dams, completely blocking rivers, and internal combustion engines, allowing boats to haul wider-mouthed nets in deeper waters, further depleted salmon populations. Despite treaties ensuring rights to subsistence harvest of salmon, the Native American nations found themselves legislated out of their historic fishing grounds or suffering under regulations and economic biases intended to prevent them from operating commercial fishing boats (Taylor 1999).

Issue: The ecological Indian and keepers of the game

Popular depictions of cultures dependent on the consumptive harvest of wild biota and academic explanations for changes in harvest patterns following colonial interference have raised questions concerning the **representation** of Native Americans and other societies subject to colonialism. Historians have asked, for example, why Native Americans cooperated with the European fur trade, which decimated populations of beaver, otter, and other fur bearers? Calvin Luther Martin (1982) argues that Christian missionaries introduced a competing religious discourse to the eastern woodland tribes, which displaced their belief in animal societies and Manitou. Repeated epidemics encouraged the abandonment of the disempowered old religion and acceptance of Christianity that, in turn, unleashed a war on the animals. Religious change thus undermined their responsibilities as "keepers of the game," that would have prevented the intense exploitation and **commodification** promoted by the European fur traders. Critics of Martin's thesis have argued the "religious change" explanation is insufficient, and the attraction of trade goods and the availability of new technologies, including firearms and metal traps, contributed to the elimination of beaver and otter from multiple river basins. Colonial governance dislocated not just family hunting territories but entire Native American nations, further destabilizing concern for the number of animals removed (Krech 1981).

A second contested **representation** is the image of the "ecological Indian," who lives in balance with natural resources and has a minimal "footprint" on the landscape. Shepherd Krech III (1999) penned a controversial critique of the idea Native Americans were the "original ecologists and conservationists." From a scholarly perspective, the concept is problematic because it is simplistic. Native American cultures occupy diverse bioregions, including ecosystems subject to climatic fluctuations like the American Southwest. The idea of a mystical balance denies the necessity of continued environmental problem-solving. Preceding European arrival, Native North and South Americans were not just hunters, but were sophisticated agriculturalists, constructing expansive ceremonial centers and managing multi-cultural trade networks. These activities generate significant environmental stresses, requiring timely societal responses to phenomena such as natural climate change.

The debate over the "ecological Indian" demonstrates the political power of representation. Non–Native American authors and artists invent Indians to suit their values. Conversely, supposedly "un-ecological" contemporary Native Americans may be largely absent from recent environmental proposals, such as the idea of establishing a "buffalo commons" based on restoration of native prairies and species in degraded regions of the American Midwest. Academics have questioned whether the "overkill hypothesis" is a **cultural construction** or a racially biased representation and have argued "overhunting" is a less biased term (Harkin and Lewis 2007).

Issue: Western versus indigenous environmental discourses

Although the question of indigenous land and fishing rights might appear to belong in parliaments and law courts, religious and scientific **western discourses** have played significant roles in displacing indigenous environmental authority and delegitimizing religious, environmental norms. Before European contact, Hawaiian chants conveyed the interrelations of deities, nature, the ruling *ali'i*, commoners, and Hawaii's sacred past. Christian missionary denigration, the displacement of the *ali'i*, and the declining use of the Hawaiian language undermined the aesthetic of chants and *hula* and their connections to the natural environment. *Hula* lost its communitarian role as religious "poetry in motion" and became an entertainment for tourists. Since the 1970s, Hawaiians as a cultural group have increasingly reasserted their **cultural discourse**. A resurgence of interest in the Hawaiian language, chant, and *hula* in its ritual context parallel and reinforce efforts to recover ceded terrains, reestablish traditional rights to forests and fisheries, and halt development projects that could negatively impact ethnic Hawaiian lifestyles (Buck 1993: 121–191).

Among the native Hawaiian ventures has been the return of the island of Kaho'olawe, occupied by the US Navy during World War II. As Hawaiians explored their heritage, older people recalled chants identifying Kaho'olawe as sacred to the sea god Kanaloa. Among the island's numerous shrines and sacred sites are two dedicated to Kāmohoali'i, Pele's brother, the shark god. One is a deep cave exiting into the ocean, and the other encompasses cliff top shrines above a bay where sharks breed. Before the military occupation, the island was a locale for teaching traditional wayfaring or non-instrument marine navigation. Aside from submitting a bill to Congress to repatriate the island, in 1976, Hawaiian protesters attempted to land on Kaho'olawe. The Navy ultimately arrested them all, but two managed to temporarily escape detection and spent a couple of days viewing the destruction caused by repeated combat training and ordinance testing. Native Hawaiian George Helm initiated a civil suit to force the Navy to reduce their destructive maneuvers (McGregor 2007: 249–285).

Advocacy for indigenous rights meanwhile achieved trend-setting legislation with the passage of the **U.S. American Indian Religious Freedom Act of 1978 (AIRFA)**. Based on US Constitutional guarantees of freedom of religious expression, AIRFA authorized additional protection for sacred sites, including those outside lands under the jurisdiction of the Native American nations (Vecsey 1991; U.S. Government 1978). In 1980, the Navy reached an out-of-court settlement that required military management to comply with the Historic Preservation Act, AIRFA, and the **National Environmental Protection Act (NEPA)**. The agreement required the Navy to protect historical features and stop the bombing for ten days each month to allow some degree of ecological recovery. Under the consent decree, about 60 Hawaiians traveled to the island monthly to initiate soil and vegetation restoration projects. They rededicated abandoned shrines and *heiau*, constructed a traditional meeting house and hula platform, and celebrated the harvest festival of the agricultural god Lono (McGregor 2007: 274–285).

Under continuing political pressure, the Navy returned Kaho'olawe to the State of Hawai'i in 1994. The State designated it as a reserve, preventing privatization and tourist developments. Among the Reserve's volunteer-staffed endeavors are restoring native plant cover, increasing seabird numbers, and instituting a bio-security plan to prevent the arrival of further invasive species. An intensive educational program for native Hawaiian college students offers land management and marine management, while Hawaiian Studies is the most popular major. Marine biologists are mapping and monitoring coral reef communities, with the intent of developing a model marine resource planning strategy that maintains biodiversity and Hawaiian cultural values. According to Hawaiian professor of ethnic studies, Davianna Pomāika'i McGregor (2007: 283), the rules of behavior relative to land and ocean care "are tied to cultural beliefs and values regarding respect of theü *āina* [love of the islands], the virtue of sharing and not taking too much, and holistic perspective on organisms and ecosystems that emphasizes balance and co-existence." The long-term goal for Kaho'olawe is to reestablish native Hawaiian sovereignty, culminating in the rebirth of the sacred (Kaho'olawe Island Reserve Commission 2018).

Issue: Ritual harvest and sacred hunts

Among the world's indigenous and regional religions, collecting wild plants and animals for ceremonial purposes or the manufacture of religious objects is normative. Today, in the face of diminishing biodiversity, religiously based hunts can have difficulty finding common ground with scientific management and species conservation. The **U.S. Endangered Species Act (ESA)**, as amended in 1973, banned not just taking and possession of species like bald and golden eagles, it prohibited any form of handling even with live release. The ESA de facto criminalized making sacred objects from the feathers, teeth, skulls, hides, or other body parts taken from endangered species, even for Native Americans residing on their ancestral lands. On the beneficial side, these prohibitions allowed federal courts to imprison and fine individuals collecting sea turtle eggs, shooting whooping cranes, or harassing manatees. The passage of AIRFA in 1978 and a series of lawsuits forced the Department of Interior to seek a compromise. The US Fish and Wildlife Service has established a permitting process to allow officially recognized Native American nations to conduct limited harvest and retain materials from protected species for religious use (Vecsey 1991).

The loss of rights to hunt key consumptive species and their disappearance due to commercial competition continue to threaten the very identity of indigenous communities worldwide. The Makah tribe of Washington state and the nearby Nuuchah-nulth groups of Vancouver Island, Canada, once conducted whaling using log canoes and hand-thrown harpoons. Blubber and oil constituted up to 80 percent of their diets, particularly in spring. Nineteenth-century government interference with fishing rights, and bans on ceremonies such as the **potlatch**, a shared community feast, began to unravel ties between religion and whale hunts. "Yankee" whaling caused populations of the gray whales to plummet, but as the Makah took only a small number, they were able to harvest up to 12 whales per year into the early 20th century. Whaling stations using steel-hulled ships operated from Vancouver Island beginning in 1917 and ending in the 1960s. These operations devastated the remaining migrating humpbacks and sperm whales. As the longhouses disappeared, and nuclear families displaced the clan-based social organization, the whaling *haw'iih* or chiefs of the First Nations could no longer locate enough whales to hunt or find enough experienced hunters to form crews (Coté 2010: 42–68).

Preceding colonial intrusion, whaling traditions were integral to Makah and Nuu-chah-nulth religious practice. The *haw'iih* leading the hunts "underwent months of complex rituals and ceremonial preparation to assure their success in whaling." Individuals undertook a **spirit quest**, seeking a spirit that would aid them in whaling, fishing, and other pursuits. Whalers progressed through *oo-simch* or **ritual cleansing**, fasting, and prolonged prayer to attract an exceptionally powerful spirit to assist in the strenuous pursuit. They would continue to honor the spirt through prescribed prepara-tory rituals, including repeatedly bathing in chilling ocean water or withdrawing to the mountains before each whaling expedition. Whalers respected taboos, including abstaining from sex for several weeks preceding the hunt. Chiefs maintained shrines as sites to conduct purification and rituals to entice dead or dying whales to drift ashore on a nearby beach. In myth, the Thunderbird T'iick'in was the first great whale hunter. Demonstrating whales could provide food and tools, he threw the Sisiutl or Lighting (Sea) Serpent as a deadly harpoon (Fig. 3.2). Thunderbird and Lightning Serpent have continued as prominent images in regional art, including carved poles and dance masks (Coté 2010: 15–41).

Figure 3.2 Sisiutl or double-headed Lightning Serpent as a principal mythic figure of the winter dance circa 1914 on Vancouver Island. His shirt is woven from hemlock boughs.

Photo: Edward Curtis, collection of the U.S. Library of Congress

The formation of the International Whaling Commission (IWC) initially removed the most heavily exploited species from legal capture. Then in 1987, the IWC imposed a moratorium on all whaling, except for scientific study or aboriginal consumptive use. The U.S. Marine Mammal Protection Act of 1972 (MMPA), prohibits capture and harassment in US waters, with exceptions made for Alaska native subsistence harvest. These constraints facilitated the recovery of grey whale populations, which by the 1990s had grown to the point where the species could reproductively compensate for minor harvest. In 1995, the Makah sent a proposal to the US government, to be conveyed to the IWC, requesting that they again be allowed to hunt whales. A problem arose as the IWC required a "continuing" tradition of aboriginal whale hunting to allow an exemption from the moratorium. In 1997, however, the IWC granted the Makah a quota of four whales providing for "aboriginal subsistence and cultural needs" (Coté 2010: 166–167).

Makah plans to renew whale hunting drew immediate criticism from the owners of whale watching boats for tourists, opponents of Indian treaty rights, and animal rights activists. Environmentalists split, some standing with the Makah attempt to recover their heritage, and some arguing against it. **Nongovernment organizations (NGOs),** intent on ending all harvest of marine mammals, like The Sea Shepherd Conservation Society, were particularly vehement. Although not all environmental NGOs (**ENGOs**) took public stands against the whale hunt, ENGOs from multiple countries sent "An Open Letter to the Makah Nation," requesting them to halt the hunt. The letter used the concept of parallel animal societies to argue that the Makah form of religious valuation of whales not be recovered. It argued that "many cultures worldwide hold whales to be sacred and consider each species a sovereign nation unto itself, worthy of respect and protection" (Coté 2010: 175–176). ENGOs worried that allowing even minor deviations from the moratorium would open the door for industrialized whaling nations like Japan to resume harvest.

As the date for the hunt neared, protestors arrived at the Makah Reservation at Neah Bay, Washington. They disrupted traffic, tourism, and village life. Tribal leaders received death threats, and the tribal police arrested protesters directly interfering with activities in the harbor. Even more problematic for the Makah, US-based ENGOs sent communications to the National Oceanic and Atmospheric Administration (NOAA), claiming that federal agencies had improperly authorized the hunt, which violated federal regulations—particularly The National Environmental Policy Act (NEPA). Despite the furor, NOAA issued a positive Environmental Assessment, finding no significant damage. In May 1999, a Makah crew who had been fasting and praying for months harpooned a gray whale and distributed the meat and blubber to tribal members. Over 3000 people attended the potlatch celebrating the event. The Makah perceived the whale as sacrificing itself participatory rituals as revitalizing community and identity (Coté 2010: 138–149).

ENGO sponsored lawsuits followed, and in 2002, a federal court determined that the authorizations for the whale hunt violated the Marine Mammal Protection Act, despite the whaling rights recognized in the treaty between the Makah and the United States. In 2007, five Makah men, frustrated by the legal barriers, undertook a whale hunt and shot a gray whale without the permission of the Makah council or the federal government. The US Coast Guard immediately apprehended the hunters and confiscated their boats. Since the MMPA prohibits taking, the Coast Guard left the wounded whale in the Pacific. Members of the Makah Nation traveled out to expiring cetacean, and sang and prayed over it, so it would not die alone. After a federal judge reprimanded the hunters for taking the law into their own hands, two received prison sentences of up to five months, and three served two years' probation (Coté 2010).

Issue: Racially and culturally dismissive rhetoric

The Makah whaling case highlights the potential dissonance between environmental care models originating in indigenous religions with those based in dominant cultures and western political discourse. The dichotomous model of 'the ecological Indian" casts animism as primitive and ecologically benign. It portrays indigenous religions as anachronistic and thereby irrelevant to contemporary policy formation. Even when environmental advocates and indigenous groups are on the same side of an issue, their motives may be divergent. Professor of American Indian Studies and member of Nuu-chah-nulth, Charlotte Coté (2010), points to the importance of **environmental rhetoric** and the willingness of non–Native Americans to define how the Makah should behave. Whites define Indians as "Other" and opposite to themselves. Mentally confining indigenous society to past centuries and undeveloped terrains, this dichotomy leads to conflicts over who should determine what is authentic and traditional, and what level of cultural change is acceptable.

A practical issue is whether a regional or indigenous culture invoking historic harvest rights may offer products for sale? Ironically, while the IWC mandated consumptive use only, the peoples of the Pacific Rim had historically traded goods extracted from salmon, whales, and shellfish among tribes. An additional question is whether only traditional methods of harvest should be allowed? In the case of the Makah whale hunt, the IWC mandated using a rifle to dispatch the harpooned whale, as this is faster and more humane. Some protesters, though, held firearms delegitimized the hunt as "cultural recovery" (Coté 2010: 156–160). Greenpeace activists opposing the killing of Arctic seals have similarly rationalized their interference with Inuit seal harvests by identifying them as commercial and thereby non-traditional. Campaigns to reduce the sale of exotic wild-caught pelts for fur clothing have indeed reduced pressure on leopards, cheetahs, and many other declining species. Dependent on seal meat for food, Inuit camps are taking seals in any case. The collapse of the market for pelts has reduced their value, eliminating income needed for tools and modern fuels (replacing oils from marine mammals). Even with rifles in hand, the Inuit hunt is a sacred pact with the seals, where the seal gives itself to the hunter and, in return, is reborn or renewed (Pelly 2001: 106, 113–115).

Colonial racist rhetoric once stereotyped Indians as savage, an image reversed by Romanticism, which stereotyped the largely defeated Native American warriors as noble in works such as James Fennimore Cooper's *The Last of the Mohicans*. Coté (2010: 158–163) argues anti-whaling rhetoric calling the Makah hunt "barbaric" and whalers as "bloodthirsty murders" revived the savage stereotype. Environmental advocates, writers, and filmmakers have brought native cultures' relationships with the land and seas into their agendas. Often, environmentalist understanding of indigenous religions is superficial or informed primarily by the popular media. When an indigenous group does not conform to their values or wishes, they blame modernization and treat the indigenous people as "sell-outs." Contemporary environmental movements like Deep Ecology award rights or intrinsic value to nature and generate ethical models that give greater weight to protecting the lives of individual whales than maintaining Makah religion, art, and culture.

Coté (2010: 164) summarizes the contrasting religious philosophy of Native American whalers:

> In my culture, we have an understanding that we all exist– humans, animals, plants, etc.—in a shared environment everything is equal. Our cultures thrived in a world of reciprocity between us and our environment. Our relationship with animals has always been one based on respect and gratitude, and there is a sense of sacredness attached to the spirit of the animal for giving itself to us for sustenance. Within this symbolic relationship was the understanding that death is ultimately integrated into life.

As of this writing, the conflict between the Makah and US government over treaty rights remains unresolved from the Makah perspective. In 2019, as opponents of renewed Makah whaling had feared, Japan left the IWC. The Japanese issued a quota for commercial whaling, citing, among other justifications, their long history in the trade.

Issue: Response to destructive commercial harvest

The intrusion of industrialized harvest methods, such as fossil fuel-driven chainsaws clear-cutting forests and beam trawl nets scouring the sea bottom, causes degradation of ecosystems. Although religious values and practices are rarely the sole motives for resisting massive disturbance of forested watersheds or seamounts, they serve as rallying banners and communication conduits consolidating local community action. As a fruit of civil rights advocacy and formation of politically active tribal councils beginning in the 1960s, the First Nations of Canada intensified their long campaigns to regain the right to guide forest management on their lands—resulting in the multi-decade "wars in the woods."

The large timber companies had been slow to reach the Pacific Rim **old-growth forests** at higher elevations or on coastal islands. As they finished clear-cutting more accessible sites, they turned their attention to licenses to fell big trees on Vancouver Island and in remote Haida Gwaii to the north. When mainland-based interests began to obtain tenure on the timberlands of Haida Gwaii in the 1950s, the Haida kept their distance. The Nation had little influence on the companies' activities or government decision-making concerning resource extraction in any case. The Haida soon found they were blocked from harvesting cedars and other preferred trees to maintain their boat-building businesses. The new landowners invoked "no trespassing" statutes, and their tree farms replaced the old-growth stands. Threatened with even larger-scale extraction operations, from the 1970s onward, the coastal First Nations began to resist (Takeda 2015: 28–78).

When the Canadian government granted a license for a tree farm to fell venerable cedars on Meares Island, British Columbia, the Nuu-chah-nulth Tribal Council reacted by filing a counter land claim. For many centuries the Ahousaht and Tla-o-qui-aht (Clayoquot) had treated the island as sacred and had cut bark and planks from the ancient trunks without killing the cedars. Three-hundred-year-old **culturally modified trees** were proof of aboriginal ownership. Teaming up with environmental groups in 1984, the Nuu-chah-nulth attempted to block the loggers by stationing protesters and barricades in their way. The timber company turned to the courts to obtain an injunction against the protestors. After an initial decision in favor of the loggers, on the grounds rescinding their license would severely damage the forest industry in the province, the British Columbia Court of Appeals reversed the decision and halted the clear-cutting until the issue of title could be resolved (Coté 2010; Magnusson and Shaw 2003). In 2005, after two decades of legal wrestling with multi-national companies, the Haida threw a blockade of truck roads utilized by the Weyerhauser Corporation and placed a seizure notice on logs awaiting milling. Incorporating traditional uses of forest products like carving a cedar totem pole and log canoes in the celebration of their successful intervention, the Haida called the blockade "Islands' Spirit Rising" (Takeda 2015: 49–78).

Issue: Co-management, community-based management, and the new political landscape

To reduce conflicts, government agencies and university-based consultants have restructured environmental planning, placing greater emphasis on local community needs and cultural resources. They increasingly recognize the validity of **traditional knowledge** and treat regional religion as a resource rather than an anachronism, thereby **legitimizing** its environmental wisdom. Indigenous residents have a **spiritual conception** of forests, rivers, and other landscape features. The coastal tribes utilize giant cedars for constructing clan houses and carving poles and masks (Fig. 3.2). Historically, shamans selected the trees for sacred projects, as the trees must willingly give themselves to the endeavor, or it will go awry. Respect for the spirit of the tree continues today. When the Kwakiutl harvest bark from a large cedar, they avoid killing the tree in the belief other cedars will curse them. Kwakiutl petition the cedar before collecting bark or felling it—addressing it as a friend and respectfully requesting to take a piece of the tree's "dress." The prayer continues: "I come to beg for this, Long Life Maker, for I am going to make a basket for lily roots out of you..." and ends with a request for good health (Stewart 1984: 179–182).

Clear-cutting, of course, dismisses this deference and does not build bonds with multiple trees in a stand. A study of the Cheam and Stó:lō Salish groups from British Columbia, found they perceived clear-cutting of forests as a failure of their spiritual duties to the Chichelh Si:yam or Great Spirit and of their duty to the forests to utilize them "without compromising their productivity." Maintaining clear streams for ritual washing and quiet areas for meditation and forest appreciation informed First Nations' consideration of whether an area was degraded or not (Lewis and Sheppard 2013).

A comparison of First Nations' cultural constructions of hydrologic cycles reveals differences with scientific constructions, including an emphasis on healing properties of pure water and the perception water has a living spirit. Employed by the Canadian Forest Service as a First Nations Relations manager, Michael Blackstock (2005) introduced the concept of **blue ecology** to reconcile First Nations conceptualizations with those of forest managers. First Nations elders have greater concerns for logging causing springs to go dry and disrupting the sponge effect provided by mosses and intact organic soils. Indigenous informants also lament the loss of beaver and the wetlands beaver generate via their dams (Blackstock 2013). Commercial logging opens the forest canopy modifying forest microclimates and microbial activity, increasing temperatures, and drying surface soils. Building roads, moving equipment, and dragging logs initiate erosion and strip humus. Clear-cutting is particularly devastating for herbs, including edible and medicinal species, and microclimate sensitive organisms like salamanders (Meier et al. 1996).

Blue ecology is less willing than "sustainable" scientific forestry, to sacrifice the diminutive, site-specific, and intermediate members of the land and aquatic communities or to allow the living spirit of water to disappear via desiccation. Oriented toward commerce, scientific forestry awards higher value to the commercial timber trees and big game. Despite the improved appreciation of indigenous wisdom, university-trained resource managers often **cherry-pick** traditional knowledge and ecologies, selecting the interpretations most consistent with positivistic science and passing over socio-cultural linkages that seem less relevant in terms of productive harvest (Stevenson 2013). More thoughtful and accepting communication does not, by itself, harmonize the visions of the stakeholders.

A second means of seeking cooperation is to develop a **co-management** system, where local or regional resource-based economies share governance and management planning responsibilities with national or provincial agencies. Co-management, however, often encounters communication gaps, differences in goals, and wrestling for authority. The New Zealand government and the Māori have continued to define access to rivers differently—leading to **ontological dissonance**. The government holds the rivers belong to no one, despite the form of privatization inherent in building electricity-generating dams. The Māori wish to recover treaty rights and the *mauri* or life force of the rivers and to reassert *māna* or spiritual authority. In 2005, New Zealand gave the Māori exclusive authority over the Nation's first freshwater reserve located at the prized eel fishery at Mataura Falls. The reserve, however, is a mere 10-km long, and the fishery remains compromised. In 2009, the Māori petitioned to close eel and whitebait fishing within the reserve. They initiated scientific research to guide fish restoration (Knight 2016: 244–280).

The Māori do not have direct authority over the sources of environmental degradation for New Zealand's watersheds. Channelization, contamination, and sedimentation are ubiquitous. The current trend is toward a form of co-management, where the national government, local governments, and Māori *iwi* (tribes) enter into agreements for joint action. In recognition of the challenges of genuine river restoration, the agreement for the seriously polluted Waiapu River has a 100-year horizon for completion, beginning with restoring forests on erosion-prone soils (Knight 2016: 244–280).

Canada has established co-management regimes between First Nations and other stakeholders across the country. Clayoquot Sound and Haida Gwaii served as early, experimental, and oft controversial projects. The Clayoquot Sound Sustainable Development Task Force, established in 1989, generated a land-use plan protecting 34% of the forested land in the Clayoquot watershed. Environmentalists rejected the plan as not preserving enough land, and the Nuu-chah-nulth rejected the scheme on the grounds they had not been adequately consulted. In 1993, cadres of demonstrators blocked roads and logging activities, resulting in the largest single arrest of protesters (800) in Canadian history. The provincial government negotiated with the Nuu-chah-nulth and created a Central Region Board, which has improved First Nations representation but did not fully relieve the potential for conflict. The Haida, in contrast, entered into formal treaty negotiations with the government that produced the legal Gwaii Hanas Agreement. It also created the Archipelago Management Board, operating in conjunction with Parks Canada. The Haida have focused on protecting heritage sites and managing tourism. The agreement mandated the symbolic recovery of the original name of the Queen Charlotte Islands as Haida Gwaii. Both co-management strategies incorporate First Nations–based sustainable harvest of commercial timber from their lands (Mabee et al. 2013).

Studies of forest co-management identify three challenges: institutional constraints and determining an effective means of governance, cross-cultural differences, and socioeconomic stratification where indigenous peoples have not had equal opportunities to train for and fund developments. The Haida, for example, achieved access to resources for subsistence and ceremonial purposes. The Clayoquot sound governance model, in contrast, did not explicitly protect Nuu-chah-nulth harvest or religious use of ecological reserves. Initially, the "highly spiritual and ceremonial context" of **traditional ecological approaches** presented barriers to understanding on the part of scientific advisors. Through time, stakeholder efforts to gain a basic grasp of First Nations worldviews have mitigated the communication dissonance. These co-management programs are still in place. In 2013, 400 people arrived at the site of the 1985 logging blockade. They erected the first "Legacy Pole" raised by the Haida in 130 years, to celebrate the "Haida Nation's continual title and occupation of the land" (Mabee et al. 2013; Takeda 2015: 187–207).

A third approach is to maintain or reestablish **community-based management**—usually where ethnic or indigenous groups are still a majority within their historic regions of residence. National parks in the Amazon basin have incorporated the peoples originally present, who continue their pre-colonial means of harvest. Parks are not intrusion free, however, and tourism and the advent of new technologies like motorized boats and rifles are givens. Further, remote parks and resource reserves have minimal infrastructure and few rangers; thus, poaching, illegal mining, and unauthorized timber cutting remain serious threats. Parks do not protect all Amazonian peoples. Rubber tappers and other extractive interests have forced the Tukano to politically organize and battle for rights to their pre-colonial lands and river access.

Issue: World religions and cooperative ecosystem management

Cooperative management strategies are applicable within the framework of world religions, particularly where regional or folk variants are embedded in communities dependent on local natural resources. Aside from leading to over-harvest, excessive capitalization of fishing fleets and increasing control by large corporations has displaced many family-operated fishing boats on the North Atlantic coasts. In the predominantly Roman Catholic Irish Republic, smaller ports and those in Irish-speaking areas are more likely to have retained such shared religious practices as pattern days (saints' days). Ports dominated by large trawlers with salaried and non-local crews have lost these traditions. Fishers from the corporate fleets are less likely to feel they are part of the local community or that they can trust others if they need assistance (Hinz and Bratton 2000; Bratton and Hinz 2002). Establishing fishing cooperatives or shared governance can protect the interests of small-scale fishers, renew community life, and retain distinctive regional cultures. Some promising strategies for fisheries, such as assigned catch shares and individual quotas (by boat or family), raise the level of expected cooperation by participants (Halpern and Agardy 2014).

Conclusion: Religion, science, and worldviews

Naïve social models equating indigenous values with contemporary environmentalism can lead to conflicts. Validation of indigenous or local discourse and understanding of diverse worldviews by scientific advisors contribute to environmental care. Ecological restoration can precipitate religious recovery. A notable pattern in co-management, community management, and indigenous reserves is the acceptance of scientific monitoring and advice, when not in conflict with cultural values. The Hawaiians are attentive to the impacts of global warming, sea-level rise, and ocean acidification on coral reefs. Canadian First Nations employ ecologically informed forest and watershed planning. The assimilation of scientific discourse and industrial technologies can, however, subtly modify indigenous bioregionally informed worldviews. The indigenous communities understand they must strike a compromise between heritage and the continuing barrage of external cultural and environmental pressures.

Suggested readings

Berkes, Fikret. *Sacred Ecology*. New York: Routledge, 2018.

Coté, Charlotte. *Spirits of Our Whaling Ancestors: Revitalizing Makah and Nuu-chah-nulth Traditions*. Seattle: University of Washington Press, 2010.

Harkin, Michael, and David Rich Lewis, eds. *Native Americans and the Environment: Perspectives on the Ecological Indian*. Lincoln: University of Nebraska Press, 2007.

Harvey, Graham. *Animism: Respecting the Living World*. New York: Columbia University Press, 2006.

Knight, Catherine. *New Zealand's Rivers: An Environmental History*. Canterbury, N.Z.: University of Canterbury Press, 2016.

Leopold, Aldo. *A Sand County Almanac and Sketches Here and There*. New York: Oxford University Press, 1949.

McGregor, Davianna Pōmaika'i. *Nā Kua'āinka: Living Hawaiian Culture*. Honolulu: University of Hawai'i Press, 2007.

Sidky, H. *The Origins of Shamanism, Spirit, Beliefs, and Religiosity: A Cognitive Anthropological Perspective*. Lanham, MD: Lexington Books, 2007.

Takeda, Louise. *Island Spirit's Rising: Reclaiming the Forests of Haida Gwaii*. Vancouver: University of British Columbia Press, 2015.

Taylor, Joseph E., III. *Making Salmon: An Environmental History of the Northwest Fisheries Crisis*. Seattle: University of Washington, Press, 1999.

Tindall, D.B. Ronald Trosper, and Pamela Perreault, eds. *Aboriginal Peoples and Forest Lands in Canada*. Vancouver: University of British Columbia Press, 2013.

4 Sustenance

Food security, agricultural innovation, and environmental degradation

Key concepts

1 The invention of agriculture about 13,000 BP initiated changes in religious organization and practice. It supported the emergence of prosocial religions, professional priesthoods, and complex ritual cycles tied to planting and harvest.
2 Social scientists have proposed rituals are valuable forms of communication, encouraging cooperation and trust within communities. They hypothesize ritual participants are more likely to sacrifice self-interest for the benefit of the greater community.
3 In their feudal, imperial, and colonial forms, prosocial religions can develop governance hierarchies that reduce equitable access to land tenure for agricultural labor and undermine food security for the lower social strata.
4 Religions develop codes and ethical principles forwarding cooperation and neighborliness among farmers. Hindu farmers practice right living by honoring *rta*, the cosmic or natural order, and *dharma*, pursuing moral action and upholding the social order.
5 Modernization of agricultural rituals or translocation to new urban settings can separate them from their agricultural context and modify their expression of environmental values.
6 Contemporary religions advocate environmentally friendly diets via practices such Jewish Eco-Kashrut or Muslims preparing a green iftar. Adherents of western religions have adopted dietary concepts of non-western origin, such as ahimsa and mindful eating.
7 Religious communities participate in urban gardening and address food deserts through the practice of civic ecology.
8 Religious sects constraining industrial agriculture technologies, such as the Amish, must still contend with the environmental impacts of modernity, such as water contamination by fertilizers and suburban encroachment on farmland.
9 In the early 20th century, US Christian concern for the welfare of farmers led them to initiate the Christian agrarian movement, develop a novel language of Christian environmental stewardship, and join with agricultural scientists and government agencies in the campaign against land degradation.
10 Both religious groups pursuing societal reforms and farmers have formed cooperative farming organizations or agriculture-centered intentional communities based on religious values. Many of these organizations practice permaculture or organic farming, and actively seek a return to place, reversing the detachment and landlessness associated with modernity.

Domestication and the earth's ecosystems

The loss of the large mammals and an increasingly unpredictable climate encouraged hunter-gatherers, who had already broadened their diet to include more small game and an expanding variety of plants, to assume a greater role in ensuring **food security.** About thirteen millennia BP, residents of the Tigris and Euphrates valleys began to gather the seeds of wild plants and to sow them in cleared plots. Not long after, separate centers of domestication arose in East Asia, central Africa, and the Americas. Overall, the emergence of agriculture would displace thousands of wild species, remove a significant portion of the planet's natural vegetation cover, initiate soil erosion, deplete nutrients, and alter **hydrology** (the water cycle). The farmers took the technological, demographic, and military advantage over the gathers of wild consumables. The languages and material cultures of the centers of domestication spread into the surrounding regions (Diamond 2002). The Indo-European language family underpinning this text migrated from South and West Asia to Europe and then to North America, along with wheat, cheese, and beef.

The rise of agriculture modified the scale, complexity, and professionalization of religion. As early forms of cultivation spread, village size expanded, and separate rooms with distinctive iconography appeared, which were likely monuments or shrines (Tauger 2011: 5). Human societies and religion **scaled up**. About 6000 to 7000 years BP, Neolithic farmers began to erect large stone tombs and structures that served as temples or platforms for religious rites. Agricultural societies must anticipate seasonal changes, and these constructions demonstrate a sophisticated knowledge of astronomy. The passage grave at New Grange, Ireland (ca 5200 BP), for example, is so precisely aligned with the annual movement of the rising sun that its central chamber is fully illuminated only at the winter solstice.

Social psychologists Ara Norenzayan and Azim Shariff (2008) have argued the emergence of **prosocial religions** facilitating individually costly behaviors benefiting other persons, including non-relatives, is the by-product of the evolution of large, stable societies. Agricultural settlements replaced the kinship-based foraging bands where members know everyone in the group. Prosocial religions support professional priesthoods, revere "big gods" concerned with morality, and promise divine reward or punishment in the afterlife. They build trust among strangers and encourage cooperative behaviors, including the sacrifice of individual benefits for the **common good**. Although the world religions did not necessarily gain an initial foothold in farming communities, they all originated in societies where agricultural production supported market towns and complex trading networks. Christianity's speedy spread from Palestine to Rome and Athens, and then to Egypt and Gaul, followed shipping routes carrying grain and wine from the provinces to Rome and to other centers of imperial control.

Domestication and ritual: Shinto and rice

Agricultural religions share features like care-taker deities, seasonal festivals, and offerings of crops. Shinto, the indigenous religion of Japan, identifies rice as sacred. A primary god or **Kami**, Inari Okami, is the protector of the rice fields and ripening grain (Box 3.1). He also takes responsibility for tea, and sake (wine fermented from rice), and thereby for general prosperity. Worshippers visiting a shrine dedicated to Inari bring offerings of rice and other foods, to please the foxes or *kitsune*, who serve as messengers

---

Box 4.1 The Shinto concept of Kami

Shinto holds that spiritual powers or **Kami** that renew life and fertility are infused in nature. Kami are more potent in some natural objects and events than others. While Kami can be deities in the polytheistic sense, with names and definite roles in natural processes, the concept of Kami extends to "anything that can fill us with wonder and awe," and thus is animistic. Kami are the essence of giant cedar trees, waterfalls, plant growth, green spaces around shrines, and sacred peaks. They also are inherent to the miracle of birth, heroic warriors, and shamans, as well as serving as protective deities for villages.

Source: Ellwood (2008: 48)

---

to the god. Inari begins his year in the mountains, which are a primary source of water greening the fields below. The loyal care-taker travels down to the rice terraces as the trees blossom in spring, nurtures his precious crop during the growing season, and then returns to the heights following the fall harvest festival. Just as both men and women participate in rice cultivation, Inari may appear as a bearded, aged man toting a sack full of rice, or as a woman bearing sheaths. Supported by 30,000 shrines, the cult of Inari remains widely popular in Japan (Ellwood 2008: 48–49) (Box 4.1).

The Shinto ritual calendar incorporates multiple *matsuri* or festivals dedicated to themes ranging from human fertility to national origins. In Osaka, the Sumiyoshi Taishi Shrine continues to hold an annual *Otaue Shinji* festival in June to petition the Kami for a successful transplanting (*otaue*) of the fragile rice seedlings germinated in flats. The festival begins when farmers driving oxen plow the sacred field associated with the temple. Following a procession accompanied by armor-attired samurai, planting maidens (*ueme*) dressed in bright green carry the symbolic sprouts around the rim of the field to the newly opened furrows. Women in colorful traditional farming clothes wade knee-deep to install the delicate plants, as a priest pours holy water to convey a blessing. The gestures of shrine maidens dancing on an elevated platform gracefully ascend and descend, capturing the flow of agricultural processes. The beat of the large *taiko* drums guides human dance steps, yet the music is supposed to improve the vigor of young rice shoots, inhabited by potent Kami. Marking the cyclical passage of the growing season, farmers make offerings of harvested rice at the Shrine in autumn (Asano 2015).

As a nexus of social relationships, shared food is prominent at Japanese *matsuri*. An officiant may present all attendees with a drink of sake or a morsel, like squid or dried seaweed, previously offered at an altar. In distributing ritual offerings, the priests urge the participants to share a feast with the Kami and build a relationship with them. Despite the formality, a *matsuri* is also entertainment. As an attendee summarized, the festivals are "an opportunity for us to get together and do something as a community" (Ashkenazi 1993: 65–77). Controlled fermentation facilitates transport and long-term storage of fruits and grains. Rice brewers donate sake to the Shinto shrines, which stack the empty barrels outside. When worshippers partake of sake, it is supposed to make them cheerful and feel closer to the deities (Gordenker 2007). For multiple religions, offerings of fermented beverages, like a **libation** or pouring of wine before an altar, and shared feasts acknowledge not just the importance of domestic crops, but their processing and provision for the populace.

Issue: Why are agricultural rituals so pervasive?

Religious scholars have hypothesized that very productive farming cultures were the basis of early interregional religions and ultimately of world religions like Hinduism. Academics reason that farming environments influence cosmologies, such as the proposal that Hebrew dryland farming and pastoralism encouraged the emergence of monotheism. Even religious movements with urban roots have adapted to the countryside. Early Christianity, for example, garnered patron saints, blessings, moral stories, and pilgrimages tied to the fields and livestock. Before industrialization, all the earth's farming cultures had generated religious rituals associated with agricultural practices.

Anthropologist Roy Rapport (1979) has argued that rituals are valuable forms of communication encouraging cooperation and trust within communities. This **functional** explanation for human activities that are not directly productive assumes religion is **socially adaptive**. Religious imagery is selective—emphasizing some landscapes, objects, and human activities rather than others. Rituals separate the positive from the negative and the desired from the feared. They convey norms of behavior and reinforce social bonds. The costuming, procession, and performance of Japanese rice festivals serve a practical purpose in promoting respectful relationships, both human and environmental. The synchronicity of the drumming and dancing enhances identification with the attending community. Farming rituals declare the intrinsic value and spirit-infused state of the plants and attest to the sacred nature of the agricultural vocations, including the critical role of women.

The logical inference that rituals build cooperation among agriculturalists is not by itself a proof of the relationship. Anthropologists Richard Sosis and Bradley Ruffle (2003) designed an experiment where they invited members of seven religious and seven secular Israeli **Kibbutzim** (cooperative farming or artisanal communities) to participate in a game where three players shared an envelope containing money. The players request a withdrawal of individual funds, but if the combined request is more than the funds in the envelope, the game is over– generating a **common-pool dilemma**. The members of the religious Kibbutzim all adhered to Modern Orthodox Judaism, where both males and females keep **Kosher** dietary rules, avoid working on the Sabbath, and attend synagogue. Participating together in public prayer three times daily, men have higher levels of synagogue attendance than women. Women focus on private rituals, such as lighting Sabbath candles and bathing at the mikveh (ritual baths) to maintain personal purity. Sosis and Ruffle hypothesized that the members of religious Kibbutzim would take less money for themselves, and the men would act more cooperatively than the women, due to their greater participation in shared daily prayers.

Sosis and Ruffle (2003) found that of 100 shekels, religious males on average removed 29.9 shekels, religious females withdrew 33.7—a statistically significant difference. Secular males selected 30.1 and secular females 30.5, which was not statistically different. Several factors, other than synagogue attendance, influenced their behavior. Making a conscious ideological commitment to a collective lifestyle, individuals who had moved to a Kibbutzim withdrew less money than those who had always lived in a Kibbutz. Demonstrating a higher commitment to communal living, members who had jobs outside the Kibbutz and transferred their salary income to the Kibbutz also withdrew less from the envelope. Male synagogue attendance was negatively correlated with the amount of money withdrawn, indicating the more a male participated in shared religious services, the more communitarian his behavior when confronting a common pool dilemma.

Social psychologists studying cultural evolution have hypothesized that if a populace believes god or gods are in control, and there is a judgment or divine retribution for anti-social behaviors, this reduces hostile actions toward others and promotes sharing. Mere reminders of divine authority, such as an image of a god, a shrine, or a call to prayers, can prompt less self-motivated ethical decision making. Psychologists Azim Shariff and Ara Norenzayan (2007) implemented experiments where one person ("the dictator") receives $10 and then decides whether to share the funds with another unrelated individual. The investigators divided their subjects into two groups and asked both to unscramble sentences by removing an irrelevant word. One group received a **religious prime** as the sentences contained the words *God, sacred, divine, spirit,* and *prophet,* and the other received no religious primes. Among the controls, "the dictator" gave the other person an average of $1.84. Among the subjects reminded of God, however, the dictator gave the other person an average of $4.22 (p<.001)—a highly significant statistical difference. These results infer shrines at the edge of grain fields or priests pouring water into flooded rice paddies have psychological functions beyond reducing anxiety concerning uncontrollable natural forces. Religious practices support **metaethics,** improving the likelihood of coordinated responses to food production and thereby of community survivorship in the long run.

One of the most widely circulated essays explaining human abuse of the environment, "**The tragedy of the commons,**" by Garrett Hardin (1968), holds that given a shared natural resource, humans are likely to take more than a fair individual portion. Hardin told the tale of a village pasture, where without regulation, individual farmers try to add just one more sheep or cow to their flock on the commons. Ultimately, too many livestock occupy a limited range, and they nibble the grass down to its roots. Forage plummets and herds starve. Given skies and rivers as **common property resources**, the same principle applies as individual households and businesses release their waste and pollute spaces belonging to all. For long-term success, however, agriculture requires sharing the irrigation water, distributing the genetic information inherent in seeds, and organizing labor for planting, harvest, and erosion control. Anthropologists have documented ritually-mediated governance systems, such as the Balinese water temple complexes, that organize very environmentally sensitive and interactive distribution of essential resources (Chapter 6). Contra to Hardin's paradigm, scientific study suggests that participants in communitarian rituals or beliefs in divine authority are less willing to overdraft common pool resources and thus less likely to add an extra sheep to the commons.

Issue: Hierarchy and empire

Agricultural festivals are not necessarily democratic or politically neutral. Expanding aristocratic control over food production has often displaced the role of the farmers in production-based rituals. In tenth-century Japan, the Emperor, deified as a direct descendant from the Kami, assumed the lead role in the *Niinamesai* or New Food Ceremony and served as the host who invited the Kami to a royal feast and entertainment on behalf of the entire nation (Hardacre 2017: 72). During the Ming dynasty, Chinese emperors commissioned a circular temple in the north of Beijing representing the heavens (ca 1420 CE), then added the square Temple of the Earth in the south (ca 1530 CE). The Temples of the Sun and Moon completed the celestial layout, reflecting medieval beliefs about the structure of the universe. Marking the solstices, planting, the rains, and harvest, the Emperor as the Son of Heaven led the ceremonies petitioning for good crops and prosperity. When conducting sacrifices at the Temple of Heaven, the Emperor and his retinue would leave the Forbidden City accompanied not by farmers and oxen but by an Imperial Guard of Honor, headed by elephants carrying massive sacred vessels. Bearing weapons and banners, ministers for military affairs, cavalry, and chariots marched to the music of pipers and drummers. Guards prevented the common people from entering the walled sacred precincts. When the Emperor stood in the center of the circular Mound Altar, where innovative acoustics produce outdoor echoes, thousands would wait outside the gates as the Emperor spoke to the gods (Tan 2008).

In acting as the high priest for his far-flung realms, the Emperor reinforced the role of imperial governmental authority over agricultural produce. Obvious differences from the Japanese rice festival include the elimination of agricultural implements, living plants, farmers and women, and their replacement with gold sacred objects, icons of empire, and an intimidating military presence. Symbols of international commerce and imperial hegemony displaced themes of cooperation among farmers. Following the revolution led by Mao Tse Tung, Communist antagonism toward traditional Chinese religion was not mere dismissal of folk superstition but based in centuries of religious collusion in the oppression of the peasantry. Despite their emphasis on **metaethics** (Norenzayan et al. 2014), prosocial religions and those with complex hierarchies, like feudal Christianity, have not ensured land equity or **food security** for people in the lower strata.

The People's Republic did not destroy the four cosmic temples but has preserved their historic architecture and symbolically opened them to the general populace as public parks. At the Temple of the Earth in Ditan Park, the best-attended festivities now occur at the Lunar New Year and feature populist forms of religious celebration like lion dances (Aldrich 2008). A troupe wearing medieval dress has reenacted Qing dynasty rites as part of the public spring festival (San Diego Union-Tribune 2016). Chinese patrons have sponsored unadvertised reenactments of the solstice sacrifices at the Temple of the Earth, presumably as petitions for prosperity rather than as events to draw tourists. Similarly, Inari's many Japanese shrines have become very popular with urban businesspeople—particularly with stockbrokers and traders, coping with the rise and fall of world commodity and currency markets rather than worrying about adequate rainfall (Ellwood 2008: 48–49). As the adaptions by investors and corporate employees demonstrate, devotees reinterpret agricultural cults in response to urbanization and changing economies.

Military invasions, imperialism, and external bureaucracies can unravel agricultural practices and local land tenure. Soil scientist Daniel Hillel (1991: 100–101) concludes that during times of peace, the vintners and grain producers of ancient Israel kept their walls and terraces in order, limiting topsoil and organic matter loss. Invading Assyrians (722 BCE) and Babylonians (587 BCE) deported Judean landholders, thereby fragmenting the social cooperation maintaining soil fertility. Breaches in abandoned terraces caused gullying. Goats allowed to run free in the vineyards dislodged retaining stonework and stripped vegetation initiating mass erosion. Isaiah 5 laments the breaking of the hedges and the wastage of the once productive slopes growing the choicest vines. Two millennia later, Europeans establishing colonies disrupted bio-regionally adapted systems of cropping in Asia, Africa, and the Americas. Colonialism treated food and raw materials as commodities serving the needs of the ruling nation. Sugar fields and tea plantations replaced local garden plots, and village or family farmer-based cropping strategies, undermining food security in the process.

Issue: Tensions concerning tillage

Removing natural vegetation and plowing the soil present a religious conundrum—if spirits infuse trees and springs, tillage disturbs the gods and their residences. Deities like Inari, who bring seeds and care for crops, sanctify the violated earth—thereby justifying the damage to natural ecosystems. A. Whitney Sanford (2012) has analyzed Hindu traditions concerning the conflict between the popular deity **Krishna**, a pastoralist protective of cowherds, and his elder brother **Balaram**, a cultivator and irrigator. The two siblings are the foci of the springtime **Holi festival** (Fig. 4.1). Sanford studied Holi in the city of Baldeo, a center of devotion to Balaram, on the Yamuna River in a region watered by monsoon rains followed by an early summer dry season.

Hinduism characterizes right living via two concepts—**rta**, the cosmic or natural order, and **dharma** (dhamma), pursuing moral action and upholding the social order. Humans are not divorced from natural functions and processes, but human *dharma* determines the continuation of *rta* or the favorable function of the environment. The concept of *rta* appears in the ancient Sanskrit text, the *Rig-Veda*, which is more than 3000 years old. Hindu farmers believe that if their *dharma* fails, the rains will not arrive, and famine will follow. The rituals conducted by Hindu priests are a form of gift exchange between humans and deities like the goddess of the earth, Prithvi. They maintain cosmic order, and thereby fertility and good harvests. As the anthropomorphic patron of agriculture, Balaram carries his sacred objects, a plow and a mace, for

Figure 4.1 Originating as a Hindu seasonal agricultural celebration, celebrants in today's urban Holi toss dry, non-toxic pigments into the air, Dallas, Texas.

Box 4.2 Balaram as a Hindu patron of tillage and irrigation

In Hindu belief, semi-divine beings, the *nagas* or serpents, burrow below ground and are analogs of plows turning the soil. They manage the soil moisture content by conveying water to their homes during the monsoon and making it available during the dry season. *Nagas*, like the rains, are capricious, and can destroy the harvests via unfavorable weather. Balaram is an incarnation of the thousand-headed serpent Shesh, the greatest of all *nagas*, who controls the deep aquifers.

Krishna threw a party for thousands of *gopis* or female cow herds, but neglected to invite his elder brother, who watched in secret. Balaram responded by organizing his own mass dance. Supplied with sweet ambrosia by Varuni the goddess of wine, Balaram became very drunk. The goddess of the Yamuna River did not attend. Balaram summoned her so he could enjoy her waters, and she hesitated. Intoxicated and angry, the god "thrust the pointed edge of his plow into the earth and dragged the Yamuna to his feet" and declared she would henceforth flow a hundred different directions. The Yamuna petitioned for mercy, and Balaram let her go, but her course changed forever. The narrative parallels male sexual conquest of women with the forceful acts of plowing the soil and diverting the broad river into multitudes of channels to irrigate the crops.

Source: Sanford (2012: loc. 1364–1368, 1518–1570)

eliminating depravity and maintaining *dharma*. In their many adventures, Krishna and Balaram defeated diverse demonic forces, but it is Balaram, not Krishna, who diverted the Yamuna River, personified as a goddess, into irrigation channel networks. The sacred stories recognize and justify tillage's violence to natural ecosystems and hydrology. (Sanford 2012: loc. 1342–1368) (Box 4.2).

Celebrating Balaram as an agricultural patron and honoring the waters of the Yamuna, the Holi or Festival of Colors is a playful if aggressive event allowing temporary relaxation of social norms (Fig. 4.1). Devotees exchange colors by gently painting friends and family with water-based pigments. Crowds roam through the streets and drench bystanders with buckets of tinted water. Holi is "a time of social renewal because this is the time when Balaram returned home to renew his bonds and to fulfill his promise to the serpent princesses," controlling the aquifers. The relationship between Balaram, the farmer, and the Yamuna river is thus one "of mutual obligation and reciprocity" (Sanford 2012: loc. 1493–1518, 1582–1595).

Contemporary interpretations emphasizing Balaram's contributions to agricultural stability have troubled Sanford (2012: loc. 1582–1607) as they rationalize exploitation under the rubric of human need, thereby paralleling "justifications for industrial agriculture." She suggests it is time to explore and rewrite the stories justifying damaging agriculture practices. Properly applied, the Holi can be a positive model of Balaram's role of protector, and human obligations to care for the hydrological regimes providing human sustenance. Sanford's proposed "greening" of the myths brings up the questions of when renovations of ancient religious practices are appropriate and who should undertake the remodeling? Like many other festivals of agricultural origin, Holi has emerged as a pleasant break for today's urbanites (Fig. 4.1). Its continuing attraction lies in its effusive sociality. Holi offers an opportunity to relax the tensions caused by economic insecurity and stratification. The Indian-heritage residents of megacities like London and Houston invite their non-Hindu neighbors to join them in a Holi frolic in warming spring weather. These transnational variants maintain ethnic identities, build neighborhood bonds, and offer a friendly introduction to Hinduism. For safety, some contemporary festivals use only dry colors, reducing the presence of water. In the process of adapting to new pluralistic contexts, Holi has become increasingly detached from irrigation and tillage.

Creating new green identities, schools in India have linked Eco-Holi campaigns to water conservation. Students conduct rallies with placards posting water-related slogans and interact with villagers concerning water management, sanitation, and environmental conservation. These programs associate Holi with plant protection, adding another theme consistent with the festival's basis in Hindu beliefs about the intrinsic value of nature (Center for Environmental Education, North Lucknow 2016). Traditionally, playing Holi deployed earth and plant-based dyes like henna. Organizers of today's festivals encourage revelers to take the pledge for Eco-Holi by purchasing organic, non-toxic colors. Eliminating plastic waste, they ban releasing multitudes of balloons (DNA Correspondent 2016). The transcontinental migration of Holi has distanced the festivities from Indian rivers. London and Houston Holi, though, challenge consumerism via friendly chaos and disrespect for clothing, cosmetics, and other symbols of personal status. Holi is rewriting its own stories while maintaining the life-supporting role of water as a keystone of Holi would be universally environmentally beneficial.

Issue: Codes and justice

In addition to the ethical modeling in myth and rituals, religions develop agricultural codes mandating shared responsibility and maintaining keystone resources. The laws in the *Torah* required ancient Hebrew farmers to compensate their neighbors for unnecessary damages caused by dangerous actions, including allowing a fire utilized to clear fields to escape, or permitting a bull to roam loose and gore a neighbor. Leviticus 25 commands a fallow year for the land every seventh year, providing a **Sabbatical rest** for the soil. As the land ultimately belongs to God, the Israelites were responsible to share its bounty with community members who were unable to farm for themselves. Leviticus 19 and 23 instruct those owning fields not to glean them (pick up fallen grain) and not to harvest the corners, but to allow those without resources—the widow, orphan, and sojourner (temporary resident)—to gather the scattered seeds and fruits. The unharvested produce is also available to the "birds of the air and beasts of the fields." Conveying divine justice, the Law requires farmers to sustain those who are landless or physically unable to raise food themselves and provide for God's creatures (Lowery 2000).

Comparative religious scholar Houston Smith has hypothesized that the leaders bringing today's world religions into existence, including Gautama Buddha and Jesus of Nazareth, were fueled by the desire to correct societal inequities generated by agricultural wealth (Ruddiman 2005: 73). During the medieval and colonial periods, repeated famines, serf or slave labor, and limited strategies for maintaining soil fertility characterized the world's grain-producing regions. Erratic production, in turn, fueled epidemics, political unrest, and economic instability, motivating religious and government leaders to structural reforms. Beginning in the 13th century, for example, the Islamic Ottoman government in Turkey attempted to protect the interests of the peasants. They abolished serfdom well before Europe banned bondage of labor to the land (Tauger 2011: 57–58). Throughout history, religious leaders have both oppressed farm laborers and campaigned for just land tenure and food security.

Issue: High-yield varieties and the green revolution

Despite the successes of scientific farming, the interface between religion and agriculture still faces the foundational challenges of famine, soil erosion, landlessness, and unjust prices for those who do the farming. In early modern Europe, a series of innovations began first to increase productivity per hectare, and then to reduce the labor necessary to this production, initiating the **agricultural revolution**. The Dutch and English enhanced soil fertility by alternating nitrogen demanding crops with nitrogen-fixing cover crops like clover. Improved methods of selective breeding resulted in higher productivity for cultivars and animals, resulting in today's controversial **high-yield varieties** (HYVs). The industrial revolution added new farm implements, the internal combustion engine, and agricultural chemicals.

Hardly on the periphery of science, religious communities made noteworthy contributions to new farming methods. The discoverer of dominant and recessive genes, Gregor Mendel, was an Augustinian friar who rose to abbot. Attempting to recover Japanese religion as practiced preceding foreign influences like Chinese Buddhism, the 19th-century Japanese nativist religious movement *Kogugaku* utilized agricultural manuals and publications to spread its teachings into the countryside. Shintoist theology treated agricultural labor as sanctified. Its ideals encouraged self-sufficient villages united around reverence at village shrines and self-cultivation regimens restoring harmony with the Kami. In the mid-19th century, the Japanese government encouraged Meiji Noho agriculture, intended to raise yields and thereby support industrialization. Japanese farmers discovered, bred, and adopted high-yield rice varieties that, like their Euro-American equivalents, consumed greater inputs of commercial fertilizer (Tauger 2011: 63–65; Hardacre 2017: 337–348).

Beginning in the 1960s, American agronomists touting the Green Revolution campaigned with government officials and scientists in India and other developing nations to adopt HYVs as a panacea to repeated famines and the growing need for food imports. The Indian program soon generated surpluses. In India, however, buying seed, fertilizer, and pesticides was out of reach for many small farmers. The purchase of thousands of tractors eliminated jobs for laborers, who left the land and migrated to India's already populous cities. Through the 1980s, several African nations sponsored research on tropical cultivars. The benefits, though, were primarily to economically advantaged operations growing for export. Droughts and crop failures during the 1970s and 1980s, including the devastating multi-year drought-induced famine in the sub-Saharan Sahel region, proved that science alone could not resolve fluctuations in production rooted in climate, human population growth, and economics. Simultaneously, the agricultural debt crisis became so severe that even in the U.S., hundreds of farmers committed suicide, and thousands of families lost their land to foreclosure. Land reforms in some developing countries have helped to counter the fiscal strains. Yet as the globalization of trade has expanded, cash-strapped growers from less and more industrialized nations have increasingly competed for markets (Tauger 2011: 152–159).

Issue: Environmental impacts of scientific agriculture

Scientifically informed agriculture has not been fully able to manage its tools or ensure the safety of the food provided. The over-application of commercial fertilizers has contributed to contamination of freshwater streams and lakes, and to fish kills in large lakes and marine ecosystems such as the Chesapeake Bay, US. Excess nutrients feed algal blooms that deplete oxygen and suffocate fish. The Mississippi River is so fertilizer-enriched that it transports thousands of tons of excess nitrogen and phosphorus to the Gulf of Mexico annually. Growth in algal and bacterial populations results in an **anoxic** (no oxygen) **dead zone** where few marine species, including the shrimp, crabs, and fish supporting commercial fisheries, can survive.

The environmental movement of the 1960s and 1970s began with the 1962 publication of Rachel Carson's book, *Silent Spring*, addressing the ubiquitous spread of pesticides like DDT and their long-term negative effects on birds, fish, and humans. The application of pesticides can incidentally damage beneficial organisms like pollinators. The most recent addition to the agriculture repertoire is genetic engineering, where genes from one species or variety may be transferred to the chromosomes of another, producing **genetically modified organisms** (GMOs) resistant to pests, adverse weather, or drought. Food activists have questioned the safety of GMOs for human consumption, resulting in bans in some countries. The engineered genes can escape into wild relatives of domestic species, threatening to propagate superweeds. Mechanized agriculture is continuing to reduce biodiversity and to eliminate habitat for native species worldwide. Despite overflowing granaries, food safety and food security are on-going issues even in Europe and the United States.

Issue: Consumerism and cultivating sustainable lifestyles through religious praxis

Religious responses to the environmental and social impacts of industrial agriculture depend on the role religionists play in farming. At one end are the urban and suburban consumers, who rarely touch humus much less shovel manure. At the other end are the professional farmers, whose livelihoods depend on productivity adequate to make a profit. **Consumerism,** as a social norm, modifies the interface between religion and agriculture. Commercial interests can extricate agricultural deities and seasonal festivities from their communitarian roles and repurpose them as icons of comfortable living. The giants of food processing utilize religious holidays for mass sales pitches, glitzy packaging, and touting new products.

Consumers who commit to **sustainable lifestyles** set an example by "greening" the food shared at religious festivals. Recognizing the ethical connection between consumption and production, Green Muslims of Washington DC (2016) publish tips for a **Green Ramadan** on their web site. They cite the Quran's instruction to "eat and drink, but waste not by excess, for Allah loveth not the wasters." (Al-A'raf 7:31) For Islam, Ramadan is the most important sacred season, as it commemorates the revelation of the *Qur'an* to the Prophet Muhammad. Lasting a month, Ramadan prescribes daily fasting from dawn to sunset terminating in an evening meal, the *iftar*. Often celebrated by extended families or with friends, the *iftar* is an expression of community. Green Muslims advocate cooking vegetarian for one or more *iftars* a week, as meat production is a root cause of climate change. Raising livestock requires clearing additional land for pasture and grain production. Vegetarian meals can reduce the use of fossil fuels for machinery and methane from burping cows. Purchasing seasonal and locally grown produce and meats from farmers' markets supports local economies. Green Muslims suggest donating unused food from community meals to shelters and food kitchens for the homeless.

Green Muslims of Washington DC (2016) recommend that mosques deliver a green **khutbah**, or sermon in the Sunni tradition, thereby encouraging believers as part of their ethical reflections during Ramadan to "examine our individual and collective impact on the earth." As Ramadan is supposed to be a time for self-reflection and attention to charity, the infusion of sustainable practice to reduce the environmental impacts of food production and sharing food with others is appropriate to its original intent. With its focus on personal restraint and right living, Ramadan is a conducive setting for environmental instruction.

Householders can express an environmental ethos by buying produce from local farmers who practice **permaculture**, without dependence on carbon-emitting fuels. Consumers can also favor **organically grown** meats or vegetables with minimal or no input of synthetic chemicals, including pesticides, fertilizers, and sewage sludge. These methods reduce soil erosion, water pollution, and land abandonment, as well as improving food safety. Sustainable diets can discourage **factory farming,** confining livestock in small spaces, and preventing animals from roaming outdoors. Factory farms lace feed with hormones and antibiotics to accelerate growth rates. Many religious environmentalists consider factory farming to be inhumane and a source of concentrated animal waste contributing to water pollution. Consumers can favor **Fairtrade** products that protect the interests of smaller landholders and family-based cooperatives in the face of competition with large plantations and the price manipulation of international corporations. The companies promoting Fairtrade assist farmers in the daunting process of marketing across national borders and obtaining a reasonable price.

Environmentally friendly grocery lists have found their way into shopping for the weekly and monthly religious observances with shared food or drink as well-loved components. Based in Buddhist philosophy, the graceful **Japanese tea-ceremony** has dispersed internationally to tea houses, Japanese gardens, and private homes. Today's provisioners of organic and Fairtrade certified teas instruct their clientele in the symbolism and preparation of ritual tea, and offer organically grown *matcha,* a finely ground Japanese green tea, in its ceremonial grade. The Jewish Shabbat ends with a special dinner, forwarding quality family time in an excessively busy world. Aside from being tasty and enjoyable, the food for **Eco-Shabbat** should be safe for the loved ones by being free from toxins like pesticides. Christian church cafes raise funds to supplement thin budgets or offer inexpensive or free meals for the needy, combining social ministry with environmental consciousness. Tourists and university students lunching in the basement of a venerable Gothic cathedral find Fairtrade beverages, organic local cheeses, or veggie-filled pilgrim's pies on the menu.

While each of these religious approaches to diet has its own theological or philosophical basis, five justifications for praxis emerge in multiple contexts. The first is either dietary self-restraint or **asceticism** leads to more virtuous behavior or greater faithfulness. Asceticism incorporates limiting the intake of food and drink or restricting the acquisition of possessions. As an ascetic season, Ramadan emphasizes self-control by the devout and the ability of the individual to make sacrifices for the **common good**. A second shared concept is how one manages the material, and consumable has effects on one's piety, spiritual state, or relationship with God. New religions emerging in the industrialized nations often advocate self-improvement and physically healthy lifestyles. They forward eco-friendly diets as foundational to wholeness or establishing a balance between the corporeal and spiritual. A third shared value is sustainable foods forward human health. Replacing red meat with plant protein, for example, reduces grain production diverted to animal feed and release of greenhouse gases while slowing the onset of coronary diseases and diabetes. A fourth mutual practice is food should be selected and distributed for the welfare of others, particularly children, farmers, or the economically-disadvantaged. Green Ramadan sponsors charitable acts, modifies diets, and promotes ethical engagement throughout the following year. The fifth commonality is food should be enjoyed in community. It is a blessing either from God or the earth.

Issue: Adapting historic dietary codes to environmental values

Historically, under **Kashrut** or the dietary laws in the Torah, Judaism has required **Kosher** preparation of meats (ritual slaughter with blood drained from the carcass) and banned aquatic species without gills, crawling invertebrates, and pork as unclean. From its beginnings, Christianity has maintained few dietary restrictions other than those concerning periodic fasts and monastic vegetarianism. Hinduism's and Jainism's concept of reincarnation, where the human soul may return to a nonhuman organism, encourages respect and *ahimsa* or compassion in relationships with all living beings, and thereby vegetarianism. Buddhism similarly teaches care for even the smallest of living creatures. Buddhist *sutras* indicate the Buddha taught consuming meat and fish generates negative *karma* and undermines the virtue of *ahimsa*.

Beginning with the Enlightenment, the academic study of eastern religions exposed westerners to Hindu and Buddhist dietary codes. It brought new arguments for vegetarianism and compassion toward animals into western philosophical discourse (Stuart 2012). Postmodern Jews and Christians are developing theological justifications for meatless diets, and for **vegan** lifestyles where no animal products at all are consumed or worn. Often the motive is respecting the right of animals to live lives free of suffering. Contemporary Buddhism and other religions historically practicing vegetarianism are integrating environmental rationales into their concepts of right diet. Visitors to major Buddhist shrines and monasteries will find their dining halls serve vegetarian fare grown by Buddhist monastics or local small plot owners. Although these dietary strictures did not originate as means for slowing global climate change or reducing the conversion of rainforests to pastures, they avoid the energy inefficiency, pollution, and the potential cruelty of livestock rearing. For today's Buddhists, mindful gardening and **mindful eating** consider how food production influences atmospheric chemistry and water quality.

Moving beyond a limited definition of eco-Kashrut, Reform Jews organized a Sacred Table Task Force to weigh constructive approaches considering "agricultural workers rights, food production, the environment, personal health, the spirituality of eating and fasting, and the challenges of eating together." Consistent with Reform **polity** (the governance model utilized by a religious organization), the task force generated guidance informing personal choices rather than inflexible prescriptions for all households. Sacred Table participants borrowed from other religions and movements, in adopting the Buddhist concept of **mindful eating** and the food activists' definition of **real food** as nourishing, non-gummy, non-processed, whole foods. Sacred Table

---

Box 4.3 Jewish foundations for food ethics

Judaism requires consideration for God's interests and commandments as expressed in:

Ritual law and Kashrut—sanitary and humane preparation of meats, <u>avoidance of unclean foods</u> like pork

Tzar Baalei Chayim—<u>kindness to animals</u> and prevention of suffering of sentient creatures

Tzedek—<u>justice</u>, ensuring none go hungry

Oshek—avoidance of *oshek* or oppression of agricultural laborers and food preparers

Sh'mirat HaGuf— guarding <u>personal health</u>

Hafrashat Challeh—food preparation as a <u>holy act</u>, providing blessings to others

Tzom—fasting

Shomrei Adamah—<u>care of the soil</u>, the earth and its fruits

Bal Taschit—<u>avoidance of wanton waste</u> and environmental destruction

Source: Zamore 2011

---

has centered, though, on ethical principles from the Hebrew scriptures, such as *bal taschit*, avoiding wanton destruction, and *shomrei adamah*, care of the soil and its fruits (Zamore 2011) (Box 4.3).

Issue: Tackling western consumerism via theology

Religious ethicists are addressing not just the process of industrialized food production but the meaning of eating in consumer culture by developing formal theological arguments supporting sustainability. In his book, *Food & Faith: A Theology of Eating*, Norman Wirzba (2011: 77–79) contrasts "Godly gardening" to "eating in exile." Wirzba notes the first human transgression was biting the forbidden apple in the Garden of Eden. Humanity is experiencing a growing separation from the Garden characterized by three forms of exile: ecological, economic, and bodily. The demands for growing profits and consolidation of food distribution into the hands of a few large corporations are causing environmental degradation. Industrialized diets are high in calories and low in nutritional quality. The variety of food offered to wealthier consumers is a "market-manufactured reality"—symbolizing prosperity and encouraging excessive consumption (Wirzba 2011: 105–107).

Wirzba (2011: 174–187) invokes the rituals of **saying grace** or thanking God before meals and the **Eucharist** (the offering of Christ's body and blood in a symbolic shared meal or morsels of bread and wine). Christian repasts should reflect God's character and plans, such as divine love for all creation. They should emphasize divine immanence as God's desire "to be *with* and *dwell among* a reconciled creation." The reconciliation inherent in the Eucharist requires the Christians living in more privileged and powerful countries to constrain their demands for low-cost food if it degrades the land or the lives of agriculturalists who are far away. Healing broken relationships requires addressing trade agreements, corporate farming, and international banking agendas that undermine food security and trap rural populations in poverty. Reconciliation also requires listening to what other species, the land, and waters are telling us. Properly saying grace is based on "the practice of delight" and "moving into gratitude"—engaging the world as a medium of God's love. Fast food undermines delight because it is boring and nothing more than a commodity. The **slow food movement** conserves the joy of dining together. It supports farmers who grow varieties adapted to local climates and soils and conserve ecosystem processes. Wirzba (2011: 79) rejects living in exile and dislocation, and admonishes other Christians to recall "the divine love and delight that brought the first creation into being."

Issue: Industrialized technology and community integrity

Globally, farming ranges from subsistence to commercial, and from family managed to corporate with owners living on another continent. Religious responses to industrialized agriculture may originate with faith-based organizations, or conversely, farmers may utilize a shared religious framework as a platform for addressing environmental care. Long established sects already living on the land often curb technology to maintain community integrity. **Old Order Amish,** Protestants who emphasize humble lifestyles, pacifism, and maintaining strong family bonds, have adopted mechanized farm machinery like threshers, but reject tractors, internal combustion engines, and electricity. Their motive is binding families and Amish meetings together via shared labor. Horse teams pull their plows and buggies; thus, the Amish make minimal use of fossil fuels (Kraybill 2001).

Planning to pass farms on to **future generations**, the Amish strive to improve the soil. Deeming husbandry a virtue, they have adopted commercial nitrogen fertilizers as well as liberally spreading livestock manure on their fields. The Amish eschew large landholdings on the grounds they encourage pride and generate social stratification via individual wealth. Due to the limited size of their farms, generally less than 110 acres (50 ha) in the eastern United States, they place as much area as possible in cultivation. Amish farm owners have cleared wood lots and thick hedgerows along streams, removing vegetation buffers that could absorb excess nitrogen and phosphorous. Their restrictions on mechanization thereby did not inherently constrain pollution of groundwater and runoff. During the 1980s, cases of blue-baby syndrome (methemoglobinemia) began to crop up among the Amish children in central Pennsylvania. Caused by the ingestion of excess nitrite in well-water, the syndrome, which can also affect livestock, reduces the oxygen-transporting capacity of blood hemoglobin (Stranahan 1995: 228–229).

The Amish believe God made them "temporary stewards of God's garden." Once the Amish understood blue-baby syndrome is caused by nitrogen pollution, they acted cooperatively to better manage fertilizer applications. To avoid government meddling in their communities, the Amish do not accept federal subsidies, initially slowing their access to capital intensive nutrient-containment techniques such as large tanks for holding manure. Despite more restrained manuring, nutrient-rich runoff from Amish farms in Pennsylvania has continued to reach the Chesapeake Bay, contributing to its algal blooms and periodic **hypoxia** (oxygen deficiency) (Stranahan 1995). Recognizing the future of agriculture depends on practical solutions to multi-causal environmental stressors, the Amish have been willing to participate in dialogs with "watermen" dependent on fish and shellfish harvest.

The Amish are facing challenges of their own due to urban expansion—particularly the tourism infiltrating market towns, suburbs encroaching on farmlands, and higher speed highways endangering their horse-drawn conveyances. The conversion of highly productive farmland to other uses is global in scope and affects densely populated regions from the European Union to the megacities of East Asia. The Amish attempt to purchase nearby non-Amish farms but cannot always compete with developers who make substantial profits by dividing properties into smaller residential or commercial parcels. Young Amish families have formed groups moving together to regions where farmland is less costly, and they can establish a new meeting house—at the cost of being separated from parents and siblings. Counties with large numbers of Amish have established farmland preservation boards and agriculture-friendly taxation policies. Both Amish and non-Amish farm owners have experimented with **land trusts** that prevent farm acres from being subdivided. These methods have slowed but not halted the conversion of farmland to other uses (Walbert 2002). Partial isolation from industrialization does not by itself resolve all modernity-generated agricultural and environmental quandaries.

Issue: Forwarding agricultural change within a religion

Environmentally informed religious organizations prefer to lead by example and engage in projects like establishing urban gardens for schools or supplying charitable food pantries curbing poor nutrition. Religious **utopian communities** committed to political change and **intentional communities** (residential groups pursuing social cohesion and an ethically sound lifestyle) demonstrate environmentally friendly farming methods through their lifestyles. Hindus committed to Mohandas K. Gandhi's ideals of justice for the disadvantaged and nonviolent social change have established *ashrams* (live-in spiritual communities) actualizing Gandhian principles. The female residents of Brahma Vidya Mandir ashram in India, for example, draw on concepts from the *Bhagavad Gita,* including *dharma*, duty, and **moksha** (liberation from earthy attachments and wrong action). Sharing chores, the women and their guests apply organic manures, and cultivate by hand to produce vegetarian fare that is *sattvik,* meeting Hindu criteria for pure light meals "that do not arouse the passions." During tillage and food preparation, the women practice *ahimsa* or compassion by carefully removing even the smallest worms from the produce (Sanford 2016).

Scientifically based extension programs have increasingly displaced religious organizations in educating farmers—a trend favoring wealthier landholders and corporations. Indians committed to Gandhian principles have, in contrast, established small, educational farms, based in animal power, cultivars adapted to local climate and soils, and sale to local markets. The farmers treat restoration of degraded land and recovering soil fertility as a *yajna*, or ritual sacrifice. Following the *Bhagavad Gita*, they emphasize faithfully doing their duty and constraining ego "to reduce greed and attachment to consumer goods." Such farms can survive without acquiring burdensome debt (Sanford 2016).

As crucibles for change, contemporary **intentional communities** purposefully jettison commercialism and identify "back to the land" as a purifying and character-building enterprise. The Israeli Kibbutz Ketura has invested in permaculture and trains interns and visiting college classes in sustainable techniques for maintaining soils and hydrology. The Jewish intentional community, Adamah in Connecticut, similarly trains residential interns in sustainable agriculture and provides fresh produce for an adjoining Jewish retreat center. Both enjoy community Shabbat services, and the agricultural celebrations in the Jewish ritual calendar. In forwarding its peacekeeping mission, Kibbutz Ketura does not require members to be Jewish.

Figure 4.2 At A'Rocha Canada in British Columbia, shared hand labor by staff and interns contributes to spiritual life and a sense of community, as well as teaching new skills like permaculture.

The Christian organization A'Rocha Canada has purchased a small farm on a tributary of the Frasier River in British Columbia, where they similarly instruct interns in crop selection, tillage, and harvest. They raise poultry for meat and eggs while emphasizing humane care and letting the animals roam in outdoor pens. Volunteers have installed a fenced garden for primary school children attending educational programs and a summer day camp. A'Rocha offers reasonably priced shares in their seasonally appropriate produce to local families who receive deliveries once a week. Interns participate in watershed protection, and environmental education as well as learning sustainable cultivation (Figs. 4.2 and 12.2). Interns and guests are welcome but not required to share morning prayer, or to participate in Imago Dei—an evening prayer service held weekly.

These communitarian farms express their environmentalism through **lived religion,** commitment to **locality,** and adherence to bioregionally informed codes. As Todd LeVasseur (2017) observes, they actively seek a **return to place**, and a reversal of the detachment and landlessness associated with modernity. Such communities intend to improve spiritual, physical, and environmental health at scales extending from the individual, to the local, to the planetary. Ethically intentional, they pursue justice—beginning with the soil, the tilled plot, and the worker—in hopes of infusing justice in the greater community.

Issue: Agriculture supporting new religions

While many intentional farming communities strive to renew or be true to historic religious values, disaffection with the culture of mass production, wage labor, and chemical proliferation can initiate religious innovation. Rudolf Steiner, whose goal was to harmonize the spiritual with the material, introduced agricultural instruction into The Anthroposophical Society's programming in 1924. Steiner rejected pesticides and chemical fertilizers, emphasized ecological processes and nurturing the soil, and "called for a holistic approach that honored the interconnections binding plants and animals to the whole of nature." Ahead of their time, Steiner and his associates forwarded organic farming and spread "biodynamic" agriculture internationally (McKanan 2018: 11–14).

A founder of the Findhorn community in Scotland, started their now famous garden in 1963 because he was unemployed, and they needed to supplement their groceries. The site is on sandy soils at the edge of maritime dunes, and not the ordinary first pick for a kitchen garden. Although the small group of mystics and folk philosophers launching the settlement did not initially consider sowing and tending as spiritual practices, their interactions with the plants soon contributed to their concept of divine action in the cosmos (Findhorn Community 2008: 4).

One spring morning, a couple of months after they had cleared the land, a member had a vision where she "contacted a spirit of the plant kingdom, the deva of the garden pea." Concerned about the elemental sources of natural forces, the Findhorn founders accepted such devas as part of "the angelic hierarchy that holds the archetypal pattern for each plant species and directs energy toward bringing a plant into form on the physical plane." As the garden diversified, so did the devas for different species and environmental elements like the tomato, foxglove, sound, and rain. Findhorn residents interpreted the communication as an offer of guidance from the devas, and they began to take the advice of these visionary nature spirits in crop selection and applying manures. The garden represented the cosmos, and the devas assisted because they wished to have the world's cooperation (Findhorn Community 2008: 78–100).

Proving that new religious beliefs can still arise from engagement in tillage, Findhorn's well-circulated writings have influenced contemporary alternative religious thought about nature. Adherents of revived variants of **Celtic religion** or the **Fairy Faith** identify the devas of Findhorn as "fairies" and hold they have always been resident along the Scottish coast. Findhorn has resisted engine-driven implements and industrial fertilizers as they believe the technology disrupts the devas. Communicating with nature via spirits is superior to following the dictates of industry-serving science. Human love and care for living beings produce a "radiance" that contributes to the health of the flowers and fruits. If all humanity would explore deva consciousness, "life on Earth would be completely changed" (Findhorn Community 2008: 46–47, 78).

Issue: Urban food deserts

A problem worldwide is the spread of urban **food deserts**—residential districts where healthy, fresh, and sustainable food is expensive or difficult to obtain. As fonts of volunteer labor, religious congregations and ministries often lead the way in clearing vacant lots for kitchen garden plots. They find spaces for farmers' markets and open groceries selling fresh fruits and vegetables at reasonable prices within walking distance of housing complexes. The All People's Church, Milwaukee, Wisconsin, for example, has installed a garden in the back of their lot, where parishioners may share the bounty for free. Their pastor Steve Jerbi believes feeding is a spiritual act, and providing healthy food is a ministry of justice. As ecologist Mallory McDuff (2010: 33–55) concludes, urban gardens create positive social feedbacks, including promoting life skills through gardening, forming relationships in faith, and teaching lessons about simpler living. Civic ecologists Marianne Krasny and Keith Tidball (2015) observe that urban gardens provide areas where neighborhoods casually gather and build a **sense of place** and affirmative identity. Youth can find constructive activities, and immigrants can build bridges to home by planting and growing familiar species.

Religious associations and charities practice gleaning or salvaging useable food that would otherwise be wasted, contributing indirectly to climate change. Both religious and secular US colleges and universities sponsor Campus Kitchen programs gathering unused food from campus dining halls, and conveying it to homeless shelters, residences for displaced women and children, and similar loci of need – many of them operated by religious charities like the Salvation Army. Some Campus Kitchen operations have cooperating volunteer gardens contributing fresh greens to free meals.

Issue: The rise of agri-business in the United States and Canada

A little-known aspect of the rise of agribusiness is the effort US Mainline Protestant and Roman Catholic organizations dedicated to mitigating its negative social impacts. Defense of family farms resulted in a diverse movement known as **Christian agrarianism.** Religious historian Kevin M. Lowe (2016) identifies an early 20th-century shift in American agrarianism (encouraging farming as a livelihood) from a primarily economic position to moral philosophy. As machines replaced hand-labor, the number of families owning their farms dwindled. Believing farm life builds character, work ethic, and moral fiber, Christian agrarians viewed "the family farm as the primary engine of Christian life." They were alarmed by declines in rural church membership and income and the difficulties of serving small scattered congregations. In an era when **millennialism** (a belief in Christ's imminent return) was increasingly prominent in Evangelical denominations, the Protestant Mainline was committed to building a visible kingdom of God within the framework of modern society. Their rubric was the **social gospel** or finding Christian solutions to national sins ranging from child labor to the poverty of **sharecropping** (tilling someone else's land and giving the owner a substantial portion of the crop).

The Mainline Protestant concern for the concrete and immediate led them to develop a novel language of **Christian environmental stewardship** and to join with agricultural scientists and government agencies in the campaign against land degradation. Despite their acceptance of applied science, Christian agrarians retained 19th-century beliefs in "the perfectibility of society, the dignity of work, and the capability of humans to cooperate with God's plan." The agrarians promoted stewardship via dedicated worship services like Rural Life Sunday, Soil Stewardship Sunday, and 4-H Sunday (4-H is an agricultural youth club). Under the God's Acre program, farmers committed the income from an acre of tilled ground or a project such as rearing a calf to the support of a rural church (Lowe 2016: 45–116).

The battles won and lost by the Christian agrarians provide still-relevant lessons about the effectiveness of religious organizations in influencing environmental outcomes. Protestant agrarians preached that the land is holy and a gift from God. Intelligent stewardship is a "divine commission." The agrarians quoted Genesis, Psalms, and Leviticus in support of conservation-conscious practices like planting cover crops to control erosion, and periodically leaving fields fallow (untilled) for a "sabbatical" year. Federal and state agricultural extension agencies supported church programs like Soil Stewardship Week. In the 1940s, the US Soil Conservation Service printed and circulated a booklet entitled *The Lord's Land*, beginning with the declaration from Psalm 24 that the "earth is the Lord's." Many of the extension agents were themselves driven by Christian zeal for rural improvement (Lowe 2016: 137–169). Although the US still has glaring deficiencies in safeguarding soil, the 20th-century conservation campaign did mitigate chronic forms of land abuse, such as gullying deep enough to swallow a mule on southeastern cornfields. A culture of mutual support and respect among the farmers, religious leaders, and scientific advisors produced genuine advances.

Christian agrarians were less successful in reaching their social goals. They attempted to relieve the plight of tenant farmers and sharecroppers stuck in debt and poverty. Agrarian advocacy for **social justice** did not undo sharecropping—the rise of the tractor and a mass-production economy did, leaving many former sharecroppers without land or livelihood. The Mainline denominations have continued to close country churches and lose ground relative to Evangelicals in rural regions. By the 1970s, denominational support for the Christian agrarian movement had faltered due to farm consolidation, the expansion of the agricultural export economy, and a theological shift away from the social gospel.

The environmental movement beginning in the 1960s contributed to the displacement of Christian agrarians by developing a new language of conservation, based on "sustainable" agriculture as an intentional counter-cultural contrast to conventional agriculture (Lowe 2016: 170–176). Critiques of Christian foundations countered established Christian models for conservation and replaced them with postmodern rubrics. Leaders of **Deep Ecology** dismissed the stewardship ethos as too human-centered to be effective. Norwegian philosopher Arne Naess (1989: 187) concluded: "The arrogance of stewardship consists in the idea of [human] superiority which underlies the thought that we exist to watch over nature like a highly respected middleman between the Creator and Creation."

American environmentalists embraced Aldo Leopold's (1949) eco-centric **land ethic,** which treats the land as a community where soil, water, and other species are also worthy citizens, thereby positioning of humans as community members rather than as conquerors or regents. Although not a church member, Leopold was familiar with botanist Liberty Hyde Bailey's treatise *The Holy Earth*, inspiring the Christian agrarians. Leopold had also studied the **Theosophy** (Lowe 2016). Theosophy originated from 19th-century European and American adaptation of East Asian thought, including Hinduism's concepts of the connectedness of all, reincarnation, and karma. Theosophists believe all souls unify in an Oversoul and anticipate the arrival of a "new age" (Albanese 2013: 193–195). In their definition of the earth as holy and their claims of divine ownership, Protestants **sacramentalized** the agricultural landscape to a surprising degree, considering the radical Reformation's rejection of holy ground. Leopold adopted the holism of religious approaches while toning down sacramentality and ritual as means for building solidarity.

Although the Protestant Mainline is no longer leading the movement, Christian agrarianism has survived and taken new forms. The best-known advocate is Wendell Berry (2007), whose books, such as *The Unsettling of America: Culture and Agriculture,* have inspired a new generation of family farmers and intentional communities—Christian or not. By the 1980s, Evangelical academics and educators were reviving the Biblical **proof-texts** (use of specific scriptures to justify policies or ethics), such as the "earth is the Lord's," and melding them with a rubric of sustainability or synthesizing them into a new version of Christian stewardship as **Creation care**. The Christian Farmers Federation of Ontario Canada (CFFO), for example, advocates for farmers' needs, while also campaigning for best environmental practices. The officers and board of directors all make their living from family-managed farms producing everything from cut flowers to boiler chickens. The scientifically conversant CFFO (2017) believes each farmer should safeguard land and water resources, participate in the implementation of appropriate technology, and protect animal and plant diversity.

In encouraging "thriving, profitable, sustainable, and responsible family farms," the CFFO (2017) seeks "to persuade governments and public agencies to adopt its public policy perspectives and to influence the broader public regarding Christian perspective on farming." The Canadian **voluntary association** recognizes that raising soil organic matter can sequester carbon, reducing the presence of greenhouse gases to the atmosphere. They accept responsibility for limiting the release of nutrients and sediments into Lake Eire and tackle the practical aspects, like reducing phosphorous in animal feeds while still providing adequate nutrition. The CFFO advocates **smart growth** based regional planning, allowing for the expansion of housing and industry, while protecting prime agricultural lands from low-density housing and excessive taxation.

Issue: Supporting agrarian movements in less-industrialized regions

In the Global South, the world religions have similarly acted as fulcrums for agricultural activism—either by anchoring grassroots movements or through consolidating farmers' cooperatives. The goals of the Buddhist-based Moral Rice Movement in Thailand, for example, are to return dignity to farmers and reduce their debt via organic cultivation methods generating high-quality harvests. Farm families join a Dharma Garden Temple where monks, elders, and volunteers maintain demonstration fields on the temple grounds and teach management tactics. The farmers commit to Buddhist precepts, self-reliance, and building food security. They strive together to make the Moral Rice brand a safe and low-cost option for the marketplace while providing fair returns for the cultivators. The agriculturalists themselves articulate a "Buddhist ecological worldview" and enhance agricultural ecosystems as a duty to society. They believe maintaining dharma and disavowing greed makes them better farmers. Pragmatic concerning questions of scale, the Moral Rice Movement has endeavored to establish a brand recognized regionally in Thailand. The movement has recovered tradition by reestablishing the local ritual where farmers venerate the Rice Goddess (Mother) by transplanting seven rice stalks infused by the Rice Soul to their fields. They have simultaneously entered a global network by joining the International Federation of Organic Agriculture and obtaining organic certification (Kaufman 2016).

Recovery of religious values and communitarianism can assist farmers in facing economic pressures. Food security expert Jagannath Adhikari (2016) argues agribusiness has displaced Hindu values among Nepalese agrarian communities.

Adhikari proposes **retrieval** of Hindu traditions and dharma as a motive for coop-eration could assist small farmers in avoiding debt and in solving problems coopera-tively. Anthropologist Pankaj Jain (2016) reasons the Swadhyaya movement in India is accomplishing exactly that—teaching a dharmic ecology or **earth dharma** as a foundation for nurturing "unity, harmony and goodwill" through entire farming villages. Practitioners accept harvests as disturbances while trying to minimize the violence to the land and adjoining vegetation. Rather than blessing or banning tech-nologies, Swadhyaya stresses four elements: "trust of neighbor, love for animals, faith in God, and respect for nature." Indian environmentalist Anil Agarwal describes the Hindu perspective as "utilitarian conservationism" rather than "protectionist con-servationism." The concept of "utilitarian conservationism" could also be applied to Christian agrarianism.

Conclusion: Feeding growing cities

Religious approaches to environmentally sound agriculture have multiple common-alities based on relationships, duties, and networks. Box 4.4. Intentional communities practicing permaculture value lived-religion and the spirituality of the day-to-day. Religious agrarians honor simplicity, land health, and shared celebration. A contin-uing concern, however, is whether religious agrarianism can respond to the scales of production necessary to feed the earth's still growing human population. Many suc-cessful eco-friendly agricultural projects based in religious organizations feed only their community or generate limited production for the market. While about 40% of working people worldwide are farmers, and the family farms still comprise 90% of all agricultural landholdings, more than half the world's population now lives in urban areas. Among the more industrialized nations, the structure of farm ownership favors large operations. In 2015, the largest US family-owned farms with gross sales of a million dollars or more were only 2.9% of the farms yet provided 42% of national production. Corporate farms contributed over 10%. Green consumers can prompt grocery stores to stock environmentally sustainable food choices, favor family farm-ers, and reduce wasteful packaging. They can visit farmers' markets. Yet, farmers working voluntarily and cooperatively to conserve the land and waters for future generations remains the most effective means for improving agricultural, environ-mental care.

Box 4.4 Characteristics of environmentally effective religious agricultural communities

Shared rituals or celebrations
Emphasis on community life
Sacramentalization of or attributing spiritual properties to land or domestic species
Emphasis on duty to both other people and the land
Concrete teachings concerning environmental practices
Means of teaching others
Concern for bioregionally compatible methods
Willingness to dialog with conservation science
Willingness to join networks within and between regions

Suggested readings

Krasny, Marianne, and Keith Tidball. *Civic Ecology: Adaptation and Transformation from the Ground Up.* Cambridge, MA: MIT Press, 2015.

LeVasseur, Todd, ed. *Religious Agrarianism and the Return of Place.* Albany: State University of New York Pres, 2017.

LeVasseur, Todd, Pramond Parajuli, and Norman Wirzba, eds. *Religion and Sustainable Agriculture: World Spiritual Traditions and Food Ethics.* Lexington: University of Kentucky Press, 2016.

Lowe, Kevin. *Baptized with the Soil: Christian Agrarians and the Crusade for Rural America.* Oxford, U.K.: Oxford University Press, 2016.

McDuff, Mallory. *Natural Saints: How People of Faith are Working to Save God's Earth.* Oxford, U.K.: Oxford University Press, 2010.

Sanford, A. Whitney. *Growing Stories from India: Religion and the Fate of Agriculture.* Bowling Green: University Press of Kentucky, 2012.

Sosis, Richard, and Bradley J. Ruffle. "Religious ritual and cooperation: Testing for a relationship on Israeli religious and secular Kibbutzim." *Current Anthropology* 44 (2003): 713–722.

Walbert, David. *Garden Spot: Lancaster County, the Old Order Amish, and the Selling of Rural America.* Oxford, U.K.: Oxford University Press, 2002.

Walters, Keey and Lisa Portmess. *Religious Vegetarianism: From Hesiod to the Dalai Lama.* Albany: State University of New York Press, 2001.

Wirzba, Norman. *Food & Faith: A Theology of Eating.* Cambridge, U.K.: Cambridge University Press, 2011.

Zamore, Mary, ed. *The Sacred Table: Creating a Jewish Food Ethic.* New York: Central Conference of Reform Rabbis, 2011.

5 Ignitions

Sacred tools, ritual fires,
and the value of "things"

Key concepts

1 Human material culture makes religion present, visible, and tangible in the world.
2 Religions, including those without metallurgy, can address any of the components of manufacturing or energy capture, such as the labor, the tools, the raw materials, and any waste, pollution, or ecological disturbance generated.
3 Not just religious professionals, but individuals and families, may sacralize manufactured objects via household altars and offerings.
4 Religions identify releases of energy and transformations of raw to refined materials as symbols of such social processes as pursuing right action, spiritual enlightenment, or joining in community. Signifying goodness, truth, or transformation, light displays and sacred fires are widespread elements in religious rituals and festivals.
5 Religions sacralize or ethically value productive labor.
6 The Reformation's desacralization and iconoclasm deemphasized religious materiality.
7 In the wake of the Industrial Revolution, Euro-American cultures adopted religious iconography to convey a meta-narrative praising the rise of modern industry as the culmination of past human endeavor.
8 Both religious organizations and commercial enterprises are attempting to "green" the energy and materials utilized in religious festivals, either by recovering traditions, such using botanical oils to fuel the Diya lamps of Diwali, or by investing in technological innovation, such as setting up outdoor solar menorahs for Chanukah.
9 Mining and energy production frequently disturb sacred sites or landscapes, or conflict with the rights and social integrity of indigenous cultures and religions.
10 Religious and socially conscious NGOs are supporting efforts to reduce the negative human and environmental impacts of artisanal mining and forward Fairtrade for extractive industries like gem mining.
11 In the United States, faith-based environmental activism resisting the negative impacts of coal extraction has three streams: an older justice and human rights-based Christian approach emerging from concerns about poverty, the more recent Christian creation care movement, and nature-venerating spiritualities.
12 Religions are exploring the ethics of consumerism in globalizing economies. Movements such as Engaged Buddhism are incorporating environmental values into concepts such as work as Right Livelihood.

Sacred tools and holy labors

Nothing characterizes humanity more than our tools and our **material culture**. Chimpanzees grasp sticks to knock down fruit and collect edible ants. Ants deploy biotechnology when they create fungal gardens to break down leaves. No other species, though, has acquired humanity's complex inventory of manufactured objects and means of harvesting and manipulating energy. Humans remain alone in their ability to intentionally ignite organic materials and generate electrical power from water and wind.

Critical to today's environmental challenges is the question of how we value "things" and the kilocalories necessary to fabricate and transport them. Manufacturing and energy capture have eight components: (1) the labor invested, (2) the tools utilized, (3) the raw materials, (4) the process of manufacturing or energy transfer, (5) the goods and services produced, (6) their trade and distribution, (7) the resulting social benefits and damages, and (8) any waste, pollution, or ecological disturbance generated. Religion may appear to be starkly divorced from bustling 21st-century industrial districts and humming electrical grids. Yet, as sociologist Dick Houtman and anthropologist Brigit Meyer (2012: xv, 1–23) have concluded: "Religion cannot persist, let alone thrive, without the material things that serve to make it present—visible and tangible—in the world." Under the influence of Protestant thought, 19th and early 20th-century academics treated "things" and religion as inherently antagonistic, resulting in reduced attention to materiality. This chapter first explores religious approaches to tools and manufacturing, then examines the extraction of fossil fuels and other nonrenewable resources and ends with the ethics of consumerism.

Sacred tools and objects

From an environmental perspective, religious materiality addresses changing states of matter, the relative value of substances, and goods as a source of human relationships. The designation of sacred objects and trades conveys messages about the conversion of natural materials to manufactured items, the permanence of the material, and the (un)importance of wealth and ownership. Societies without metallurgy, for example, do not just sacralize unworked natural objects and processes, they sacralize tools and manufactured objects. Anthropologist Bud Hampton (1999: 47–49) lived with the Dani in remote Irian Jaya, Indonesia, during the 1980s when the forest-dwelling culture had little access to trade goods and was still fabricating stone tools. The Dani believe in a diverse realm of ghosts and spirits, incorporating evil and dangerous entities that inhabit natural objects, animals, and habitats. The adult and initiated juvenile males reside separately from the women and younger children in the men's compounds and houses, which form an *axis mundi* excluding women.

Dani men choose sacred stones or *ganeke* from a variety of natural and manufactured sources. Favored natural forms are quartz crystal, fossils of coiled ammonite shells, and river-polished pebbles. Outstanding craftsmanship, ancestral ownership, and exceptional service characterize sacred tools and weapons. In the wake of careful ritual, a male spirit enters the stone, which is no longer used for its profane purpose. The big men or leaders of the men's groups supervise the rituals and construction of a *ganeke* cabinet to preserve the stones in the rear of the men's house. The cabinet also collects the weapons, regalia, tufts of hair, and, more rarely, other body parts of enemy warriors killed. As ancestor worship is a core feature of the Dani religion, the ancestor stones, which they decorate with feathers and other colorful materials, are the most revered and hold an honored place in the cabinets. The living descendants "revitalize the spirits' superhuman energy (life) through a continuum of renewal rituals." The process of sacralization is thus **patrilineal** and **patrilocal**. It follows the male lineage, and the sacred objects reside in spaces identified as male (Hampton 1999: 126–130, 143–144).

The Dani use these empowered objects to "fertilize" their crops, encourage large litters of pigs, and regulate the rains. Both men and women wear amulets or carry bags of "power stones" to ward off evil spirits, illnesses, and injuries. Along with river polished pebbles and crystals, the forest dwellers favor chisels and adzes for amulets (Hampton 1999: 126–137, 198–208). The Dani *ganeke* cabinets esteem quarrying and craftsmanship, reinforcing the importance of manufacturing itself, and recording design successes and innovations. Yet, sacralization also blurs sharp distinctions between unmodified natural objects, raw materials for human implements, and creations of superior artistry. The entrancing products of unfettered nature and human invention reside in the same sequestered, sacred space. Despite Dani belief in spirits infusing natural features, technology is a fulcrum of religious power where tools and weapons transform into **hierophanies** or manifestations of the sacred. Lynn White, Jr. accepted the dualistic assumption that animist spirits reside in trees and not in stone axes, missing the complex religious interpretation of **materiality** in cultures like the Dani.

During the Bronze and Iron Ages, the rise of metallurgy and tools with moving parts modified portrayals of supernatural beings, who acquired implements and professions appropriate to their earthly spheres of influence. Depictions reflect the increasing specialization of social roles, such as belonging to a caste or a skilled trade. Among the Hindu pantheon, Balaram carries a plow and mace, and Shiva wields a trident. Hardly an exclusively male responsibility, goddesses like Durga carry tools and weapons deployed to defeat evil and sustain devotees. In their multi-armed persona, deities can hold a dozen or more sacred objects. For the Abrahamic faiths, God, as the creator of all things, inspires the crafts. In the Hebrew scriptures, honored ancestors are founders of critical manufacturing processes. Cain built the first city, and among his lineage, Jabaal made tents, Jubal "was the father of all those who played stringed instruments and pipes," and his brother Tubal-Cain "forged all kinds of tools out of bronze and iron" (Genesis 4: 20–22). Religions can sacralize or demonize the eight components of manufacturing and convey social messages about the relative value of the technologies and their environmental costs and benefits.

Household and family altars

Even among religions where priests or other professionals consecrate the material, folk or household devotional practices sacralize objects via the construction of shrines for making offerings to deities or remembering ancestors. The Mexican Day of the Dead or *Día de los Muertos* syncretizes Aztec iconography and beliefs about the annual return of departed souls with the Christian All Saints Day. Families assemble a household altar displaying pictures and keepsakes of deceased relatives along with bouquets of living flowers, statuettes of saints, and offerings of fruit and food so the deceased can share a meal with loved ones. Adults and children bring garlands of marigolds, bread, and freshly cooked food to cemeteries, and hold watch beside family graves. Like Mardi Gras and Carnival, the popular celebration accommodates industrially manufactured objects. Musical instruments, handicrafts, and images of automobiles serve as mementos of the dead and their passions (Carmichael and Sayer 1992). The placement of a baby's toy or a bottle of a favorite beer of a deceased loved-one on the altar sacralizes not just the item but the interpersonal relationships it represents.

The altars can be organically themed, yet they offer a dialog about materiality regardless. The vibrant colors and fresh petals of the flowers and sparkling skins and green hues of the fruits are proof not just of the afterlife but of the worth of life itself—unmodified by human processing. The ubiquitous skulls or *calaveras* conversely remind participants that life and its trinkets are ephemeral, and, in the end, it is the familial and social bonds that continue beyond the grave. Skeletons wearing mock-ups of formal dress or expensive clothes capture the inadequacy and ultimate futility of ownership and the prerogatives of wealth. The holiday both rejoices in lives well lived and mocks the vanity of the corporeal. The altars honor **attachment to place**, the beauty and beneficence of nature, and fond remembrance.

Holy illumination, sacred energy

Aside from raw materials, manufacturing, building, and transportation require energy. Solar deities and solstice celebrations are common worldwide, as are supernatural masters of natural energy sources, like Pele, representing fire, winds, rivers, tides, and volcanism. The most potent human means of modifying natural environments—fire—can initiate a creative event, and in altering states of matter, it can purify, regenerate, or destroy. **Eschatologies** (beliefs about the end of life or the end of time) prophesy unquenchable flames as the ultimate fate of the earth or evil-doers. Light symbolizes ethical illumination, goodness, or renewal (Box 5.1).

Box 5.1 Symbolism of sacred fire

Metaphors and representations

  Original element or source of the universe: Zoroastrianism's three sacred flames in ancient Persia

  Life giving energy of the sun: Cherokee sacred fires

  Eternality or omnipotence of God: Ancient Hebrews' ever-burning fire at the Outer Altar of the Tabernacle.

  Eternality of human souls: Buddhist lanterns to remember the dead

  Religious illumination: Diwali lamps

  Termination of the cosmos or an age: Christian apocalyptic belief God will destroy the earth with fire

  Eternal damnation: Images of hell

Rituals

  Communicating with deities: Votive candles

  Purifying ritual participants: Native American rites wafting sage or cedar smoke over dancers

  Releasing the dead from the material body to another life: Hindu cremation rites

  Purifying the community of infection: Hebrew burning of objects contaminated with mold

  Purifying the community of evil doers or ideas: Burning of supposed witches and heretics, the culturally destructive practice of burning books

---

Figure 5.1 During the South Asian Mela Diwali festival, lighting lamps symbolizes the return of Rama, goodness and truth. Here at a celebration held in Houston, Texans Energy, an electrical power provider and event sponsor, advertises on a screen behind Indian dancers on the main stage.

Diwali or the Festival of Light is of Hindu origin with variants celebrated by Sikhs, Jains, and some Buddhists (Fig. 5.1). The fall new moon, at the end of October, determines the date for Diwali, marking the onset of winter. Homeowners light small multi-colored *diya* (lamps) made of vegetable oil and clay. Temples glow with thousands of colored lanterns. Families' position geometric *rangoli*, made of dyed seeds and other natural materials, at the door of their homes. Birds then consume the colorful symbols of protection. The festival commemorates the return of the god Rama, and the victory of good over evil. As the solar days shorten, Diwali reaffirms hope (Watson 2016). Like most pre-modern sacred fires and lights, Diwali lamps traditionally utilized renewable sources of energy, like botanical oils.

Religious practices also draw on renewable geophysical energy and animal power. East Asian religions fly kites in thanksgiving ceremonies. The wind lifts Buddhist prayer flags strung in high mountain passes in the Himalayas. River currents and ocean tides transport offerings to the gods or carry the deceased to the habitation of the dead. Horses, donkeys, and elephants participate in religious processions by bearing human impersonators of gods or saints and pulling vehicles bearing sacred images.

Sacred smelters

Most ritual ignitions parallel household or agricultural activities, such as preparing a feast. In contrast to a cooking fire, metallurgy requires high-calorie fuels and skilled handling. The smelter's furnace and the smithy are in the realm of technological specialists, transferring religious interpretation to the trade itself. In Bantu regions of Africa, the reduction of the raw ore is associated with human reproduction. Smelters may thus decorate furnaces with female anatomical features, like breasts. Much as a baby exits the womb, the refined metal emerges between the "legs" at the base of a clay oven. A few furnaces display the image of an infant above the port for removing the metal. Some

smelters work in isolation away from settlements, and remain celibate during the process, avoiding "adultery"—adding to the trade's mystic (Chirikure 2007). The parallel
to childbirth allays fears of witchcraft or uncontrolled magic in the metalworkers' art.
It identifies the smelter as the "father" of a material converted from its natural state into
cultural objects, ensuring the value of the finished product. Fire becomes a metaphor
for the mystery of the sexual act. Religious **rituals of transformation** align the processes of violating the earth to extract ore and generating the temperatures necessary to
separate the elemental materials with iconographies of conversion, power, and gender
(Herbert 1993).

Products acquire the mystique of the manufacturing, and technologies assume the
ritual status of their products. In pre-colonial Africa, select iron objects were religiously
empowered. Before the British rule of the Indian subcontinent, military and economic
leadership by Sikh **gurus** forwarded steel production and the establishment of smithies,
along with the construction of fortresses for defense against Islamic Mughals. English
regulations forced their colonies to export raw ore, thereby transferring metal manufacture and profits to British corporations. Khalsa Sikhs (a sect defined by initiation
rites) utilize five external symbols of membership including the *kirpan* or sword, the
kara (a circle of iron or steel and a metaphor for attachment to God), and the *nisan sahib*,
a pole or pendant bearing a symbol made from interlocking curved swords and the *kara*
circle. In Sikh scriptures, the portrayal of iron is equivocal. It is an elemental material
with great potential as it can be reshaped, and a substance that can be transmuted into
more worthy gold via the philosopher's stone. Sikh religious sites house weapons and
enshrine swords, symbolizing their commitment to community protection, and sub-
ordination of Sikhs to gurus. A historic Sikh rallying cry translates as "Victory to the
cauldron and the sword..." declaring the importance of well-made household utensils
and weapons (Nesbitt 2016). Such practices de facto sacralize metalworkers, forges, and
foundries, along with the finished implements.

Other faiths exhibit metal objects at sacred sites or incorporate them in sacred art. A
walk around St. Paul's Cathedral in London, U.K., encounters multiple stone monuments to military heroes, wearing swords, holding navigational instruments, or even
standing over a cannon with shot. Like the Sikhs, Jews and Christians invoke the trans-
mutation of base ore as a spiritual metaphor (Box 5.2). Religious codes may require
pure or uncontaminated materials, including fuels and containers, to sustain sacred
flames. Following a divinely mandated design, Moses constructed the prototype of the
Jewish **menorah** of pure gold (Exodus 25). The ancient Israelites carried the seven-
branched lamp into the wilderness as a portable shrine. They then placed it in the
permanent temple in Jerusalem, where it represented the continuing presence of God.

Box 5.2 The Refiner's Fire

Jewish and Christian texts extoll God's protective power and the value of spiritual preparedness
through images of weapons and armor. (See Psalm 28 and Ephesians 6:10–18.) They invoke
the refiner's fire or removal of dross (impurities) as metaphors for the purity of God's word or
for growing spiritual strength or maturity. In a reference to the priesthood in ancient Israel,
Malachi (3:2–4) states God is like "a refiner's fire,…and he will purify the descendants of Levi,
and refine them like gold and silver, until they present offerings to the Lord in righteousness."

Labor as sacred

In addition to materials and energy, religions guide the valuation of human labor. Trades may have their shrines, processions, and patron deities or saints. **Ordinary religion** addresses the meaning of work—both its trials and benefits. For Jews, work complies with God's commandment (Exodus 20:9, 34:21): "Six days you shall you labor, and on the seventh, you shall rest…." Jews understand work as joyful, meaningful, fatigue-inducing, distracting, sometimes burdensome, and inherent to being human. The mandate to stop labor for the Sabbath does not deem labor profane but recognizes its critical role in community welfare. To avoid work or to leave one's family unsupported is to disobey God. For Orthodox Jews, the forms of labor that must halt on the Sabbath are the same as those used to construct the Tabernacle and the first temple in Jerusalem. The Sabbath is a gift and the holiest of days, when even labor committed directly to God must cease (Eisenberg 2004: 130–132, 157; Heschel 1951).

Utopian and monastic religious communities identify manual labor as a foundation of the fully committed life. Theologian Stephen Meawad (2017) has found that for Egyptian Coptic Christian monastics, work does not distract from personal holiness but is necessary to it. The monastic community should be self-sustaining, not drawing resources from the churches. Ideally, labor becomes uninterrupted praise of the Triune God, and integral to a life of joy and sacrifice. The monastics believe they are **co-stewards** with God. They thus avoid **commodification** in favor of pursuing work as a form of self-giving love. Coptic Christians comprise many of the garbage recyclers in Cairo, Egypt, where the recycling rate is a high 80%, compared to the 30 to 40% typical in the United States. Despite their lowly social status and income, these Copts believe recycling is an expression of their faith and an inherently sacred task.

Issue: Reformation, iconoclasm, and economics

The Reformation's **desacralization** and **iconoclasm** deemphasized religious materiality. The radical reformers eliminated not just statues but brass candlesticks and lamps from churches and homes. They argued that expensive church furnishings were wasteful and proud, and diverted funds that should be committed to charity. Removing costly sacred objects supported a humane and equitable Christian economy. The distinction between the sacred and profane no longer concerned things or physical spaces, but the relationship of the individual believer with God and "witnesses" gathering for teaching and worship. True religious virtue or piety could only "inhere in a life of ascetic denial of physicality" (Wandel 1995: 190–191; Crew 1978). The **radical Reformation** fostered an aesthetic of plainness and **simplicity**. Calvinists, Baptists, and Friends built solid brick or wood meeting houses that looked more like inns or homes than churches. Ostentatious displays of wealth or envy of others' possessions were sinful (Bratton 2016: 1–48).

In a still contested thesis, German sociologist Maximillian "Max" Weber (2001) asserted that the Reformation was central to the rise of market-driven capitalism in the west. The Protestant ethic encouraged work, thrift, self-development, and concern for economic futures. These values, in turn, called for efficiency and fiscal accountability actualized as profits and the production of goods for sale. Protestant theology sanctified "earthly vocations," a concept reinforced by "the priesthood of all believers." The godly had a duty to acquire a trade or profession, establish a comfortable residence for their families, and invest in their children's education. Despite the minimalist architecture of their meeting houses, Protestant homes and businesses were not necessarily small **footprint** (the cumulative environmental cost) in terms of size or materials. Historians have considered whether Protestantism accelerated the rise of experimental science and whether Protestants played a disproportionate role in designing the new machines replacing handcrafted production of commodities, during the 19th century (Harrison 2016).

At the onset of the industrial revolution, Christian attitudes toward the worth of the labor, while far more democratic than feudal norms, generated a dichotomy that has continued to afflict environmental decision making into the 21st century. On the one hand, the Protestant ethic of frugality and of "waste not, want not" was a foundation of the 19th-century American conservation movement. On the other, Protestants admired entrepreneurship and invested in banks, canals, and factories. Today, the ethos of continual economic improvement often runs afoul of environmental planning. While lowering the cost of goods, campaigns for efficiency and ever-multiplying profits can result in labor abuses and dodging environmental regulations.

Issue: Sacralizing modern industry

Built on coal and steel, the industrial revolution (ca. 1790) resulted in drastic changes in Euro-American landscapes within a generation. A superficial reading of this speedy economic transition might conclude the proliferation of factories and new modes of transportation was one of **secularization**, separating religion from manufacturing. Christians, however, awarded moral efficacy to industrial innovations, such as railroads that allowed penetration and "civilizing" of new territories, be it through American deserts or African plains. Railroads carried missionaries and Christian settlers into the hinterlands and brought rural products back to national markets. Railroad companies incorporated religious myths and sacred natural features into their advertising. One firm happily interpreted Pulpit Rock as an iconic scenic feature by the tracks. Reputedly, Brigham Young sermonically emboldened the Latter-Day Saints (Mormons) to journey onward to new enterprises in Utah from this natural podium (Walker 2017).

Industrialists appropriated religious motifs to glorify their endeavors. Although Victorian factories were often architecturally austere and steel mills lacked the decoration of Bantu furnaces, ambitious plant owners commissioned a Byzantine-revival façade or rows of lotus-topped "Egyptian" columns bracketing the front office door (Pearson 2016). Magnificent rail stations installed marble floors and entrance halls with soaring vaults mimicking cathedral naves. Passengers entering London's Euston station (ca. 1837) walked through a grand propylaeum, lifted by massive Doric columns 13 meters tall. The propylaeum was the gatehouse or entrance to an ancient Greek temple housing a deity. (British Railways demolished this preservation-worthy entrance in 1962.) London's Paddington Station conserves cast-iron columns in Moorish style, imitating the alignments creating dramatic open spaces in medieval mosques. The designers of London's St. Pancras station and hotel (begun in 1865) chose Gothic revival for the eye-catching exterior and 270-foot clock tower, which looks like a church façade (Christopher 2015). International examples include the Baroque central station in Antwerp, Belgium, Neo-classical Union Station in Washington, D.C., and, more recently, Kanazawa Station, Ishikawa, Japan, with a controversial massive wooden gate, much like a **tori** or Shinto sacred gate.

The railroad **meta-narrative** (big or all-encompassing story) praises the rise of modern industry as the culmination of past human endeavor, worthy of the same aesthetic recognition as a temple or cathedral. Religiously-inspired designs laud the finished product rather than the raw materials. Centered at the consumer end of production, they invite corporate stockholders and ticket purchasers into sacred terrain, rather than sanctifying the realm of the miners or smelters. The eclectic geographic origins of the London rail station architecture parallel the accumulation of monumental souvenirs of colonialism, like the Egyptian obelisk known as Cleopatra's needle relocated to the British capital. **Implicit religious associations** valorize high-speed transportation and consumer culture.

Issue: Sacralizing industrial evil

As the National Socialists rose to power in Germany following World War I, they drew on religious traditions of ignition when they set public bonfires to burn books, including many hand-illuminated Torah scrolls removed from synagogues by force (Box 5.1). During World War II, the Nazis deployed railroads to deport Jews, gypsies, gay and transgender individuals, and other *Untermenschen* (less than humans) to extermination camps. The camp at Auschwitz, Poland, had 41 parallel tracks for unloading the prisoners from cattle cars—more than any urban rail station in Germany. Prisoners became items in inventories—demoted to mere freight (Gigliotti 2009). Guards herded entire families into fake showers, where they released toxic Cyklon-B gas, an industrial chemical product. They then forced *Sonder Commandos*, who were prisoners themselves, to incinerate the corpses in ovens, which smoked like a coal-burning factory. The Nazis invoked the ideal of industrial efficiency as moral efficacy to disguise industrial-scale evil.

Religious praxis relative to illumination can, however, directly address technological and industrial wrongs and abuses. In original Biblical usage, the term **holocaust** referred to making burnt offerings to God where flames entirely consumed a sacrificial animal. Its modern definition recognizes the Jewish families who died in Nazi concentration camps as a profoundly tragic yet holy offering to God. Today, memorials may maintain an "eternal light" as a continuing reminder of **the Holocaust**. Synagogues keep a perpetually lit lamp, or **Ner Tamid**, above the ark containing the Torah scrolls, as a symbol of the eternality, the continuing presence of God, and the light of the menorah in the original temple in Jerusalem (Eisenberg 2004: 336).

Religious commemoration can invoke the dual symbolism of fire as the eternal energy of the divine and as the ultimate destroyer. Japanese Buddhists end the Bon festival honoring their ancestors with the **Toro Nagashi ceremony**, where families set paper lanterns afloat on rivers. Hiroshima conducts the Toro Nagashi on the date the atomic bomb fell at the end of World War II, thereby replacing the fierce tower of radiation with the gentle reminiscence of beloved souls lost and hope for the future (Lowe et al. 2018: xii). The symbolic release of energy may be subtle, such as a single candle in an otherwise dark room. It may also be very demonstrative, demanding thousands of kilocalories, as in the case of fireworks or American Christmas. The low-key applications inspire contemplation, ethical consideration, or remembrance. Dramatic displays encourage social unity and group identification, demonstrate political or economic authority, or attract commerce.

Issue: Religious symbolism and sustainable energy

In concert with stripping or removing altars, Protestant reformers eliminated lighting candles as a votive offering to the saints and dropped Advent candles as a precursor to Christmas. The most stringent rejected the festive ignition of a Yule log as pagan retention. No longer sacred, the purpose of candles or gas lamps in a meeting house was merely practical. They provided illumination to read scriptures, just as stoves generated warmth to make the sermon more tolerable. Almost from the beginnings of public electrical grids in the early 20th century, however, Christians of multiple denominations, including the heirs of the radical Reformation, began to use electric "candles" and colored lights as substitutes for renewable wicks and tallow in celebrating Christmas.

In 1923, US President Calvin Coolidge welcomed the first outdoor National Christmas Tree sparkling with 250 bulbs to the Whitehouse lawn (U.S. National Park Service 2017). At the time, electrical lighting was replacing gas lights in US cities and homes, but many rural regions still did not have electrical service. In the first half of the 20th century, looping electrical wiring around a living evergreen tree, imported from a remote corner of the country, symbolized national industrial progress and federal support for economic improvement. Today, the practice of Christmas lighting has become so competitive that some shopping districts or residential neighborhoods decorate the exteriors of dozens of homes with thousands of sparkling bulbs.

Other faiths have similarly adopted electrical energy as a surrogate for sacred fires. Hindu temples celebrating Diwali install strings of electrical lights as safer and easier to manage than open flames. In the America and Europe, Diwali gatherings in public spaces have grown in popularity. Thousands of Hindus, Sikhs, Jains, and tourists converge on London's Trafalgar Square on the Saturday closest to the October new moon. All-city festivals stage traditional dances, fireworks, Indian cuisine, and Rangoli contests. Providing multiple civic benefits, they encourage children to enjoy their heritage, maintain religious equity in civic terrains, support charities, and build understanding among people of different ethnicities.

Electrical and communication companies have long acted as sponsors for public light displays, thereby sharing in Christmas as a metaphor for Christ as the Light of the World. Similar support for Diwali associates the power grid and business acumen with light as truth (Fig. 5.1). Stage lights allow thousands of attendees to view a production of the **Ramala**, a religious play relating how the god Rama, as an incarnation of the creative deity Vishnu, defeated the forces of evil. In other contemporary adaptations, attendants bring an image of Krishna on stage, and the crowd performs an *aarti* (a rite honoring a deity) by waving the glowing faces of thousands of cell phones. Christians have similarly drawn on flashlights, glow sticks, and cell phones as points of illumination in outdoor worship, sacralizing the technology in the process. Like the fanciful railroad stations, the synthesis of religious symbolism with industrialization is at the consumer end of the production chain.

An environmental challenge for sponsors of religious festivals like Diwali and Christmas is to maintain light as a symbol of goodness, hope, and community while encouraging sustainable energy use. Growing public environmental consciousness is slowly modifying the political **subtext** (embedded meaning) of municipal and corporate Christmas trees and light displays. Although construction workers first decorated the original Depression Era 20-foot tree with tin cans and pieces of paper in 1933, the Christmas tree in Rockefeller Center, New York City, now ranges from 70 to 100 feet in height and sparkles with a spectacular 30,000 bulbs. In 2007, the Center transitioned to a sustainable holiday season by installing roof-mounted solar panels at the top of Rockefeller Plaza to compensate for the elevated energy use and illuminate a constellation of energy-efficient multi-colored LED lights. In recent years, Rockefeller Center has donated the tree to Habitat for Humanity, who mill it, and symbolically use the lumber for building new homes for families who could not otherwise afford to own their own. The Center now purchases the tree from nearby states, reducing the energy utilized to transport it (Baker Electrical and Solar Systems 2017; Rockefeller Center 2017). Playing the Grinch, *The Huffington Post* critiqued the "greener" tree as faux-sustainability, on the grounds, the display still uses 1300 kilowatts per day (saving 3500 kw) and would be better replaced by a farmed tree or one growing in place (Silver 2011). The symbolism has none-the-less metamorphosed from national progress to national responsibility and precipitated public dialog concerning carbon emissions.

Public menorahs are also going solar. In 2011, Rabbi AB Itkin of Chabad of Ulster County, New York, connected a previously unlighted menorah on the Woodstock Village Green to solar panels. Rabbi Yitzchok Hecht reported that the local Jewish community was supportive, and "the concept of taking the energy of the sun and using it to bring light into the darkness of night is a beautiful complement to the miracle and story of Chanukah" (*Inhabitant* 2011).

Hindu websites are circulating ideas for Green Diwali, among them returning to the traditional *diya* lamps – made of biodegradable clay and fueled by renewable vegetable oil – rather than fossil fuel-based options. Other suggestions are buying real rather than artificial or plastic flowers, and making a *rangoli* by using organic materials, like flower petals, thereby avoiding chemically-based paints. For homeowners using dyed rice and spices will still generate an avian feast. In 2019, BAPS Hindu **mandirs** (temples) joined in **Earth Hour** (an internationally shared event celebrating respect for the earth) by darkening their lights, except for candles illuminating shrines. They posted attractive images of deities in bathed in a shimmering glow rimmed by the muted frames of temple arches and niches on their websites. The approach accentuated the issue of energy generation and climate change without violating the ritual tradition of maintaining perpetual light and turned the darkening into a thought-provoking engagement with Hindu spirituality.

The Sioux at Standing Rock maintained a sacred fire burning day and night. Fueled by clean, renewable materials, the respected flame was a statement of resistance to the massive pipeline carrying water-contaminating petroleum interstate. A lesson about scale, the smaller council fire was supportive of community and life, while the "great snake" DAPL disrespected both. Today's Native American Pow-Wows have recovered the sacred fire as a symbol of unity and cultural continuity, and as a connection to natural materials drawn from the living landscape.

Issue: Opening the earth for nonrenewable resources

In clan-based and village societies, miners, smelters, and smiths are high-status individuals. Since ancient times, however, feudal and imperialist cultures have depended on slaves, serfs, or the socially disempowered to perform the arduous tasks necessary to quarrying and mining. Pre-industrial metallurgy stripped thousands of hectares of forest near furnaces, for charcoal. Despite Protestantism's democratic leanings and modernity's concern for individual rights, the industrial revolution worsened rather than relieving many of the negative impacts of **nonrenewable resource extraction**. Corporate management and government regulators turned a blind eye to the environmental and human costs of critical economic sectors like coal mining. Boys too young to shovel ore drew minimal pay hand-picking slate out of the coal or leading the mules pulling coal cars from sunless tunnels. Thousands of children died in the explosions and cave-ins plaguing deep mining (Richards 2006).

Early industrial coal mines did not restore denuded hillsides and left their tailings or waste rock in barren piles near abandoned entrances. Subterranean fires might burn for years. **Acid leachate** tainted with sulfur compounds trickled into streams, exterminating fish and making the water unfit for drinking or agriculture. Even today, coal miners have multiple environmental health concerns as they age, such as black lung disease caused by chronic exposure to coal dust. Despite improved safety practices, devastating accidents, like the Deep Water Horizon petroleum spill in 2010, continue to plague the extraction of nonrenewable materials.

Issue: Destruction of sacred sites and disruption of indigenous communities

From a religious perspective, international and state-run corporations have frequently ignored or over-ridden the interests of cultural groups residing near or on mineral and fossil fuel deposits and have disturbed sacred sites worldwide. Today, an estimated 50% of extractive operations have indigenous peoples living near their wells or mines. The Subanen of the Zamboanga Peninsula, Philippines, for example, encountered a flawed approval process, where the government recognized a selected council of elders who gave consent to the mining of sacred Mount Canatuan. The "council" incorporated neither the leadership elected by the Subanen nor representatives from the Mount Canatuan community. Security forces harassed and jailed Subanen representatives. The Subanen sought recourse through the United Nations Committee on the Elimination of Racial Discrimination, who strongly recommended that the Philippines government address the human rights violations. The national government acknowledged they had approved mining without obtaining proper consent but then delayed instituting appropriate remedies (Doyle and Cariño 2013).

In 2007, the Subanen judicial body, the *Gukom*, invoked their religious heritage and conducted a ritual to "condemn the destruction of sacred Mount Canatuan." Following a trial, the *Gukom* imposed fines on the mining company. Four years later, the company finally agreed to "conduct a cleansing ritual in atonement for desecrating Mount Cantuan..." and opened negotiations concerning reparations. For the Subanen, religion was a means of seeking justice and reestablishing right relationships with their homeland. The conflict convinced the Subanen that their communities should have the right to close their lands to mining and that once they had decided to do so, the matter was not open to repeated renegotiation (Doyle and Cariño 2013).

A better resolved but equally complex example of extraction affecting a sacred site concerns the Argyle Diamond Mine in the Kimberly region of Australia. The Rio Tinto conglomerate has dug the mine into Barramundi Gap, a locale with deep mythic and ritual significance, particularly to the women of the Miriuwung and Gija peoples. According to sacred narratives, women fishing for barramundi below the gap had huge fish jump over their grass nets, and the scattered fish scales became multi-colored diamonds. Initially, the mine overrode Aboriginal land claims and closed sacred ground to visitation. Appropriating Aboriginal **Dreamtime**, Rio Tinto named a collection of diamond jewelry "Dreamtime" associating their products with unique Australian landscapes and cultures. For aboriginal Australians, Dreaming is the process of telling stories describing the creation of the world, the land, its climate and creatures, and their cultural values. Dreamtime is about ancestral origins, and a life lived in the present (Barrett 2013; Rio Tinto Corporation 2018 a,b).

In 2005, traditional landholders completed negotiations for an **Indigenous Land Use agreement** granting them increased benefits from the mine, including a return of land rights, and more training and jobs for the indigenous workforce. Both the mine staff and Aboriginal guides have offered tours for visitors, thereby cooperating in building the tourism sector. The Argyle mine, though, is running out of diamonds and, depending on prices, will terminate operation circa 2020. The mine raised aboriginal employment from 7% to 25% and provided royalties to fund indigenous trusts. The trusts are now depleted and have not significantly diversified economic opportunities for indigenous communities. Despite improved communications between the mining company and indigenous stakeholders, careful planning is necessary to prevent the negative social and environmental impacts of the inevitable pit closures (O'Faircheallaigh 2008; West and Smith 2017; Rio Tinto Corporation 2018a).

Although substituting sustainable energy generation for fossil fuels might appear to resolve extractive concerns surrounding sacred sites and indigenous peoples, the construction of hydroelectric dams and wind turbines also threatens religious terrains. Dams with extensive reservoirs drown temples, churches, and cemeteries, like the Māori ancestral sites (Chapter 3). As major national projects, Aswan Dam in Egypt and Three Gorges Dam in China salvaged temples of exceptional historic worth and transported religious objects to preservation zones or museums. Villages, scattered burials, and recently-constructed houses of worship do not fare as well. Sacred waterfalls, springs, rapids, and caves are particularly vulnerable. In the United States, the Tennessee Valley Authority has disinterred individual burials at churches and family plots and relocated them before dam completions. They were unable, however, to move Chota or Tanasi, the pre-colonial Cherokee towns now submerged beneath Tellico Lake.

Issue: Artisanal and small-scale mining

Worldwide 10% of miners are corporate employees, and 90% are independent or work in small scale operations, most of them in the Global South. Dependent on muscle, shovels, and sluices, artisanal mining incorporates children as part of family operations or recruits vulnerable minors without stable guardianship (Hilson 2008; World Health Organization 2016). Women comprise 40% of artisanal and small-scale miners and often receive less income for their efforts. Environmental impacts of mining, such as forest clearing and stream contamination, can cause women to walk further to gather firewood or draw water (Bashwira et al. 2014). Small-scale miners use poisonous chemicals like mercury in extracting precious metals and turn-up lead and other contaminants. Youthful laborers and children playing around operations suffer toxic exposures. In remote regions, artisanal miners have attacked indigenous peoples and caused fish kills with poisonous chemicals. Environmental scientists Daniel Marcos Bonotto and Ene Glória da Silveira (2009) have documented **biomagnification** raising levels of methyl-mercury in fish tissue, in the Amazon basin. Cultures such as the Yanomami and Kayapo, who draw much of their protein intake from the aquatic food chain, are at risk for elevated mercury ingestion. Once mercury enters the rivers, it binds to sediments, thus remains within riparian and lake ecosystems for many decades.

Artisanal mining is often unpermitted and uninspected, if not a priori illegal. In multiple countries, however, police and military units have evicted or arrested small-scale miners, who are historic landholders or are already living in poverty and have few other alternatives for cash income. The Embera Chami (Katio Indians), for example, are indigenous to Columbia, where 32 communities occupy an area of 50,000 hectares. They have historically mined gold on their lands using artisanal methods. The government criminalized unpermitted mining, arrested numerous Embera Chami miners, and granted international corporations mining concessions effectively covering Embera Chami lands. Asserting customary law, the Embera Chami developed a mining association and protocols governing extraction within their territory, excluding some areas critical to their livelihoods from excavation, and banning industrial-scale mining entirely. They also banned any mining, including artisanal, deploying cyanide or mercury. As is the case in forest management, retention of indigenous religion or cultural traditions does not preclude establishing scientifically informed environmental regulations (Doyle and Cariño 2013).

The United Nations, organizations forwarding responsible mining, and social-justice NGOs, like Oxfam, are exploring means for mitigating the negative features of artisanal mining without placing the miners in even more trying fiscal circumstances or exacerbating unjust treatment of women. The Ecumenical Council on Corporate Responsibility, a religious NGO based in the United Kingdom, supported the publication of a report on indigenous rights cited by this chapter (Doyle and Cariño 2013). Development agencies and NGOs are encouraging mining corporations to assist artisanal miners, by providing safety training, instruction in methods not requiring toxins, purchase of ores and gems, and permission to mine areas adjoining corporate pits (CSAM 2009). Because small-scale mining is low tech, low capital, and low income, environmental health, and environmental restoration remain two of its greatest challenges.

Issue: Extraction, peacebuilding, and Fairtrade

Beginning with colonial governments, elites and international corporations drained the profits from mineral and petroleum extraction, associating mining with oppressive governance and inequitable distribution of national wealth. Resistance movements and insurgencies have operated extractive enterprises to fund military operations, such as the faction-controlled diamond exports from Sierra Leone during the civil war (1991–2002). Not infrequently, conflicts over natural resource ownership and management align with religious identification, as has been the case when ISIS (DESH) as a religiously framed insurgency captured and operated petroleum fields and refineries in Syria. Governing to correct environmental abuses and distribute benefits from high-value natural resources harvest, such as utilizing income to improve schools and roads, conversely contributes to post-conflict peacebuilding, a process in which religious organizations are often participants (Lujala and Rustad 2012).

The application of **Fairtrade** principles to gems and minerals began with the international outcry concerning "blood" or conflict diamonds. Profits from the illegally traded precious stones fund rebel groups and interethnic or interreligious battling. Mining companies, cutters, and dealers cooperated in developing a certification system restricting the sale of diamonds of questionable origin – a process supported by socially-conscious religious NGOs and congregations. The Fairtrade organization, which now certifies gems and gold, has conducted an entrepreneurial project in east Africa intended to guarantee a reasonable price to artisanal miners. The pilot is experimenting with loans to improve the technology via the purchase of centrifuges, replacing the less efficient and hazardous separation of gold from dross via polluting mercury and cyanide. The associated Dragonfly Initiative has developed prototypes for environmental restoration in South America, where affected residents plant fruit trees on mined sites (Butler 2017).

Issue: Mountain top-removal coal mining

In most countries, the nation owns mineral and fossil fuel rights, often in shared arrangements with regional or local governments. Under US laws, mineral rights belong to the landowner and may be sold separately from the surface land plats. In the Appalachians, mining companies once paid relatively small amounts to acquire rights to coal seams under farms and residences. The property owners retained "use rights" to their land, but most did not realize they and their heirs had no legal protection from the disturbance caused by coal extraction. As surface or strip mining replaced deep mining due to lower costs per ton, the coal companies began to practice mountain-top removal mining (MTM), where they blast away the overburden with its productive soils and bulldoze it into adjoining valleys. Operations have arrived unexpectedly with their machinery and left farmers staring at piles of rubble where their fields had been (Hirsch and Dukes 2014: 15–25).

Today, federal regulations require mining corporations to recontour the slopes and plant them with vegetation preceding closure. The mountains, however, remain flat-topped, and their forests need many decades to recover. Property owners and even entire towns downslope have limited protections against the concomitant erosion, pollution, and burial of streams. Like many types of mining, coal companies construct slurry impoundments to contain the wastewater generated by cleaning ore before shipment. Dam breaks are a threat, as proven by the Buffalo Creek, West Virginia, flood that killed 125 people, and the massive slurry spill in Inez, Kentucky, in 2000 (Hirsch and Dukes 2014: 15–25).

Increased mechanization has dramatically reduced the person-hours required per ton, causing layoffs of miners and unemployment throughout Appalachian coal-producing regions, which remain among the poorest in the United States. The coal companies have claimed the regional reserves will support thousands of jobs for the next 50 years. Opponents of MTM argue the prime production period will be about 20 years or about half the working life of a typical American (Hirsch and Dukes 2014). In either case, the projected duration of employment is less than two generations. Environmental recovery from MTM is critical to the Appalachian region's economic future, as it directly or indirectly affects agriculture, forestry, and recreation, along with the willingness of other businesses and industries to move into former coal towns.

As with other environmental conflicts of this scale, stakeholders represent diverse interests, and some are more empowered than others. Coal companies and labor unions employ professional lobbyists and conduct outreach to state legislators, who tend to favor mining as a source of jobs and tax revenues. Some miners, however, are opposed to surface mining and support the "Dig It Deep" movement as tunnel-based mining requires larger crews and causes less damage to the land's surface. Federal and state regulatory agencies, including the Environmental Protection Agency and the Army Corps of Engineers, are responsible for compliance. Both landowners and environmental NGOs have sued coal companies and have managed via the courts to constrain some negative impacts, like the release of coal dust from processing facilities. In a process termed **micro-mobilization**, regional residents have formed **grassroots activist** groups based in individual watersheds or states (Hirsch and Dukes 2014: 27–52; Bell 2016).

Evangelical Protestant churches are the most common centers of worship in the Southern Appalachians, yet coal mining's past dependence on immigrant labor has diversified the Christian denominations present. Catholic and Orthodox churches are also staples of coal country. Both sides in the political battles over MTM are concerned about maintaining the cultural character and regional lifestyles of the Appalachians—one from the perspective of the mining with its higher wages, and the other from the heritage of small farms and picturesque landscapes. Gospel standards like "Build Me a Cabin in Glory Land" idealize the "old home place" and mountain culture. Country hits have lauded the stoic and struggling miners and have also protested the environmental and social impacts via compositions such as Kathy Mattea's "Hello, My Name Is Coal" (Hirsch and Dukes 2014: 43).

Religious scholar, Joseph D. Witt (2016: 69–79) has investigated the roots of resistance to MTM in Appalachia. He divides faith-based, environmental activism into three streams: an older justice and human rights-based Christian approach emerging from concerns about poverty, the more recent Christian creation care movement, and nature-venerating spiritualities. Since the 19th century, mainline Protestants and Roman Catholics have operated schools and **home missions** in the southern Appalachians. The Catholic Glenmary Home Missionaries began sending both ordained religious and laity to the Appalachians in 1939. Their original focus was relieving human suffering and the combating poverty, causing families to fragment and migrate to industrial cities. As Sister Mary Cirillo has summarized: "everything has to do with the coal, gas, oil, and timber being needed to supply the consumers…" For Cirillo, resource exploitation has ruined the landscape and "the morale of the people," including "the sense that we are part of nature." Shoddy environmental protection perpetuates the social injustices limiting the futures for the upland communities the sisters serve. Under a rubric of **eco-justice**, fair treatment for the mountaineers requires care for the mountains.

Rather than acting through coalitions of local churches, Christian denominations with a national presence often address social–ethical issues via statements from governing bodies or participation in ecumenical organizations. The Episcopal Church, the United Methodist Church, and the Unitarian Universalist Association, among others, have released public statements condemning MTM. Regional bodies have enhanced credibility and influence at the state level. Already advocating reform of the coal industry, in 1998, the Catholic Council on Appalachia became the first regional religious organization circulating a resolution forwarding stewardship. They perceived the companies as outsiders taking benefits while Appalachia unjustly bears the damages and social costs. In 2011, the West Virginia Council of Churches assumed a more moderate position that did not reject coal mining per se. The Council did assert current environmental regulations should be more strictly enforced. Other anti-MTM activists, though, found the "more effective regulation position" too weak. Opposing additional government oversight, the coal companies have been unwilling to admit they are not in compliance (Witt 2016: 80–95).

Regional religious councils and individual denominations have met with both industry and activist leadership and participated in protests. In addition to visiting grassroots organizations, representatives of the West Virginia Council of Churches engaged legislators and elected officials, and the West Virginia Coal Association chairman. Meanwhile, the Earth Quakers initiated a campaign intended to "out" banks that provided funding for MTM. They staged protests against the PNC Bank, and in 2010 conducted a sit-in at a Washington, DC bank branch, where they built a symbolic mound of dirt in the center of the lobby. Other denominations began to divest their holdings of stock or accounts in PNC, which responded to the bad publicity by eliminating loans for surface mines (Witt 2016: 80–95).

Many Appalachian Evangelical churches have members both for and against MTM. They thus have avoided wading into the political fray and remained silent as institutions. The rise of the contemporary Creation Care movement, with its deeper roots in Biblically justified land stewardship, has, in contrast, provided both a platform and allies for Evangelical Protestants opposed to MTM. The most common theological approach is termed **theocentric** (God-centered) and credits environmental activism as service to the Creator of both humanity and the mountains. Religious theorists, such as Episcopalian Andrew R.H. Thompson (2015) have argued the mountains should be considered sacred or holy, and that the intersection of place and regional identity has moral weight. Thompson invokes both the social ethics of Reformed theologian Richard Niebuhr and theocentric approach for addressing issues such as the legitimacy of environmental reclamation, which may not fully recover the ecological health of mined terrains. In the early 2000s, advocates for Creation Care began to establish Christian environmental organizations in the Appalachians, both through more progressive churches and as free-standing RENGOs (religious, environmental NGOs). Formed in 2005, Christians for the Mountains grew out of a network of environmental activists, many of whom had already gleaned experience in endeavors like the Religious Campaign for Forest Conservation (Witt 2016: 97–144).

The third group of activists identified by Witt (2016: 145–194) is the biocentric or **dark green** contingent, whose primary goal is "defending Mother Earth" (Taylor 2010). Witt defines this orientation as pursuing an intense spiritual relationship with nature, and putting biological conservation and regional environments first, rather than organizing in terms of denominations. Many dedicated Anti-MTM activists fit this characterization as they discuss their childhood experiences on mountain creeks and utilize religious vocabulary, like "sacred," to describe the slopes and summits. Some biocentrists are traditionalist Native Americans, others are Christians, Buddhists, adherents of metaphysical religions, or have no identification with a faith. Witt's analysis depends on profiles of groundbreakers in an array of organizations, while this wing has not, as of this writing, established specifically dark green RENGOs or national political networks countering MTM.

Meanwhile, the independent churches and Evangelical denominations have become more politically active, particularly concerning family values. This wave of civic engagement has aligned denominations, like the Southern Baptists, with conservative political platforms advocating steady economic growth, opportunities for large corporations, and elimination of environmental regulations that might constrain profits. The venerable Protestant tropes of self-improvement and achieving financial success are common sermonic themes for television evangelists and megachurch pastors. When campaigning in 2016, Donald Trump maintained outreach to Evangelical voters as favorable to his pro-industrial, anti-regulatory platform. National Evangelical support for Trump cast votes in favor of MTM and deregulation of coal extraction, whether or not a majority of Appalachian wage earners agreed.

MTM points to the importance of seeking consensus and forming alliances to resolve regional environmental conflicts. Religious stakeholders must interact with other interested parties with different goals and values. As Witt (2016: 135–137) notes, theocentric environmentalists encounter other Christians who share their Biblicism but who are environmentally ambivalent. Although Appalachian residents may reject intervention by "outsiders," national RENGOs, such as ecumenical Interfaith Power and Light, assert that the coal mining clears forests and releases pollutants into the earth's atmosphere—thereby modifying the global carbon cycle (Hirsch and Dukes 2014: 35). Closure of coal-fired power plants or installation of emission controls in Kentucky reduced asthma disease burden, including hospitalizations and emergency room visits, in the surrounding area (Casey et al. 2020). What happens in West Virginia mines effects homes and bioregions elsewhere via fuel pricing, respiratory illnesses, and global warming. Faith communities have the potential to link the regional and the global, and, conversely, to become stuck in the narrower frame of their membership. Environmental care and management operate in hierarchies of scale, institutional organization, economy, and governance.

Issue: Sacralizing a damaged mountain—Buddhist monks save Khao Chi Chan

As western environmentalists prefer to preserve little disturbed landscapes, they rarely attempt to award sacred status *di novo* to mined terrains. In Thailand circa 1996, the Supreme Patriarch of Buddhist monks, Somdet Phra Yannasangwon, moved to prevent mineral extraction from demolishing a mountain. During the Vietnam War, the US military began quarrying Kheo Chi Chan with heavy equipment to support the construction of an airfield. After the war, local roadbuilding created further demand for limestone and threatened to level the peak. Countering the wastage of a perfectly good and lovely mountain, Yannasangwon arranged for royal purchase and the craving of a 109-meter image of Sakyamuni Buddha on the quarried cliff face. Working at night with lasers, crews etched a simple, dramatic outline and filled it with gold leaf, blessing the peak with permanent status as a sacred site (Fig. 5.2). A small lake, floral plantings,

Figure 5.2 "The Buddha that enlightens and shines with brightness and sublimity," outlined in gold at Khao Chi Chan, Pattaya, Thailand—a former limestone quarry.

and shrines now grace the base. Aside from serving as a popular devotional destination, Khao Chi Chan attracts tourists and income for local businesses and has become much too admired to disappear as truckloads of paving material. As a sign at the site indicated in 2020, the fractured earth has given birth to "The Buddha that enlightens and shines with brightness and sublimity".

Conclusion: Consumerism, values, and religious materiality

Among the greatest conundrums for religious environmentalism is how best to raise awareness that the warm glow of ceremonial lighting strips mountains, and gold statuettes pour cyanide into tropical rivers. The problem is embedded in the religious understanding of the material and, as a corollary, of **consumerism**. Hindu activist, Mahatma Gandhi summarized the central characteristic of modern civilization as "a multiplicity of wants." The political philosopher believed ancient civilizations like that of India, were distinguished by their "their imperative restriction upon, and strict regulating of these wants." Western industrial cultures have "a mad desire to destroy distance and time, to increase animal appetites, and go to the ends of the earth in search of their satisfaction." Gandhi declared: "If modern civilization stands for all this… I call it satanic." He advocated a commitment to voluntary simplicity as a conscious alternative to modern values. Gandhi's much-repeated aphorism "the world has enough for everyone's need, but not enough for everyone's greed" has become a rallying cry for eco-justice (Guha 2006: 231–232).

Christian ethicist Laura Hartman (2011: 61–63) links the purchase and consumption of food and material goods to self-love, love of close others, love of somewhat distant others, love of faraway others, love of place, and cumulatively, love of God. For Christians living faithfully relative to consumption cultivates virtues forwarding a healthy community, including sharing, moderation, generosity, hospitality, gratitude and providing for those who have less. Love of others at a distance incorporates consumer decisions that protect the livelihood of farmers, miners, and factory workers in other nations. Gratitude and thanksgiving raise appreciation for the most basic of meals and material possessions.

Hartman (2011: 165–166) believes the production and consumption of energy flowing when she flips a light switch "shares many factors with the **Eucharist**: it comes from and strengthens the community; it is a vital resource that is distributed and accessible to many; it is an occasion for thanksgiving and closeness to God, and it brings the world that much closer to (one ecological version of) the vision of its fulfillment." Hartman (2011: 169–193) proposes four considerations for moderating consumption: avoiding sin (damage to others), loving neighbors, embracing creation, and envisioning the future. An ethic of **discernment** should frame consumer choices. Making a purchase is the effort-demanding process of selecting among and synthesizing moral alternatives.

For Buddhists, the material is *maya* or constantly changing illusion. Craving expressed as desire and attachment is the cause of suffering. Craving arises as a manifestation of basic human inclinations identified as the "**Three Poisons**: greed, aversion or hate, and delusion." Buddhist scholar Stephanie Kaza (2019: 101–117) critiques consumerism as a state where the Three Poisons "become wanting *more* of something, wanting *less* of something and wanting something that doesn't exist." Consumerism continually reinforces the ego-identity, propagating delusion, and causing a misunderstanding of "the empty nature of self." It spawns "a never-ending field of desire" fed by senses saturated by cultural conditioning anchored in advertising, slogans, and self-identify formed around manufactured goods. For individuals immersed in consumerism, grasping generates becoming, further distancing the self from enlightenment and the craving free state of *nirvana*. A remedy is the Buddhist concept of *santutthi*—pursuing contentment and satisfaction by following the Eight-Fold Path. Cultivating *metta*—"the capacity to offer positive well-wishing or lovingkindness on of one's self and others"—also relieves consumerism generated suffering. Consumerism promotes harming of other people and other creatures; thus, Buddhists should exercise restraint and take responsibility for the damages done.

The **Engaged Buddhism** movement encourages Buddhists to tackle social issues at scales from local to global. Engaged Buddhism integrates the concept of work as **Right Livelihood** to approaches to mass production and economies where meaningful work is not available to everyone. Environmental activist John Negru (2019: 114–131) proposes that Buddhists actualize their values by establishing better workplaces and by starting humane businesses that are fulfilling places to be employed. One of the routes out of consumerism is to "reframe ourselves as makers." Right Livelihood accepts the need to earn a living while striving not to cause harm. Buddhist entrepreneurship can forward Fairtrade certified suppliers, offer gender-equitable salaries, establish employee cooperatives, and invest in businesses with positive social impacts. Negru concludes: "A Buddhist model for economic activity cannot simply be a negation of worldly work, because that would be cruel to literally billions of people. Buddhist economics must simply put healthy lives and a healthy planet at the center of its economic model."

Suggested readings

Doyle, Cathal, and Jill Cariño. *Making Free, Prior & Informed Consent a Reality, Indigenous Peoples and the Extractive Sector.* www.piplinks.org/makingfpicareality, 2013.

Guha, Ramachandra. *How Much Should a Person Consume? Environmentalism in India and the United States.* Berkeley: University of California Press, 2006.

Hampton, O.W. *Culture of Stone: Sacred and Profane Uses of Stone among the Dani.* College Station: Texas A&M Press, 1999.

Hartman, Laura. *The Christian Consumer: Living Faithfully in a Fragile World.* Oxford, U.K.: Oxford University Press, 2011.

Houtman, Dick, and Birgit Meyer. *Things: Religion and the Question of Materiality.* New York: Fordham University Press, 2012.

Kaza, Stephanie. *Green Buddhism: Practice and Compassionate Action in Uncertain Times.* Boulder, CO: Shambhala Press, 2019.

Witt, Joseph D. *Religion and Resistance in Appalachia: Faith and the Fight against Mountaintop Removal Coal Mining.* Lexington: University of Kentucky Press, 2016.

6   Watersheds

Scale, place, and consilience

Key concepts

1 Religious environmental problem-solving must adapt to geographic and social scales.
2 Religious-based watershed management has evolved systems sustaining bottom-up management and mediating water sharing for agriculture. Religions can sacralize headwaters or essential water sources, protecting them from overharvest and abuse.
3 When colonial authorities or government agencies supersede religiously-based, self-organizing managerial systems, they often undermine sustainable practices.
4 Contemporary environmental planning attempts to adapt to ecosystemic scales, engage diverse stakeholders, avoid top-down management, and correct mistakes.
5 Bottom-up movements, such as Thailand's Buddhist ecology monks, have developed strategies for organizing villagers and other disempowered stakeholders. They prevent the degradation of forests and watersheds by working cooperatively with civic government and ENGOs.
6 Like other ENGOs, religious environmental organizations must prove their capability and accountability. RENGOs must build the capacity and expertise to instill the best environmental practices in faith communities.
7 Practicing eco-peacekeeping and cultivating consilience among stakeholders of different faiths are essential to environmental planning in multi-cultural contexts. Implementing methods like alternative dispute resolution is especially critical to resolving transboundary conflicts over natural resource allocation and conservation at international scales.
8 Environmental planning for resources like water can enhance post-conflict peacebuilding.

An exercise in environmental scale

Like civic, environmental governance, religious engagement with the environment is sensitive to social and geographic **scale,** and stakeholder diversity. This chapter investigates two related topics: how religious organizations address environmental management, integrating local with regional scales, and how consilience evolves among stakeholders. A practical exercise is to examine how religions adapt to the essential geographic unit for protecting water quality and aquatic biodiversity—the **watershed**. A watershed has a catchment collecting precipitation in groundwater, which in turn percolates into underground aquifers. The water reemerges at the surface in springs and first-order or primary streams. These converge into second and higher-order streams and finally into major rivers flowing into deltas and estuaries. The chapter begins with two historic cases—Balinese **water temples** and New Mexico **acequias** (communal irrigation systems)—where religious institutions and traditions directly regulate water sources or assist in maintaining the cooperation necessary to ensure the quality and quantity of water. The chapter then explores contemporary ecosystem-based management and watershed planning with culturally and economically diverse cadres of stakeholders and finishes with transboundary, environmental peacekeeping.

Issue: Self-organizing managerial systems, Balinese water temples

When the Green Revolution arrived in the volcanic landscape of Bali, Indonesia, agricultural scientists assumed they could improve irrigation efficiency and raise production via high-yield rice varieties. Government reorganization of rice farming for continuous cropping increased application of commercial fertilizers and overrode traditional irrigation schedules—resulting in decreased production! Water shortages and unprecedented outbreaks of pests and diseases off-set any gains. Bali's volcanic soils are rich in nutrients such as phosphate and potassium, leached into the paddies by monsoon rains. The "scientific" cropping scheme introduced superfluous (and expensive) levels of commercial fertilizers, releasing excess nitrogen into the rivers. Levels of nitrogen rose downstream and contaminated nearshore ocean waters, leading to macroalgae mats covering and killing reef corals (Lansing 2007).

Preceding Dutch colonization of Indonesia, a system of regionally distinctive Hindu water temples, rather than the royalty of multiple kingdoms who were often at odds with each other, had primary authority for irrigation on Bali and Lombok. Farmers divide into *subaks* of around a hundred members each, organized around an irrigation channel and a local water temple. Water temple systems begin at crater lakes on volcanic summits and end at temples on the seacoast. The boundaries of the temple networks do not correspond with those of former kingdoms; they align with the topography of the watersheds.

The temple networks are effective in maintaining rice production because farmers act cooperatively to take optimal advantage of ecological processes. The irrigation systems pass through weirs directing controlled levels of water flow into channels and aqueducts delivering water to terraced hills. Farmers work simultaneously to create pulses of wet and dry conditions, which in turn stimulate microbial activity—especially of nitrogen-fixing cyanobacteria providing an essential nutrient to their crops. Coordinating irrigation via temple membership, farmers synchronize their fallow periods, which dry the paddies, reducing pests and inhibiting outbreaks. The temple network avoids completely simultaneous action, however, as that would cause all farmers to demand maximum amounts of water at the same time when they reflood the paddies. Anthropologists J. Stephen Lansing and James Kremer (1993) describe the temples as **complex co-adaptive systems** or **self-organizing managerial systems**. The constant cropping recommended by scientists disrupted both the fallow and water sharing.

The summit Temple of the Crater Lake and the lake goddess, Dewi Danu, on Mount Batur, Bali, forms the center of the natural **mandala** of "power and interlocking

Figure 6.1 The Hindu Ulun Danu temple in the caldera Lake Bratan, Bali, Indonesia. The temple is the fulcrum of a system incorporating multiple shrines associated with irrigation channels. The Hindu procession celebrates the full moon.

Photo: Rolf Zimmerman, Licensed by Getty Images

religious cycles," encompassing the springs feeding the lake and thereby the water source for the entire watershed. A virgin priestess selects the 24 priests, maintaining the temple. The Jero Gde or high priest adjudicates disputes and allocates water rights, maintaining water availability for all *subaks*. Thousands of farmers annually make offerings at the Temple of the Crater Lake and participate in seasonal rituals at their local water temples and shrines adjoining rice fields (Fig. 6.1). The water temples are summit to sea, providing a communication network concerning the timing and amount of water releases (Lansing 2007). Religious pilgrimages and processions map and connect the branches forming the mandala.

As the farmers are self-organizing at the *subak* and local temple level, the network is not predominantly top-down hierarchy run by priests, but one of solidarity forming a **"resilient system** of **bottom-up management** that increases and equalizes harvests." The farmers adjust the size of the paddies relative to the terrain in a pattern that is "non-uniform and scale-free." They optimize the trade-off between water releases and pest control via a process of **self-organized criticality** (Lansing 2017). The management is "scale-free" because bureaucracy has not forced a poorly adaptive hierarchy of land and water allocation on the farmers. Scientific planners initially dismissed the temples as archaic and unnecessary to reasonable agricultural practice. Applied science should, however, have avoided untested assumptions and investigated how the existing system of water distribution and soil management functioned before renovating it. Government agricultural extension now cooperates with the venerable religious management network.

Issue: Scientific management versus headwaters as sacred space, Taos Pueblo, New Mexico

In contrast to the religious unity of the water temples, today's watershed management for American southwestern pueblos and acequias transpires in a multi-religious context. The Pueblo people had developed sustainable dryland farming techniques and irrigation systems many centuries before the arrival of the Spanish. The Spanish then introduced new forms of irrigation and aqueduct construction, based on Moorish (Islamic) designs (Arellano 2014). As colonists moved into New Mexico, they displaced Native Americans from the lower reaches of the watersheds and nutrient-rich flood-plain soils. The colonial administration applied Spanish water law, forcing the Pueblos to defend their water rights. Both the Pueblos and the Spanish colonists sacralized **hydroscapes** and utilized religious rituals to encourage water sharing. After the US annexed the region, the federal government placed much of the land in the public domain. It increasingly asserted the authority of land and water management agencies, causing yet another shift in legal oversight. With its hunger for natural resources and Protestant-influenced dismissal of sacred landscapes, the US government initially had little motivation to preserve religiously moderated irrigation networks.

Before the conquest, Taos Pueblo had sacralized Blue Lake and the headwater springs feeding the Río Pueblo de Taos—their source of drinking and irrigation water. The Taos conducted an annual two-day pilgrimage to the translucent, undisturbed lake nestled in the forested slopes above the cluster of adobe homes. As the Pueblo believe disclosure to non-Pueblos disempowers their religion, the private pilgrimage and ceremonies have never been open to outsiders. When the U.S. Forest Service (USFS) established Taos National Forest in 1906, they acquired what had, from the US government's perspective, been "vacant" lands in the public domain. The USFS took control of 50,000 acres surrounding Blue Lake that had under treaty belonged to the Pueblo. The federal agency promised to maintain Blue Lake and the surrounding property only for the use of the Taos people (Gordon-McCutchan 1991: 1–14).

Beginning in 1915, a new forest supervisor mandated trail-clearing and transport of non-native trout to the lake to make it more enticing to recreationists. Miners were visiting the Blue Lake area to scout claims. During the 1920s under The Religious Crimes Act, federal authorities made engagement in traditional Native American rituals a criminal offense, further diminishing Blue Lake's sacred status. Pueblo elders, however, resisted and went to jail rather than abandon the instruction of their youth in Pueblo ways. In hopes of improving the situation, the Pueblo signed a cooperative use agreement with the USFS in 1927, which gave the agency the authority to manage the timber and vegetation and build roads. Ignoring the Pueblos' religious strictures, the USFS officially permitted recreational companies to enter the area. Even worse, the Forest Service built a ranger cabin with an outhouse and garbage dump near the lake (Gordon-McCutchan 1991: 15–22). Disrespectful visitors were soon tossing beer bottles and food wrappers around the shores of Blue Lake and interfering with Pueblo rituals. The recreational public stole or vandalized sacred objects placed at the site, such as wooden prayer sticks decorated with feathers. For the Taos people, the prayer sticks were a form of respectful communication with the land and waters; for non-Pueblos, the prayer sticks were mere souvenirs (Keegan 1991: 13–17).

In 1926, the US government offered payment for treaty lands illegally taken or sold, but the Taos Pueblos did not want cash for Blue Lake; they desired a clear title. The

Indian Claims Commission did not have the legal authority to return the land, only to pay for it. As part of the movement beginning in the 1960s to restore the rights and dignity of Native Americans, the Taos intensified their efforts to regain the headwaters of the Río Pueblo. In response, the Indian Claims Commission reiterated an offer of $297,684.67 in fiscal compensation. Rejecting the concept of the lake as a commodity, the Taos people replied: "We will not sell our religion, our life." As the political battle to regain the lake continued, the National Council of Churches issued a formal statement, arguing Blue Lake was the religious analog of a cathedral or mosque. President Richard Nixon supported the return of the lake, but as redress for grievances rather than an acknowledgment of the lake's religious value. Ultimately in 1970, Congress voted to return Blue Lake and 48,000 acres to the jurisdiction of the Taos Elders, who granted a request for 2,000 acres to become part of a USFS wilderness area. The Pueblo celebrated with dances, sacred songs, prayers, and a feast (Keegan 1991: 49–51).

Thinking themselves better able to manage the lake than the Pueblos, the professional foresters defined virtuous action as utilizing the natural resources in ways that allowed them to replenish through time and provided the greatest good to the greatest number of people. The government focused on the lake as property, and Taos articulated **blue ecology** (Chapter 3) in the belief that "all that surrounded it was sacred. The animals and plants, as well as the earth itself, were seen as living creatures whose integrity was intimately bound up with that of the tribe." For the Taos people, who believe their souls return to Blue Lake after their death, loaded logging trucks could never replace the lake's connection to their ancestors. They believe the loss of the lake and degradation of the Río Pueblo watershed would ultimately result in the disintegration of the religious fabric holding the community together—scattering the Pueblo (Keegan 1991: 50–52). The Pueblos' relationships rested on duty to the land, waters, and family rather than in transferable property rights.

Issue: The acequias, the role of tradition

Under Spanish governance in the same arid watersheds, wealthy landowners maintained private irrigation systems. Protecting their water rights, smaller farmers developed clusters of irrigators forming *acequias de comun*, a type of water association. The autonomous irrigation communities originally depended on a process of *repartimientos de agua* or *repartos* based on Spanish **customary law** (established patterns of water access). Participants conduct annual meetings and renegotiations for water distribution. *Reparto* underpins a proportional, transparent, and accountable system of water allocations, making the system elastic and adaptive. Acequias cooperate in cleaning ditches, maintaining aqueducts, and managing headgates controlling flow. Following US annexation, the New Mexico State legislature required the acequias to appoint three commissioners and to operate under a *mayordomo* (Rodríguez 2006: 3–5).

Southwestern cultural scholar Sylvia Rodríguez (2006) identifies a **moral economy** as a critical foundation of equitable access to water and fair contribution of labor. The acequia ethos anchors in *respeto* or traditions of interpersonal and inter-family respect, and customs of benediction and blessing. Regionally distinctive Roman Catholic devotional gatherings celebrate **novenas** and **rosaries** and share prayers and hymns in Spanish. These rituals are **paraliturgical,** as a priest is usually not present. They transfer ritual power to the local community and foster social cohesion. Parish churches and the associated acequias participate together in feast days and processions honoring patron saints of villages and San Isadore (Ysidore) patron of cultivators. As Rodríguez (2006: 81–103) observes: "A procession traces a specific path in space and gives meaning to the particular territory it traverses. An annual procession reinscribes its pathway of spatial extension through a mapped cosmos." In the Taos basin, these rituals connect artifacts of human occupation, which coalesce largely "around or in relation to water sources," forming a **sacred landscape–hydroscape**. The religious system does not manage the water directly; it contributes to the consilience and solidarity necessary to maintain its equitable availability.

US water law asserts prior appropriation as the basis for water rights restricting flexibility in allocation, while Pueblo and Spanish practices apply equitable apportionment. As urbanization around the City of Taos (downstream from the Pueblo) has increased, the demand for water for non-agricultural uses and privatization of water sources has accelerated. In response, government agencies have attempted top-down apportionment. Overdraft of water from the US tributaries of the Río Grande has caused the river to run dry at its delta at Brownsville, Texas, during drought years, and has water-starved Mexican farms along the Border. Through a series of lawsuits, the acequias fought to maintain customary water rights, which the US District Court affirmed in 1991 (Rodríguez 2006: 115–131).

The City of Taos once depended on *sobrantes*—water left over after irrigation. Through time the municipality has acquired rights to half the river. Taos Pueblo and the Río Pueblo acequias must, therefore, draw water rotationally with the city. Although fewer youth are taking up farming, the sacred landscapes of the Taos Pueblo and the acequias remain as moral systems and religious forms of attachment to place. The future of watershed planning for the Taos Valley is not merely a matter of optimizing water availability down to the last drop or ensuring the Río Grande reaches the Gulf of Mexico, it is also one of intercultural negotiation, and hopefully *respeto* (Rodríguez 2006: 115–131). For the American southwest and the Border region, as demand intensifies, apportionment at all scales remains contested.

Issue: Science and policy addressing scale

Meanwhile, scientifically informed environmental leadership and governance have experienced philosophical and organizational turmoil of their own. Rooted in 19th-century worldviews, the early agricultural and natural resource conservation movements borrowed industrial ideas of efficiency and attempted to optimize farm produce, timber extraction, and fish harvest. Invoking the **balance of nature**, they assumed ecosystems could heal or restore themselves given time. During the 1970s and 1980s, biologists mounted a critique of environmental planning norms and proposed the science itself was flawed. Ecologists challenged the theory of ecosystems or biological communities, attaining a predetermined composition and self-regulating state. Previous scientific advisement had frequently been deficient in its knowledge of ecological and geophysical processes and made errors with its predictions, as was the case with Bali's rice terraces. Maturing from a simple dichotomy of preservation (no use) versus conservation (wise use), contemporary environmental discourses favor **adaptive** management—dynamic, interactive, and willing to address mistakes (Meffe et al. 2002).

Simultaneously, legislators and policy experts began to doubt the wisdom of conventional regulatory approaches and allowing "scientific management" free rein. In the United States, ENGOs demanded the right to comment on federal agency plans. In Canada, the First Nations stoically insisted that they could serve as responsible caretakers for their lands and waters. Conversely, pressures from business interests have resulted in modifications of environmental statutes, and resistance to government agencies operating by fiat. The court cases and legislative battles surrounding Blue Lake and the acequias are examples of **top-down** decision-making alienating rather than incorporating **stakeholders**. Out of the political storms and economic cross-currents, more inclusive forms of environmental management began to emerge.

Ecosystem-Based Management (EBM), for example, approaches environmental problems at supra-local but less than national scale, and requires monitoring of outcomes. EBM allows the stakeholders to "establish rules of engagement, define issues, design data collection, and analysis, and help develop solutions" (Layzer 2008). It appreciates the **resilience** or ability to recover from stresses and the **bottom-up problem-solving** evident among the Balinese *subaks*. The planning protocols attempt to expand the scale from municipal to regional, extending cooperative environmental management across watersheds. These more holistic methods for reaching environmental consensus also have weaknesses. Landscape and bioregional scale environmental planning are fraught with questions concerning jurisdiction, demands for development, and the weighting of one interest against another. EBM management can marginalize outlying views while seeking a common denominator and may give way to business interests, stalling conservation programs (Layzer 2008).

From a religious perspective, it is critical to recognize how strategies like EBM or its sibling **adaptive environmental management** operate and to know what is in force among governmental entities. Professional planners set goals representing desired future outcomes and identify specific, attainable **objectives** as components of a strategic plan. Management teams revise and adjust these objectives as an environmental project proceeds. Administrators conduct formal evaluations utilizing **metrics** or **benchmarks** to determine if an environmental program is effective. In EBM, religious organizations are welcome, while rather than claiming universal authority, their positions should be consistent with their direct stakes and actual constituencies. Adaptive management values experience over opinion and intends to provide environmental guidance in perpetuity. Religious communities thus need to arrange continuing representation. Indigenous councils and institutions like faith-based universities can easily accomplish this; ad hoc committees and self-appointed spokespeople, in contrast, are inherently unstable. As is the case with all participants in consortia, religiously based organizations are more likely to make constructive contributions if they are well versed in the issues and their scientific foundations and are willing to dialog with people with differing views.

Issue: Ownership, accountability, and watershed structure

In the United States and Canadian context, where organizations like acequias are rare, faith-based motivation to participate in watershed management often materializes at the level of families and neighborhoods. **Civic ecology** is increasingly a means for providing labor for aquatic clean-up and restoration projects, and for educating the citizenry in watershed care. Becoming practitioners, volunteers and school classes plant prairies, restore urban streams, and reestablish oyster beds in the polluted waters (Krasny and Tidball 2015). Mosques, churches, and temples are all legitimate sponsors.

Cultivating a **sense of place**, religious youth and educational organizations have participated in wetland plantings and initiated river clean-up using kayaks to clear plastic waste from shorelines. Faith-based educational institutions sponsor student teams participating in citizen science, and at the college and university level, train water professionals. Religious intentional communities can become stellar examples of watershed care at the local level. Findhorn treats its wastewater via greenhouse aquaculture, where aquatic plants take-up the excess nutrients and other pollutants flushed down toilets and drains.

In 1983, an Anglican priest and impassioned ornithologist, Peter Harris (2008), established the A'Rocha Charitable Trust in the U.K. to raise funds for a Christian conservation center on a species-rich estuary in Portugal. When that prototype project was successful enough to fall under national management, A'Rocha began to develop a network of international subsidiaries in countries with a high need for biodiversity initiatives and those with interested Christian sponsors (Harris 2008). A'Rocha Canada's farm on a tributary of the Frasier River trains interns in ecological surveying and ecosystemic restoration. The residential community maintains the forest vegetation along its stream corridor, contributing to its value as a salmon nursery. Interns have been cooperating with government scientists in monitoring the endangered Salish sucker (fish), native salmon, exotic invaders like bullfrogs, and other aquatic species (Fig. 6.2). Investing in public education, A'Rocha invites other property and business

Figure 6.2 Stream corridor protection at A'Rocha Canada's farm in British Columbia includes leaving forest and wetland around the creeks as buffers. Volunteers carry fish traps to the creek to monitor for the presence of the endangered Salish sucker and young salmon. The fish will be released alive.

owners to view their watershed conservation strategies and offers aquatically themed school programs and children's summer camp activities (Fig. 12.2). The non-profit has employed environmental professionals and educators, thereby developing the **expertise** and **capacity** to address the complex planning required to preserve watershed function and integrity.

Issue: Tackling major watersheds

Where religious hierarchies have regional or national authority, they can display leadership at broader, even international, scales. In 2001, the United States and Canadian Roman Catholic bishops of the Columbia River basin released an international pastoral letter to their parishes and schools entitled *The Columbia River Watershed: Caring for Creation and the Common Good.* The bishops underwrote a pamphlet available in three languages, English, Spanish and French, and funded an educational video suitable for use in schools and churches to accompany the letter. Aside from providing a theological rationale for caring for the entire Columbia watershed, the directive considers the eco-justice aspects of maintaining the health and ecosystem services of the river (Box 6.1).

A more bottom-up approach has emerged in Thailand, where Buddhism has been an integral part of daily life for many centuries. "Ecology" monks have resisted the degradation of forested watersheds caused by government grants of corporative logging concessions. Villagers who do not own the land have suffered as streams have dried up, and consumptive resources have disappeared. Revising long-established practices, like adorning a sacred bodhi tree with a colorful cloth or blessing individuals by sprinkling water, the monks instituted new rituals, including the **ordination** of trees as monks, intended to engage both villagers and government officials (Fig. 2.1). In wrapping trees in orange robes, the rituals anthropomorphize nature, yet equilibrate the status of trees with that of humans. The ceremonies incorporate sanctification of water by placing a Buddha image in water in alms bowls and having village headmen imbibe of consecrated water in front of a Buddha statue, thereby sealing an oath to protect the forest and its watershed. As anthropologist Susan Darlington (2012: 1–92) concludes, these symbolic religious actions have expanded into village-based conservation projects and

---

Box 6.1 Roman Catholic Bishop's (2001) recommended actions for the Columbia River watershed

1 Consider the common good.
2 Conserve the watershed as the common good.
3 Conserve and protect species of wildlife.
4 Respect the dignity and traditions of the region's indigenous peoples.
5 Promote justice for the poor, linking economic justice with environmental justice.
6 Promote community resolution of economic and ecological issues.
7 Promote social responsibility among reductive (extractive) and reproductive (agriculture, forestry, fisheries)-based enterprises.
8 Conserve energy and establish environmentally integrative alternative energy sources.
9 Respect ethnic and racial cultures, citizens, and communities.
10 Integrate transportation and recreation needs with sustainable ecosystem requirements.

cooperation with ENGOs, directly engaging key stakeholders. Begun in rural terrains, they have attracted the attention of the middle class, energizing Buddhist conservation commitment at the national level.

Issue: Multi-faith projects

Multi-religious RENGOs adapt well to the all watershed scale, where municipalities and river authorities play essential roles in regulating water quality. As the largest estuary in the United States, the Chesapeake Bay receives water from multiple states and cities, including Washington, DC. Pollutants originate from farm manure, fertilizer, urban runoff, vehicle exhaust, power plants, shipping, fracking, trash, and industrial effluents. Dams have interfered with fish spawning, and overharvest has depleted the oyster reefs that once filtered phytoplankton. Hypoxia, fish die-offs, and highly contaminated zones like Baltimore Harbor, Maryland, continue to plague the Bay (Horton 2003).

In response to complex jurisdictions, two overarching organizations strive to maintain fruitful communication, advise legislators, and educate the public. The Chesapeake Bay Commission, founded by the US EPA, coordinates policy. The Chesapeake Bay Program coordinates the efforts of federal and state agencies, local governments, educational institutions, and NGOs. Several ENGOs, the most prominent of which is the Chesapeake Bay Foundation, raise funds for conservation and public outreach. Strategies for recovering the Chesapeake Bay's water quality and fisheries productivity correspond to EBM in their continual reappraisal of concrete goals, like the reduction of nitrogen inputs, and their interactive relationships with the watershed's stakeholders.

In techno-industrial societies, religious organizations rarely develop new conservation methodologies; instead, they contextualize and expose their members to established **best practices**. Regionally, the Interfaith Partners for the Chesapeake (2019) has been acting as a hub for religious networking and education. Among their sponsored activities are interfaith nature walks, creek clean-ups, educational film showings, panel discussions, and training for Sunday School and Vacation Bible school teachers. Interfaith Partners establishes "One Water Partnerships" based in cities or counties. Their purpose is "igniting and equipping the faithful to restore our shared waters, honoring creation and acting justly in broader communities." Becoming One Water congregations, Roman Catholic cathedrals, Buddhist meditation centers, Friends meetings, Reform synagogues, and African American churches have invested in **rain gardens**, cisterns, rain barrels, pollinator gardens, and additional trees, thereby reducing flash runoff and **non-point source pollution**. Acting as a bridge to the Chesapeake Bay Program and ENGOs, Interfaith Partners trains houses of worship to apply for mini-grants to fund their water-conserving improvements.

Multi-faith RENGOs must tackle inherent social barriers to being inclusive. The presence of a historically prevalent religion can inhibit participation by minority or new religions. In the American context, mainline Protestants often dominate multi-faith dialogs due to their many denominations and commitment to civic engagement. The rhetoric of "interfaith" can be problematic for religious groups firmly committed to internal orthodoxy. Although shared work events pose few barriers other than respecting different sacred calendars, multi-faith worship and festivals require tact and mutual understanding. Educational materials may of necessity be faith specific, as not everyone sponsors a Sunday School. Pastors, imams, and rabbis sometimes perceive religious

NGOs as preempting their moral authority or diverting sparse donations. Conversely, family-friendly environmental activities can attract new members to congregations.

Internationally, ENGOs accomplish much community outreach and on-the-ground problem-solving. In comparison to government agencies, ENGOs are very entrepreneurial and adaptable to local cultural settings. Large ENGOs ordinarily have better **capacity** than religious institutions or church councils to address chronic environmental issues and organize networks, as ENGOs employ ecologists, planners, lawyers, and other professionals. Further, larger ENGOs are adequately empowered to gain the cooperation of government agencies. Due to their dependence on fluctuating public interest and the economics of donations and grants, smaller ENGOs, religious or not, may suffer from instability in leadership and focus.

A RENGO, like Interfaith Partners for the Chesapeake, must prove its **capability** and **accountability**, both relative to the goals of its funders and partners, and relative to the needs of the local faith communities it serves. In a maze of religious governance models, RENGOs face challenges in terms of how to cultivate community acceptance. The planning concepts of **attainable objectives** and **objective metrics** improve outcomes for their projects, just as they do for other NGOs. ENGOs experience pressure to **scale up** to reach an entire watershed, or, in the case of A'Rocha, to represent Christianity globally. Scaling up requires careful strategic planning, as it can cause loss of connection and credibility at the local level, multiply programming in excess of available funding, and result in the inability to maintain capacity for action at expanded scales (Balboa 2018).

Issue: Trans-boundary water management and peacekeeping

For some countries, religion and national governance are strongly aligned. Within Israel, Jews of all sects have supported a national strategy for water conservation. The Hebrew language is rich in aquatic vocabulary, and the Hebrew scriptures discuss water 580 times. Water features like springs, wells, and cisterns appear as metaphors and locales for historically significant events, such as Joshua leading the returning Hebrews across the Jordan River. Jewish law prescribes water for ritual purification (Tal 2002: 199).

As environmental historian Alon Tal (2002: 199–200) has documented, **Zionism**, the movement forwarding immigration of Jews to Palestine, and 20th-century Jewish nationalism have emphasized water as critical to greening Middle Eastern terrain and to ecological restoration of the land itself. Zionists idealized the return of Jewish farming to The Land of the sacred scriptures after a 2000-year diaspora, thereby incorporating water management in their **ideology** (the values, ideals, and ideas informing governance or political policy). As Tal summarizes: "Water resource development was both a symbol of technology's unlimited potential and the prosperity that the Jewish revival could bring the land."

Water indeed led to several early political victories. In 1939, in response to the British government blocking Jewish settlement in better watered northern Israel, hydrologist Simcha Blas proposed piping water from the north to Jewish agricultural settlements in the Negev desert in the south. World War II delayed the project, but following a British mass arrest of Zionist activists in 1946, the Jewish resistance created eleven new settlements in the Negev on Jewish National Federation lands. Acting so quickly the British bureaucracy did not have time to interfere, the water entrepreneurs installed surplus pipes from London's wartime firefighting to divert water to the Negev. After gaining independence from Britain, the newly formed sovereign nation invested in irrigation. Israel achieved a remarkable 500% increase in agricultural production during the 1950s and became an exporter of fruits and other produce (Tal 2002: 205–207).

The modern state of Israel has, at various points, permitted non-sustainable practices. The first irrigation projects were based entirely on groundwater withdrawal. Drilling wells lowers the water table, and in coastal regions, seawater fills the vacuum. Tel Aviv's wells had become too saline to provide drinking water by the 1950s. As industrialization began to outstrip farming and agriculture fell from 30% to 3% of the national product, the farmers continued to demand 70% of the available water. The emphasis on development and the lionization of agriculture created a regulatory blind-spot concerning growing levels of water pollution. Toxic chemicals poured into Lake Kinneret (the Sea of Galilee) and tainted wells. Tal (2002: 205–232) concludes Zionist ideological zeal for hydrological "progress" countered prudence and "left rivers filthy and subjected aquifers to a contaminant bombardment."

Conversely, Israel took a conscious lead in developing technology to conserve water. A leaky pipe inspired Simcha Blas to experiment with delivering water via plastic pipes with small holes. "Drip irrigation" has since become a favored method for conservation worldwide, reducing the evaporation and wastage of sprinklers. Today, Israel has desalination plants providing freshwater for cities. National planning is tackling the issue of overdraft and attempting to anticipate increasing drought caused by climate change. The question of competing demands remains incompletely resolved, however, and opposing claims can leave wetlands and natural habitats without water (Tal 2002: 205–236).

Among its negative impacts, ideology has contributed to a series of geo-political "water wars." Of the Jordan River's three main headwater tributaries, only the Dan is entirely within Israel's boundaries. The Hatzbani originates in Lebanon, and during the 1950s, the headwaters of the Banias belonged to Syria. The Jordan and the Yurmuk Rivers, critical to Israel's national strategies for water availability, are also the most important sources of surface water for the nation of Jordan. Five **riparians** (countries within the watershed), including the Occupied Palestinian Territories, have a direct interest in the Jordan watershed. When Israel attempted to divert the Jordan River in 1953, Syria massed troops on their side of the river facing the construction zone. In the convoluted diplomatic maneuvers that followed, including a stand-off between the United States and the Soviet Union, the United States assisted in creating a water-sharing agreement that made Lake Kinneret the primary reservoir for the Jordan and allocated 45% of the water to Jordan and 15% to Syria. Although the Arab League backed out before signature, the plan was a first step toward formalizing **trans-boundary water allocation** (Tal 2002: 209–211).

In the course on the Six-Day War in 1967, Israeli troops occupied the village of Banias on the Golan Heights with the specific goal of securing rights to the watershed. During the 1960s and 1970s, both Israel and Jordan developed irrigation projects that diverted water from the Jordan River. They depleted so much of its discharge that, by the 1980s, it was seasonally running dry. The loss of river volume, along with climate change, has contributed to the recession of the Dead Sea. Even as political conflicts continued, Israeli and Jordanian water managers were meeting at "picnic table discussions" to deal with variations in the Jordan's flow. In 1993, the Declaration of Principles for Interim Self-Government for Palestinians established an independent Palestinian water authority. In 1994, Israel and Jordan negotiated a Treaty of Peace without the other riparians, which included a section on water (Krieger 2016: 187–190).

Competing demands for water among Israel, Palestine, and Jordan have continued to both strain international relations in the Jordan River Valley and stimulate constructive efforts towards transboundary cooperation. Reduced flow due to overdraft threatens the watershed's unique natural ecosystems and role as a stopover for 500 million migrating birds. Constricted freshwater input is lowering the level of the Dead Sea and is reaching the point of causing irreversible damage. The percentage of people employed in agriculture is continuing to decline in all three countries. Israel has higher family incomes, smaller families, and a lesser proportion of its population employed as farmers than Palestine and Jordan. Israel thus has the socio-economic profile of a more industrialized nation. International problem-solving concerning the Jordan watershed engages **economic disparity**. Water remains closely linked to food security (Yasuda et al. 2017).

On the positive side, Israel's expansion of wastewater reuse and construction of five desalination plants has reduced dependence on the Sea of Galilee and the Jordan River. New technologies are ensuring water security in an era of decreasing rainfall and climate change. As of 2020, Israel was upgrading all wastewater facilities from secondary to tertiary treatment, making the effluent useable for irrigation of food crops, and lowering the price below that for freshwater. Accepting students from Palestine, Israel, Jordan, and other countries, the Arava Institute of Environmental Studies is teaching courses in transboundary water management and sponsoring research on water cooperation. Religious NGOs, like the Jewish National Fund, support water projects in Israel, including lake and river restoration. Eco-Peace Middle East has sponsored a regional master plan outlining multiple strategic objectives, including pollution control, sustainable water management, urban infrastructure improvement, and expanding sustainable tourism. The proposal allocates set amounts of flow for the restoration of the Jordan River (Krieger 2016: 24–86).

Investing in bottom-up participation, Eco-Peace has engaged mayors and other local officials and youth groups in their planning and activities. In 2010, administrators in shorts joined student volunteers in a symbolic big-jump into the Lower Jordan, where stakeholders of different nationalities and faiths plunged into the critically stressed river together. Other internationally cooperative initiatives include the Red Sea-Dead Sea desalination project, planned on a 20-year horizon, which will pump treated water inland to the Dead Sea region and partition the water to Jordan, the Palestinian Authority, and Israel. As of 2020, Palestinian communities on the West Bank recycle about 10% of their wastewater, while Israeli communities downstream recycle 80%. Government and institutional stakeholders are attempting to cooperatively close the water treatment gap and bolster the health and economies of all parties (Mehyar et al. 2014; Krieger 2016: 24–86).

The religious significance of the Jordan and the economic benefits of religious tourism, such as Christian pilgrims traveling to receive baptism in the river, generate advocacy for watershed restoration. As environmental writer Barbara Krieger (2016: 235) summarizes: "The Israeli, Jordanian, and Palestinian ministries of environment and tourism have also committed themselves to participate in the renewal of the river, a good deal of this progress being due to the perseverance of Eco-Peace." Eco-Peace has drawn financial support and expertise, not just from the five riparians but from international sources, such as the German-based Konrad Adenauer Foundation (Eco-Peace

Middle East 2017). The situation remains dynamic, and each outbreak of fighting in the region slows cooperative environmental problem-solving. Nevertheless, a focus on water has bolstered the post-conflict peace process for the Jordan watershed. Just negotiations for access to water continue as a critical component of **inter-religious peace-keeping**, not only in the Middle East but in other political geographies, such as the Indian sub-continent where Hindus, Muslims, and Buddhists share major watersheds both within nations and between them.

Conclusion: Religious models for conflict reduction and shared accountability

Instead of inflaming divisions, religious values and praxis can contribute to sustainable eco-peacekeeping and shared accountability. Geoscientist and water mediator, Aaron T. Wolf (2017: 1–28) proposes that rather than divide the scientific and the spiritual, religiously informed methods of conflict resolution can support techniques, like **alternative dispute resolution**. A tool of corporate bargaining, alternative dispute resolution emphasizes negotiations where all parties gain something via mutual gains bargaining or win-win solutions. Multiple religious traditions have creeds and coda appropriate for resolving competing environmental claims and interests. Wolf found that the Bedouin of the Negev (Muslim) did not recognize past disputes. The Bedouin did sometimes squabble over access to a well, but following negotiations, they performed a *sulha*—a ceremony of forgiveness erasing the disagreement from community history.

As a trained facilitator, Wolf (2017: 34–54, 91–132) suggests a Four Worlds model, based on four perceptual scales and levels of social interaction. The physical (body) is at the base, followed by the emotional (heart), knowing (mind), and ultimately the spiritual (spirit). Relieving interpersonal tensions, the first transformative step is tackling the internal anger and self-righteous that are barriers to communication. In calming discord, developing a listening heart allows a clear perception of the hurts, issues, and needs of others. This concept parallels the *Lev Shome'ah* (listening heart) of Judaism, the "deep listening" of Buddhist teacher Thích Nhất Hạnh, and the Christian practice of *Lectio Divina* (divine reading) when conversing with God.

At the group level, practices for building group harmony include Buddhist invocation of the Four Foundations of Buddha's teaching. A phased approach by the Christian Evangelical Peacekeeper Ministries begins by glorifying God (looking to what God would desire for everyone involved) and getting the log out of one's eye (being realistic about personal faults and desires). It proceeds to gentle restoration (respectfully engaging other participants), and reconciliation (joining in lasting solutions). The Baha'is provide robust guidance for group consultations by identifying seven virtues and seven detriments (Box 6.2). Wolf (2017: 144–166) holds that shared religious staging without forcing compromise over individual beliefs facilitate consilience. He notes "that on the occasions that Christian, Muslim, and Jewish leaders have opened with a prayer and some reflection of what water means to their tradition, the conversations tend to ease more readily in shared values and harmony rather than starting with divisive positions." Today, the multiple national and international offices representing different faiths and peacekeeping initiatives are increasingly addressing the environment as a potential element in every stage of international conflict development and resolution.

As the cases in this chapter demonstrate, faith-based commitment and scientifically informed methodologies are capable of forming synergistic partnerships resulting in

---

Box 6.2 Baha'i virtues and detriments in consultation

Virtues facilitating consultation

Motive: Working together for the same thing without hidden motives

Spirit: Enthusiasm, positive outlook, and setting aside personal preferences

Detachment: Ideas belong to the group, present yours, and let them go

Attraction: Eagerness to hear the contributions of others

Humility: Modesty aids consultation

Patience: Allows the best answers to develop

Service: Attitude gives priority to the group over self

Countered by detriments

Discord, stubbornness, pride of authorship, discounting, advocacy, criticism, and dominating.

Source: Wolf (2017)

---

model programs for watershed-scale conservation. Scriptural and ritual significance can fuel water activism, while a well-constructed social ethos is necessary to adjudicate contentious allocation issues and build responsible conservation planning for a limited resource. Broader scale consortia and cooperative networks can elevate religious response by translating science, providing training, and demonstrating the best environmental practices. The ultimate challenge is forming successful trans-boundary partnerships and forwarding respectful peacekeeping in multi-religious contexts.

Suggested readings

Balboa, Cristina. *The Paradox of Scale: How NGOs Build, Maintain and Lose Authority in Environmental Governance*. Cambridge, MA: MIT Press, 2018.

Darlington, Susan. *The Ordination of a Tree: The Thai Buddhist Environmental Movement*. Albany: State University of New York Press, 2012.

Krieger, Barbara. *The Dead Sea and the Jordan River*. Bloomington: Indiana University Press, 2016.

Lansing, J. Stephen. *Priests and Programmers: Technologies of Power in the Engineered Landscape of Bali*. Princeton, NJ: Princeton University Press, 2007.

Rodríguez, Sylvia. *Acequia: Water Sharing, Sanctity, and Place*. Santa Fe, NM: School for Advanced Research Resident Scholar Books, 2006.

Tal, Alon. *Pollution in a Promised Land: An Environmental History of Israel*. Berkeley: University of California Press, 2002.

Wolf, Aaron. *The Spirit of Dialogue: Lessons from Faith Traditions in Transforming Conflict*. Washington, DC: Island Press, 2017.

7 Sanctuaries

Preservation of species, ecosystems, and natural features

Key concepts

1 Faith-based sanctuaries such as sacred groves or wooded temple grounds can protect regional as well as local biodiversity.
2 Human population growth, modernization of communication and transportation infrastructure, decline of religious tradition, displacement of indigenous religions by world religions, and other forms of cultural change threaten the ecological integrity of sacred natural terrains and species. Cultural change can relax religious constraints on practices threatening wild species populations, such as the collection of bushmeat.
3 Cooperative and socially flexible strategies incorporating the local populace in conservation planning are usually superior to government or NGO disruption of existing religious structures, in managing sacred landscapes and hydroscapes.
4 Religious utilization of organic materials such as elephant ivory contributes to population declines of wild species.
5 Romanticism, transcendentalism, and other cultural movements emphasizing the aesthetic or spiritual value of nature have been foundational to securing the preservation ethos a role in modern environmental management.
6 Conservation interventions and participatory management of community reserves should consider the religious values of participants and seek cooperation among faiths in pluralistic contexts.
7 Although both biologists and philosophers have challenged the application of intrinsic or inherent value rather than instrumental value to resolving biodiversity dilemmas, sociological research has found that in actual environmental planning contexts, stakeholders may invoke intrinsic, instrumental, and relational values.
8 Religiously motivated biodiversity conservation is important in more industrialized countries and to recent preservation trends like the expanded designation of marine parks and reserves.

Preserving biodiversity

Conserving **biodiversity**, including genetic, species, and biotic community diversity, is a critical component of successful environmental management. **Preservation** encompasses designation and protection of representative natural areas, geologic monuments, and sites of scientific interest. Preservation does not deal with locales in isolation but depends on watershed and landscape-scale models of ecosystem structure to determine which areas are the most critical to protect. Today, government agencies and ENGOs (environmental nongovernmental organizations), like the World Wildlife Fund and the International Union for Conservation of Nature (IUCN), take the lead in determining whether species are endangered or threatened and which landscapes and seascapes are worthy of status as nature reserves. Long before the US Congressional designation of Yellowstone as the world's first national park in 1872, however, the world's religions established natural sanctuaries, ranging from single springs, to monastic grounds, to unoccupied sacred peaks.

This chapter describes how formal and informal belief systems make significant contributions to **biocultural conservation** of genetic and species diversity. Expanding the discussion of harvest in Chapter 3, it investigates religious prohibitions on extracting wild species or disturbing natural ecosystems, and, conversely, explores cases where religious esthetic, devotional, or ritual use is depleting populations of threatened or endangered species. Case histories document the religious roots of the national park and wilderness movements and weigh religious considerations in managing designated community conservatories, nature reserves, and similarly protected landscapes. The final sections examine the application of ethical models such as inherent value and the practice of ahimsa or compassion relative to biodiversity conservation.

Sacred ground, sacred species

Touting pagan sacred groves as exemplars of religious environmental care, Lynn White, Jr. (1967) presented the natural sanctuaries as if they were untouched ancient woodlands, protected by animist spirits. As forest historian Oliver Rackham (2015) has documented, sacred landscapes are not all managed the same way and the degree of preservation varies. In the case of the ancient European groves, Greco-Roman deities could own land. Written records prove that Dionysus leased property in southern Italy to tenants who could not cut the god's oaks for sale. Yet the pragmatic god of wine allowed tenants to take wood for domestic building and household use, thereby permitting subsistence harvest.

Conversely, an anthropomorphic deity can designate a biotic or natural feature as off-limits to exploitation or closed to entry at his or her temple. As sacred spaces frequently encompass unique biophysical landscape features, such as caves, oases, and alpine summits, they innately serve as protected habitat for species rare elsewhere. Although the size varies, sacred natural locales form networks across the wider landscape, supporting broader scale conservation. The perception that such spaces frequently conserve trees is correct. Woody species are particularly valuable to biodiversity conservation because they provide **microhabitats** conducive to other animals and plants, increasing species diversity overall (Ruelle et al. 2018).

The sacralization of individual species and sites combines symbolic, ritual, and consumptive values. Mythic portrayals of biota as conduits between this world and the realm of the gods, as fonts of creative events, or as supernatural fulcra convey exceptional status. The pre-Colombian Maya of Central America retained sacred ceiba trees within their villages and cities, where the ceiba symbolically linked the living settlement to the underworld and the heavens. A frequent image in Maya funerary art, the ceiba with its spreading roots represents the descent to the realm of the dead and the ancestors, and the eternal resprouting of crops and human families. The stout trunk and broad crown are **archetypes** of the primal creative event, with paradise blooming under sweeping branches. The ceiba or kapok is a source of fiber and oil-rich seeds; thus, the sacred tree acts as a connection between the city and forest, and between commodity and natural resource. The productive plant serves as a metaphor for the strength and beauty of Maya culture itself. It declares the efficacy of the priestly hierarchy and the gods. Mayan farmers, in turn, maintained mature ceiba instead of toppling them as they cleared plots for agriculture. Even today, Mayan loggers are hesitant to fell a ceiba (Carrasco 1990: 98–103; Altman 1994: 71–85).

Temples and monasteries maintain populations of rare wild species for practical purposes. Chinese Buddhist monks planted ginkgo trees at monasteries, conserving the species for its edible nuts, distinctive fan-shaped foliage, and applications in medicine. The ginkgo represents the oldest known linage of broad-leaved trees, going back 200 million years to the Tertiary era. Western botanists were shocked to discover a living representative of a **taxon** (category of related organisms) they had previously encountered only as a fossil was already extirpated from native east Asian forests but prospering within Buddhist precincts. In addition to its scientific and commercial pharmaceutical values, the ginkgo has found a niche as a stress-resistant street tree in modern cities (Crane 2015).

Religious grounds similarly protect fauna by disallowing hunting and harassment as contrary to the pious behavior expected from visitors to the home of a deity. Like foxes at Shinto shrines, a living creature can hold protected status as a confidant, assistant, or messenger of a god or goddess. Alternative faunal persona or **avatars** of supernatural beings share the power and wisdom of anthropomorphic forms. Animals are thus welcome at temples, which in essence belong to them. Freedom from harvest and harassment can apply to potentially dangerous species living in undeveloped habitats. In sacred lakes of the Niger River delta, where sacred species embody deities and ancestral spirits, customary codes prohibit the killing of the now nationally threatened crocodile, who is "the peoples' brother." If a crocodile becomes entangled in a net, the fishers carefully extricate and release it (Anwana et al. 2010).

Issue: Evolution of religious terrains, the sacred groves of Tamil Nadu

Having conducted repeated observations of village interactions with sacred groves in Tamil Nadu, India, religious scholar Eliza Kent rejected a priori projections the safeguarded woodlands are relics of ancient animism. She also discarded the idea that the religiosity protecting the groves is primitive, based on ancestor or nature worship. Careful examination dated the groves to government decentralization in the 18th century, when local chiefs taxed the villages and protected them from cattle raiding. Forest temples originally functioned as integral components of "village-based non-Brahmanical Hinduism that organizes space, time and village society in complex, fascinating ways." The groves in Tamil Nadu are not relics of simple superstition, nor are they primal stands. Villages built temples in forests modified by prior human use, and they have continued harvest of fruits and branches from the woodlands. Just as Indian religion and village life are changing, the groves are ecologically and culturally dynamic (Kent 2013: 10–11).

As Kent concludes, changes in sacred groves are "almost always lamented" and misunderstood by conservationists. In Tamil Nadu, the days of armed chieftains are past, and the villages are integrating into more extensive social networks, exposing them to secularism and new religious perspectives. Studies by environmental historians Subhash Chandran and J. Donald Hughes (1997) found the on-going process of identifying forest deities with gods and goddesses from the Sanskritic tradition, like Vishnu and Shiva, has increased the focus on the temples, resulting in inattention to the surrounding forests. The expansion of roads has been a primary driver of landscape change. A new highway near a grove supports temple development as well as reducing the wooded area around the shrine. Kent (2013: 11) notes that roads also open villages to contact with environmentalists, who, along with transportation infrastructure, "are particularly important vectors of change."

Other social variables influence the vulnerability of the groves to decline and species loss, as does the size of the sanctuary, with larger stands of forest being more stable. High levels of community solidarity, strong local temple associations, and traditional leadership enforcing prohibitions on harvest are superior to more diffuse and less supervised utilization of the sacred forests. Identifying the god as the proprietor is far better for conservation than having the grove divided among human landlords. Kent (2013: 115–116) concludes that "...when people start to view the management of temple property (including forests) as a monopoly held by a particular faction of the village, the temptation to poach waxes and the fiction of divine ownership wanes." Firewood gathering and loping of green branches for livestock fodder accelerate and chew away at the forest boundaries.

Colonial governments disrespectful of regional religious practices and village authority fragmented sacred groves and similar holy terrains by privatizing or nationalizing such public domain properties. They awarded them to plantation owners, split them into plots for villagers, or managed the forests via "scientific" schedules of planting and logging. In the face of perceived declines, today's government agencies and ENGOs may be tempted to deem themselves better protectors of biodiversity and ecosystem integrity than the religious interests which have been keeping the deity's arbor for the past few centuries. Cooperative and socially flexible strategies incorporating the local populace in conservation planning are, however, superior to disrupting existing religious structures. In cases where younger community members are losing interest in religiously based conservation, environmental education may assist in integrating them into longer-term landscape-level biodiversity conservation endeavors, as well as raising appreciation for their cultural heritage (Kent 2013).

Issue: Monastery and church forests as models for community conservation–Ethiopia

By implying Christianity had not forwarded biotic protection in holy locales, Lynn White, Jr. (1967) forwarded a false dichotomy between the Abrahamic faiths and other religions, already prevalent in romantic depictions of ancient societies and indigenous peoples. Christian protection of wild species has deep roots in the monasticism emerging in the arid mountains and wadis of Egypt, Palestine, and Syria in late antiquity. **Hagiographies** (biographies of saints) demonstrated the holiness of the desert ascetics by lauding their care for wildlife. Seeking peace with other creatures, the saints allowed lions, leopards, and wild asses to remain around their hermitages (Bratton 1988, 2009). Many centuries ago, in Ethiopia, monks selected inaccessible ridge tops surrounded by cliffs to secure their solitude. Groves provide a shaded ambiance for ascetics "seeking seclusion in their attempts to approach divinity." Ethiopian Orthodox churches similarly maintain arbors shading service attendees who remain seated outdoors. The forests shelter the replica of the Ark of the Covent or *tabot* within the churches. As fuelwood gathering and intensive grazing have stripped Ethiopia's woodlands, the monasteries and churches have become forested islands of biodiversity, succoring tree-nesting birds and forest-dwelling mammals. Because the growing rural population and deforest-ation of adjoining properties are threatening these de facto reserves, the Ethiopian government has sponsored surveys of monastery flora and fauna in hopes of preventing impending species losses (Orlowska and Keppei 2018).

Biodiversity managers Morgan Ruelle, Karim-Aly Kassam, and Zemede Asfaw (2018) investigated congregational motives for conscientiously maintaining trees and native vegetation within the walled enclosures of Ethiopian Orthodox churches. Botanical inventories prove numerous species rare in the surrounding countryside sur-vive at these heavily-visited centers for worship, even though the average religious "forest island" is less than 5 ha (11 acres). Interviewees reported the congregants had planted most of the trees present. Among the favored species are symbols of tradi-tion and witnesses to church history. Other selections provide building materials for church repairs and income from the sale of firewood. Local informants believe founders planted the now mature trees at the time of church construction. The oldest honored indigenous olives and cedars thus date to the 15th century. Direct religious uses for the trees include rubbing with leaves during foot-washing marking Holy Week (at Easter), making charcoal to burn incense, and smoking the containers for *tella*, a beer produced at the churches for consumption during feasts and celebrations. Communities value the wooded, shaded church compounds as comfortable social spaces. Ethiopian traditions sacralize both trees and the communitarian act of planting them.

The Ethiopian government's Green Policy has encouraged the restoration of forest cover and erosion control nationwide. Both government and ENGO-based conserva-tionists have initiated outreach to the churches and conducted sessions for priests in the importance of maintaining woody cover. As the borders of church forests are eroding, ENGOs have funded building walls. Communities welcome the investment in church infrastructure as it supports their core values of preventing livestock from disturbing graves and raising the status of the church. Conservation assistance to local communi-ties is more likely to generate cooperation when it forwards pre-existing cultural values and addresses genuine community needs (Orlowska and Keppei 2018).

Conservationists believe churches can serve as education centers and generate indig-enous religious ecological narratives supporting forest restoration. The extension of **in situ** (within site) vegetation protection, to **ex situ** (off-site) or greater landscape programs does face multiple logistic barriers. Church leaders are often unprepared to instruct the general populace in planting seedlings, and communities may not fully understand forest restoration's potential economic benefits. The churches need to con-sider contemporary values, such as the role of forests in sequestering carbon in the face of rising carbon dioxide levels in the atmosphere. One of the currently favored trees is a eucalyptus from Australia that can displace native vegetation and lower water tables with its deep roots. Churches find the fast-growing eucalyptus produces fire-wood for sale. Conservationists, in contrast, are concerned about the collateral damage the non-native tree causes to biodiversity (Tilahun et al. 2015). As Ruelle et al. (2018) have concluded, however: "Ethiopia's church forests nurture the knowledge neces-sary to promote plant diversity in the rest of the landscape and serve as archetypes for community-driven conservation."

Issue: Interpretive caution–Muslim burial grounds in Morocco

Islam strictly prohibits devotions focused on natural objects or worship of any entity other than Allah. These bans do not mean, however, that Muslims do not conserve native species associated with religious sites. Investigation of regional praxis finds that Moroccan Muslims protect trees at burial grounds, particularly those surrounding the tombs of respected Islamic scholars. The people conserve the arbors "because such sites are important to for the identity and social organization of the people that live with them." As denser woodlands in heavily grazed landscapes, the plots shelter rarer herbaceous plants, such as orchids and thistles extirpated elsewhere by voracious livestock. Exempt from commercial logging, they sequester locally adapted ecotypes of trees of interest to forestry. Accommodating vestiges of pre-Islamic religious practices, the groves host pilgrimages or *moussem*, often held at the end of the farming season and tied to traditional markets (Deil et al. 2008).

As is the case with Kent's study in Tamil Nadu, assuming clusters of trees are ancient and arose from animist groves on the same sites requires careful documentation. Lacking representative art, both rural and urban Muslim cemeteries frequently support native forest species and large trees, even if a graveyard is newly opened or a century or two old (Fig. 1.1). In Morocco, the supposition that the groves are animist risks identifying the woodlands as heterodox, which could undermine their conservation value. For the Moroccan burial sites, concerns about correct ritual practice probably rest more with honoring deceased "saints," than with the trees, which are not devotional foci.

Issue: Changing religious beliefs and protection of species, Nigerian sacred primates

Displacement of indigenous or regional religions by world religions or modernization of communication and transportation infrastructure can undermine the preservation of sacred species. Teams of scientists based in Nigerian universities have studied changes in the population status of primates in Igboland. Averaging 2.06 ha in size, the sacred groves of Igbo Traditionalists are conducive habitat for tantalus and mona monkeys (Fig. 7.1). Field appraisal in the early 2000s found, however, that although most shrine groves were still extant, they were declining in size due to agricultural encroachment. Igbo priests were actively maintaining some forest sanctuaries, but several priests had died, leaving groves without caretakers. Some families were no longer interested in replacing deceased priests or perpetually protecting unharvested forest. Among species with sacred status, the threatened Sclater's guenon (Sclater's monkey) has been surviving outside of either nature reserves or sacred groves. Already pressured by habitat loss and hunting for **bushmeat**, Sclater's monkeys engage in crop raiding, placing them in conflict with farmers (Baker et al. 2009).

The growing influence of Christianity in Igboland has eroded indigenous beliefs about sacred primates. Some Christians do not protect primates due to their association with traditional deities. Yet, many villages have continued to observe taboos against killing monkeys. The motives differ by site. Farmers fear supernatural retribution in one locale and avoid community disapproval in another (Baker et al. 2014). The Igbo are more protective of Sclater's monkeys in villages where they retain **totemic** or symbolic status (Box 7.1). Favorable folklore, such as tales of monkeys sounding the alarm if dangerous animals are near children, discourages punitive actions against crop raiders. The idea that

Figure 7.1 Local community members serve as forest monitors surveying sacred groves in Igboland, Nigeria. Note the richness of the vegetation and the intact forest canopy, suitable for primates and other vertebrates as habitat.

Photo: Lynne Baker

monkeys give a village a positive image and attract visitors also inhibits their removal as agricultural pests (Baker 2013). As neither Christianity nor Traditional religion influences the interactions between people and monkeys in uniform ways, an understanding of the religious dynamics assists in constructing practical conservation responses to the continued conflicts over the economic costs of preserving primate species and their habitats. Conservation biologists have developed programs integrating community members in the inventorying and monitoring of Igbo sacred groves, to enhance local commitment to maintaining the groves' irreplaceable biodiversity (Fig. 7.1).

Box 7.1 Traditional ruler's explanation of Igbo taboos

There are two major clans in Akpugoeze: Ihite and Ezi. Long ago, during the time of the forefathers, the Ezi clan said that the gods declared monkeys should never again be harmed or eaten, as monkeys belonged to the gods. However, one man did not agree, and he was supported by the entire Ihite clan and one Ezi village. The remaining two Ezi villages declared monkeys as the property of two shrines, located in Umuokpasialum and Amagu villages. Over time, monkeys learned that they were safe within the borders of these villages and took refuge there. Residents of other villages in Akpugoeze did not kill monkeys in Umuokpasialum or Amagu out of respect for their kindred.

Source: Baker et al. (2009)

Issue: Tourism and preservation, temple monkeys of Bali and Lombok

Historic sacred sites draw tourism. Those incorporating protected natural habitats can be more attractive to visitors due to their wildlife and scenic values. Both casual and professionally-guided **ecotourism** can modify animal behaviors, disturb breeding populations, and trample sensitive root systems. In Asia, Hindu and Buddhist temples allow monkeys to reside unmolested on their grounds. On Bali and Lombok, Indonesia, priests, and worshippers have historically protected long-tailed (crab-eating) macaques residing at temples; thus, humans and macaques live in **sympatric associations**. Lombok villages have set aside sacred forest stands, including a natural area at Ubud, protecting monkeys (Fig. 2.2). Conserving a diversity of native organisms, these "monkey forests" are home to nearly two hundred tree species and a variety of birds and lizards. In increasingly developed landscapes, these religious forest "islands" can accommodate several hundred adult primates, making them refugia for reproductively viable populations of species facing continuing attrition in the surrounding countryside. Anthropologists have hypothesized the macaques may not be sacred per se but protected by their association with temples (Louden et al. 2006).

Primates acclimate to fascinated humans, who offer food to entice them into camera range. Monkeys do bite, defend their young, and speed up the process of foraging by grabbing food from people's hands or backpacks. They can carry the rabies virus and other infections. Along with climbing on or defacing art, tourists thoughtlessly drop food tainted plastic wrappers and other trash around temple grounds, where the monkeys can find the waste. Temple complexes may maintain areas closed to tourists and reserved for religious activities, which improves the habitat for fauna resident at the site, and respects visitors whose primary visitation goals are religious. The temples encourage proper trash disposal and post signage to discourage meddling with wildlife. Settling disputes should favor the monkeys while orienting them toward natural foods and keeping them a safe distance from nosy people. In changing **religioscapes**, tourism can generate funds for religious organizations and motivate species protection, while spawning new challenges for environmentally sound preservation of sacred terrains.

Issue: Bushmeat and zoonotic diseases

Religious prohibitions on killing primates have an additional value—they reduce the probability of disease transmission to humans from our near biological relatives. With roads and settlements penetrating what were once unbroken forests or wetlands, and firearms ever more widely available, the harvest of **bushmeat** has accelerated, often radically reducing populations of vertebrates. Inadequate human food security may even tempt collecting dead or dying infected animals found on the forest floor. Some types of animals pose far more risk of harboring pathogens transmissible to humans, and these taxa often converge with those of elevated biodiversity conservation concern. High on the list are primates, carnivores, and bats, which carry infectious diseases like HIV (human immunodeficiency virus), Ebola, Coronaviruses, and rabies.

Human contact with a West African species of chimpanzee transferred HIV to humans. Although the exact means of transmission of a simian immunodeficiency retrovirus remains unknown, human contact with chimpanzee blood or body fluids was necessary to initiate a pandemic that has killed over 30 million people (Sharp and

Hahn 2011). The bare-handed butchering of bushmeat poses more risk from zoonoses (animal-borne diseases) than eating well-cooked meat. Mislabeling or misidentifying wild-caught meat puts the purchaser – and the neighbors – in danger.

In the case of Nigerian sacred monkeys, traditional religion requires burial of dead monkeys (Baker et al. 2009)—providing safer removal. Known health risks may not initially have informed such religious practices, yet respecting primates as mythic or totemic analogs of people does reduce human consumption. Religious codes and concepts like ahimsa guide food selection and handling, either eliminating some or all meats or requiring careful preparation. Conservation awareness encouraged a traditional ruler of four villages in Igboland to ban killing monkeys after he stopped eating them himself—likely resulting in improved survivorship for Sclater's monkey in the area (Baker et al. 2017). Interviews of Balinese temple goers, however, have found that some but not all communities have relaxed prohibitions on killing macaques, particularly those becoming agricultural pests. A few people are either consuming the flesh or covertly selling the carcasses to illegal animal markets, including on Java. Balinese are also transporting macaques to unsanctioned pet and live animal markets (Louden et al. 2006).

Among zoonoses of continuing grave concern, the World Health Organization (2014) has identified fruit bats as the original natural viral **hosts** for Ebola, while a diversity of mammals may contract and carry the virus, including chimpanzees, gorillas, and porcupines. Religions like Christianity and Islam that have been expanding in the Global South do not have dietary regulations precluding all the potential host species for lurking zoonoses. Christianity does have a history of demonizing bats, which were the source of the 2014–2016 Ebola outbreak, and probably of the 2019–2020 coronavirus pandemic, originating in an animal market in Wuhan, China. Satan wearing a bat's muzzle or wings or vampires turning into bats, though, originated in folklore, rather than from Biblical texts or formal theological process. From a conservation perspective, demonic associations discourage touching bats and hunting them for food, but they have the negative impact of prompting householders to exterminate colonies and disturb bat roosts and nurseries. Religious stereotyping of species as evil can lead to the killing of declining species for no purpose, as sometimes occurs in the case of snakes and wolves.

For both Traditional and world religions, educators and leaders can cooperate with public health officers and conservationists by addressing right relationship to animals and raising the harvest of bushmeat as a multifaceted ethical concern. A balanced approach understands bats as offering critical ecosystem services, including pollination of flowers and capture of insects. Primates and bats spread the seeds of trees and contribute to the productivity and ecological integrity of forest and savannah ecosystems. Religious institutions like churches, temples, and pagodas can avoid calling the exterminator and conserve the bats in their spires or have a youth group install safe roosts by building houses for beneficial species like bats and owls on their grounds.

Issue: Religious materiality and endangered species

Socially and economically related to the harvest of bushmeat, poaching of endangered and threatened species for the manufacture of religious objects or ceremonial uses similarly threatens biodiversity. With their passion for beautiful crafts, the world religions have sought elephant ivory for Christian crucifixes, Buddhist devotional statues, and

Islamic inlays in stands or boxes holding the holy *Qur'an*. Today, most countries have passed laws protecting species in severe decline. The **U.N. Convention on Trade in Endangered Species of Wild Flora and Fauna** (CITES) coordinates enforcement of bans on the collection and sale of materials originating from endangered species among nations. International traffic in declining biota for religious purposes incorporates rhinoceros horns, orange and black corals, rare tropical hardwoods, medicinal and incense plants, and living organisms such as turtles and birds. Markets can be "white" or legal, "grey" of uncertain legally, or "black," meaning illegal (Gao and Park 2014). Legal trade may still betray major conversation concerns, such as temples in south-east Asia purchasing teak or mahogany from other countries for craving large sculptures. The temples import rare woods because their home forests no longer house trunks of sufficient size. Procurers focus on the fiscal rather than the spiritual aspects. Poachers, for example, kill African elephants not just at village boundaries but in National Parks and wildlife reserves. Like "blood" diamonds, ivory funds insurgencies and weapons purchases. Buyers arrange shipment to workshops, particularly in Asia, where carvers convert the ivory into jewelry and art.

Today in countries with consistent enforcement, religious institutions no longer commission sculptures or furnishings incorporating elephant ivory. Tourists, in contrast, purchase ivory objects and attempt to bring them through customs, where inspectors confiscate illegal imports if they locate them in luggage. Ironically, popular objects include images conveying compassion, sacrifice, happiness, and natural beauty, such as representations of the Buddha, the dying Christ, and the Chinese goddess of mercy Quan Lin. Trade in endangered species ignores principles like *ahimsa*. Wildlife agencies both in Africa and trade-linked countries, including the United States, periodically burn confiscated ivory regardless of its potential religious or artistic significance. Religious leadership can provide ethical guidance concerning the purchase of religious objects for personal wear or household shrines. Temples, cathedrals, and monasteries displaying antique religious art incorporating rare organic materials or providing habitats for species under excessive human harvest pressure can develop educational exhibits or add educational vignettes to tours explaining the consequences for biodiversity. Both educators and guides can similarly develop conservation-friendly strategies for interpreting sacred art and texts demonizing or negatively portraying wildlife or native flora.

Issue: Western Romanticism and Edenic constructs

Nineteenth-century **Romanticism**, American **Transcendentalism**, and other cultural movements emphasizing the aesthetic or spiritual value of nature have been foundational to securing preservation ethos a place in modern environmental management. As Mark Stoll (2015) has argued in *Inherit the Holy Mountain*, American thought about wildland aesthetics has deep roots in Calvinist theology. For the colonial Puritans, God's glory and beauty infused all nature, and observing nature could deepen ones' understanding of God. In his treatise, *Nature* published in 1836, the Transcendentalist philosopher Ralph Waldo Emerson recognized the natural realm as font of insight into human existence. Advocates for preserving American wilderness, like John Muir, often had Calvinist backgrounds. Although he abandoned Presbyterianism, Muir's short book on his residence in the Yosemite region of California, *My First Summer in the Sierra*, makes frequent use of religious language and imagery. Not confined to Congregationalists, naturalists from other Christian sects contributed to the emergence of an intense aesthetic appreciation of nature. The wildland-trekking Quaker bota-nists John and William Bartram counted such luminaries as Thomas Jefferson and the English Romantic poets among their readers (Bartram 1955; Muir 2003).

The British critic and watercolorist, John Ruskin identified "truth in nature" as a metric for the most accomplished art. His aesthetics influenced 18th- and 19th-century Euro-American painters to seek out **sublime** landscapes little modified by human presence. The works of Thomas Cole, Fredrick Edwin Church, Thomas Moran, and other painters of the American Hudson River Valley School feature religious motifs such as divine light shining over the wilderness, or God's blessings flowing from the well-watered summits. Landscape painters like Church (Dutch Reform) traveled to the tropics or the Arctic and created dramatic scenes of rainforests, volcanoes, and icebergs for public exhibition. The depictions were Edenic, capturing the untainted wild free of human influence. Thomas Moran (Roman Catholic) visited the Rocky Mountains and accompanied an expedition exploring the Yellowstone region of Wyoming (Fig. 7.2). Placed on public display, his watercolor and oils of geysers and the Grand Canyon of the Yellowstone helped to convince the US Congress to exclude the region from distribu-tion to homesteaders and designate Yellowstone as the first national park (Novak 2007).

The infusion of religious values into landscape painting and nature poetry was, on the one hand, beneficial, as it made Euro-Americans more aware of their rich natural heritage and justified preservation of landscapes and seascapes for their biodiversity and

Figure 7.2 Thomas Moran, *Mountain of the Holy Cross, Colorado*, ca. 1876. This print (original in color) prepared for popular sale depicts a mountain in the Rockies, with a cross formed by nat-ural glacial and erosive processes. The landscape directly invokes the role of the Christian God in creating the resplendent American landscape.

Collection of the US Library of Congress

geologic features. As the United States developed its national park system, however, the notion of "Edenic" or "untouched" contributed to the removal of Native Americans from the newly designated preserves. The US Army evicted the resident Blackfoot and Shoshone and their camps from Yellowstone before the tourist hotels and campgrounds arrived. Along with the national park idea, policies removing a range of regional cultures from nature reserves spread internationally (Keller 1999).

A second problem generated by Edenic ideals was a misunderstanding of the importance of predation in parks and reserves, accompanied by stereotyping of good and "evil" species. While sparing bears, the early administration of Yellowstone National Park mandated the extirpation of "evil" wolves and mountain lions that preyed on elk and bison. Predator control inside and outside the park eliminated the timber wolf populations from Wyoming. All North American wolf species and subspecies are now endangered in the United States, south of Alaska. The protected Yellowstone elk and bison populations expanded, causing increased browsing on deciduous trees (Boyce and Keiter 1991). The Edenic model has also contributed to ignorance concerning the role of natural disturbances, like fire, in maintaining biodiversity in native grasslands and savannahs.

An additional lesson from Eden, however, is that a religious ideal that is inflexible in one planning context can be highly valuable in another. Conservation biologists, Dereje Mosissa and Birhanu Abraha (2018) have found recreating the lush greenery of the Biblical Eden is a primary motive for maintaining Ethiopian church forests. Beneficial reintroductions of locally extirpated species sometimes invoke the "Edenic" original complement of species, as a rationale for the expense. Israel has protected species mentioned in the Hebrew scriptures and sponsored reintroductions of extirpated taxa like the Arabian oryx. The Israeli government acted to restore the populations of the Nubian ibex, which had collapsed to a few individuals by the 1950s. The ibex, with its spectacular horns, is the "wild goat," roaming mountains crags in Psalm 104 (Fig. 12.1). A healthy herd has recovered in the Ein Gedi Nature Reserve. When David fled from King Saul, the enraged regent took 3,000 men and sought David in the wilderness of Ein Gedi near the Crags of the Wild Goats (1 Samuel 24:4), making the reserve itself a Biblical terrain.

Issue: Religious pluralism and wilderness values

From their beginnings, the preservationist movements in the more industrialized nations explored cosmologies outside of Christianity. Romantics delved into texts from Asian and ancient religions and engaged the perceptual cycles of death and rebirth of Hinduism. Buddhist Gary Snyder became the poet laureate of the movement in the 1970s and 1980s to expand the US system of officially designated wilderness areas. Discovering Asian landscape painting as a meditative exercise, Snyder immersed himself in Zen in Japan. Having trekked over ridges of the Cascades and the Sierras in the western United States and worked as a fire lookout and a logger, Snyder pens poems ringing of the unencumbered spirituality of summers spent along the vast skylines of the high elevations. As recorded in *Mountains and Rivers without End*, Gary Snyder (1996) and his fellow poets Allen Ginsberg and Philp Whelan circumambulated Mount Tamalpais in California, following the Asian ritual of the "opening" the mountain. Snyder describes the practice as "circling and climbing—chanting—to show respect and to clarify the mind."

Buddhist environmental scholar Stephanie Kaza (2019: 38–52) identifies *Mountains and Rivers without End* as an instructional discourse drawn from Zen master Eihei Dōgen's 13th-century *Mountains and Water Sutra*. Snyder weaves Buddhist conceptualization of place or where we are, being or how we should behave, and the nature of reality into Western spaces and language. "The Big Scale setting of where we are is the same distant, abstract, cosmic revelation reified by religious consideration. Instead, the Big Story is made up of many smaller stories, each a history of specific moments and places." Behavior, in turn, is less about who we are, and more about where we are and our understanding of the Big Story—"which determines what is necessary for low impact survival in a particular place." The practice of "being in the present" and **mindfulness** inform the Big Learning. Snyder believes right behavior and compassion arise from the understanding everything is insubstantial and impermanent. Interpreting the land as a transient, if entrancing mandala, he reminds his readers even the soaring sierras and unfordable rivers will pass way. Snyder's poetic gift has served as one of many nature-based conduits for introducing Buddhism to Euro-Americans. His work has been particularly influential in the spheres of preservation and simple lifestyles.

Issue: Preserves and wilderness as elite spaces

In a study of long-distance hikers on the Appalachian Trail, USA, Susan Bratton (2012) found, despite the rocky ground and perpetual drizzle, the experience generated multiple spiritual benefits like building friendships. Engagement in prayer and meditation enhanced positive outcomes of the journey, such as feelings of self-worth. The Trail accommodated religious pluralism, and hikers were more likely to subscribe to Asian and alternative religions than would be expected for a cross-cutting sample from the general American populace. Yet, hikers were much less likely to report African American denominational membership than the expected percentage in national surveys. As geographer Carolyn Finney (2014) documents, the de facto definition of American recreational spaces as white continues to characterize more remote wilderness and park areas. Access to wildlands is biased in favor of those from socioeconomically advantaged backgrounds; thus, religious valuation reflects the preferences of ethnic majorities and the more affluent classes. Bratton (2020) suggests that smaller and more democratically accessible suburban and urban natural areas can provide many of the spiritual benefits of the most dramatic national parks and wilderness areas and support a more equitable framework for spiritual exercise.

Issue: Religious roles in conservation organizations and community conservatories

A recent phenomenon is the formation of RENGOs (religious environmental nongovernment organization) intending to conserve threatened species and biodiversity. In founding A'Rocha, Rev. Peter Harris's original goals were to engage Christians in biodiversity conservation, establish field research and education centers, and to integrate science-based conservation "with Biblical values." As A'Rocha stabilized, its international network geographically enlarged. As of 2020, they had launched Tropical Forest Programs in Kenya, Ghana, India, and Peru, as well as expanding an initiative for the severely stressed Mediterranean biodiversity hot spot. Their tropical programs offer instruction in sustainable livelihoods, such as raising snails for sale in concert with retaining coastal mangroves (A'Rocha International 2019).

Today, natural parks, marine reserves, and other nature reserves may retain indigenous populations or maintain zones for their consumptive use. In a geographically inclusive program, Namibia allows communal societies to manage land without establishing private ownership by forming **Community Conservancies**. Each conservancy must define and negotiate boundaries and submit a conservation plan. The first African national parks and game reserves excluded indigenous management, and only opened hunting to European-heritage residents and visiting trophy seekers. The Community Conservancies, in contrast, can build tourist camps, apply for and take the profits from a trophy hunting quota, and continue subsistence hunting of wildlife with adequate populations. Namibian community conservatories support traditional and communitarian religious praxis and family-scale farming (Naidoo et al. 2015). While conservancies are successful in increasing populations of species like warthog and kudu, some residents are hesitant to join the cooperative ventures. Conservancy economic benefits and jobs are, therefore, not equally distributed. Increased numbers of large animals raise the potential for human-wildlife conflicts ranging from garden-raiding, to livestock depredation, to fatal attacks on children. Women can be more vulnerable due to their roles in farming and household management. When facing food insecurity due to crop losses caused by wildlife, female agriculturalists have articulated their need for adequate compensation (Silva and Mosimane 2012).

As these community conservancies are recent innovations, the role of religion in their operation and social acceptance remains little studied. Differences in values emerge between Traditional religionists and adherents of world religions like Christianity or Islam who are stakeholders in managing natural areas or mixed-use landscapes. Conservation policy analysts, Grant Murray and Andrew Agyare (2018) investigated community perceptions of CREMAs, **Community Resource Environmental Management Areas**, in religiously diverse Ghana. CREMAs emphasize community participation in managing designated conservation areas with a mix of social and ecological goals. Murray and Agyare (2018) first administered a survey and then followed with focus groups at constituent communities, including one that was entirely Traditionalist, and one that was predominantly Christian. Religion intersected socioeconomic variables – Christians were more likely to have attended school, and Traditionalists were more likely to be directly dependent on natural resources for their livelihoods. Respondents considered religion, regardless of faith background, to be part of an individual's basic identity, to "foster good moral values" and to guide interaction with the non-human world.

Differentiating among religions, respondents described Traditionalists as closer to and more dependent on natural resources. They perceived Traditionalists as more knowledgeable about resources and local ecology and more able to provide accurate evaluations of the success of CREMAs. Stakeholders in the conservation areas perceived Christians as better educated and more open to modernity and new ideas. They also expressed sentiments that Christians tended to resist traditional knowledge. Some respondents reported that elders had attempted to teach Christians about fundamental taboos, "but that Christians were adamant about not listening/believing because those beliefs were not congruent with Christian tenets." Participants identified Christians as "less connected to the natural world," less resource-dependent, and disposed to make liberal use of resources. The informants perceived Christians as more likely to contribute to environmental degradation. Traditionalists viewed themselves "as conserving the environment for a long time." Some respondents, however, thought that Traditional religion was too rigid in its religious demands and that Traditionalists "took conservation outcomes for granted." Surveys indicated Christians gave greater importance to CREMA planning and outcomes than did Traditionalists, who were more likely to consider ecological conditions and conservation outcomes as divinely ordained (Murray and Agyare 2018).

Deep rifts and division into factions are not conducive to effective environmental planning. A **conversation intervention** which overrides religious values in settings where religion is strongly linked to personal identity risks public rejection. Prior conversations with stakeholders and appraisal of their potential contributions can assist in seeking fruitful compromises and mutually beneficial participation. A'Rocha Ghana, for example, organized teams of Islamic and Christian scholars to assist in implementing the Murugu Mognori CREMA, outside Mole National Park. Possible means of reducing conflict and forwarding stakeholder support for CREMAs, include having religious experts or applied anthropologists find ways "to incorporate traditional practices and beliefs that resonate with Traditionalists," that are "palatable to Christians." A second juxtaposition for action is finding ways to take advantage of the greater acceptance of conservation programs by some participants, without alienating more skeptical stakeholders or encouraging unrealistic expectations of benefits (Murray and Agyare 2018).

Issue: Intrinsic value and conservation planning

A difficult question is how the world religions, with their intercontinental geography, should value biodiversity? Human exceptionalism tempts awarding worth only to **instrumental values**. The instrumental-only favors species, natural features, and processes having consumptive or productive uses. Small populations of endangered species may have no market price, or their fragile status precludes harvest. During the 1970s and 1980s, philosophical environmental ethicists and the **Deep Ecology** movement forwarded **intrinsic value** as a universal model for **non-anthropocentric valuation**. Biblically inclined ethicists have argued that God's declaration in Genesis 1 that the newly created creatures are all *tob* - good and beautiful—conveys intrinsic value to all life (Bratton 1984). A second related strategy is to treat all species as having **existence value**. In religious terms, the argument is God or gods made them; therefore, all species are worthy of human respect and care.

A third strategy is to consider benefits to **future generations** or **bequest value**. Religions are concerned with inheritance and passing teachings and blessings on to children. Bequest value encourages setting aside natural areas and protecting irreplaceable species like Sclater's monkey from further population decline. As scientists do not know all the possible benefits of individual genes or chemical compounds produced by living species, a rare species may be of greater human interest in the future. Once considered a nuisance by foresters, for example, Pacific yew has become pharmaceutically prized due to its production of taxol, a compound effective in anticancer therapies. The ginkgo has also been a source of commercial pharmaceuticals. Maintaining genetic and species diversity thus has **option value**.

Despite its widespread application, conservation biologists Lynn Maguire and James Justus (2008) have critiqued intrinsic value as vague and inherently noncomparative, offering little guidance for realistic conservation decision-making. Considering all nature to be "sacred" or infinitely valuable poses similar problems—environmental planning requires relative valuation of geophysical or ecological processes, terrains, and elements. The practice of conservation biology focuses on specific species, species relationships, or biotic communities. In protecting an endangered species, for example, environmental managers may eliminate or reduce the populations of a competing or predatory invasive species. Restoration ecologists may ignite prescribed fires, forwarding the reproduction of some species while inhibiting the survival of others. Conservation projects compete for funds, requiring trade-offs and compromises.

Maguire and Justus (2008) point out that instrumental value is comparative, thus allows concrete weighing of public "goods" in favor of protection. People do not award equal value to all endangered species or ecosystems and favor those perceived as beautiful, charismatic, economically productive, or of high scientific interest. Donors to conservation organizations are more likely to contribute funds to protect whales, eagles, and orchids than to protect cave spiders and diminutive mosses. In a public policy framework, inherently instrumental "cost-benefit analyses and multi-criteria decision-making frameworks can aid stakeholder negotiations convened to adjudicate controversies about conservation actions." Planners can award aesthetic, religious, and cultural heritage values definite weights (for example, by using surveys).

Philosophers and social scientists have also become disaffected with intrinsic value. Philosopher Bryan Norton (2000) has objected to utilizing a combination of "Economism" and "Intrinsic Value Theory" as bases for biodiversity conservation because they do not work well in tandem. Aside from being "polar opposites," the two models seek **monistic approaches** to values that will form a unified, coherent set of principles, unilaterally logically defensible that can resolve all moral quandaries. Norton doubts such a monolithic theory "will prove rich enough to guide difficult, real-world choices regarding what will be saved…" or that monisms can properly inform adaptive environmental management. Norton deems the **entity orientation**, or focus on objects rather than processes, and **placeless evaluation** or the removal of valuation from its human, environmental and ecological context to be equally flawed. In practical applications, the sharp philosophical distinctions between intrinsic and instrumental value confuse decision-making. Norton suggests incorporating both instrumental and noninstrumental reasoning and striving to "recognize, respect, and attempt to reconcile a whole range of varied values" in environmental planning. Practical problem solving should determine "whether good reasons can be given for invoking a particular value in a particular situation."

Bruce Morito (2003) has called intrinsic value a "modern albatross" born of insulating western intellectual traditions. The concept places the interests of individual humans in conflict with those of other living creatures. Morito summarizes: "When used as a basis for determining moral considerability, these Modern foundations engender contradictory and self-defeating ways of thinking about the individual/ecosystem relationship. As a result, formulations of moral sensibilities and principles become self-defeating and, vis-a-vis the ecological context, incoherent." Social scientists have hypothesized intrinsic value as a universal ideal remains disconnected from actual human motives for pursuing sustainability or engaging in preservation. Alternate models suggest cultivating experience with nature, a love of nature, and a sense of place elicit a much stronger commitment to environmental care than accepting the idea of intrinsic value does.

Recent sociological research has found that in actual environmental planning contexts, stakeholders may invoke all three forms of value– intrinsic, instrumental, and relational. The transdisciplinary sustainability research team of Paola Arias-Arévalo, Berta Martin-López, and Erik Gómez-Baggethun (2017) collected questionnaires from 589 respondents from the Otun River watershed in the central Andes of Columbia. The interviewees were representative stakeholders in a regional environmental planning process, where urban residents had different concerns from rural householders who were more likely to make direct use of the river and its extensive wetlands.

The investigators categorized values as either egoistic or altruistic and by specific motivation, such as aesthetic, cultural heritage, or the river as a source of life. Respondents could express multiple values. In this **socio-ecological system**, 34% of respondents articulated moral duties to other organisms and ecosystems, a form of intrinsic value, as the desired foundation for planning. A smaller 2.4% utilized religious language directly, by mentioning God or the sacred nature of the river in their replies. The relational value of subsistence and livelihood was the most prevalent at 76.2%. The second most frequent was the relational value of altruism or the care for other people, including future generations and people who lived downstream and depended on the river for water at 37.0%. The study concluded "intrinsic, instrumental, and relational values coexist in people's narratives about the importance of ecosystems" and that all are relevant when tackling social conflicts and weighing the needs of different cohorts of stakeholders (Arias-Arévalo et al. 2017).

Religiously informed values emerge in all three categories, including instrumental. Scoring the use of religious language alone underreports the impact of religion in environmental decision-making, as religious participation may foster altruism and other values like concern for cultural heritage. Further, academic terms, like "intrinsic value," may not inspire interest among religionists who prefer language drawn from sacred texts or stories. Relational values are frequently more prominent than intrinsic values in a religious context. Christians, for example, have discussed which forms of love are most appropriate to relationships with other species, with James Nash (1991) and Susan Bratton (1992) arguing *agape*, or divine love is appropriate. Love for the nonhuman is not limited to friendship (*philos*) or desire (*eros*), the love of the physical or material. Bratton (1988, 2009) has documented the invocation of *agape* relative to wildlife protection in the hagiographies of the first Christian monastics residing in north Africa's arid ecosystems. The totemic role of Sclater's monkey is a form of relational valuation, as is ahimsa.

Issue: Universal models of compassion

An additional universal model posing ethical quandaries for biodiversity conservation concerns compassion for other living creatures. The pro-social religions all have formal codes and sacred texts endorsing compassion as a pro-active virtue. Religions have, however, historically differed in terms of which creatures are considered worthy of compassion. Judaism, Christianity, and Islam permit hunting and raising of livestock. Christians monastics, in contrast, have banned hunting on monastery grounds or have rescued animals from hunters. Lynn White, Jr. (1967) recommended Saint Francis of Assisi as a Christian environmental role model. Francis released birds from traps and, extending compassion to invertebrates, cared for bees during the winter (Sorrell 1988; Bratton 2009). Strictly practiced, **ahimsa**, or compassion as found in Hinduism and Buddhism avoids killing any form of animal extending to small insects and worms.

Concepts like ahimsa and dharma play protective roles relative to wildlife around temples and inhibit the harvest of bushmeat.

One of the most pervasive threats to endangered species is the introduction of new species into their habitats. These invasive or exotic species increase in numbers, displacing or reducing native species populations in the process. The Polynesians brought rats and pigs to oceanic islands. Europeans then transported livestock and species like the mongoose, causing intense predation and habitat degradation for endemic birds and reptiles. More recently, owners of saltwater aquaria have released Pacific lionfish into Atlantic Ocean coral reef ecosystems. Defended by poisonous spines, the lionfish have preyed on other reef fish, like tomtate, depleting their populations. Indigenous reef predators avoid the lionfish, allowing them to outcompete native species occupying the same ecological niche (Ballew et al. 2016).

Attempting to restore biodiversity, reef conservation organizations have organized teams of volunteer divers who spear the lionfish and reduce their numbers. Religious compassion is predominantly **entity oriented**—it concerns the welfare of individual organisms, rather than population processes or a species' reproductive viability. Strict adherence to ahimsa precludes dispatching the lionfish. St. Francis's straight forward applications of compassion to other creatures as brothers and sisters did not address cases where one animal species was reducing the populations of multiple others.

Advocacy for animal rights, including on a religious basis, has generated political conflicts with conservation projects, removing or controlling invasive or "overpopulated" species. Native and exotic deer and elk herds graze and browse heavily on grasses, herbs, and tree seedlings and in the process modify forest or prairie structure. Feral animals like house cats can extirpate endangered species and eliminate fragile colonies of nesting birds. Most issues with invasive species, overgrazing, and mass starvation are rooted in human intervention in ecological processes or human transport of species to new regions. In applying concepts of compassion and humane treatment, the question becomes, is it the survival of the species or of individuals that is central? Should compassion be entity or process-oriented? Since humans have caused threats to coral reef biodiversity, like the arrival of Pacific lionfish in the Atlantic, do humans have an obligation to mitigate the damage to other species? How does "loving nature" actualize as conservation practice in the case of threatened coral reef ecosystems?

Conclusion: Sacred landscapes—an anachronism, or contemporary strategy?

Development and cultural change have increasingly destabilized religious systems intentionally or coincidentally conserving biodiversity. Preservation of sacred landscapes, species, or ecosystems is not, however, old fashioned or out of sync with scientific biological conservation. A keystone issue is often **custodianship**. Government agencies and ENGOs replace or manage local guardians and influence community decision-making. Differences in values between conservation professionals and religionists and between Traditionalists and adherents of world religions complicate future planning for biodiversity. Supporting the autonomy, rights, and contributions of regional societies fosters greater buy-in and increases the effectiveness of community-based conservation programs. Cultivating respect, seeking mutually beneficial paths, and balancing biodiversity with economic imperatives are necessary to maintaining the efficacy of religiously based biodiversity conservation (Vershuuren et al. 2010). Government agencies and NGOs can share preservation of pilgrimage foci or historic religious sites with conserving biodiversity or vice versa.

The British National Trust, for example, manages the Farne Islands as a seabird sanctuary, with breeding puffins and a healthy population of eider ducks. Medieval saints lived in hermitages on Inner Farne, where St. Cuthbert instituted protective regulations for seabirds in the 7th century C.E. Although the original hermitages disappeared long ago, Christians join bird watchers and travel by boat to visit a ruined chapel dedicated to Cuthbert. The Farne Islands are well-patrolled, but the boat and walking traffic still repeatedly flush nesting and foraging birds. Tourists disturb puffins entering their subterranean burrows. Cooperation between pilgrims and wardens is necessary for pursuing long term preservation of the islands' natural values.

Deeming religiously motivated biodiversity conservation an anachronism, surviving primarily in animist, indigenous, or rural contexts undervalues its importance to the more industrialized countries and to recent preservation trends like the expanded designation of marine parks and reserves. The establishment of marine reserves in the Philippines and the South Pacific, for example, has legally formalized protections for preexisting ancestral domains or sites protected by oceanic deities (Vershuuren et al. 2010). Today's religious communities and institutions are capable of creating sacred terrains like Thailand's Buddha Mountain di novo (Fig. 5.2), and managing gardens, cemeteries, and grounds for biodiversity. Retreat centers, camps, intentional communities, colleges, monasteries, and similar organizations with property holdings have increasingly set-aside mini-reserves sheltering wetland plants, cacti, migratory birds, butterflies, or wildflowers.

In the most industrialized nations, religiously based institutions are sponsoring conservation initiatives. The Findhorn Ecovillage in Scotland, with its alternative religious foundations, has improved nature corridors and created the Hinterland Trust to conserve local species diversity. Serving a consortium of Christian colleges and universities by offering off-campus field courses, Pacific Rim Institute (2019), Whidby Island, Washington, monitors and protects rare plants on its grounds and has constructed a Native Plant Center to provide stock for prairie restoration. The IUCN's Delos Initiative begun in 2004 has reviewed the obstacles to conserving religioscapes within protected areas in countries like Japan, the United States, Spain, and Finland. Delos sponsored workshops concluded: "The sacred remains potentially one of the more powerful drivers for conservation, inspiring feelings of awe, veneration, and respect…[and has] been an effective form of nature conservation over the ages, even in the most technologically developed countries" (Mallarach and Papayannis 2010).

Suggested readings

Arias-Arévalo, Paola, Berta Martin-López, and Erik Gómez-Baggethun. "Exploring intrinsic, instrumental, and relational values in sustainable management of socio-ecological systems." *Ecology and Society* 22, no. 4 (2017): 43.

Baker, Lynne, Oluseun Olubode, Adebowale Tanimola, and David Garshelis. "Role of local culture, religion, and human attitudes in the conservation of sacred populations of a threatened 'pest' species." *Biodiversity Conservation* 23 (2014): 1895–1909.

Bratton, Susan P. *The Spirit of the Appalachian Trail: Community, Environment, and Belief on a Long Distance Hiking Path.* Knoxville: University of Tennessee Press, 2012.

Finney, Carolyn. *Black Faces/White Spaces: Reimagining the Relationship of African Americans to the Great Outdoors.* Chapel Hill: University of North Carolina Press, 2014.

Kent, Eliza. *Sacred Groves and Local Gods: Religion and Environmentalism in South India*. Oxford, U.K.: Oxford University Press, 2013.

Maguire, Lynn, and James Justus. "Why intrinsic value is a poor basis for conservation decisions." *Bioscience* 58 (2008): 910–911.

Murray, Grant, and Andrew Agyare. "Religion and perceptions of community-based conservation in Ghana, West Africa." *PLOS ONE*, (2018) doi.org/10./101371/journal.pone.0195498.

Muir, John. *My First Summer in the Sierra*. New York: Modern Library, 2003.

Norton, Bryan. "Biodiversity and environmental values: in search of a universal earth ethic." *Biodiversity and Conservation* 9 (2000): 1029–1044.

Ruelle, Morgan, Karim Aly Kassam, and Zemede Asfaw. "Human ecology of sacred space: Church forests in the highlands of northwestern Ethiopia." *Environmental Conservation* 45 no. 3 (2018): 291–300.

Sheridan, Michael, and Celia Nyamweru. *African Sacred Groves: Ecological Dynamics & Social Change*. Athens, OH: Ohio University Press, 2018.

Snyder, Gary. *Mountains and Rivers without End*. Berkeley, CA: Counterpoint, 1996.

Stoll, Mark. *Inherit the Holy Mountain: Religion and the Rise of American Environmentalism*. Oxford, U.K.: Oxford University Press, 2015.

Vershuuren, Bas, Robert Wild, Jeffery A. McNeely, and Gonzolo Oviedo, eds., *Sacred Natural Sites: Conserving Nature & Culture*. Abingdon, U.K.: Earthscan, Routledge, 2010.

8 Megacities

Sacred space, urban planning,
and built environments

Key concepts

1 Religions have influenced urban planning since cities first appeared.
2 Understanding religious cosmology and symbolism can assist in reading urban landscapes.
3 In today's megacities, religious spaces can become public spaces, where tourism, recreation, and other activities compete with religious and devotional uses.
4 Religious values, such as neighborliness, can support planning for family-friendly, walkable, livable, and sustainable cities.
5 Historic religious ideals for urban planning may be dissonant with modern norms for design, construction, or economic development.
6 Religions sacralize urban nature within and outside sacred spaces, contributing to urban green spaces, wildlife habitat, and biodiversity.
7 Established and majority religions may discriminate against minority religions in the allocation and management of urban spaces. Conversely, religious advocacy for civil rights or justice for the marginalized can forward equity in urban environmental planning.
8 Civic spaces are platforms for religions in the public sphere. Civic spaces can become occupied spaces when dominance or governmental control by one religion excludes or confines other faiths.
9 In adapting to urban change, houses of worship can become centers for environmental action and demonstration sites for sustainable institutional management, such as installing photovoltaic cells on rooftops.
10 In suburban settings, houses of worship can worsen environmental stresses by clearing vegetation and constructing massive parking lots, or they can contribute to environmentally sound urban watershed and microclimate management by pursuing best practices, such as reducing impermeable paving, building rain gardens, and maintaining vegetated stream corridors.
11 Successful urban renewal and development planning can inadvertently modify religious spaces and receptacles of religious and cultural memory. Conversely, culturally sensitive planning can identify means of protecting or enhancing religious spaces, such as establishing a vest-pocket park adjoining a temple or mosque.
12 Religious NGOs and consortia tackling environmental problems in today's pluralistic megacities need viable strategies for incorporating different faith perspectives.

Cities as sacred centers

Religion has been a powerful influence on urban planning, ever since market towns and governmental hubs expanded into multi-functional human population centers. Cities have, in turn, shaped religious values and practices. Christianity, Buddhism, and Islam all arose where cities anchored interregional trade routes, and all fashioned new approaches to urban spiritual life early in their histories. St. Francis of Assisi is known as a "natural saint," yet Francis committed his ministry to the dispossessed poor in the flourishing market towns of early modern Europe. In the 21st century, increasing urban populations and socio-economic stratification continue to propagate the very problems St. Francis confronted, from families living on the street to entrenched infectious diseases.

Environmentally, cities act as energy and natural resource **sinks**, drawing fuel, water, and sustenance from the surrounding countryside. Metropolises are pollution nexuses spewing sewage and runoff into adjoining rivers and estuaries and sending airborne particulates across mountains ranges. The density and height of the buildings modify **urban microclimates** and form **heat islands**, where temperatures are higher than those in rural districts. Proposals for garden cities go back to the 19th century. Today, urban designers visualize walkable, non-polluting **eco-cities**, and **sustainable cities**. This chapter investigates religious contributions to urban green spaces, nature conservation, and sustainability.

Reading the religious urban landscape—Jade Island, Beijing

Many 21st-century megacities began as sacred centers. Reflecting medieval cosmology, Beijing's major temples mark the city's quadrants and serve as termini of processional routes. As a former private imperial garden, today's Bahai Park attracts adherents of Buddhism and Chinese religion, along with family outings, recreationists, and international tourists. A Tibetan-style Buddhist structure, the White Dagoba (or **stupa**) crowns the lake encircled Qionghua Isle or Jade Island (Fig. 8.1). For Buddhists, the climb to the dagoba symbolizes freedom from *samsara*, receiving Buddha nature, and accepting *anitya* or impermanence (Box 8.1) (Qingxi 2008: 158–159).

The visitor first crosses a bridge over a lotus filled lake, and, rising above the mud representing material existence, enters the Hall of the **Wheel of the Law**, calling for adherence to right thought and actions (dharma). The pink-flowered lotuses symbolize the perfection of Buddha's teaching. Modeling care, waterfowl glide quietly along with their hatchlings. Chinese esthetics balance **yin and yang** via curved and three-dimensional interdigitation of land and water. The visitor then ascends to the Hall of Righteous Understanding, where the Buddha sits among **bodhisattvas** and **arhats**. Artificial caves flank the Hall, where a gaunt, fasting Buddha faces a smiling, plump Maitreya Buddha, teaching the importance of self-control to accepting the joys of the Buddha nature. Above them, awing Tibetan gods and the *chakras*, populate The Hall of Universal Peace. Topped by a golden ball appearing as a flame and a box containing Buddhist relics, the dagoba at the apex contains only a single tall pillar. A letter denoting the **Heart Sutra**, embossed on the exterior, summarizes the meaning of the climb (Shu and Peijin 2002; Qingxi 2008: 172–174).

Western tourists sometimes complain when they reach the top because they cannot enter the dagoba. As the park is a public zone, they expect it to function like the

Figure 8.1 Bahia Park in Beijing centers on a Buddhist temple complex constructed on a hill in the center of a lotus filled lake.

Eifel Tower or the Washington Monument and offer an enhanced vista, rather than a cumulative statement of impermanence. On average, tourists **read the landscape** as an eclectic, museum-like assemblage of art instead of an integrative whole. For Chinese offering incense, money, and flowers, the walk fulfills duties and accesses the spiritual guides lining the walls. **Multiple-use** presents challenges concerning behavioral

---

Box 8.1 Buddhist concepts informing the design of Bahai Park, Beijing

Anitya—impermanence, physical existence is transient

Bodhisattvas and *arhats*—Buddhas who return from Nirvana to instruct humanity on the eightfold path

Chakras—centers of spiritual energy within the human body, important to contemplative exercise as channels to emptiness

The Heart Sutra—applies wisdom to the emptiness of all the phenomena comprising the five aggregates of human experience (*skandas*): form, feeling, will or volition, perception, and consciousness

Maitreya Buddha—a bodhisattva who will return in the future to teach pure dharma

Samsara—suffering in the cycle of birth, death, and rebirth

Stupa/dagoba—shrine conserving religious relics

Wheel of Law or Dharmachakra—a symbolic wagon wheel with eight spokes, representing the eightfold path to dharma

Yin and yang—existence is composed of opposites complementing each other, like male (yang) and female (yin), or squares (yang) and circles (yin); harmony arises from their balance

dissonances, such as prayer versus photography, and maintaining silence versus constant chatter. In pluralistic megacities, cathedral closes, temple grounds, and pilgrimage routes become contested **public spaces**, where religious users must compromise with the interests of economic development and the greater citizenry. Today, the gleaming and ethereal dagoba rising over modernized Beijing symbolizes the ascent of the new China, respecting her worthy history, while freeing the people from the bonds of imperial and foreign reign. Although not all Jade Island users experience the **religioscape** in the same way, the layers or **palimpsest of meaning** enrich urban life.

The environmental value of religious spaces—Islamic gardens

Urban residents have complex needs in terms of outdoor facilities and **green spaces**. A recent Harvard study found that US women residing near or adjoining green spaces were healthier and lived longer than those who did not. Adjusting for other factors, women who resided in the highest quantile of greenness within 250 m of their homes had a 12% lower rate of non-accident mortality. Cancer, respiratory illness, and kidney disease all displayed significant reductions. The reasons are not completely clear why curtains of leaves reduce illness, but a green milieu encourages exercise, filters particulate air pollution, supports social engagement, and reduces depression (James et al. 2016). People need places to socialize with others—away from the rigors of work and commerce. Green spaces contribute to people-friendly neighborhoods.

A mosque does not require an outdoor space, yet from their beginnings, larger mosques incorporated a courtyard (*sehan*) as a place to prepare for prayer. After Abad al-Rahman I established an independent emirate in Cordoba, Spain, in 756 CE, he removed a Christian basilica and commissioned the Aljama Mosque to accommodate a growing Muslim population. The initial plans positioned a courtyard as a generous entryway covering an area nearly equal to the mosque's colonnaded interior. The Islamic rulers of Cordoba enlarged the mosque three times and increased the area of the garden to parallel expansion of the building's dimensions. When Christians reconquered Cordoba, they converted the mosque into a cathedral, but having no argument with pleasant patios, left the garden intact (Hussain 2014).

Planted with oranges, palms, and cypresses, the Court of the Oranges is on the side away from and parallel to the **qibla wall** that usually faces Mecca, but in Cordoba faces more directly south. Under Muslim rule, the devout entered through the beauty, fragrance, and pleasant shade of the trees and performed purifying **ablutions** (*wudhu*) before prayer (*salah*) at a fountain that is still in place. They then walked under open arches and through the forest of colorful columns to face the **mihrab** in the qibla wall where a hand-copied *Qur'an* rested behind a doorway decorated with shining glass mosaics laced with vegetative motifs. Today's tourists crowding the fountains and jostling to take snapshots of the entrancing mihrab grasp the architectural elegance, but miss the sense of corporate belonging immersing the worshippers when Cordoba's Muslims gathered at Aljama to share Friday prayers.

Islamic gardeners adopted the techniques and cultivars of prior civilizations, including Roman irrigation systems and Persian parks. Rather than being sprayed across the Orange Tree Courtyard surface, water still courses through narrow stone-lined channels to the bases of individual trees, reducing wastage via evaporation. This engineering might appear to be a modern eco-innovation, but the methods are ancient. Runoff from the roofs of the Cordoba mosque and water from a subterranean aquifer collected in underground cisterns formerly fed the sophisticated irrigation system (Rogers 2001: 104–108).

Garden historian Emma Clark (2010: 38–45) concludes that beyond the striking geometry of Islamic designs lies the "force that draws them all together into a satisfying and harmonious composition: the concept of unity, *at-tawḥīd*, the profound message of the Quran, which penetrates every aspect of a practicing Muslim's life." Mirroring cosmological differences, Islamic layouts are more linear and make more use of contained water sources than Buddhist gardens do. A diversity of religious teachings informs not just garden layouts but their ethos, forwarding eco-dimensionality. The sayings of the prophet Muhammad support the cultivation of edible species as a form of charity to both humans and wildlife: "No Muslim who plants trees and from their fruits the human being or the beasts or birds eat, but that would be an act of charity on the Day of Resurrection" (Khan 2001: 45). Islamic gardens do not separate plantings for visual enjoyment from those that are fragrant or delicious. The garden evokes all the senses: aural in the sound of birds, running water and rustling vegetation, touch and olfaction in running the fingers over fragrant herbs, and taste in drinking its water and consuming its vegetables and fruits. Beauty bolsters rather than diminishing fresh provisions for urban kitchens (Clark 2010: 57).

Religious conceptualization of urban community—the *'ummah*

The Prophet Mohammed understood the importance of cities to religious life and personally supervised planning for the holy centers of Medina and Mecca. According to architectural historian Hisham Mortada (2003: 17–45), the concept of *'ummah* or a society where Allah's code guides all aspects of the political, economic, and legal organization was central to early Muslim cities. Islam encourages frequent and respectful social interactions; thus, the creation of neighborhoods building strong interfamily relationships characterizes traditional Muslim city planning. Islamic cities favor multi-story homes accommodating extended families, and thereby interactions among generations. **Neighborliness** is a virtue, and beyond respecting property boundaries, neighbors should build or act in ways that do not disturb adjoining residences. Everyone should have access to fresh air and light as well as to personal privacy conserving modesty. Islamic courts have regulated the positioning of walls that would block a neighbor's windows and disallowed shops where they could generate a disturbance. Conversely, attached flat roofs in "old" cities like Isfahan, Iran, both increase urban open space and extend trust to close neighbors. Islam teaches clemency and neighborly relations toward other religions; thus, rulers and courts permitted the construction of synagogues and churches within city limits.

A western suburbanite visiting the "old city" in Tunis, Cordoba, or Jeddah (Saudi Arabia) will find the alleys are narrow, and the buildings close or attached via shared walls. Plain facades disguise the simple yet comfortable living spaces within. Houses of similar size and structure reduce social stratification and forward equality among the faithful. Unlike many modern suburbanites, families in these neighborhoods do know the other people living on their street. Meeting the contemporary architects' desire for "walkable districts" and ensuring equity of access, the homes are all a stroll away from a central mosque and markets and shops ringing the mosque or forming clusters where they do not disturb residences. Valuing cleanliness, Islamic law historically prohibited depositing excrement on the streets and mandated careful management of sewage and unpleasant smells. Industries operated outside the city walls, thereby keeping the dust of mills and the strong odors of tanneries away from residential areas and religious public spaces. Islamic strategies allow for palm groves and riparian corridors within the urban matrix, as well as for gardens and orchards adjoining the exterior walls (Mortada 2003: 47–118).

A *hadīth* or saying of the Prophet forwards buildings with climate control: "If one of you was in shade and soon was partly in the sun and partly in the shade, then he should rise." Islamic architects adopted means of moderating **microclimates** of built environments from other cultures as well as experimenting with regionally appropriate improvements. Among them are the multipurpose walled open roofs for sleeping outdoors, channels cooling buildings with underground streams, and the structural wings or wind catchers that divert breezes (Mortada 2003: 118–121). Using flowing water, plantings, and shade to reduce temperature and humidity extremes for urban residential and public courtyards, Muslim builders have become masters of the "outdoor room." The household's enclosed garden is a place to sit in the evening, share food with family, read the *Qur'an*, and engage in prayer and contemplation. Islamic design norms enhance **livability**.

Cities not only form large heat islands but they also generate internal hot spots where solar radiation warms walls and becomes trapped between structures. Today, this elevates energy demand via the increased need for air conditioning. Islamic planning, in contrast, limits the effects of direct solar exposure, reradiation, and drying winds. In comparison to broad thoroughfares, for example, narrow streets remain shaded throughout the day and limit direct radiation on building walls. The networks inhibit wind while allowing air to gain buoyancy, thereby reducing the heat retention caused by the "street canyon" effect, while cooling both homes and thoroughfares. Islamic teachings encourage respect for God's blessings, discourage waste, and support careful use and recycling of building materials such as wood and coral rock (Mortada 2003: 47–118). In Islamic practice, sustainability and eco-justice are integral to *'ummah*.

Religious differences in the sacralization of urban nature—Bengaluru, India

From the perspective of today's urban administrators, religion is one of many influences contributing to positive social environments and the welling being of city dwellers. Understanding the **sacralization of urban nature** is critical to intelligent planning. The speedy growth of Bengaluru (Bangalore), as the technological center of India, has put building space at a premium. Predominantly Hindu, Bengaluru has a reputation as a "garden city" with tree-lined streets and numerous lakes and ponds. The consolidated villages that initially merged to form the megapolis formerly maintained village forests and sacred groves. Bengaluru residents have adapted these traditions to the urban context and preferentially select sacred tree species, like the pipal or bodhi, as street or household plantings. Urbanites continue to protect plants, birds, and insects due to their religious associations (Nagendra 2016).

Sustainability scholar and Bengaluru native, Harini Nagendra (2016: 153–157), has studied the biodiversity of contemporary Bengaluru's sacred spaces and found the different faiths have different landscape preferences. Hindu temples, ashrams, and *mathas* (monasteries) favor high-value timber trees and orchard-like configurations of flowering species, particularly fruit-producers and those used in worship and rituals. Many Hindu institutions are residential and have kitchens; thus, they cook or process what they grow, explaining their **utilitarian** plantings. Muslims often select species of cultural significance, such as date palms. Christians preferentially construct central houses of worship surrounded by landscaped gardens, characterized by large, flowering trees, while Muslims create large open spaces for outdoor worship.

Interestingly, Nagendra (2016: 153–157) found that the density of trees around churches was similar, at a mean of 92 per ha, to the density around Hindu temples at an average of 88. In contrast, Muslim cemeteries had about three times greater density of trees per hectare at 161, than Christian graveyards at 59, or Hindu burial grounds at 48. (In this region of India, many Hindu families bury rather than cremate their dead.) Some resting places for the deceased harbor massive trees, whose spreading branches house diverse urban wildlife, a pattern common elsewhere in Asia. Further study would be necessary to determine why Bengaluru's Muslim burial grounds have more trees. However, as Nagendra (2016: 155) points out, cemeteries are often less disturbed than other religious sites and display "perseverance of character." As Muslims avoid representative art and complex grave markers, they may leave native trees standing to separate the site from its surroundings, or to give it a verdant aspect (Fig. 1.1). Burial grounds are also social locales. Bengaluru's Hindus celebrate festivals in cemeteries, and families cook food to place on the graves of loved ones. Demonstrating the "tenacity of nature" in Indian urban life, the religious grounds contribute to urban biodiversity and Bengaluru's environmental **resilience** in the face of rapid population growth.

Issue: Sacred nature and the marginalized—Bengaluru's slums

In global megacities, slums are usually in marginalized zones in terms of infrastructure access and the quality of the building sites. Bengaluru's poor live on old lake beds and dumps, or along stormwater drainages. Half of Bengaluru's slums are flood-prone, and a third affected by active garbage disposal. The city has engulfed numerous peripheral villages, which have then grown in population and absorbed recent immigrants from other rural areas. Nagendra (2016: 79–97) has found slum residents continue to raise livestock and to tend gardens, even if they must salvage old pots and cans to act as planters. Small trees grow in cramped spaces, providing shade for playing children and holding up clotheslines. Half of Bengaluru's slum trees have medicinal uses, and many produce edible fruits like coconuts and mangos. Having come from agricultural backgrounds, residents transfer their **traditional knowledge** of plants into backyards and open niches between buildings. Going beyond consumptive utility, the poor plant flowers and sacred trees to add a touch of beauty and connection to the divine to otherwise oppressive milieus. Religiously meaningful plantings are not confined to temples but appear throughout the entire urban matrix. Stunted sacred trees reach for the sun in stressed and unexpected places.

The ecojustice literature often focuses on exposure to environmental pollutants and hazards, yet access to nature is also crucial to the well-being of the economically marginalized. Women and children are the most vulnerable to health threats, including lack of clean water and sanitation, and exposure to insects, rats, and snakes. Despite their elevated risk, women often take the lead in cultivating plants for food, fuel, medicine, and otherwise unaffordable beauty treatments. As Nagendra (2016: 79–97) concludes, resettlement projects that concentrate on improving physical infrastructure for the economically marginalized can neglect the importance of green spaces. Asking the residents of slums—particularly the women—what is important to them will improve professionally planned renovation of their neighborhoods and new housing projects.

Issue: Religious pluralism and urban planning

Despite civic commitments to the co-existence of faiths in cities like Bengaluru, religion has been a potent source of discrimination in urban planning. **Established religions**, where members of one religion or sect lead civic governance or receive state support via taxes, normatively repress other faiths or restrict them to designated areas within cities, if not banning them entirely. Both Muslim and Christian rulers in medieval Spain practiced exclusion or suppression of minority or conquered religious populations. Under medieval Islamic rule, **Sephardic Jews** (of Spain and North Africa) could build synagogues—in locations restricted to the Jewish quarter (*Juderia*). Permission was difficult to obtain. The construction might fall under other regulations, such as Jewish and Christian buildings not exceeding Muslim owned structures in height. The surviving Spanish medieval synagogues demonstrate Jewish incorporation of walled courtyards and gardens as comfortable shaded green spaces attached to houses of worship distinguished by rich carvings and mosaics. In 1492 CE, the Christian monarchs Isabella and Ferdinand forced Jews and Muslims to either convert to Christianity, leave Spain, or be burned as heretics. Christians seized synagogues and mosques and remodeled them as churches or commercial buildings (Fernández-Morera 2016: 179).

Established religions and those with aristocratic hierarchies have historically justified the separation of the rich from the poor or excluded the common people from sacred precincts. Religious reformers and leaders favoring **disestablishment** or **religious tolerance**, in contrast, have utilized urban planning as a means combatting social and economic injustice. Eighteenth-century Christian reformer James Oglethorpe established the colony of Georgia with the intent of transplanting debtors and other disadvantaged commonfolk into more economically optimistic circumstances. His strategy for the city of Savannah added additional public squares as the city grew, thus ensuring that all the city's residents, regardless of the social class composition of their neighborhood, could enjoy civic green spaces within a short jaunt from their residences. Two of the oldest African American churches in the United States and Mickve Israel Synagogue now front on these salubrious live oak groves. The colonial plan for Savannah was so foresighted the city remains one of the most charming and walkable in the American South (Rogers 2001: 224–226).

An argument in favor of secular planning is it limits the hegemony of dominant religions. Yet, in the 21st century, discrimination against immigrants and religious and ethnic minorities as "outsiders" remains widespread. The barriers can originate with current landowners or the citizenry rather than with municipal governments. Muslims in Germany and other European countries have experienced difficulties purchasing structures and obtaining building permits for mosques large enough to accommodate all participants in Friday prayers. Jocelyne Cesari (2005), who studies contemporary Islam in western countries, concludes that the transition of Islamic practice from the private to the public spheres underpins many of the tensions. Construction of new houses of worship is a statement of growing political and economic influence, especially if the structures are in central districts or face on public squares or government buildings. Aware of damages caused by past interreligious exclusion and violence, Jewish and Christian leaders in Germany and other countries have spoken in favor of Islamic projects or supported Muslims by providing meeting halls in their facilities. Representatives from different faiths have joined dialogs to understand the perspectives and needs of stakeholders from culturally diverse backgrounds.

Religious discrimination in purportedly secular urban planning can be subtle and indirect. In 2017, a US court settled two lawsuits precipitated by Bernard Township, New Jersey, when the township refused a zoning permit allowing the Islamic Society of Basking Ridge to build a new mosque. The federal judge ruled that the town planning board had acted unconstitutionally and violated the right to "free exercise of religion" by asserting "vague parking requirements" as a rationale to block the mosque. The Islamic Society had persisted through 39 public meetings, and a hostile atmosphere fueled by "anti-Muslim vandalism, fliers, and social media posts." Aside from awarding permission to build and 3.25 million dollars in compensation to the Islamic Society, the court required the town government to modify their zoning restrictions on houses of worship and to train managers to implement laws protecting "religious land-use" (Reilly 2017).

Issue: Socioeconomic divisions and green space

Unfortunately, individual access to urban green and civic spaces remains a serious **eco-justice** concern, even in the United States. Before the passage of the Civil Rights Act of 1964, states and cities in the southern US legally segregated public parks and beaches. In many municipalities, African American children could not use public swimming pools and did not have equivalent facilities available. Exclusion was also due to location, such as limiting pool construction to white neighborhoods, and privatization, such as requiring a membership fee. African American churches, the Nation of Islam, and numerous other religious organizations were leaders in protests and political campaigns that eliminated prejudicial regulations designating whites-only playgrounds and beaches (Lawson 2014).

Urban African American religious institutions have, for many decades, acquired and designed spaces suitable for community gatherings, education, and recreation—in the process compensating for civic inequalities. Hopewell Missionary Baptist Church, at the margins of Atlanta, Georgia, expanded from a small chapel constructed by freed slaves following the Civil War to over 16,000 members. Bishop William Sheals led the purchase and clean-up of a junkyard, where they built a new sanctuary, community building, and senior and youth facilities. Aside from their spacious lawn, congregants have installed a prayer garden and safe recreational spaces for children. Mainstream environmentalists often miss the creativity and environmental values these local projects display (Bratton 2016: 133–135).

Civil rights activism has made urban civic terrains more inclusive, yet today US children from low-income neighborhoods on average still have less green space per child than those from higher-income districts. **Environmental rhetoric** can forward socioeconomic or ethnic discrimination when "greening" supports the interests of the financially advantaged or wealthier neighborhoods at the expense of lower-income stakeholders (Box 8.2). Installation of **greenways**, clean-ups of river corridors, and restoration of industrial **brownfields** (areas requiring removal of toxic contaminants) can result in **gentrification**, which raises rents and property taxes. Greenspace projects engineered for wealthier populations can thus displace the less affluent from their neighborhoods. Conscientious environmental planners use census data, surveys, and contact with citizens, including outreach to religious congregations, to ensure inclusive access and consider needs and preferences, such as the picnic areas and playgrounds popular with families with young children (Hellmund and Smith 2006).

Box 8.2 Sources of eco-justice concerns in green and civic space planning

Urban decay and deterioration of infrastructure

Deindustrialization—the loss of factories and manufacturing due to changes in labor
  costs, demand for products, or technology
Economic recession and unemployment for workers earning hourly wages
Minimum budgeting for public housing projects and infrastructure like schools
Higher income populations favoring green infrastructure for their own neighborhoods
Under representation of minorities and recent immigrants in neighborhood associations
  and local ENGOs
Gentrification where improvements in older neighborhoods including addition of parks
  and greenways, draw higher income residents – raising housing costs, and displacing
  lower income families

Issues: Religion in the public sphere

Civic spaces are platforms for religions in the **public sphere**. Equitable and perhaps
non-traditional access supports democratic city governance and affable relationships
among cultural groups. Cities can benefit from preserving pilgrimage routes, festival spaces, and religious vendors. San Antonio, Texas, for example, supports seasonal
Latinx-heritage festivals and processions, such as the outdoor Holy Week passion play
following the original Spanish language script. Beginning on stage in a public park
dedicated to the revolution against governance by Mexico, the play turns into a procession, winding down city streets to the Main Plaza, where Christ hangs on a cross
in front of San Fernando Cathedral. The mini-pilgrimage connects civic and sacred
spaces, allows anyone who wishes to participate, and acknowledges the importance of
its Spanish heritage to the city's character. Such festivities contribute to **livability** for
residents of diverse heritage (with the drawback that pre-modern European church dra-
mas such as the Passion Play incorporate anti-Jewish statements and characterizations).

   The author encountered an example of peaceful sharing in Hong Kong on a Saturday
when the dragon dance societies were holding a major festival in a center-city park.
Honoring Chinese heritage, the costumed dancers paraded, drums beating, down the
sidewalk into an open square, where tourists and proud parents could view the competition among the troupes. Believed to bring good fortune, the dances are associated
with seasonal religious celebrations, yet bridge the sacred and the secular. Nearby, small
groups of Muslim women were enjoying a pleasant January day, as they sat on blankets
at various tree-sheltered sites in the same park, which adjoins a large mosque. Some
were reading the *Qur'an* or studying together; others were just chatting with their
friends. So many women were getting out of Hong Kong's apartments and enjoying the
fresh air, they spread up the hill onto level spots toward the center of a forested knoll,
and found seats in the canopied pedestrian overpasses nearby. The lion dancers and the
Muslim woman represent implicit religious uses of the municipal grounds and the infusion of lived religion into the civic fabric. The overflow on the pedestrian overpasses,
however, suggests a need for more shaded outdoor nooks near the mosque—difficult
space to acquisition in Hong Kong's densely developed downtown.

   Conversely, as leader of inter-religious dialog Mitri Raheb (2015) documents, public spaces accommodating processions, symbols of religious identity, and prayers can

become **occupied spaces**, discouraging religious expression. In Israel, even the mobile aspects of urban management, like the placement of Israeli security checkpoints, inhibit Palestinian religious activity by restricting routes to mosques and churches. Palestinians have resisted by praying in streets and open fields.

Issue: Integrating with the modern city—downtown houses of worship

As metroplexes expand, commercial districts often engulf religious institutions and communities. Members of long-established houses of worship move away from central districts to the suburbs or new housing projects. The ethnic composition of older neighborhoods often shifts in favor of new immigrants with different faith preferences. The U.K., for example, has an inventory of **"redundant" churches**, which have lost membership due to urbanization, or changes in neighborhood demography. Whether thriving or struggling to survive, for urban religious institutions, environmental sustainability is a multifaceted issue, demanding adaptation to the growth of the city itself—often as one institution among many.

The architect of St. Paul's Cathedral, Sir Christopher Wren designed St. James's Piccadilly, London (ca. 1676) as the "model" of an Anglican town church that "may be found beautiful and convenient, and as such, the cheapest I could invent." London's taller buildings have since encircled the parish once on the outskirts. Following German bombing in 1940 and post-war restoration of the burned-out, partially roofless house of worship, the congregation did not immediately recover its former vigor. Heading into the 1970s, an imaginative and socially committed vicar saved them from "redundancy" by welcoming and engaging London's ethnically diverse and politically active populace (St. James Church 1966; Summerson 1993: 197).

During the post-war restoration, a charitable donor funded conversion of churchyard and burial ground to an urban garden space with sculpture and fountains. Today, blackbirds, a migratory thrush species, sing melodically in between forays to forage fresh fruits from shrubs, rimmed by mature London plane trees. The garden provides a stopover for wildlife inhabiting other urban islands of vegetation, such as nearby St. James Square. Red-breasted English robins hop about on the grass and bumblebees explore open blossoms. Churchgoers, tourists, neighbors out for a walk, and café patrons lounge on the benches. Quiet enough for prayer or a private chat between friends, the garden is a social alternative to crowded coffee shops. A statue of Peace stands with hands outstretched in a shaded recess.

In 2003, St. James's was ahead of its time in installing photovoltaic cells on its roof, thereby reducing its carbon emissions. An indoor meter informs congregants and visitors of the kilowatts gleaned. Demonstrating high eco-dimensionality, St. James's celebrates an outdoor Eco Liturgy once a month. They sponsor educational speakers on topics like climate change, support rituals like blessing the bicycles, and schedule one-day eco pilgrimages to urban green spaces and sustainable communities. The church joins with the greater London environmental community in celebrations, including a candlelight vigil in nearby Piccadilly Circus to mark the globally celebrated **Earth Hour**. The lights in the Circus darken for an hour to honor human connection to the earth and nature (St. James Church 2019).

St. James did not develop its environmental strategy at a single point in the congregation's history—their efforts have matured through time. A foundation of St. James's

---

Box 8.3 Environmental administration for an urban house of worship

St. James's Church Piccadilly (2019) has utilized the following administrative strategies to improve environmentally accountability:

- Retitling the warden to Warden and Sustainability Champion
- Having the warden and gardener act as coordinators
- Forming a highly committed Eco-Group from members active in urban food cooperatives, neighborhood sustainability organizations, and zero-carbon energy initiatives
- Organizing environmental liturgies
- Identifying as a Fairtrade Church
- Participating in **citizen science** through urban bird counts
- Establishing an Eco Group cooperating instead of competing with other ministries including Walking Boots for hikers and the Animal Welfare Group
- Managing an informative eco-website
- Publishing an environmental calendar a year in advance
- Participating in all-city events and neighborhood community service

---

achievement is their recognition that organizational style and continuity matter (Box 8.3). The congregation encourages members to be active in their neighborhoods, supporting their **commitment to place**. Integrative eco-programing grounds the church in its urban matrix and returns benefits to the overall membership while keeping the church in touch with planning trends within the city.

Issue: Suburban sprawl and urban watersheds, US megachurches

The contra location to downtown is the scattered suburbs. Nineteenth-century conceptualizations for suburbs were supposed to produce healthy and affordable environments for raising families away from the crowding and grit of the inner city. Rather than being inherently green, though, the US-style single-family home, with a two-car garage and encircling lawn, encourages the destruction of natural ecosystems, heavy use of fossil fuels to support personal vehicle commuting, demand for irrigation water, and land-gobbling **suburban sprawl**. Suburbanization decentralizes and compartmentalizes neighborhoods, making it necessary to drive to shopping malls or parks and playgrounds. At their worst suburban developments are un-walkable, hemmed in by high-speed roads. While more likely to retain vegetation cover, elite-gated suburbs are inherently economically stratified and are frequently de facto racially exclusive as well (Bratton 2016).

Originally, a city center phenomenon, Christian megachurches, with 2000 or more in weekly attendance, have increasingly emerged in suburban settings. Land at city margins is less expensive and available in more extensive tracts. US suburban congregations often purchase 20 ha (45 acres) to 100 ha (220 acres), thereby occupying former ranches or woodlands, and contributing to the loss of agricultural acreage and wildlife habitat. Other budding megachurches have, instead, rented empty shopping malls, or, like Hopewell Missionary Baptist Church, purchased outdated industrial plants, brownfields, or abandoned quarries—thereby reducing sprawl, restoring degraded sites, and improving their residential neighborhoods.

On average, suburban megachurches favor a style of landscaping termed **corporate pastoralism**, providing a tidy, safe, image-generating ambiance to business and public spaces by clearing native vegetation and installing wide swaths of mowed lawns around buildings. Megachurches have become one among many culprits in the degradation of **small urban watersheds**, particularly when paving over much of their property to provide easy parking. Rainfall runs off the asphalt and lawns, causing flash-flooding and transporting nitrogen fertilizer and pesticides into creeks. The treeless lawns and dark asphalt contribute to the urban heat-island effect, raising temperatures. In arid climates, the "corporate pastoralist" grass sward, border shrubs, and fountains demand a steady supply of precious water (Mozingo 2011; Bratton 2016).

Some institutions such as Willow Creek Community Church in South Barrington, Illinois—a Chicago suburb—are demonstrating environmental responsibility by conserving natural ecosystems on their holdings. Downstream from a **capped landfill** (closed garbage dump), the Nondenominational Evangelical congregation has conserved the wetlands along its namesake Willow Creek. The patches of willows and tall grasses provide a biofilter for the runoff from their lawns and parking areas, thereby maintaining clean urban streams and the quality of water reaching nearby Lake Michigan. The congregation manages a small prairie populated by indigenous wildflowers. Birds that have difficulty finding nesting and foraging sites in the suburbs frequent church property. Hawks, herons, and woodcocks find food and cover.

Willow Creek Church has cleared an unpaved worship trail with benches and signs displaying Biblical verses along their wetland corridor, inviting strollers to enjoy the ducks and cattails. The grounds staff have established native marsh plant species in the medians of their entry road. These **bio-swales** reduce runoff and filter pollutants. Just as Willow Creek's urban watershed and riparian zone management recognize the environmental needs of the greater community, volunteers maintain a large vegetable garden to provide fresh tomatoes and greens for the church's charitable food pantry. Some Christian denominations give greater precedence to waterscapes than others, and, not surprisingly, megachurches practicing full immersion or adult baptism are more likely to invoke water as a potent religious symbol (Bratton 2016: 149–177, 255–285).

Similar urban religious institutional projects, sponsored not just by megachurches but by diverse faiths, include revegetating runoff detention ponds with native plants, building **rain gardens**, and installing grass sward or water-permeable materials in less-used parking zones. Retaining mature trees around buildings and along roads mitigates changes in microclimate and filters pollutants. These enhancements beautify institutional grounds, assist in stabilizing water tables, and reduce urban flash-flooding damaging homes and businesses. In arid climates, religious institutions are increasingly practicing **xeriscaping** or landscaping with cultivars requiring little or no irrigation water. Installation of water-saving irrigation systems, such as drip irrigation, that releases water only at the base of trees or timed-irrigation that releases water at night has higher initial costs while lowering water bills in the long run. Houses of worship are reducing the areas of water-demanding grass sward in favor of leaving indigenous desert vegetation in place (Bratton 2016: 221–251).

The Kadampa Meditation Center of Baltimore (2019) is a participant in the "One Water" program of Faith Partners for the Chesapeake (Chapter 6). The Center offers instruction in modern Buddhism via classes, retreats, and festivals. Their complex shelters the world Peace Café serving vegetarian cuisine and a 1.75-acre urban garden open to their neighborhood. Within the Peace Garden are a mediation garden and three rain gardens funded by a grant

from the Chesapeake Bay Trust. Moving beyond Buddhism's history of designing exceptional contemplative spaces, the Meditation center has posted educational signage explaining the reason for installing native species in the rain garden and elucidating how rain
gardens reduce stormwater runoff. The Center believes "that investing in our local community and environment creates a strong and vibrant city for everyone to enjoy…," and the
gardens improve environmental health and "create a lush and beautiful atmosphere at the
temple." In 2017, the temple won the Best of Baltimore Contest for Best Urban Garden.

Issue: Planning for social connectivity

The question remains, why US houses of worship demonstrate such varying levels of
participation in urban and suburban environmental planning, ranging from begrudging
compliance with county ordinances to integrating environmental accountability fully
into congregational ethos? Senior clergy usually have little facilities training and depend
on the same architects and engineers who design shopping malls. Differential openness
to municipal bike trail and footpath networks among megachurches suggests that they
have varying conceptualizations of their role in the surrounding neighborhoods and
their interface with city government. **Polity**, or the form of religious governance, often
influences connectivity with the greater neighborhood and civic processes. Greenways
and trails provide recreation and exercise and maintain wildlife corridors. If linked with
shopping, schools, and offices, greenways reduce automobile use and carbon emissions.
Some megachurches express a "gated mentality" or **political alienation** where they
build enclosing fences that "protect" their members from "outsiders." They erect barriers to greater neighborhood connectivity, such as fencing out adjoining public bike
trails. These churches view themselves as safe, welcoming alternative communities, free
of the unsavory aspects of urban life (Bratton 2016: 287–303).

   Other churches treat nearby greenways and natural areas as amenities, conducive to
an after-service family ramble. A third cohort offers trail easements to municipalities
or participates actively in environmental planning for their immediate neighborhoods.
A few churches have opened wooded or wetland vest-pocket parks to their neighbors.
These institutions believe they should contribute to civic well-being, and their religious
community should serve the greater metroplex. This genre of religious polity encourages
participation in other forms of shared environmental welfare, including urban gardening,
assisting the elderly, and providing for the economically-disadvantaged. Unfortunately,
many suburban megachurches continue to plan for corporate norms rather than for the
common good. The sectarianism and independent polity of American Protestantism
contribute to the inconsistencies (Bratton 2016: 287–303, 341–356).

Issue: Adapting religious values
to modernity—Islamic urban plans

One of the greatest challenges for religious participation in urban planning is construc-
tively addressing modernity and oft secular administrations while remaining true to
tradition and religious values. In countries where Islamic principles still guide civil law,
modernity and globalization have introduced new technologies and demands for infrastructure. Modern steel-framed skyscrapers and elevated real estate costs suppress the
installation of courtyards and patios within newer construction. One-bedroom apartments do not comfortably house extended families. Cities experience increased social

---

Box 8.4 Four Islamic criteria for adopting foreign material culture or thought under *Shari'ah* codes

1   Enhances human roles as God's *khalīfah* or vicegerent
2   Benefits other Muslims or the *'ummah*
3   No behavioral or physical offence to others
4   Compatibility and adaptability with Islamic principles.

Source: Mortada (2003: 130–131)

---

stratification as displaced rural populations move into make-shift housing around the margins. The rapid growth, division of districts into commercial and residential, and anonymous nature of megacities all undermine *'ummah*. Modern urban design poses a challenge to Muslim planners, as Islamic codes forbid adopting foreign concepts and non-Islamic behaviors and culture, without weighing their compatibility with Islamic teachings and values (Box 8.4). Muslim traditionalists may perceive modernity as a threat to the foundations of the faith, and thereby resist urban renewal. **Islamists**, in contrast, treat urban planning as a means of making modern cities truly Muslim.

The award-winning rebuilding of the Hafsia Quarter, Tunis, utilized Islamic conceptualization to recover and stabilize older architectural forms in a deteriorating "old city" slum, and transform it into a contemporary livable neighborhood. Hafsia was originally a mixed district of Sephardic Jewish, Arab, and Christian business owners and traders. In the 1860s, the wealthier families began to move to the suburbs to be replaced by more impoverished immigrants from rural areas. By the 1930s, crowding, infrastructure decay, and health hazards caused French colonial authorities to develop a master plan mandating destruction of most of Hafsia's buildings, and replacement of the north African layout characterized by zigzag passageways, courtyard homes, and mixed land use. The French plan called for a European style street grid and large blocks of housing. World War II halted the French-led demolition and bombing battered the district (Mortada 2003: 148–149).

In the 1970s, the municipality decided to recover the "old urban fabric" and social homogeneity of the quarter, while upgrading infrastructure and accommodating new residents. Depending primarily on unskilled labors and low-technology methods due to fiscal constraints, the new streets and alleys retained the irregularity and cul-de-sacs restricting some passages to pedestrians only. The plan connected two pre-existing bazaars and facilitated the opening of shops and offices in buildings also used for housing. It retained rooms built over alleys and courtyard homes with open arcades while building new housing units in a range of sizes to encourage the integration of residents with a range of incomes. New support for community life incorporated accessible daycare, public baths, and health care facilities (Mortada 2003: 148–149). In this locale, Islamic values provided a sense of place, enhanced walkability, and conserved the shade inherent in the historic layout.

Issue: Christian theology and the new urbanism

Despite their role in driving western economies, Christians are also wrestling with the values embedded in postmodern urbanization. Roman Catholic theologian Philip Sheldrake (2001) prioritizes "the art of community" for urban plans, accompanied by

---

Box 8.5 Christian proposals for urban social ethical values or functions

Timothy Gorringe's (2002) five key values for Christian alternative visions of the built environment:

1 *Justice*, eliminating slums and poverty
2 *Empowerment*, citizens guide their own futures
3 *Situatedness*, people are rooted in constructed spaces
4 *Diversity*, accommodating different cultural heritages
5 *Enchantedness*, freeing spaces from banality and secularization, replacing these with beauty and delight

Eric O. Jacobsen's (2003) Christian contributions to the evolution of the good city:

1 *Patient vigor*, in pursuing civic processes
2 *Focal practices*, including sustainability
3 *Celebration*, including communal events
4 *Good citizenship*
5 *Intentional community*

---

redemption, reconciliation, hospitality, and seeking the common good. Presbyterian Eric O. Jacobsen (2003) wishes to redeem the city, which should rise to the ideals of the Biblical New Jerusalem. Christians should participate in the **new urbanism** and construct "sidewalks in the Kingdom." Social ethicist Timothy Gorringe (2002: 248–255) accepts 21st-century cities as multi-cultural and imbedded within the "global village." He believes, however, both capitalism and **postmodernism** can limit architecture's virtue. For Gorringe, postmodernism's advocacy for "community, locality, place, and regional resistances, social movements, and respect for otherness," are worthy, yet the relativism can undermine "moral focus." The religious voice too often articulates "backward versions of identity politics." Gorringe imagines a Christologically-informed architecture "refracted by the cross and resurrection." Interestingly, all three theologians develop their overall philosophy of urban design in an explicitly Christological framework. They emphasize Christian **eschatology** via rhetoric of redemption and the New Jerusalem—thereby asserting Christian authority over the multi-cultural and multi-religious demography of the megacity. The social virtues they propose, in contrast, are widely applicable in secular planning contexts (Box 8.5).

Issue: Secular planning and accommodating multi-religious heritage, Singapore

Among the most successful programs for urban development worldwide has been the multi-decade effort in Singapore to remove substandard housing, clean the river and harbor, expand public transportation, forward commercial development, enlarge civic space, and enhance sustainability. Confronting cobbled-together shanties lining the river, Singapore constructed public housing projects offering electricity, running water, and larger living areas. Most slum residents willingly relocated to better quarters that the city organized as multi-ethnic. The municipality then cleared the debris from the water-front, controlled the infusion of garbage, and eliminated the hog farms draining animal waste into the river. Today, the Marina Bay district is a tourist magnet, with world renown gardens (Ho et al. 2013; Tortajada et al. 2013).

Although the urban development program is secular and bids projects to international architectural firms, Singapore remains distinctive in its **religious pluralism**. Under colonial administration, the British deployed a divide-and-conquer approach to the city's cultural diversity. Malays lived predominantly in Kampong Glam, the Chinese in Chinatown, and Indians in Little India. After becoming an independent city, urban renewal initially tore down relics of colonialism with little thought to cultural values. Recognizing its disregard for its distinctive heritage, Singapore then moved to the conservation of individual significant buildings, unfortunately removing them from their historical context, as the areas surrounding them were demolished and rebuilt. Via a 1985 Conservation Master Plan, Singapore ultimately evolved from salvaging isolated monuments, temples and mosques, to planning for multi-block districts to give its citizens a sense of place and national identity (Muzaini 2013).

According to urban planner Hamzah Muzaini (2013), however, the conversion into "historic and cultural" districts still constricts religious expression and practices. Public reactions to state-led efforts to heritage and historic districts remain ambivalent. High rents have pushed lower-income families and traditional trades out of older neighborhoods. A policy of **adaptive reuse** of historic structures by modern businesses has, for instance, displaced the Chinese craftspeople who made paper houses for ancestral prayer offerings, and the coffee shops where the Chinese once met and socialized in Chinatown. As **"receptacles of collective memory,"** what is in the buildings is as important as outward appearances. The sights, sounds, and even the smells have changed.

Encirclement by high rises demotes mosque domes and temple gates that once were visually dominant features. Pressure for land acquisition encourages the removal of cemeteries and unwalled religious green spaces, thereby diminishing their function as wildlife habitat or social spaces (Fig. 1.1). Conversely, the historic courtyards of mosques and temples have helped to buffer the effects of enclosure. Municipal planners have turned areas adjoining religious buildings into municipal parks, creating constellations of spiritual and social terrains adjoining housing and businesses (Fig. 8.2). The Marina Bay Gardens incorporate cultural heritage gardens with religiously informed designs. Religious celebrations and decorations are welcome in public spaces, like street medians and building plazas. Although Singapore has proven megacities can replace slums with comfortable housing and offer brighter economic futures to all its citizens, resolving conflicts between development and heritage remains part of the on-going planning process.

Issue: Effectiveness of multi-religious RENGOs—Faith in Place, Chicago

The multi-religious aspects of megacity environmental planning bring up the question of whether multi-faith RENGOs (religious environmental nongovernment organizations) can contribute to urban problem-solving at scales beyond the individual institution? Religious scholar Amanda J. Baugh (2017) acted as participant-researcher when she volunteered for Faith in Place (FIP), a RENGO (religious environmental

Figure 8.2 Telok Ayer Green provides a pleasant public space framing two historic religious structures, Nagore Darga Indian Islamic Heritage Center (left), and Thian Hock Keng (right),
a Chinese temple, dedicated to the Queen of Heaven (Ma Zu), Singapore.

nongovernment organization) committed to raising environmental awareness
among Chicago, Illinois, religious communities. Rev. Clare Butterfield, a Unitarian
Universalist minister and founding director, was serving as the senior administrator at
the time. Baugh investigated how FIP, which like many US ENGOs (environmental
nongovernmental organizations) has founders and membership primarily drawn from
white Protestant backgrounds, has navigated the ethnic and religious diversity of the
megacity. During Baugh's research, core FIP projects were bringing healthy organic
foods into food deserts by establishing urban gardens, educating the public in installing
weatherstripping in their residences to reduce energy loss, and locating grants to assist
religious bodies installing solar panels and other sustainable technologies.

From its beginnings, FIP viewed Muslims and African Americans as relatively disinterested in the environment, thus attempted to develop outreach first to mosques
and then to African American churches (Baugh 2017). African Americans indeed
have been reticent to join large ENGOs, which, on average, have white leadership
and reflect white middle and professional class priorities. Reclaiming the deep well of
non-white US environmental contributions, however, historian Dianne Glave (2010)
argues African Americans had to navigate trans-Atlantic deportation and adaptation to
the hostile culture of slavery. Beset by hardships, African Americans retained a legacy
of working the land, gardening, and observing nature. They have nurtured leadership
for the pursuit of environmental justice and taken demonstrative stands against urban
spatial discrimination and pollution (Glave and Stoll 2006).

Baugh (2017: 109–127) did observe dissonances in religious values that were erecting barriers to coalition building. At an environmental conference with presentations by members of different faiths at Chicago's Lutheran School of Theology in 2010, for example, participants challenged imam Skeikh Eshaal Karmini when he discussed the practice of animal sacrifice in conjunction with **Eid Al-Adha**, concluding the **Hajj**— the annual pilgrimage to Mecca. Pilgrims consume part of the meat and convey the remainder to the poor. One of the critics was Omar Ahmadi, a Muslim and professor of environmental studies who thought Islam should reinterpret the ritual due to the environmental impacts of raising livestock. A professor from the Lutheran school was concerned about the contributions of animal waste to global atmospheric carbon. Karmini countered that the sacrifice ending the Hajj was a small number of animals compared to worldwide annual livestock slaughter.

Baugh (2017: 109–127) interprets these opposing views as progressive versus more traditional religion and points out that FIP, with its liberal Protestant underpinnings, "insisted that religious teachings must adapt to be relevant to modern times…" Like the objections to the Makah whale hunt, both environmental rhetoric and mainline Protestant values dismiss tradition as worthy of consideration and compromise. Christian theology, for example, does not consider ritual animal sacrifice as effective or as required by God, and Islam does. Protestant dismissal of pilgrimage and desacralization of sacred locales in their ritual practices can subtly delegitimize international community-building celebrations, such as the Hajj. Meanwhile, US Christian seminary cafeterias and cafes serve animal products from turkey sandwiches to yogurt. Muslims in Euro-American cities are already struggling to remain faithful in unsympathetic social settings, that sometimes treat Islam as backward and old fashioned.

Baugh observes the members of FIP were committed to religious pluralism, yet had a vague concept of how it should be actualized. FIP leadership passed over possibilities for incorporating Pagan organizations in their network, likely due concerns for religious respectability. With its dismissal of magik, liberal Protestantism continues to cast Paganism as unscientific and irrational. For their part, Pagans are often anti-structural and avoid hierarchical organizations. Despite the presence of environmentally committed Evangelical congregations in the Chicago metroplex, FIP initially made little effort to recruit their more conservative co-religionists or overcome their concerns for orthodoxy. FIP did conscientiously diversify its staff in terms of ethnic and religious background. Despite successes in encouraging mosques to install solar panels, FIP experienced difficulty in retaining Muslim administrators. Conversely, they hired a highly effective African American educator, Veronica Kyle, who gained the trust of African American institutions and incorporated African Americans in FIP's sustainability initiatives. Increasing black membership was a major step toward inclusivity within the socioeconomically stratified realm of ENGOs (Baugh 2017: 128–147, 168–171).

FIP's success in drawing diverse urban religious populations to the environmental cause has been greatest among Protestants, and groups, like mainstream Roman Catholics and Reform Jews, who share their presuppositions about modernity and the role of religion in civic life. As Baugh concludes, FIP began with the assumption that a "core religious message" based on Protestant universalism could simply be translated into "the language of other religious traditions." The RENGO positioned itself as "an authoritative religious voice representing all the communities of faith" but, in fact, "represented the concerns of a particular segment of progressive, modern religious groups." Under Butterfield's leadership FIP's "work embedded theological understandings characteristic of liberal, modern theology, including the commitment to modern intellectual inquiry (especially modern science), belief in the authority of reason and experience, and understanding of Christianity primarily in ethical terms, and a priority on making religion believable and socially relevant in contemporary terms."

Conclusion: Organizing within the metroplex

Religious expression, aesthetics, and diversity contribute to the vitality and character of today's metropolises. Yet, megacities have also retained the problems of the past, including confining religious minorities and the poor to unhealthy neighborhoods. The world's cities conserve well-loved religious spatial-alignments and designs. Megacity population densities, social diversity, and infrastructure, though, challenge religious conceptualizations of built environments. Amada Baugh (2017) does not answer the question of how best to coordinate multi-faith urban RENGOs. The FIP case suggests that more religiously open coalitions encouraging the participating faiths to recognize their rich environmental heritage could ease tensions. Allowing participants to bring forth the issues most significant to them, and address environmental concerns through the means they prefer, including ritual and prayer, could achieve even greater inclusivity. FIP has developed new strategies for inclusivity as they have gained experience. As of 2020, FIP has grown to nearly 400 institutional partners—predominantly Protestant mainline and Roman Catholic with smaller numbers of Evangelical, Jewish, Buddhist, Muslim, Zoroastrian, and Bahai bodies. They have opened offices in the suburbs, increased their focus on water protection, and trained volunteer Green Teams from houses of worship throughout the metroplex.

Suggested readings

Baugh, Amanda J. *God, and the Green Divide: Religious Environmentalism in Black and White*. Oakland: University of California Press, 2017.
Bratton, Susan. *Churchscape: The Iconography of Megachurch Lawns*. Waco, TX: Baylor University Press, 2016.
Glave, Dianne. *Rooted in the Earth: Reclaiming the African American Environmental Heritage*. Chicago, IL: Lawrence Hill Books, 2010.
Gorringe, Timothy. *A Theology of the Built Environment: Justice, Empowerment, and Redemption*. Cambridge, U.K.: Cambridge University Press, 2002.
Ho, Elaine, Chih Woon, and Kamalini Ramdas. *Changing Landscapes of Singapore: Old Tensions, New Discoveries*. Singapore: National University of Singapore Press, 2013.
Mortada, Hisham. *Traditional Islamic Principles of Built Environments*. London, U.K.: RoutledgeCurzon, 2003.
Nagendra, Harini. *Nature in the City: Bengaluru in the Past, Present, and Future*. New Delhi, India: Oxford University Press, 2016.
Sinn, Simeon, Mouhamad Khorchide, and Dina el Omari, eds. *Religious Plurality and the Public Space: Joint Christin-Muslim Theological Reflections*. Leipzig, Germany: Evangelische Verlagsanstalt, 2016.

9 Healing

The iconography of pollution and planetary wellness

Key concepts

1 Religions can support environmental wellness in six modes: precautionary, regulatory, responsive, healing, restorative, or compensative.

2 Religious cultural constructs of pollution may or may not parallel scientific definitions.

3 The environmental movement beginning in the 1960s has learned from and shared issues with other social reform movements, including anti–nuclear, civil rights, and labor movements.

4 Minority, economically-disadvantaged, and socially marginalized populations often sustain greater exposure to environmental pollutants than majority or economically advantaged populations. Religious organizations support campaigns against polluting industries and toxins, such as lead, and join coalitions striving for eco-justice.

5 Labor leader César Chávez creatively combined Mexican devotional piety with strategies originating with the civil rights movement in organizing the United Farm Workers, who have tackled multiple issues concerning environmental safety.

6 In Hinduism, river goddesses like Yamuna and the river are one in the same, and a river can be both dirty (*gandi*) and pure (*pavtra*). Pilgrims' encounters with industrial pollutants as they bathe in or drink water from sacred rivers such as the Yamuna and the Ganges have inspired the formation of organizations to clean the rivers of sewage and industrial contaminants.

7 Contemporary Mongolian Buddhists associate the "lack of spiritual clarity," and the corruption that followed capitalism as having karmic effects "in opposition to enlightenment," including unhealthy levels of particulate air pollution.

8 As a model of planetary health, the Gaia hypothesis, named for the Greek goddess of the earth, asserts that the thin organic layer covering the earth's surface and infusing the oceans interacts symbiotically to maintain conditions favorable to life itself. New Age, contemporary "goddess religion" and other alternative faiths have similarly featured a universe with a preprogrammed end or installed Gaia in their eco-friendly pantheons.

9 Beginning with early Greenpeace, radical environmentalism adopted the Quaker strategy of bearing witness to societal wrongdoing. They utilize religious language of conversion, martyrdom, and the earth transfigured.

10 Following the Fukushima nuclear accident, Japan has become more open to revalorizing Buddhist teachings. These include moderate lifestyles, knowledge of

self-sufficiency, understanding of causality through dependent origination, and environmental conservation through an ethic of non-violence.

11 Misunderstandings concerning the roles people of color have played in battling pollutants are partially rooted in the rhetoric of the ENVIRONMENT as a consolidated cause defined by overarching threats like climate change. Socially disadvantaged groups frequently engage in micro-mobilization to correct the environmental abuses that wage laborers, immigrants, and ethnic minorities bear.

Religion and health

Religions have long fostered rituals and codes, avoiding contamination, and promoting healing. Faith-based organizations manage hospitals, public health initiatives, and disaster relief. Much like today's medical and legal professionals, religion can support environmental wellness in six modes: (1) **precautionary** or avoiding hazards, (2) **regulatory** or creating codes to limit pollutant exposure, (3) **responsive** or mitigating threats, (4) **healing** injuries and illnesses, (5) **restorative** or repairing long term impacts, and (6) **compensative** or mitigating damages that cannot be repaired—including the death of the patient.

Preceding the modern era, religious approaches to environmental hazards were often precautionary. Taboos or demonization of dangerous natural phenomena like river rapids and whirlpools serve to reduce human entry, preventing potential injury. Indigenous peoples residing along the tectonically active zones encircling the Pacific Ocean retain myths describing seismic sea waves. As an earthquake-generated tsunami raced toward South Asia in 2004, the Moken or sea gypsies living on the islands of Thailand and Burma observed the ocean retreating far back from the shore and reacted by climbing to elevated knolls. A Moken who realized the birds and other animals had suddenly become silent, stopped fishing and ran to warn others. This fisherman later explained: "The wave is created by the spirit of the sea. The Big Wave had not eaten anyone for a long time, and it wanted to taste them again." Although the monster wave named La Boon—the breaker that "eats people"—originates with angry ancestral spirits, the resulting flood is a cleansing force, and the world is reborn after the waters recede. Such narratives convey detailed traditional knowledge concerning life-threatening natural disturbances and dictate quick action (Elias et al. 2005; Leung 2005).

Like the Mauri ban on depositing fish waste back in the stream, religions evolve codes defining pollutants and regulating their handling. Frequent concerns are human excretions, animal and human corpses, blood, foreign matter in water, smoke, and substances contaminated with microbes. The Hebrew scriptures mandate that soldiers carry a shovel or paddle to bury their excrement outside camp boundaries (Deuteronomy 23:12–14) and that any materials coated with spreading mold be burned (Leviticus 13:47–59). Mere entry of a human or animal into a sacred hydroscape may be polluting, as when the Roman emperor Nero disturbed the purity of Aqua Marcia's shrine by taking a swim in its healing waters (Lennon 2012).

Anthropologists have questioned whether **religious constructions of pollution** and "dirt" parallel health risks. Purification and cleansing of temples, households, and private spaces may not discourage outdoor disposal of wastes that science identifies as unsanitary (Lüthi 2010). **Liminal** objects, representing an edge or transgressing a boundary, may be physically dangerous—or not. In *Purity and Danger: An Analysis of Pollution and Taboo,* Mary Douglas (2003) investigated the foundations of **ritual purity** and proposed the Kosher dietary codes in Leviticus were not public health regulations. Clean animals are those having unambiguous roles in the natural order. Fish with gills and herbivorous cattle are edible. The ocean creatures without gills and pigs with their cloven hoofs and omnivorous diets are conversely unclean. In a later edition, Douglas reconsidered her original explanation and replaced it with a theory of "clean" animals as those utilized as sacrifices and cared for by herders. In either case, dirt was "matter out of place," indicating "dis-order" (Bradley 2012). Ritual purity defines symbolic boundaries, including who is a faithful Jew and who may enter holy precincts. The **iconography** and **semiotics** of the clean and unclean parallel those of good and evil, order and disorder, and life and death.

In contrast, Kimberly Patton (2007: loc 642–674, 878–892) concludes that "impurity itself is real and is not simply a socially constructed vehicle for the experience of disorder." The religious historian argues that modern industrial marine pollution assumes that the seas in their massive size, impenetrable depths, and constant motion can neutralize poisons and carry way all forms of waste. Religions from animist to world have these same concepts embedded in their **dialectics** (examination of metaphysical contradictions, or discussions determining what is true). Their myths portray the oceans as purifying, absorbing evil, or as "a supreme means of catharsis." However, religious conceptualization of the ability of oceans, or of the earth in general, to infinitely absorb human messes frequently entrain counter-themes, such as the oceans revealing what was hidden or rejecting the discarded in myths of "unwanted return." Human transgressions, for example, enrage the Inuits' Great Sea Woman, Sedna. Misdeeds scatter debris and lice among her long black tresses waving on the Arctic seafloor and coat her eyes and mouth with irritating dirt. In response, she hides the sea creatures the Inuit hunt. To stave off impending starvation and release the seals and walruses, the Inuit must repent. A shaman or *angakoq* in an entranced state must travel to the depths and clean Sedna's countenance and flowing hair. Religious definitions of purity and pollution are not simple dichotomies but may demand complex responses involving moral restitution, cultural renewal, or behavioral restraint (Patton 2007: loc. 1722–1858).

Combining causes

Preceding the 1970s, much religious response to scientifically defined pollutants was a component of other missions, particularly peacekeeping, assisting the disenfranchised, responding to disasters, and protecting children. Nineteenth-century Christian reformers campaigned for better working conditions for mine and factory employees beset by accidents and respiratory diseases caused by coal dust, textile fibers, and chemicals. Ironically, during the era when Lynn White, Jr., the Deep Ecologists, and many other activists drew attention to the deficiencies of Abrahamic cosmologies or doubted the environmental efficiency of religion, the **historic peace churches**, such as the Society of Friends, were lobbying against the proliferation of atomic armaments, and thereby against insidious radioactive fallout. Members of the Catholic Workers Party, Buddhists affected by the destruction of Hiroshima and Nagasaki, and many others motivated by religious conscience joined them in protesting nuclear arsenals (Fig. 9.1). Although the primary issue was preventing devastating wars, peace activists increasingly wove the long-term health impacts of radiation exposure and bioaccumulation of strontium-90 and other radioactive isotopes from above-ground nuclear testing into their arguments. Rachel Carson's *Silent Spring* (1962) described the sad fate of the crew of a Japanese

Figure 9.1 A US protest against using federal monies to develop nuclear arms in 1950. The man's placard reads, "Catholic Worker, Let's do it Gandhi's way—not Truman's," referring to Mahatma Gandhi and President Harry Truman.

Photo: Fred Palumbo, Collection of the U.S. Library of Congress

fishing boat downwind of a hydrogen bomb detonation. The exposé encouraged an already nervous American public to support nuclear disarmament treaties.

During the Vietnam War, religious leaders from college chaplains to Buddhist monastics condemned aerial spraying of the herbicide **Agent Orange** tainted with carcinogenic **dioxin** on farm fields and rainforests. Modern weaponry caused immediate losses of Vietnamese religious heritage, such as the carpet bombing-inflicted damage to the Cham Hindu temples and sculptures at Son Puy, now recognized by UNESCO as a World Heritage Site. Although the Vietnamese government began to demine unexploded ordinance at Son Puy in 1975, this hazardous aspect of site restoration remains incomplete (UNESCO 2020). More than a half-century after the war's end, Vietnamese religious bodies continue to support restorative and compensatory responses to the chemical nightmare, by raising funds to care for the estimated three million victims of Agent Orange, including children born with congenital disabilities caused by parental exposure to residual dioxin in soil and water. Signs on today's temple collection boxes urge, "Let us ease the pain of Agent Orange together." *Silent Spring* captures the insidious nature of the post-industrial organic toxins and radioactive isotopes. These health threats are invisible, persistent, and global.

Both the movement to ban nuclear weapons and Rev. Martin Luther King, Jr.'s advocacy for non-violent, steadfast protests against legislated racial exclusion drew on Mahatma Gandhi's Hindu-based ethos of peaceful resistance (Fig. 9.1). These crusades helped to frame the greater environmental activism following *Silent Spring*, by contributing justifications, tactics, and political savvy. The accompanying candlelight vigils, prayer services, and gatherings in houses of worship are all forms of implicit or explicit religion sacralizing political action. This chapter focuses on four religious aspects of environmental health—the cooperation with other social reform movements, cross-cultural perceptions of pollution, planetary models, and the iconography of healthful versus polluted nature.

Issue: Vulnerability of minorities and the economically-disadvantaged to toxins

Freedom from environmental health risks is inherent to guarding the civil rights of the economically disempowered and vulnerable women and children. Yet cultural majorities often stereotype ethnic minorities, migrants, or the poor as inherently "dirty" or "unclean." New Zealanders, for example, have attributed littering in crowded downtowns to "morally inferior behavior" exhibited by foreigners—particularly Asians—thereby casting them as less committed to modernity. Anthropologist Eveline Dürr (2010) observes some Kiwis of Asian heritage have responded by publicly displaying environmental care. Others have, unfortunately, appropriated cultural constructions independent of any measurable form of pollution. These negative depictions represent "a symbolic and material struggle over social positioning and national identity" and over majority-culture access to resources and power.

Polluting industries select factory or refinery locales where land is cheap, and effluents are weakly regulated. Corporate management may avoid expensive processing of hazardous waste by disposal in ponds, streams, or vacant lots adjoining plants. In *Dumping in Dixie: Race, Class, and Environmental Quality*, sociologist Robert Bullard (1990) documented the elevated exposure of African Americans to environmental hazards, due to differential legal protection. For African American heads of household, the most prevalent **voluntary association** membership is a church, making houses of worship the most frequent place for African Americans to gather and discuss neighborhood concerns. As platforms for civil rights activism, African American churches have aided neighborhood organizations and public health departments battling elevated levels of lead in older apartments and homes where owners applied toxic paint before current bans. Congregations have joined campaigns to rescue entire districts from **chronic pollution exposures**.

Beginning in 1934, the RSR Corporation operated a lead smelter in predominantly African American West Dallas, Texas. In 1956, the city opened a 3,500 unit public housing project just to the north of the auto battery recycling facility that was annually releasing approximately 270 tons of lead into Dallas's air. The prevailing winds dusted windows, yards, sidewalks, and playgrounds with metal-laden particulates. In 1968, Dallas passed a strict ordinance limiting lead compounds in the air but failed to enforce it in West Dallas. In 1981, a lead-screening study found that children living near the smelter had higher levels of lead in their blood than those living in a control study area away from the plant. Grassroots citizen's organizations and the City Council-appointed Dallas Alliance Environmental Task Force petitioned for tighter compliance (Bullard 1990: 54–61). Pastors spoke out against the inequity of the pollution, and West Dallas churches participated in organizing neighborhood response.

Belated enforcement and a series of lawsuits against RSR finally closed the plant in 1981. As Bullard (1990) summarizes, "the plant closure was a tribute to the tenacity of the low-income black neighborhood to withstand the assaults of pollution, inept government officials, and institutionalized discrimination." In circumstances like West Dallas, faith-based institutions do not necessarily head the environmental action, while playing supportive roles by offering organizational space, sending community leaders to public meetings, circulating educational materials, and offering prayer and affirmation to participants. Congregations assist in the vital political processes of forming coalitions and aligning constituencies to take a unified stance. As of 2020, unresolved issues with residual lead in soils and lack of compensation for medical expenses for those with elevated exposures continue to drive West Dallas church-based activism and calls for additional restorative projects.

In Flint, Michigan, a supposedly cost-saving, 2014 municipal switch in water supply pumped highly corrosive water through lead pipes and delivered it to thousands of Flint households. Health impacts extended from rashes, to a shigella outbreak, to a tripling of lead levels in affected children. A "rust belt" city recovering from the loss of automobile manufacturing plants, Flint had a declining population and many families living below the poverty line. Initially, state water regulators dismissed complaints from the public and physicians. Tap water was turning an unattractive brownish-orange as it picked up corroded pipe coatings. Finally, recognizing the gravity of the management error, the state, and the federal government declared a public health emergency in January 2016 (Deland 2020).

Emerging from the mire of miscommunication, environmental health professionals from government agencies and NGOs (nongovernmental organizations) drew on community leaders and voluntary associations to assist in educating the public in stop-gap measures like installing filters in faucets. Environmental managers requested cooperation from religious bodies in holding public forums and distributing supplies. Conversely, religious leaders became spokespeople for their congregants. Houses of worship, including churches, mosques, and synagogues, often framed contributions in distinctively religious ways. In the spirit of civil rights, Flint's churches acted as gathering places for participants in public demonstrations. One predominantly African American Baptist Church distributed over five million bottles of water. The pastor of Flint's First Church of the Nazarene delivered a donated water filter to partner church, Joy Tabernacle, whose members were refusing baptism in city water (NCN News 2019). Moving toward healing and restoration, in 2016, the Muslims of Hamtramck and Detroit raised $10,000 from six cooperating mosques, which they donated to the Flint Child Health and Development Fund to support "long term care and development for Flint children exposed to lead" (Emery 2016). The multiple faiths and denominations aiding the stricken city acted based on pre-established social-ethical priorities, particularly care for children, justice for the injured, and neighborliness. (Note: Plastic bottles are also a form of pollution, and the failure of the municipal water system left limited alternatives.)

Religious support for environmental justice extends to regional chemical exposure scenarios. A stretch of the Mississippi River between Baton Rouge and New Orleans, Louisiana, has earned the nick-name Cancer Alley due to the concentration of petrochemical plants, and indifferent state regulation of their effluents. Most residents of the river flood plain near the chemical companies are African American or have limited family incomes. Although the corporations create jobs and pay taxes, their immediate residential neighbors are disadvantaged in obtaining employment in the chemical industries. They receive minimal benefit and absorb maximal risk. To attract industry, the state and parish governments have offered corporations tax incentives, further reducing benefits to the community (Bullard 1990).

Resistance to the health hazards, odors, and watershed degradation of Cancer Ally began during the 1980s. Citizens of predominantly African-American Alsen, Louisiana, mounted a class action suit against the Rollins Environmental Service facility, a hazardous waste incinerator, and disposal site that spewed smelly, chemical-laden air into the unincorporated hamlet. Greenpeace, the Sierra Club, and other ENGOs (environmental nongovernmental organizations) joined grassroots organizers in opposing a permit allowing the disposal facility to burn PCBs (polychlorinated-biphenyls) toxicologically verified as carcinogens (Bullard 1990: 65–69). Unfortunately, in the more than 30 years since the waste disposal facility paid damages to the citizens of Alsen, odors, contaminated groundwater, and reports of elevated cancer cases have remained the norm. In 2019, churches again operated as organizational locales for protesting "cancer ally's" environmental inequities. Their focus was blocking the opening of new plants, including one owned by a Taiwanese plastics manufacturer, that would contribute to the pollution burden in an election district that is 80% African American. Traveling from his church in North Carolina, civil rights activist, Rev. William Barber asserted the environmental health threats originate with greed. The companies "decide who we can make the money off of that will give us the least resistance. It's evil economics" (Laughland 2019). In Cancer Alley, the campaign for civil rights as divine justice has merged with the struggle for pollution-free neighborhoods.

A challenge for communities suffering from toxic exposures is transitioning from the oft news-worthy responsive mode to less dramatic but disease-reducing precautionary and regulatory strategies. Founded in 1787 as a move toward racial equity in Methodism, the African American Methodist Episcopal Church (AME) has incorporated meeting environmental needs in its mission statement. The AME's Social Action Committee recognizes climate change as causing and exasperating illnesses like asthma, which already pose higher risks for people of color (Box 9.1). In 2018, environmental justice was the topic for the AME's annual national conference (AME 2019).

Box 9.1 The environmental mission of the African American Methodist Episcopal Church

Overall Mission Statement of the AME (2019): The Mission of the African Methodist Episcopal Church is to minister to the spiritual, intellectual, physical, emotional, and environmental needs of all people by spreading Christ's liberating gospel through word and deed.

AME statement on climate change: Climate change hurts God's creation and people. Black people are unduly impacted. The health of children, elderly, and those with chronic diseases like asthma is at greater risk. Our faithful in the Caribbean, Africa, and rural communities are suffering from floods, drought and disease. The AME is supporting climate policies and action that will move us away from dirty fuels that make us sick and toward safe, clean energy.

Issue: Protecting farmworkers—Mexican popular piety and *La causa*

Along with employees in extractive industries, farmworkers have elevated risks of exposure to toxins on the job. Accidental **acute exposures** (causing immediate illness or death) to pesticides have been widespread—and are a recurrent problem in developing nations where applicators may not be formally trained or able to read the warning labels. Pesticides remain on treated fruits and vegetables, drift into adjoining residential areas, and contaminate soil and water for multiple growing seasons. Studying the interactions between the churches and the farmworkers in California and Texas, historian Alan J. Watt (2010) has traced the transition from missionary service to the poor in the early 20th century to the political mobilization for better pay and more humane working conditions emerging as **La Causa** in the 1960s. Rarely the sole issue, environmental health is one of a constellation of farmworker concerns.

Initially, socially active Christians drawn from the economic elites sponsored home missions and service organizations conducting outreach to farm laborers. The activists' origins were in northern liberal Protestantism and Catholicism, and a more quietist southern Christian ethos. As the farmworkers themselves became more engaged, their own regional or folk religious practices became a mainstay of the movement. Watt (2010: loc. 2002–2014) credits labor leader César Chávez with creatively combining Mexican **devotional piety** with strategies originating with the civil rights movement. The synthesis expressed pride in the workers' heritage and promoted solidarity (Fig. 9.2).

When a strike by California grape harvesters was losing momentum, the strikers borrowed from the civil rights repertoire and undertook a march to the state capitol, Sacramento. Coinciding with **Lent** and **Holy Week**, the rally became *La Peregrinación*—the pilgrimage. As the marchers set-out, a farmworker at the head of the procession

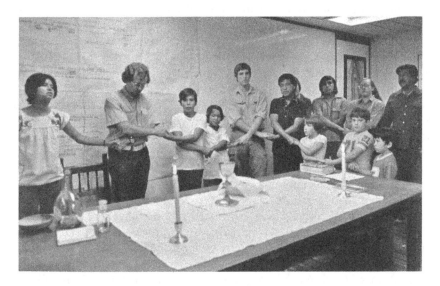

Figure 9.2 César Chávez (sixth from left) attends mass with other Farm Workers Union organizers at their headquarters in La Paz, California, ca. 1970s. An image of the Virgin of Guadalupe hangs on the wall (rear right).

Photo: Cathy Murphy, licensed by Getty Images

elevated a banner displaying the **Virgin of Guadalupe**, who first appeared to the poor and dispossessed farmer Juan Diego, following La Conquistá. The very last *peregrino* bore a cross, wrapped in black cloth—the symbol of Christ's death for the world's sins as displayed in some churches on Good Friday. When Christ rises, the church removes the dark veil. Participants in *La Peregrinatión* reported experiencing "a newfound self-confidence and self-respect." The integration of Catholic iconography did, however, have the negative consequences of causing Pentecostals to drop out of the march, and alienating more secular labor organizers. Vineyard owners "accused Chávez of profaning the holiest day in the Christian calendar." Liberal Protestants supporting Chávez, in contrast, were unconcerned about elevating a female saint in the vanguard (Watt 2010: loc. 981–1025).

Not long after, César Chávez again invoked popular piety, when he began a public fast in response to the strike's continued stalling. He identified the fast "as an act of penance in response to the feelings of discouragement, impatience, and hatred among strikers." Filipino farmworkers turned the union office into a temporary chapel—even coloring the windows to look like stained glass. A Franciscan priest, Mark Day, celebrated daily mass at "the chapel," which attracted several thousand pilgrims through the duration of the fast (Fig. 9.2). When Chávez ended his ordeal after 25 days, thousands, including Senator Robert Kennedy, joined the procession to a flatbed truck acting as a temporary altar and speakers' platform (Watt 2010: loc. 1031–1075).

Movements like La Causa have contributed to improved federal and state environmental protections for workers, via regulatory agencies like the EPA and **OSHA** (the U.S. Occupational, Health and Safety Administration). In the mid-1980s, Chávez, as president of the United Farm Workers, led a campaign to raise public awareness concerning the toxicity of pesticides used on grapes in hopes of having the five most hazardous to farm workers banned. Unfortunately, as recent lawsuits concerning herbicides demonstrate, manufacturers may not fully inform purchasers and applicators of known risks, and environmental regulations do not unilaterally curtail long term health impacts of pesticides. In 2018, for example, an NGO sponsored lawsuit forced the EPA to ban chlorpyrifos-based insecticides, after EPA director Scott Pruitt had delayed implementing new regulations. Chlorpyrifos is a nerve agent that can cause acute toxicity in agricultural workers and neurological damage to children. Among the NGOs acting as plaintiffs were the League of United Latin American Citizens, the Natural Resources Defense Council, Farm Worker Justice, the National Hispanic Medical Association, and Green Latinos (U.S. Court of Appeals 2018).

La Causa strengthened the interface between the environment and religion by forwarding the Virgin of Guadalupe as an icon of both liberation and healthy human–nature relationships. An unknown 16th-century Aztec scholar wrote the original poetic account of her mysterious appearances in Nahuatl rather than Spanish, constructing it as an inherently **Mezito** (mixed-ethnic) narrative. An indigenous Aztec, Juan Diego, encountered the dark-skinned "Mother of Creation" in an other-worldly garden, at Tepeyac hill, a pre-colonial Aztec temple site in Mexico City. Following his mystical experiences, Juan Diego returned home to find his uncle miraculously cured of a mortal illness. Clad in a star-decorated, deep blue robe, Our Lady of Guadalupe symbolizes new cosmic life comprised of healing, beauty, and friendship emerging from the womb of the earth. She offers relief from the collective trauma and diseases of the conquest, and a splendor arising from *flor y canto*—flower and song (Elizondo 1997). The patronage of the Virgin counters negative cultural constructions of farmworkers as dirty, unhealthy, or morally inferior and shifts the responsibility for work-induced illnesses to the responsible parties, including farm owners and chemical manufacturers.

Issue: Water as sacred—religious resistance to water pollution in south Asia

Religions sacralize rivers, lakes, and springs in a variety of ways. The Māori deem the *mauri* and *māna* of a stream critical to its health. In contrast, the churches of Flint were searching for water pure enough to baptize, but they did not link baptism with the spiritual essence of the Flint River. For Hindus, the deities, such as goddess Dewi Danu on Bali or the river goddess Yamuna, are "one in the same" with the water bodies in which they reside (Fig. 6.1) (Haberman 2006: 104). Hindus undertake pilgrimages to sacred rivers to perform **aartis** and **pujas** (acts of ritual worship) on the **ghats** (large steps or platforms leading to the water) or by wading into the flow (Fig. 11.1). Unlike baptism as a one-time initiation, these ritual practices continue through the life of a Hindu. Aside from offering direct contact with the goddess, bathing in and drinking the water of the Yamuna River purify the devotee, facilitating a deeper relationship with **Krishna**, and freeing the devotee from the goddess's brother, **Yama**—Death. Hymns to Yamuna articulate her beauty, generosity, compassion, and transformative nature. The *Yamunashtakam* by Vallabhacharya proclaims: "Joyously I honor Yamuna, the source of all spiritual powers. Her expansive sands shine as bright as the lotus feet of Krishna. Her waters are fragrant with lovely flowers from the lush forests on her banks.... She shimmers as her abundant foamy water cascades down from the peak of Mount Kalinda. Playfully she descends the high rocky slopes, moving eagerly for love..." (Haberman 2006).

Anthropologist Kelly D. Alley (2005: 75–93) has investigated the semantics of **multivalent or polyvalent terms**, including purity–impurity and cleanness–uncleanness for Hindus of Varanasi (Banares). Residents of the holy city have an especially close relationship with the Ganges River—spiritually, economically, and politically. The goddess *Gaṅgā* and the river itself are sources of purity and cleansing. The opposite is **gandagī** or anthropogenic waste materials entering the river, including human excrement, trash, soap from washing, and industrial effluent. Residents believe the sacred river can transport or dissolve the gandagī "via her purifying power." Many Hindus do not categorize offerings deposited in sacred waters as gandagī, but treat them as blessed objects. Among sacred materials cast into the Ganges and Yamuna are food, flowers, religious texts, and statues of deities (Fig. 11.1).

Although some residents of the Ganges' banks classify corpses as gandagī, the deceased have different properties relative to ritual purity than sewage or garbage. The purpose of cremation is to reduce the corpse to the five basic elements of earth, air, water, ether, and fire. Priests then immerse the ashes in the river to draw on her cleansing power and purify the soul of the deceased. Alley's (2005: 93–98) interviews found the pandas, religious specialists who assist pilgrims and conduct many of the rites along the river, classify corpses as gandagī. They, however, "insist that bodies and all other forms of gandagī cannot alter *Gaṅgā*'s power to give liberation (*mukti* or **moksa**) or to purify the ashes of the deceased. The power is eternal (*acyut*) and not subject to fluctuations in material reality." The purposes of bathing and ablutions with the waters of sacred rivers are similar—to remove sin and generate **moksa** (moksha) or liberation from **samsara**, the eternal cycle of death and rebirth. As Haberman (2006: 131–132) concludes, a river can be both dirty (*gandi*) and pure (*pavtra*), and Hindu concepts may not correlate with scientific definitions of water pollution or public hygiene.

Despite the inconsistencies between scientific and religious definitions of pollution, Hindu concern for ritual environments has motivated river clean-up campaigns. Economist Gopeshwar Nath Chaturvedi and lawyer M.C. Metha, for example, instigated litigation in the public interest to halt the release of untreated sewage effluents into the Yamuna River. Chaturvedi had a rude awakening when he led a group of pilgrims to the Vishram Ghat on the Yamuna in 1985. As they entered the river to bathe, they found themselves surrounded by red and green industrial dyes and floating dead fish. Dogs and crows were chowing down on carrion along the banks. On investigating effluent releases, Chaturvedi discovered that all the domestic sewage from the cities of Mathura and Vrindaban was reaching the river untreated. The problem had not been the absence of public health regulations but a lack of enforcement. Chaturvedi met with Metha at the holy center of Vrindaban in 1998 to launch the Indian National River Conservation Campaign (Haberman 2006: 141–149).

Metha has pursued environmental legal action since 1983, when he learned that acid rain was corroding the exterior of the Taj Mahal and damaging human lungs. Acting to protect India's people and architectural treasures, he filed his first environmental court case to constrain insidious air pollutants. Metha then tackled factories releasing industrial effluents after the Ganges caught on fire near the sacred pilgrimage center of Haridwar, in 1985. The discharges from merely two of the factories were so volatile that a mile-long stretch of the sacred river exploded in flames. Metha's arguments caused India's Supreme Court to order factories throughout the country to install pollutant controls protecting both air and water quality (Haberman 2006: 141–149).

Expressing relational values, Chaturvedi holds: "Yamuna is my Mother, and love for her is in my blood." All the key festivals for his family begin with a drink from the Yamuna or with bathing in her water (Fig. 11.1). They appreciate her blessings, and the intimacy of their relationship with the goddess. Metha similarly states: "I have a love for *Gaṅgā*.... Whatever Lord Krishna has said about Yamuna or the *Gaṅgā* is based on truth." Integral to Hindu heritage, the rivers are where the great sages have done *tapasay* (spiritual practices). Metha believes that imitating Western materialism is the root of India's environmental failures and that Americans are spiritually deficient as they "want something they don't have." For Metha, "the difference between the West and India is we love and worship our rivers" (Haberman 2006; 143–147).

Agency administrators have similarly recovered Hindu cosmology to forward pollution reduction. District Magistrate R.D. Paliwal describes Indian religion as "basically-nature loving," but believes the populace no longer treats the Yamuna as "a pious river"—a concept that "has to be utilized to achieve environmental health." In his public presentations, Paliwal has encouraged his audiences to emulate Krishna, who in the *Bhagavata Purana* rid the Yamuna River of the giant, poisonous serpent Kaliya (Box 9.2). Today, the industries discharging toxic waste are like the many poisonous heads of the serpent. Citizens must free Krishna's great love, the Yamuna from this grave danger, just as Krishna dispensed of Kaliya (Haberman 2006; 148–150). The power of ancient deities to inspire citizen activism suggests "modernizing" religion is not invariably necessary to tackling contemporary environmental health threats.

Not every Indian water manager, however, is optimistic about religion's ability to force recovery of sacred rivers. Unauthorized colonies and unsewered slums in India's sprawling cities continue to taint holy waters, despite court orders. Government-sponsored

> **Box 9.2 Versatile environmental recovery of religious stories**
>
> Indian environmentalists have recovered the story of Kaliya casting Krishna as an "eco-hero." The monstrous serpent's effusive poison had sickened the cattle of Krishna's cowherds and withered trees on the Yamuna's banks. Even birds flying over fell dead from the sky. Hindu gods and goddesses have vehicles or animal associates called ***vahanas***. When the god Krishna battled Kaliya, Krishna appeared briefly in his persona as the supreme deity, Vishnu. Vishnu's animal associate is Garuda, a serpent-eating eagle. As eagles and hawks do hunt and capture snakes, natural history parallels cosmic history. Here, divine merger with natural process returns balance to the aquatic system.
>
> Source: Sanford (2012: loc. 1404–1405)

treatment projects fall short of their deadlines. Corrupt officials divert funds, and bureaucracies fail to coordinate their efforts. Indian environmental researcher Gopal Krishna has concluded: "The claim to being religious and spiritual is fake, bogus. If people were really spiritual they would not let the rivers get polluted." He notes that although sacrilege adjoining a temple causes a public outcry, religious leaders do not respond in a timely way to water diversions or emerging pollution sources. Water specialist Himanshu Thakkar observes that stakeholders living along the rivers are no longer sharing river governance with the authorities. As urban lifestyles displace rural, Dehli's population has lost its connection with the Yamuna (Colopy 2012: 75–76). In 2018, toxic foam coated sections of the Yamuna and left intrepid pilgrims wading head-high into deep layers of white bubbles as they entered her holy flow (Fig. 11.1).

Yet Hindu religious leaders continue to promote environmental optimism and persistence. As the holy man and Ganges-advocate Pujya Swami Chidanand Saraswati exhorts: "The journey will be from filth to faith….The river has spoken for us for ages, for centuries. And now we must speak for her. We have taken baths in her for ages and now it is time for us to give her a bath." For the swami, replacing the day's aarti with a pledge to thwart cholera, hepatitis, and other waterborne diseases killing up to fifteen hundred Indian pre-school children daily, is a worthy exchange (Mallet 2017: 251–252).

Issue: Pollution obscuring iconography—Mongolian Buddhism and toxic air

Twisting semiotics, pollution can obscure or modify religious connections to natural features. Before the advent of air-blackening smokestacks and sprawling urban encampments of felt tents (*ger*) heated by soot-spewing stoves, Mongolian Buddhists looked to the crystal blue sky above them as a symbol of spiritual **enlightenment**. The sun's radiation pierced the crisp mountain air bathing the entire country in sparkling light. During the period when they governed Mongolia in the mid-20th century, the socialist administration brutally repressed Buddhism and persecuted the lamas. The secular government attempted to disassociate "enlightenment" from a spiritual state of perfect understanding and to redefine it as receiving academic education and aspiring to societal progress. The Marxist regime modernized by constructing coal-fired power plants with negligible pollution controls, which they called "Lenin's light." As Mongolia has converted to capitalism, unsustainable industries have contributed to the Marxists' perpetual brown haze in Ulaanbaatar. Periodic droughts decimate livestock on overgrazed steppes and blow tons of eroded soil into the city, further darkening the sky. Health professionals estimate that one in ten people who die in "the gasping city" are casualties of air pollution (Abrahams-Kavunenko 2019: 1–82).

Buddhist scholar Saskia Abrahams-Kavunenko (2019: 40, 120–121) finds many contemporary Mongols associate the "lack of spiritual clarity" and corruption that followed capitalism as having karmic effects "in opposition to enlightenment." The strangling haze is a product of greed rather than pure intentions. Buddhists "link environmental pollution (*bokhir*) to spiritual contamination (*buzar*)" and, in turn, to ill-fortune. The city is illness-inducing because minds are polluted. The contra process is purification and cleansing motivations, beginning with studying Buddhist teachings. The devout then implement visualization practices, such as focusing on an image of Bodhisattva Vajrasattva, often pictured in a scene with a clear flowing stream and a radiant blue sky. Regulating breathing as a meditative practice, Buddhists are deeply aware "the air we breathe is a foundation for life" (Abrahams-Kavunenko 2019: 198–199).

Much of Ulaanbaatar's populace view pollution and their inability to halt it as a "sign of moral degeneration." Other Buddhists, though, interpret pollution as "a condition of ignorance that, like the globalized economy, is something the urban population cannot see their way around or through." Ulaanbaatar is one of many cultural settings worldwide, where there is religious agreement concerning the undesirable spiritual roots of pollution. Yet lack of funds, insufficient technical expertise, and economic inequities act as barriers to instituting low-pollution energy alternatives. Contemplating an experience with dense winter smog in Bodh Gaya, India, where Buddha received enlightenment under the bodhi tree, Abrahams-Kavunenko summarizes: "As pollution literally smothers light and breath, it proclaims the urgency of our situation" (Abrahams-Kavunenko 2019: 119–141, 198–202).

Issue: Globalizing environmental health—the Gaia hypothesis

The growing recognition that environmental pollution is global in scale has resulted in repeated calls to maintain planetary health. In the 1960s, atmospheric chemist James Lovelock attached the name of the ancient Greek earth goddess, Gaia, to the planetary processes circulating gases like oxygen through living ecosystems. The **Gaia hypothesis** asserts that the thin organic layer covering the earth's surface and infusing the oceans interacts symbiotically to maintain conditions favorable to life itself. Author of *Lord of the Flies,* William Golding, suggested to Lovelock that Gaia, as an "earth mother," summarized the idea of a self-regulating biosphere (Ruse 2013: 4–7). Inventing instrumentation to measuring increasing CFC (chloroflourocarbon) levels in the atmosphere, Lovelock explicated the role of anthropogenic chemicals in generating the growing hole in the ozone layer over the Antarctic. The Gaia hypothesis helped to precipitate the regulations eliminating the release of destructive refrigerants and aerosols (Lovelock 2009: 209–210).

Cosmologists, evolutionary biologists, and other scientists have criticized the **monism** and **teleological assumptions** of the Gaia hypothesis. Theorists do not agree that the biosphere has goals of its own or any means to seek a perpetual balance (Box 9.3). Some scientists have been uneasy about the mythic roots of the name. The moniker did not, however, originate with contemporary Paganism. Repurposing Greco-Roman deities to generate memorable technical terminology is a normative scientific practice (volcanology, *Artemesia* as a botanical taxon, for example). Less skeptical than

Box 9.3 Teleology and monism

Teleological—In philosophy, the term means explaining phenomena, including the cosmos, in terms of their purposes. In theology, the term refers to God's design and purposes for material reality, or the difficult to prove assumption that the universe serves a divine purpose and has a predetermined end.

Monism—In philosophy, the concept that two different entities are one in the same. In theology, the concept there is only one deity, or more commonly, that there is no distinction between God and the world, or between the physical body and the soul. The German zoologist Ernst Haeckel, who coined the term ecology (*ökologie*) identifying the scientific field, was a leading 19th-century proponent of Monism as a personal belief system.

the scientific establishment, popular environmentalism has enthusiastically adopted the Gaia hypothesis. New Age, contemporary "goddess religion," and other alternative faiths have featured a universe with a preprogrammed end or installed Gaia in their eco-friendly pantheons. As the philosopher of science Michael Ruse (2013: 107) points out, the **organicism** or **holism** and invocation of **homeostasis** (system balance) so evident in the Gaia hypothesis have precursors in the formation of scientific ecology. Early 20th-century ecologist Warder Clyde Allee, for example, drew on his religious upbringing in the Society of Friends who emphasize the inner light and service in community. Allee played down the Darwinian emphasis on nature red in tooth and claw in favor of stressing the cooperation and integration critical to life.

Having little knowledge of the philosophical precedents, Lovelock was likely thinking of the world in terms of stark mathematical and physical models when he shaped the Gaia hypothesis. Brought-up as a Quaker, however, he remained open to the emphasis placed on transcendental experience during his childhood and retained a spiritual side receptive to William Golding's literary imagination. For his part, Golding was hardly a "conventional Christian," but had, as a young man, embraced Rudolf Steiner's **Anthroposophical** ideals and resided for a short period in one of Steiner's communities (Box 9.4). Believing in an accessible and rationally comprehensible spiritual realm,

Box 9.4 Anthroposophy and ecology

As a movement founded by Rudolf Steiner, **Anthroposophy** is an esoteric understanding of human existence that believes there is a spiritual realm accessible to the intellect and rational understanding. Anthroposophists took an early interest in **biodynamic farming** advocating the methods underlying permaculture. The movement has founded Camphill communities in multiple countries, where the residents seek "to connect care for the natural world with the other dimensions of their shared life." Rather than intentionally scaling-up, they pursue a symbiotic relationship with the life around them. Camphillers engage in **therapeutic ecology**, providing healthier lives for people, the land, and both domestic and wild species. While the movement has made major contributions to spiritual Gaianism, Dan McKanan (2018: 213) notes: "For Gaians, the earth is the ultimate object of devotion, and humans are merely a component of it. For Steiner, human evolution is the ultimate value, and the earth is merely one stage in that process."

Source: McKanan (2018 153–174, 204–214)

Box 9.5 William Golding's cosmology

Excerpt from Golding's 1983 Nobel Prize acceptance speech

[We] have been caught up to see our earth, our mother, Gaia Mater, set like a jewel in space. We have no excuse now neither for supposing her riches inexhaustible nor the area we have to live on limitless because unbounded. We are the children of that great blue white jewel. Through our mother we are part of our solar system and part through that of the whole universe. In the blazing poetry of the fact we are the children of the stars.

Source: Ruse (2013)

Steiner wished to "bridge the world of science and spirit." Golding, in contrast, held "both worlds are real," but there is no inherent bridge between them. For Golding, the language of religion and human relationships best conveys the beauty of the earth and human responsibility to her (Box 9.5). As an additional tie to Steiner, George Trevelyan, who had helped to translate anthroposophical ideas and convey them to the public, became an early religious advocate for Gaia. Trevelyan was a founder of the Findhorn Foundation and forwarded concepts of the New Age and the Age of Aquarius in the 1970s (McKanan 2018: 83–84).

Lovelock asserts his invocation of Gaia has helped to fill the moral vacuum left by mechanistic and indifferent science, as Gaia gives us "something to which we were accountable" (Ruse 2013: 171–186). Lovelock (2009: 159–162), however, considers the birth of the Gaia hypothesis coincident with the appearance of New Age religion as a reason "why so many scientists still regard it as part of the plethora of New Age nonsense that was around at the time." Having become a staunch advocate for curtailing climate change, the atmospheric chemist admits he was tempted to adopt a more scientifically pedestrian identifier, like earth system science. He is glad, though, he remained faithful to the name Gaia as it attracts attention to "the true nature of the climate threat we now face." In light of human reticence to limit greenhouse gas emissions, Lovelock credits Gaia's homeostasis with buffering humanity's foolishness. Lovelock (2009: 239) warns, though: "If we think of Gaia as old lady still quite vigorous but nowhere near as strong as the young planet that carried our microbial ancestors, it should make us realize more seriously the danger that we are to her continued healthy existence."

Today, the field of **environmental health** refers to human health, while **ecosystemic health**, **One Health**, and **planetary health** refer to living systems in general, expanding the quest for wellness to other species. One Health is based on the concept that environmental conditions harming flora and fauna are also damaging to humans.

Issue: Institutionalizing holism—early Greenpeace and the rise of Rainbow Warriors

Countercultural environmentalism has also contributed to holistic depictions of planetary health. Emerging from the social movements of the 1950s and 1960s, the ENGO Greenpeace launched its first ship in 1971. Departing Vancouver, Canada, the refitted fishing boat headed toward Amchitka, Alaska, carrying a message of peace into maritime zones where underground nuclear testing was imminent. Greenpeace's first venture drew on the Quaker anti-nuclear pacifism of the 1950s, and on the Friends' mode of "bearing witness"—"registering one's disapproval of an activity and putting moral pressure on the perpetrators simply through one's presence at the scene." British Friend Harold Steele was the first to envision sailing a yacht into a nuclear test zone. He failed, though, to raise a boat and crew when he attempted unsuccessfully to "bear witness" to a British weapons trial on Christmas Island in 1957 (Zelko 2013: 13–17).

In route, the Kwakiutl people of Alert Bay invited the Greenpeace crew ashore and offered a blessing for the mission and a gift of salmon to sustain the peacekeepers. The Kwakiutl assured the socially conscious sailors, "the wishes of all the Native Americans of the west coast went with them." Arrested by the US Coast Guard, Greenpeace's pioneer expedition never reached Amchitka. Standing around a sacred fire encircled by carved poles, the Kwakiutl initiated the all-male Greenpeace crew as brothers of the tribe on their return journey. The US government did detonate a nuclear weapon as planned but announced not long after they would conduct no further tests on Alaskan islands (Mompó 2014: loc. 495–542).

Five years later, Green Peace began using similar tactics to interfere with the capture of whales by factory ships—expanding the anti-nuclear NGO's environmental agenda. As historian Fred Zelko (2013: 151) summarizes: "Drawing on an eclectic and at times confusing mixture of biocentric thought, Eastern religion, New Age romanticism, and some controversial neuroscience, Greenpeace embarked upon a radically new way of protecting wildlife." President of Greenpeace Bob Hunter had taken a book entitled *Warriors of the Rainbow* with him on the first expedition to Alaska. Gathering narratives from Native American traditions, Native Alaskan William Willoya and nature writer Vinson Brown (1962) relate a prophecy attributed to Cree grandmother Eyes of the Fire who passed it on to her grandson. At some future time, Native Americans will recover their spirit, and instruct whites in ending war and halting the destruction of the earth (Zelko 2013: 87). In 1976, when a Greenpeace ship was preparing to launch a mission to interfere with whale hunting, Cree medicine man Fred Mosquito appeared at the farewell ceremony. He confirmed a Cree prophecy foretold of warriors of the rainbow, inclusive of the Greenpeace crew, who would unite all humanity in the protection of the earth. The following year, Greenpeace Britain acquired a faster ship to deploy in dividing the whalers from their quarry. Bob Hunter had passed his well-worn copy of Willoya and Brown (1962) on to the British, who decided to christen the versatile vessel the *Rainbow Warrior* (Weyler 2004: 397; Mompó 2014: loc. 557–578).

Consistent with New Age cosmology and Christian eschatology, *Warriors of the Rainbow* assumes a cosmic plan. A great light from the east will enlighten the warriors who introduce a new and far more beautiful civilization, clearing the polluted rivers and replacing wastelands and slums with forests. Echoing Isaiah, the prophecy declares: "In that day all peoples will be able to walk in wilderness flowering with life, and the children will see around them the young fawns, the antelope and the wildlife as of old. Conservation of all that is beautiful and good is a cry woven into the very heart of the new age." (Willoya and Brown 1962: 119) In promulgating rainbow iconography, Bob Hunter was merging the basics of systems ecology with a teleological view of time, promising ultimate universal success for Greenpeace's endeavors to protect the planet. For Hunter, ecological awareness was critical to a more holistic consciousness. Greenpeace would lead in mending a dysfunctional society and moving the earth toward an "organic and highly defined state of organization," which Hunter identified as "convergence" (Zelko 2013: 45–48).

Aside from playing a formative role in internationalizing environmental activism, early Greenpeace cultivated alternative religious perspectives within countercultural environmentalism. This mixture was to inspire a variety of forms of social resistance, including tree-sitting to prevent loggers from felling old-growth forests, gate-blocking at nuclear construction and fracking sites, and camp-outs intended to protect endangered species habitat from extractive industries. The image of the eco-warrior spread to even more aggressive organizations, such as Earth First! and Sea Shepherd, which engage in "**monkeywrenching**" or physically damaging the tools and vehicles of lumbermen, whalers, and drillers. While Greenpeace matured into a BINGO (big international nongovernmental organization), smaller ENGOs with specialized missions, like saving the redwoods, developed eco-rituals and celebrations. Often borrowing from indigenous religions, typical elements include sacred fires or smoke, drumming, and building altars with natural materials.

Comparative religious scholar Sarah Pike (2017) found that radical environmentalism has adopted the language of conversion and the earth transfigured. Rites of passage and initiation feature isolating forest experiences and nurture inclusivity via shared gatherings. Commitments to the cause are themselves a form of spiritual transformation. Eco-activists idealize childhood landscapes of "wonder and awe" and primal, untrammeled nature. They grieve the loss of old-growth, endangered species, and healthy ecosystems through ritual mourning and memorial poetry. The warrior mentality is associated with love for the wild, calls to holy war, martyrdom, and narratives of fallen combatants. **Apocalyptic doom** and its opposite, **contingent hope**, fuel warrior courage, and the belief primal beauty will rise again from the wastelands of misguided civilization. In an oft retold story, the first *Rainbow Warrior* fulfilled its destiny and became a martyr for the cause when French intelligence agents covertly planted explosives on her hull and sank her in Auckland harbor in 1985, killing a journalist in the process. The wrecked *Rainbow Warrior* had been on her way to bear witness at a French nuclear test (Zelko 2013: 111).

Issue: Continuing exposures—Buddhist response to the accident at Fukushima, Japan

Despite the regulation of CFCs, the termination of above-ground nuclear testing and other environmental successes, the 21st century has been facing equally sinister threats to environmental health. The 2011 tsunami-initiated "meltdown" and release of radioactive at the Fukushima powerplant in Japan evoked self-reflection among Japanese Buddhists, who have strived to eliminate nuclear armaments since the end of World War II. Much as modernity has constrained the role of Christianity in Britain, Japanese Buddhism has lost part of its cultural authority and become increasingly marginalized. With a declining number of active participants, Japanese Buddhism suffers from a distorted public image as "Funeral Buddhism"—a faith only relevant when departing the current life. Aligned with more traditional aspects of Japanese culture, Buddhism has assumed a socially conservative stance, thereby responding slowly to the risks of domestic nuclear power (Watts 2012: loc. 80–101).

For Buddhists, the healing and restorative outreach following the disaster of "3/11" consisted not just of attending to the material welfare of victims, but in offering **psycho-spiritual aid**. Priests immediately opened temples that were still standing as shelters for the displaced after the earthquakes and tsunami. Monks prepared meals and cared for the homeless. Priests conversed with the bereaved, conducted funerals, and sought out the scattered members of their temples. Engaging in restoration and mitigation, Buddhists sought to maintain the dignity and humanity of the suffering evacuees—often by small acts of support, such as holding a modest birthday celebration or a children's day camp. The laity pitched in, and as the crisis progressed, victims themselves became volunteers (Watts 2012: 886–1290).

The other half of coping with nuclear risks is the prevention of another disaster like Fukushima. For Buddhists, the precautionary is inherently linked to the philosophy of the material, eschewing unrelenting accumulation of wealth, and encouraging **Engaged Buddhism**, actively addressing social change. Professor of Asia-Pacific studies, Jun Nishikawa (2012) proposes carefully weighing Japan's plans for future development and rediscovering Buddhist spiritual values while forwarding autonomy, participation, and conviviality through the sangha. Nishikawa reasons the Buddhist philosophy of autonomy and self-sufficiency is contra to the individualistic value system and globalization, supporting the massive expansion of economic capital and material affluence. Buddhism is compatible with more endogenous (in place) community, where people find "their own meaning of life (*ikigai*) through the realization of a more non-violent (*ahimsa*) and sustainable type of development…," which is a step toward "a more convivial and peaceful world."

The crisis at Fukushima has opened Japanese society to **revalorizing** Buddhist teachings, "such as the personal attainment of universal truth, a moderate lifestyle and knowledge of self-sufficiency, understanding of causality through dependent origination, and conservation of the environment through an ethic of non-violence." In December 2011, the All Japan Buddhist Federation declared "the necessity of abolishing all nuclear power plants in the country." The Buddhist ethos makes this a realistic option for reducing environmental risk. Buddhist values can guide the nation toward finding greater personal satisfaction in *bhavana* or opening the self to enlightenment and converting the *tanha* or "grasping" driving the unrelenting desire for material possessions and wealth into *chanda* or "right effort to abandon grasping and the will to find out the truth" (Nishikawa 2012).

Conclusion: From iconography to action

These pollution cases prove the power of individual religious belief to sustain and inspire societal leaders from César Chávez to Gopeshwar Nath Chaturvedi. Popular piety, religious iconography, and shared rituals foster solidarity and the patience necessary to tackle persistent environmental failures. Religious expression can be deeply traditional, popular, alternative, or post-modern and serve as an anchor for constructive action. Centuries-old stories and symbols remerge as environmental lessons and means for enculturating the prognoses of environmental science. As voluntary associations within the context of modern secular states, Buddhist temples, African American churches, and other religious bodies act as foci of relief in emergencies, provide infrastructure, and contribute to the formation of larger coalitions. Articulating the interconnectedness of human actions with planetary outcomes, environmental scientists and political organizers have, in turn, adopted religious language to share their ideas with the public and to recruit new adherents to their causes. Global concerns like CFCs draw on religious imagery to forward holistic problem-solving. Synthesis of elements from diverse faiths, as in the origins of Greenpeace, has been evident in recent environmental campaigns, like the camps at Standing Rock. Apparently secular ENGOs like the Indian

National River Campaign and Greenpeace have arisen from unapologetically religious "aquifers."

In these pollution cases, idealizations of health-preserving human-nature relationships are often demonstratively gendered. Iconography invokes the divine feminine or the earth/river as maternal. The images evoke feelings of comfort, safety, and assurance of life's perpetual renewal. The ever-caring mother envelopes the world in peace and wellness. Drawing on visualizations of philosophical constructs such as enlightenment and purity prompts the examination of human motivations and responsibility for darkening skies and stinking waters. More universal conceptualizations of virtues such as non-violence, support practical solutions like Buddhist applications of *ahimsa,* and the economics of sufficiency to nuclear futures. Interestingly, Greenpeace and radical environmentalists, who owe much to the non-combative Quakers, adopted the persona of cosmic warriors and martyrs as they shifted their tactics from simple bearing witness to harassing whaling ships.

Considering the roles African American churches and Latinx popular piety have played in battling poisonous metals and misapplied pesticides, the assumption that people of color are not "interested" in the environment appears even more dissonant with reality. This misunderstanding is partially rooted in the rhetoric of the ENVIRONMENT as a consolidated cause defined by overarching threats like climate change, versus micro-mobilization to correct the specific economic and environmental abuses that wage laborers, immigrants, and ethnic minorities bear. Ritual immersion in Hinduism, African American churches defending of civil rights, and other community-building aspects of lived religion are natural conduits to tackling threats to environmental health. Informed by values like neighborliness and compassion, religions contribute to all six modes of addressing environmental health concerns from precautionary and regulatory, to responsive and healing, to restorative and compensatory.

Suggested readings

Abrahams-Kavunenko, Saskia. *Enlightenment and the Gasping City: Mongolian Buddhism at a Time of Environmental Disarray.* Ithaca, NY: Cornell University Press, 2019.

Alley, Kelly. *On the Banks of the Gaṅgā: When Wastewater Meets a Sacred River.* Ann Arbor: University of Michigan Press, 2005.

Bullard, Robert. *Dumping in Dixie: Race, Class, and Environmental Quality.* Boulder, CO: Westview Press, 1990.

Haberman, David. *River of Love in an Age of Pollution: The Yamuna River of Northern India.* Berkeley: University of California Press, 2006.

Patton, Kimberly Christine. *The Sea Can Wash Away All Evils: Modern Marine Pollution and the Ancient Cathartic Ocean.* New York: Columbia University Press, 2007.

Pike, Sarah. *For the Wild: Ritual and Commitment in Radical Eco-Activism.* Oakland: University of California Press, 2017.

Ruse, Michael. *The Gaia Hypothesis: Science on a Pagan Planet.* Chicago, IL: University of Chicago Press, 2013.

Watt, Alan. *Farm Workers and the Churches: The Movement in California and Texas.* College Station: Texas A&M University Press, 2010.

Watts, Jonathan, ed. *This Precious Life: Buddhist Tsunami Relief and Anti-Nuclear Activism in Post 3/11 Japan.* Yokohama, Japan: International Buddhist Exchange Center, 2012.

Zelko, Frank. *Making it a Green Peace: The Rise of Countercultural Environmentalism.* Oxford, U.K.: Oxford University Press, 2013.

10 Networks

Tackling global climate and sea change

Key concepts

1 The world's faiths are not mere spectators or ethical accountants relative to climate change but share in the consequences, such as sea level rise threatening thousands of religious communities and structures.
2 Climate and oceanic changes are stressing human communities by generating food insecurity, increasing environmental hazards like droughts, and modifying regional economies. Religious service organizations are already offering support to climate migrants and advocating for climate justice and relief for at-risk cultures.
3 Current technological containment strategies are not adequate to buffer the effects of atmospheric and oceanic changes.
4 Religions can build metaphysical resilience to address atmospheric change and its effects.
5 Faiths with higher degrees of organization and centralization may be better equipped to direct local social capital toward constructive responses to global environmental dilemmas like climate change.
6 Climate change inaction can originate from ontological insecurity, skepticism rooted in ideologically fueled distrust of science, or an embattled mentality driven by religious suspicion of secular culture.
7 Political ideologies supporting free-market economies encourage religiously based climate skepticism.
8 Climate stresses contribute to religious insurgencies and sectarian violence.
9 Religious directives addressing climate change advocate for humanitarian action relative to the economically disempowered and care for other species.
10 Religious institutions are experimenting with zero-carbon and green building planning.
11 Three principles of climate justice are the polluter pays, the beneficiary pays, and the stakeholders should remedy climate wrongs based on their ability to pay or capability to act.
12 Faiths are participating in climate change conversations, meetings, and declarations at the international level.

The challenge of zero emissions

The idea that anthropogenic releases of **greenhouse gases** could change the earth's climates precedes the environmental movement of the 1960s and goes back to the 19th century when physicists first verified the **greenhouse effect**. Today, computer models predict that industrial and agricultural emissions in concert with accelerated forest clearing will raise the earth's temperatures on average, albeit differentially among geographic regions. Rainfall and flooding will increase in some locales, and drought frequency will intensify in others, generating critical stresses on agriculture and creating conditions favorable for forest and grassland fires. Tropical diseases are likely to invade current temperate zones. The input of freshwater from melting ice caps and the expanding volume of warmer surface waters contribute to rising sea levels. As the oceans exchange gases with the atmosphere, they will absorb more CO_2, raising ocean pH (acidity), and modifying patterns of shell and skeletal formation for marine organisms like corals. Terrestrial and oceanic species will have to speedily relocate or suffer extinction by remaining in increasingly hostile habitats.

Production of **clean and renewable energy** continues as the most daunting challenge for sustainable industries. Alternatives to burning coal and petroleum also have negative environmental impacts. Renewable organic fuels, like wood and dried cow manure, degrade air quality via particulate matter. Production of ethanol from sugar cane and other crops requires inputs of energy and fertilizer, as well as removing tillage from food production. Construction of large dams generating hydroelectric power interferes with fisheries and submerges productive farmlands. Accidents have afflicted nuclear reactors. Wind and solar energy are both clean and renewable, although turbines do kill flying animals, and solar "farms" displace vegetation. Current technologies have substantial footprints in terms of the mining and transport of the materials required. On the positive side, in the United States, both wind and solar electricity are surpassing coal-generated power in cost-effectiveness. Chapter 5 examined religious interactions with fossil fuel extraction, the sacralization of modern industry, and programs to "green" religious symbols related to energy production. This chapter addresses the impacts of atmospheric and sea change on religion, reviews the religious roots of climate-change skepticism, and explores zero-carbon strategies at scales from those of faith-based institutions to international agreements.

Issue: sea level rise as a shared cultural heritage dilemma

The world's faiths are not mere spectators or ethical accountants relative to climate change but share in the consequences. A 2018 study of UNESCO (United Nations Educational, Scientific and Cultural Organization) world cultural heritage sites in the Low Elevation Coastal Zone encircling the Mediterranean Sea found 37 of 49 already at risk for a 100-year flood and 42 suffering from coastal erosion due to sea-level rise. In Istanbul, Turkey, the former Eastern Orthodox cathedral of Hagia Sophia, converted to a mosque under Ottoman rule, stands close to the harbor, and thus is subject to saltwater intrusion. Conservators are already dealing with subsidence under its massive dome, constructed over a geological fault. Istanbul's architectural treasure, the Blue Mosque (Sultanahmet), with its bold mountain-like profile, is nearby and equally vulnerable. Mediterranean World cultural heritage sites in danger include the Baha'i holy places in Haifa, Israel, Neanderthal cave paintings in Spain, and "old city" districts of Corfu, Acre, and Dubrovnik (Reimann et al. 2018). In the United States, religious, cultural heritage on receding shorelines incorporates such diverse properties as the archeological remains of the oldest English church at Jamestown settlement, Hawaiian coastal heiaus, and venerable houses of worship in subsiding cities like New Orleans (Fig. 1.2).

Sea level rise is a too edged threat because even if the earth's nations immediately eliminated carbon emissions, the climatological impacts of the greenhouse gases already released into the atmosphere and the melting of glaciers will continue for decades into the future. Technological defenses have their limitations as the floundering programs to defend Venice, Italy, and its historic churches prove. Exasperated by industrial groundwater pumping, Venice's elevated water table has been seeping into buildings and penetrating vulnerable materials like brick. The corrosion now reaches 6 meters and more up the walls of the Basilica di San Marco, an 11th-century Byzantine masterpiece. Architects have historically raised the church floor to keep up with sea change, but under current conditions, this would damage significant architectural features. In November 1966, a gale drove water from the adjacent lagoon into Venice. It flooded buildings, eliminated electrical power, and emptied sewage and oil storage into the streets. The polluted deluge washed over historic church frescos, furnishings, and marble facades (Fig. 10.1). Venice is losing population, and its tax base is eroding. Tourism rules the economy, as other businesses and industries disappear (Goodell 2017: 116–135).

Having banned groundwater pumping, the government selected among six options for action, ranging from raising the city further, to building a huge sea wall. They chose a proposal for mobile barriers at the three inlets to Venice's lagoon that could be raised in the face of an impending storm and block a surge of 3 meters. Beginning construction in 2003, Modulo Sperimentale Electromechanico (MOSE) planned for a mere 22 cm increase in sea level, while current predictive models indicate the increase could reach 180 cm by 2100. The acronym MOSE invokes the Biblical Moses, who commanded the sea to retreat, but technology does not have the divine authority of a prophet. The

Figure 10.1 St. Mark's Square, Venice, Italy, on the Adriatic, is already suffering from repeated inundation. A flood of two meters damaged many historic structures in 1966, and St. Marks experienced serious flooding again in 2019. The Basilica di San Marco is the church in the background.

Photo: Nov. 15, 2019, Filippo Monteforte, License from Getty Images

project has suffered from corporate corruption and fiscal overruns, raising the cost to over $6 billion (Goodell 2017: 116–135). In 2018 and 2019, autumn storms again inundated St. Mark's Square, as MOSE remained unfinished (Fig. 10.1). A first deployment of the 78 flood barriers in October 2020 did hold back storm driven surge, while the future of Venice's churches remains uncertain. Due to superior access to economic and scientific resources and more stable substrates, some world regions like the Netherlands or the New York City metroplex may be able to keep the ocean out of churches, temples, and mosques until the end of the century. Others, like Jakarta, Indonesia, are already planning to relocate or disperse in the face of unrelenting sea change.

Issue: Population impacts and climate migrants

The impacts of climate change and sea-level rise reach far beyond historic resources, as entire religious communities are in danger of life-threatening flooding. In the Mediterranean region, Alexandria, Egypt, with its beautiful mosques, Coptic churches, and archeological sites, is in a vulnerable geographic location. Due to upstream dams, the Nile delta lacks adequate input of transported sediments to counter erosion and subsidence. Fresh groundwater water is already becoming saline, and fishing villages are experiencing repeated inundation of homes. Marine scientists Mohamed Shaltout and Anders Omstedt (2015) have found 25% of the land area in the Nile delta region is already at or below the current mean sea level. Even a 10 cm increase will dramatically damage the north side's tourist beaches and fertile farms. Scientific models predict sea-level rise could eliminate 12.5% of Egypt's grain-producing lands and displace eight million of Egypt's citizens by 2100.

Climate change exasperates the food insecurity already faced by small farmers. The highlands of Central America, for example, are a region of seasonal rains, subject to **El Niño-La Niña cycles**. Current climate models predict an increase in low-rainfall years and deficient annual precipitation. Mayan family farmers are already cultivating small plots. They do not have adequate acreage to practice traditional **milpa**, where farmers clear openings in a forest on a rotation that allows organic matter and nutrient levels to recover as native trees reestablish on abandoned plots. According to climate scientists, average temperature could rise by 3–6 °C, and increasingly unpredictable rainfall could decline by 10–30% for Guatemala by 2100. Seven of ten of Guatemala's farmers already live below the poverty line, and about half of their children under five years old are malnourished. Guatemala has already suffered from a coffee blight encouraged by warming conditions and changes in coffee markets that have put many farm laborers out of work. Guatemala's government is assisting in installing new irrigation systems, but small-scale agriculturalists lack resources to switch cropping schemes (Pons et al. 2017; Moloney 2020).

An irony of these impacts is the failure of small farms generates more resource-bereft families who leave the land and seek other means for making a living. Worldwide, tens of thousands will join the ranks of climate migrants attempting to reach the US or European countries that have already contributed more than their fair share of greenhouse gases to the atmosphere. The countries diverting more government funds to "border crises" or "refugee crises" are caught in negative feedbacks as they withdraw monies that could be invested in programs for societal advancement, including those forwarding scientific research on sustainable energy. Social scientists have estimated between 50 and 200 million people will become climate migrants by 2050 (Pilkey et al. 2016).

Issue: Religion and resilience

Religious institutions and constituencies can perceive themselves as passive recipients of state guardianship, as potential sanctuaries and rescuers in the wake of natural disasters, or as active participants in building community **resilience**. In the United States, denominational offices provide packages advising houses of worship concerning preparation for hurricanes. Religious NGOs (nongovernmental organizations) assist evacuees. In dealing with climate and sea-level changes, environmental planner Timothy Beatley (2009) recommends against depending on hard structures, like levees and sea walls, as forms of intransigent **resistance**. A superior strategy enhances **environmental resilience** by closing high-risk zones to development, promoting building designs that can survive physical stresses, and maintaining protective ecosystem services that reduce erosion and flooding. For farmers, resilience requires expanding irrigation and planting genetic varieties and species adapted to changing temperature, rainfall, and invasive diseases. Anticipating and responding creatively to disturbances, planning for resilience emphasizes flexibility, adaptability, and durability.

Well-informed about current science, the First Nations of the Pacific coast have been studying their salmon and shellfish harvests relative to anticipated changes in rainfall, hydrology, and sea level. Recognizing their shoreline along the Skagit River delta is at increased risk for flooding, the Swinomish Indian Tribal Community (2010: 11–12) of Washington State has undertaken a climate change initiative. The Swinomish hold indigenous peoples are disproportionately vulnerable to climate change. Native Americans need to be free to utilize their indigenous knowledge for improving their circumstances without risk of misappropriation of that knowledge. The Swinomish perceive climate change as a threat to food security and community fabric—particularly ceremonial lifeways (Box 10.1). Their strategies emphasize relocation of organisms like clams that can be moved in response to shoreline recession, restoring depleted species like oysters, and protection in place—as feasible—for sacred ground and ritual locales.

Box 10.1 The importance of maintaining Swinomish ceremonial resources threatened by climate change

The climate plan approved by the Swinomish Indian Tribal Council (2010: 21) states:

"Ceremonial use [of natural resources] is more than the ceremonies and gatherings themselves. It also means the importance of giving thanks to the spirits of the natural resources when harvesting and preparing them, and the necessity to feed the spirit of oneself by consuming natural resource foods or feeding the spirit of a relative who has passed away by offering natural resources. Ceremonies, also referred to as gatherings, involve natural resources such as salmon, duck and clams are viewed as an important part of the food-sharing network. Ceremonies provide an environment in which healing can take place.... Community members look forward to ceremonies for the natural resources and the company as well as the spiritual significance. Ceremonies are the best way to reinforce ties to other community members and members of other tribal communities, and are especially important to elders, many of whom only have access to natural resources at these events throughout the year."

The precarious topography of The Alliance of Small Island States demonstrates the growing vulnerability of indigenous and regional religions to severe disruption and even extinction via sea-level rise. Their call to action is "1.5 to stay alive," as a global temperate increase of greater than 1.5 °C will cause a critical loss of land surface for the 44 member countries. The residents of islands at risk have been protecting reefs, beaches, and mangrove forests, thereby preserving resilient buffers against storm tides and salt-water intrusion. They have also sought trans-national platforms for drawing attention to their plight. In May 2014, Pacific islanders coordinated with Australian environmental groups who had been holding an annual climate protest. They formed a flotilla and paddled into the world's largest coal terminal, Newcastle, Australia. Australian mining companies have been exporting millions of tons of coal to Asian countries to fuel steel production and power plants. Australia continues to depend on domestic coal reserves to generate electricity. The Pacific Climate Warriors, as the protesters call themselves, hand-carved and decorated canoes to lead their fleet. Their maxim has been "we're not drowning, we're fighting" (Davidson 2019; Regan 2019).

In organizing for climate protests in 2019, the Pacific islanders composed a chant, *Matagi Mālohi*, identifying themselves with strong oceanic winds from "sacred spaces and revered places." They are "stewards of gifts from our old peoples," while the same ancestors who are calling them to belief also call them to unbelief so their "faith can take a new form." Recovering sacred crafts, the Climate Warriors celebrate the natural world with mats and *masi* (cloth) handmade from pounded and stained mulberry bark. They have selectively adopted Christian terms like the word "stewardship" and the Quaker tactic of "bearing witness," while at the same time reclaiming their narratives and traditional knowledge. The Islanders recognize, however, that other nations like Australia must act to curtail fossil fuel extraction to ensure **climate justice** (350 Pacific 2019).

Widely established in the South Pacific region via colonialism, Christianity can contribute to or undermine **metaphysical resilience**. A sociological study of adaptation to climate change in Tuvalu found that some Christian informants believed that Biblical promises made to Noah never again to flood the earth, and God's special relationship with the island would protect them. On the adaptive side, churches are more proximate locations for deploying **social capital** in response to disasters than government agencies are. In Samoa, the Red Cross has cooperated with church networks to distribute disaster and climate educational materials. As women are already part of the social fabric, working through churches has the benefit of being more gender inclusive than delivering education via government extension services. Conversely, church-based programming can exclude Muslims, Hindus, and other non-Christians. The reverse has occurred in predominantly Muslim Bangladesh, where the Christian minority has found themselves excluded from disaster preparation (Haluza-Delay 2014).

As sociologist Randolph Haluza-Delay (2014) reasons, faith traditions can be more expansive than their local manifestations. By forming affiliations across widely scattered islands and connecting to organizations outside their home region, churches extend their scale of activity and influence in time and space. Faiths with higher degrees of organization and centralization may be better equipped to direct local social capital toward constructive responses to global environmental dilemmas like climate change. Christianity, Islam, and other more strongly institutionalized faiths can mobilize aid networks and communications infrastructure linking the local to the national and transnational. The Australian Roman Catholic bishops have contributed monies to develop disaster and climate education for the Islands, as has Caritas, a coalition of

Catholic social ministries. The National Council of Churches in Australia has supported climate change initiatives for the Pacific Island States. The Pacific Conference of Churches has repeatedly articulated the critical nature of the growing threat to low-lying coasts. In turn, the World Council of Churches and the Geneva Interfaith Forum on Climate Change, Environment and Human Rights have distinguished Polynesia and Micronesia as regions of gravest concern relative to **climate justice**.

Issue: Ethical disinterest and skepticism concerning climate change

Not every faith community supports weaning the earth's economies of fossil fuels. The reasons religionists remain disengaged range from competing priorities for action to **climate fatalism**—the belief that little can be done to halt the inevitable. The most politically virulent barrier is **climate skepticism** (denial) that holds recent climate change is not due to anthropogenic causes or that its impacts are minor and over-stated by scientists. Based on survey data, sociologist Kari Norgaard (2011: 63–93) argues that lack of information does not explain the behavior of Norwegian citizens who know about climate change and do not take action. **Hierarchy of needs** explanations can account for rationalizations like "the need to drive automobiles" but are insufficient "to explain public apathy on the larger social level." Nor were her Norwegian informants failing to respond because they were "too greedy or individualistic, and suffer from incorrect mental models or faulty decision-making processes…" Global environmental change "raised fears for the future, feelings of helplessness, and feelings of guilt, some of which were, in turn, threatening to individual identity." Well-educated, media-savvy citizens were not implementing social correctives because the issue is generating risk and threatening their **ontological security**, incorporating the construction of personal meaning and a collective sense of identity. Norwegians who have benefited financially from North Sea petroleum extraction do not wish to be identified as "bad people" or as harming others. They thus avoid discussing emissions, and, as a consequence, delay collective action.

A survey conducted in 2011 by the Public Religion Research Institute in cooperation with the American Academy of Religion found that a mere 5% of US respondents thought climate change is the most critical issue facing their country. Only 33% of Americans believed they would experience significant harm from climate change, while 56% of respondents believed that people living in developing nations would experience severe damaging impacts. Americans did not find the issue to be of critical importance to their futures. Only 36% of Americans (all faiths) who attend religious services at least twice a month reported that their clergy preach or teach about climate change often or occasionally. A third indicated their clergy never spoke on the topic (Jones et al. 2014: 1–3).

A potential source of climate misunderstanding is **apocalypticism** or **millennial beliefs** supported by Biblical interpretation predicting the proximate return of Christ's divine rule following a series of planet-wide catastrophes. In this genre of climate fatalism, termed "end-time apathy," protecting the atmosphere is a low priority as God will destroy the sin-riddled sphere in any case. Christ, as regent, will create a new natural order and new earth. According to Jones et al. (2014), 62% of Americans overall believed recent natural catastrophes are fueled by climate, while 49% viewed them as signs of the Biblical "end times."

For Americans, political alignments and party membership are better predictors of individual beliefs about climate than theological preferences like Calvinist or

Methodist. The survey administered by Jones et al. (2014) divided respondents into climate Believers, Sympathizers, and Skeptics. Not surprisingly, approximately two-thirds of Democrats (65%) were Believers, as opposed to 22% of Republicans and 23% of members of the now partially defunct Tea Party. The Tea Party had the highest percentage of skeptics at 53%. Ethnicity was significantly correlated to perspectives on climate with 71% of Latinx Americans, 57% of African Americans, and a mere 43% of whites very or somewhat concerned (Jones et al. 2014). The AME statement recognizing climate as differentially harming blacks is a part of a greater matrix of variable Christian perception of climate risks (Box 9.1).

Issue: Industrial lobbies and the credibility of scientific findings

In the throes of the Cold War, scientists, engineers, and government administrators who believed communism was a dire threat to the political and personal freedoms of the west promoted the well-stocked nuclear arsenals of NATO (North Atlantic Treaty Organization). According to historians of science Naomi Orestes and Erik Conway (2010), federally employed scientists initially challenged the scientific evidence supporting nuclear risk assessments to counter the anti-nuclear movement. Atomic energy advocates, such as Fred Singer, cast doubt on scenarios predicting nuclear winter could turn the earth into a sunless, freezing terrain. Seeking alliances with corporations and conservative think-tanks, some of the detractors aided tobacco companies in their efforts to discredit evidence that inhaling nicotine elevated the risk of cancer and other illnesses. More recently, fossil fuel corporations interested in slowing legislative action on climate change have funded the contrarians. Sociologists Riley Dulap and Peter Jacques (2013) examined 108 books contesting climate change published by 2010 and found 72% received backing from conservative think tanks, who had either funded the authors or disseminated their ideas.

Orestes and Conway (2010) posit nuclear and climate risk skepticism has two ideological bases: communism and socialism are insidious threats, and the **free market economy** is critical to the American way of life. The opponents of climate science depict environmentalists as "watermelons"—green on the outside and red (leftist) on the inside. Inherently anti-regulatory, the contra-environmental agenda intends to hobble the EPA (Environmental Protection Agency) and tone down climate impact assessments by the US National Academy of Science and advisories like the **IPCC** (International Panel on Climate Change). Organizations with an Evangelical Protestant base also participate in and bankroll conservative think tanks and political coalitions. Utilizing rhetoric mirroring the "merchants of doubt," Christian climate skeptics spread the message—the science is uncertain, scientists do not agree, and the experts are self-interested.

Issue: Religious campaigning against climate action—the Christian Right

Interdisciplinary environmental scholar Robyn Globus Veldman (2019: 69–85) has weighed the end-times apathy hypothesis. She found that some Christians taking anti-environmental positions have publicly articulated the "God's going to burn it anyway" argument. Others, however, have been misquoted. American Evangelicals can be **pre-millennial** (Christ returns before the earth's demise), **postmillennial** (Christ returns after the onset of catastrophic events), or **amillennial** (the return of Christ is figurative and is a transformation in the heart of believers). Veldman utilized research focus groups in premillennial and amillennial churches to conduct an in-depth inquiry into the impacts of these beliefs on the environmental ethical values of individuals. While encountering "hot millennialists" for whom the prophesied end times were a consuming interest, she found most of her informants were "cool millennialists" for whom "end-time beliefs were not a daily preoccupation."

Norgaard (2011: 79–80) found **political alienation** was not prevalent enough among Norwegians to explain indifference to climate change. Veldman (2019: 86–113), in contrast, hypothesizes another American Evangelical characteristic, "the embattled mentality" or sense of continual attack from the secular culture, is a significant driver of climate skepticism. Christian fundamentalists have been wrestling with the perceived secularization of American education and the "godless" universities since the late 19th century. Favoring a "big god," Evangelicals picture a parental giant in control of the physical realm. The concept of anthropogenic global change is thus an offense to divine sovereignty and denies God's **omnipotence**, replacing it with human authority. Climate change becomes a competing eschatology, undermining the belief that God's power directs the future. For "embattled Evangelicals," environmentalists arise from the secular elites threatening to displace Christian values. Evangelical alignments with politicians who favor free markets, deregulation of corporations, and restraint of an overly controlling government spur the distrust.

The initial Evangelical theological response to the post-1960s environmental movement was predominantly supportive. Respected Presbyterian theologian Francis Schaeffer (1970) penned a reply to Lynn White, Jr., rejecting the concept that Christianity was hopelessly anthropocentric. He argued that Christians were responsible for halting degradation as God was the "true owner" of the planet. A mix of scientists and theologians, including ecologist Calvin DeWitt and Reformed theologian Loren Wilkerson, furthered rubrics of "earthkeeping" and "creation care." In 1993, the Evangelical Environmental Network (EEN) consolidated as a subsidiary of Evangelicals for Social Action. Cooperating with ENGOs (environmental nongovernmental organizations), the EEN mounted a successful political campaign to deter the US Congress from weakening the US Endangered Species Act. Ideology began to splinter Evangelicals when theologian E. Calvin Beisner countered the earthkeepers by casting doubt on their Biblical interpretation and justifying the Christian duty to "forceful rule" of the Creation. Like the "merchants of doubt," Beisner's polemic lionizes the benefits of **neoliberal** industrial capitalism. His Cornwall Alliance has garnered funding from ExxonMobil and politically conservative foundations. As the anti-environmental Christian backlash strengthened, the newly formed Evangelical Climate Initiative published an "Evangelical Call to Action" in 2006, with the supporting signatures from a multi-denominational cadre of Evangelical ministers and academics (Zaleha and Szasz 2014).

Veldman (2019: 161–189) found that rather than encouraging Christians to adopt sustainable energy, several influential evangelists, television personalities, and political pundits replied to the Evangelical Climate Initiative by utilizing their sophisticated media platforms to promote climate skepticism as the Biblically correct position. Among them were Pat Robertson, who founded the Christian Broadcasting network, James Dobson, who established the parachurch ministry Focus on the Family, and Jerry Falwell, Jr., who had taken over the presidency of Liberty University from his father. Falwell invited

Lord Christopher Monckton to speak at a university convocation, where Monckton proclaimed the intellectual deficiencies and fallacies of climate science. With Falwell's blessing, Monckton referred to Al Gore's widely viewed film, *An Inconvenient Truth*, as a "Mawkish, sci-fi, comedy horror movie dreamt up by a P.R. guy" (Mayhew 2009).

The Evangelical Climate Initiative statement elicited a strong reaction because it challenged the authority of the Christian Right, who were protecting their hold on the laity and their well-cemented political ties. In supporting the climate initiative, "New Evangelicals" and more progressive pastors resisted, in the belief that ultra-conservative agendas dismiss critical social issues and contribute to political polarization in an already divided Christian populace (Veldman 2019: 190–214). In toto, the inconsistent American Christian response to climate change is rooted in complex political alliances, vulnerability to pseudo-science, the influence of large corporations, perceived economic self-interest, and the fragmented sectarianism of American Protestantism.

Issue: Religions forwarding violence under climate stresses

Climate skepticism is not the only negative or ill-adapted religious response to climate change. Natural and anthropogenic climate stresses are drivers of political instability resulting in intrastate and international conflicts. Social scientists Cullen Hendrix and Idean Salehyan (2012) have found that extreme fluctuations in rainfall serving as environmental shocks are precursors to violent events in Africa. They concur with the IPCC that "Climate change and variability are likely to impose additional pressures on water availability, water accessibility and water demand in Africa." The fringes of the Sahara Desert are experiencing declining rainfall, which, in combination with deforestation, is stressing Muslim populations. They abandon their lands and move south into regions where Christians have settled. Nomadic pastoralism can no longer weather the drought cycles, and young householders are unable to support their families. Deficient access to land tenure, insufficient infrastructure, unemployment, and unresponsive governments act synergistically with crop failures and water shortages to ignite civic unrest (Griswold 2018). Preexisting interreligious tensions and the formation of religiously framed or sectarian insurgencies contribute to civilian deaths and the generation of refugee populations, straining civic resources and burdening neighboring countries. Prolonged warfare, in turn, exacerbates environmental degradation and stymies economic recovery from environmental stresses. Among the climate-related events contributing to the "Arab Spring" with its concomitant flood of refugees beginning in 2010 were poor harvests in Russia raising food prices internationally and prolonged droughts in the Middle East and North Africa (Perez 2013).

The economic fallout from climate stresses fueled the emergence of ISIS (Islamic State of Iraq and Syria) as an Islamic insurgency. Claiming standing as a sovereign state, ISIS captured high-value extractive resources—ironically commandeering petroleum production. Circa 2015, ISIS controlled the territory surrounding Syria's oil fields, and smuggled oil to local traders or over the border to Turkey and Iraq, receiving an estimated 40 million dollars per month in revenue (International Wire 2015). The ISIS strategy perceived foreign and corporate economic interests as the problem, and Arab management of natural resources via the "caliphate" as the solution, without addressing fossil fuels as a potential driver of deteriorating regional economies. As investigate journalist Eliza Griswold (2018) reasons, "labeling the violence simply 'religious' obscures our role and responsibility in creating the conditions for conflict, which lies in part in the wreckage of the colonial project and in postcolonial support for despicable puppet leaders. The factor unfolding right now is the pressure brought by the extreme weather of a rapidly warming planet. We blame the creeds when the conflict is driven by the failure to address the man-made environmental crisis unfolding around us."

Issue: Seeking solidarity within a denomination—*Laudato Si'*

Despite turmoil among conservative American Protestants, multiple Christian denominations have issued statements identifying climate change as a critical moral concern. Pope Francis's Encyclical Letter, *Laudato Si'* carefully selects Roman Catholic teachings concerning the Creation and presents them in language accessible to the laity. The title originates with a canticle by Saint Francis of Assisi, which begins "*Laudato si', mi' Signore*"—"Praise be to you, my Lord, through our Sister, Mother Earth, who sustains and governs us, and who produces various fruit with colored flowers and herbs." For Pope Francis (2015: 7–54), the earth is "our common home," and climate is "a common good, belonging to all and meant for all...linked to many of the essential conditions for human life." Identifying nature as a locus of divine presence, Pope Francis gently but directly addresses problematic interpretations of Christian cosmology. He handles the question of "the last days" by reminding Catholics the risen Christ has already "attained the fullness of God," available in the present as well as the future. Legitimizing the non-human as moral subjects worthy of ethical consideration, the Encyclical declares, "The Spirit of life dwells in every living creature and calls us to enter into relationship with him" (Box 10.2).

The leader of the planet's 1.2 billion Catholics laments the co-occurrence of human and natural environmental deterioration afflicting "the most vulnerable people on the planet..." For Francis, "a true ecological approach *always* becomes a social approach; it must integrate questions of justice, so as to hear both *the cry of the earth and the cry of the*

Box 10.2 Cosmology in *Laudato Si'*

Pope Francis (2015: 40–63) corrects multiple points of theological confusion concerning the environment:

The concept of creation is not limited to the material

In *Laudato Si'*, "the word 'creation' has a broader meaning than 'nature' for it has to do with God's loving plan in which every creature has its own value and significance."

God did not mandate wanton exploitation of the earth

Pope Francis writes, "We are not God. The earth was here before us and it has been given to us. This allows us to respond to the charge that Judeo-Christian thinking, on the basis of the Genesis account which grants man dominion over the earth (cf. Gen. 1:28), has encouraged unbridled exploitation of nature by painting him as destructive and domineering. This is not a correct interpretation of the Bible as understood by the Church....The biblical texts are to be read in their context, with an appropriate hermeneutic, recognizing that they tell us to 'till and keep' the garden of the world (cf. Gen 2:15)."

Divine futures do not justify environmental neglect

The encyclical states, "The ultimate destiny of the universe is in the fullness of God, which has already been attained by the risen Christ, the measure of the maturity of all things."

poor." One of the strengths of the Encyclical is it establishes a theological foundation for tackling environmental issues of all origins, from land tenure to toxics, while also being very definite about the urgency of curtailing industrial modification of atmospheric chemistry. The directive acknowledges climate change is anthropogenic. It identifies barriers to global environmental progress, including the foreign debt of poorer nations, weak international political response, and "many professionals, opinion makers, communications media and centers of power being located in affluent areas...." Reducing greenhouse gases will be challenging and requires the mature virtues of "honesty, courage, and responsibility" (Pope Francis 2015: 17–39).

Catholic political and theological conservatives find Pope Francis too oriented toward modifying the economic order, and too welcoming of socialists and suspected Marxists. On the liberal side, critics identify *Laudato Si* as anti-modernist. Many environmentalists disagree with the Encyclical's (2015: 32) assertion that "while it is true that an unequal distribution of the [human] population and available resources creates obstacles to development and sustainable use of the environment, it must nonetheless be recognized that demographic growth is fully compatible with integral and shared development." Yet *Laudato Si'* elevates climate change to a high ethical priority for all Catholics and calls explicitly for humanitarian action relative to the economically disempowered, and as a corollary to climate migrants. Parishes worldwide have responded via programs ranging from eco-retreats to solar-powered parochial schools.

Protestant moderates have also focused on economics as spawning climate wrongs. Accentuating the political context of the New Testament and Jesus's and St. Paul's resistance to Roman oppression, Lutheran Carol Robb (2010) asserts Christianity's call to relieve the poor and free the captive justifies climate activism. Anglican Michael Northcott (2007) identifies mindless Neo-liberalism and western affection for unregulated free markets as fonts of dependence on fossil fuels. He believes Christians should respond by slowing their pace of life and rooting themselves in their home communities. Northcott (2013: 206) questions the Neo-liberal assumption that "the only proper way in which rival conceptions of the good can be arbitrated is in the marketplace itself." He argues (2013: 243–258) liberal economic theory provides inadequate defense against climate change because it holds "individuals achieve flourishing only when they are free to maximize their interests by maximizing their preference for goods which they themselves individually chose." Instead, Christians should situate virtue in "the history of divine creation and redemption" emerging from divine love and forgiveness.

Issue: Seeking consilience within a world religion—Buddhists unifying over climate change

Other religions with multiple philosophical schools have not split as dramatically along sectarian lines concerning climate change as American Christians have. Buddhists have striven for consilience, among national branches in Asia and between East and West. Such diverse figures as American Buddhist scholar Joanna Macy, the Fourteenth Dali Lama, and Vietnamese Zen Buddhist monk Thích Nhất Hạnh have offered guidance (Stanley et al. 2009). Buddhism, though, has many strands, ranging from the Thai ecology monks with their grassroots activism to the leaders of military governments or insurgencies, for whom the environment is a low priority.

Like the pursuit of a non-nuclear Japan, Buddhist decision-making concerning climate draws on their philosophy of the material. Bhikkhu Bodhi (2009), an American

Theravada monk, asserts the "two complementary pillars, wisdom and compassion" can serve as diagnostic tools, and expose "underlying causation." Compassion provides new insights, as "through compassion, our hearts feel the danger vividly and personally, and thereby expand to embrace all those exposed to harm: All who, like ourselves, are subject to suffering, who seek peace, well-being, and happiness." Unmitigated greed on the part of energy corporations and fear of their industries' collapse, unfortunately, hamstring wise governance. Entrenched delusion and the general population's insatiable desire for the material prevent humanity from recognizing their behaviors are leading to the catastrophic modification of the earth's atmosphere. The **Buddhist principle of sufficiency** would, in contrast, displace "the principle of commodification" and the hegemony of the free market with the idea that "the key to happiness is contentment rather than an abundance of goods."

Exiled Tibetan lama, Ringu Tulku (2009) similarly explains climate conflicts arise from the human inability to understand interdependence, and "our failure to understand phenomena are impermanent." Truth promotes selflessness, concern for collective welfare, and gross national happiness. Delusion breeds "greedy consumerism and its side effects of competition, dissatisfaction, anxiety, and pollution." Taking the **bodhisattva path** means relieving suffering. Tulku concludes: "Clearly it is a vitally important bodhisattva activity to prevent a universal disaster like the collapse of our living world."

Issue: Different paths to climate accountability

Buddhism's emphasis on contentment points to a division in approaches to grappling with the practical aspects of **carbon neutrality**. The world religions all forward sharing material wealth, and all practice some form of self-restraint or asceticism. One path is reducing consumption of problematic products—not just gasoline but wood from threatened forests and grain-fed beef. Constraining food waste is climate-friendly, as is limiting air travel. Different religious traditions, however, have different spiritual goals and different baselines for "moderation." Buddhists, Hindus, and Roman Catholics distinguish between the stricter standards set for ascetics and monastics and expectations for the laity. Protestant simplicity has not historically been low footprint in terms of materials (Chapter 5). Historic rationales for simple lifestyles center on self-control, reduction of desire, personal purity, and service to the poor. They thus require adaptation to the global context of greenhouse emissions. In practical terms, however, reducing consumption of fossil fuels by a third or a half, delays rather than halting anthropogenic climate change.

A virtue of religion is its community-building capabilities. A second path is to implement restraint via sustainability-based social units. Designated in 1998 by the UN-Best Practice Unit as a model for sustainable living, Findhorn has grown into an **Ecovillage**. As of 2018, Findhorn had roughly 700 members living in the original settlement and surrounding area and welcomed 12,000 residential guests annually, who enjoy sustainable meals as a form of spirituality. The Ecovillage manages a woodland for firewood production. In struggling to cap its carbon emissions, Findhorn takes responsibility for the burning of fossil fuels supporting the travel of its residents and transnational visitors. They run a carpool and have purchased electric vehicles they power from their windmills. A 2006 study rated Findhorn as the community with the lowest **ecological footprint** of any they had measured in more industrialized nations. Although many idealistic utopian settlements disband in a few years, a core of practical visionaries and a religiously framed commitment to changing the world have sustained Findhorn's evolution from caravan camp to an internationally recognized demonstration site for carbon neutrality (Forster and Wilhelmus 2005; Meltzer 2015: 3–18; East 2018).

Issue: Tradition and innovation—sustainable technology for historic ecclesiastical buildings

Embedded in Findhorn's strict carbon accounting is the acceptance of technological innovation. The third path to curtailing modification of atmospheric chemistry is furthering sustainable engineering. In the more industrialized nations, public resistance to collateral damage in constructing photovoltaic arrays and wind farms has spatially displaced or even halted alternative energy initiatives. Gleaming white turbines have been particularly controversial looming over quaint villages and nearshore locations on scenic coasts, like Cape Cod, US. Religious institutions similarly find themselves seeking thoughtful accommodation of the contemporary within the framework of tradition. They face challenges in adapting historic buildings to sustainable technology. Religious architecture is not mere drama or convenience but conveys cosmology, values, community identity, and relationships to nature.

Gloucester Cathedral of St. Peter and the Holy Indivisible Trinity (Anglican) has been exceptionally adventurous in their erection of a solar array on their central vaulted roof topping a massive **nave** dedicated in 1100 CE (Fig. 10.2). The Cathedral has multiple unique or irreplaceable features, including the largest surviving medieval stained-glass window in the U.K., the original stone vaults over the quire (choir) and altar, the tomb of King Edward II, and entrancing gargoyles. Readers of this text may have seen this Cathedral serving as an authentic filming location for such diverse productions as three of the Harry Potter series, a Doctor Who Christmas special, and the 2018 film *Mary Queen of Scots* (West 2011; Gloucester Cathedral 2019).

Despite support by stout stone pillars from the Norman era, adding additional weight to the roof required cautious engineering. Twentieth-century strengthening of the vaults by removing oak beams and replacing them with steel (no longer an approved method of historical restoration) has contributed to adequate loadbearing. A local solar energy firm, Mypower, carefully aligned the photovoltaic cells on a nonpenetrating fixed-rail frame to avoid damaging the medieval lead roofing (Fig. 10.2). The relatively

Figure 10.2 Gloucester Cathedral, U.K. The dean blesses the new solar panels over 11th-century nave and the historic lead roof.

Photo: Mypower, Inc., U.K.

low angle of the eaves and the high stone pediment enclosing the roof ensure the solar panels are invisible from the street. Visitors taking a guided tour and climbing the 269 steps to the mid-15th century tower can glimpse the photovoltaics if they peer down over the edge of the stonework. Most explorers, though, are unconcerned about "Gothic solar."

With its origins as an Anglo-Saxon abbey, Gloucester Cathedral is one of the oldest buildings in the world to generate electricity from the sun's radiation. In 2016, the Dean of the Cathedral put on a hard hat and climbed to the roof to bless the completed photovoltaic array, adding ecodimensionality to the endeavor (Fig. 10.2) (West 2011; Mypower 2016; Gloucester Cathedral 2019). Not all U.K. historic church or cathedral plans for energy sustainability have garnered approval, and new applicants must successfully pass through a multiphase process of formal review. In addition to affirmation from consulting historic architects and a Diocesan Advisory Committee, a church with bats in its belfry must ask Natural England for a bat license, before placing solar panels on the roof.

Issue: Energy infrastructure and religious polity

In 2003, St. Olaf's College, Minnesota (Lutheran) became the first US liberal arts college to join forces with a corporate wind provider, Xcel Energy, and invest in a utility-grade wind turbine. Named for a saint, Big Ole accounts for about a quarter of campus electrical demand. In pursuit of a zero-carbon campus, St. Olaf's have renovated their steam plant that heats campus buildings to improve efficiency. Achieving 100% carbon-free electricity, the college rents about 20 ha of land to solar developers and subscribes to a solar "garden," providing about 40% of their power. The staff manages the St. Olaf Natural Lands for carbon sequestration. They have restored many acres formerly in tillage to carbon gobbling native vegetation (St. Olaf's College 2020). Luther College, Iowa, cares for historic campus grounds planned by Jens Jensen, an influential American landscape architect who designed environments for Frank Lloyd Wright's buildings. In conjunction with their stewardship of Jensen's mix of meadows and woods, Luther College (2020) has also invested in a campus wind turbine. They intend to be "a place that joins pragmatic action with academic exploration and moral courage in the area of environmental sustainability." Both Lutheran colleges have turned the potential visual intrusion of an industrial-scale turbine into an icon of community care. Wooden farm windmills pumping water are symbolic of pioneer adaption to the mid-American prairies, and Big Ole continues the tradition.

In encouraging Luther College students to participate in Climate Justice Week, ethicist James Martin Schramm (2019) invoked German theologian Dietrich Bonhoeffer, who was executed by the Nazis during World War II. In 1942, Bonhoeffer lamented the German Christians who thought it "impious to hope for a better future on earth and to prepare for it…," and who withdrew "in resignation or pious flight from the world, from the responsibility for ongoing life, for building anew, for the coming generations." Synthesizing Lutheran history with current dilemmas, Schramm expressed his concern that 21st century Christians were similarly withdrawing from the struggle to curtail climate change and abjuring their duties to future generations.

To raise capital for institutionally owned power generating technology, English houses of worship combine monies from diverse sources, including donations, grants, and even national lottery profits. In return for the fiscal outlay, Gloucester Cathedral's solar will reduce energy costs by about 200,000 British pounds over 25 years. As Mallory McDuff (2010: 57–70) documents, smaller and less affluent religious congregations find the high cost of commercial energy drains their budgets. They consult with RENGOs (religious environmental nongovernmental organizations), like Interfaith Power & Light, to devise green building plans. Pullen Memorial Baptist Church, Raleigh, North Carolina, for example, calculated geothermal heating for a new parish hall would cost $170,000, but savings of $6,000 per year in utility bills would recover $300,000 to the church budget over 50 years. On-site zero-carbon technology has the advantage of making the environmental commitment obvious to members and visitors. It avoids the hypocrisy of encouraging members to personally sustainable lifestyles, without taking action institutionally.

As St. Olaf's participation in a solar garden demonstrates, a practical, lower capital investment strategy is to join a consortium. Religious universities and colleges can obtain favorable commercial contracts at reduced costs as they are relatively large users, expending as many kilowatt-hours as a small town. Located in central Texas, where wind power is a thriving enterprise, Baylor University (Texas Baptist Convention) has received environmental recognitions, like becoming a Sierra Club "Cool School" for contracting wind-generated electricity from a corporate distributor. In 2007, Baylor initially estimated savings of two million dollars per year or 20 million over ten years from its wind power agreements. Joining a consortium is less obvious to the public yet builds the market for zero-carbon power and stimulates technological innovation.

All the above emissions reduction projects have the commonality of strategic plans which are compatible with the **polity** of the denomination. Baylor University was the first academic institution in the central Texas region to encourage its architects to sketch blueprints worthy of energy-saving **LEED certification** (Leadership in Energy and Environmental Design). Their initial sustainable building venture was part of a campaign to construct the new George W. Truett Seminary during a period of theological battling among Southern Baptists and within regional Baptist conventions. Through the early 20th century, Truett, as the namesake, was active in raising funds for Baptist schools, orphanages, and hospitals, thereby modeling civic responsibility. Certified in 2009, the university's first LEED building with its embedded chapel is a symbolic synthesis of Baptist commitment to participation in local civic welfare and the centrality of shared worship and preaching in Baptist life. Baylor has since hired a sustainability coordinator and extended LEED initiatives to the new business school and the Allison Practice Field, a LEED-certified indoor football facility receiving commendations for innovation (U.S, Green Building Council 2020).

The inherent Evangelicalism of Baylor and Baptist emphasis on community service prompt environmental action in spheres bridging church and state, and building the regional clean energy economy. Blessing the photovoltaics and referencing Dietrich Bonhoeffer open similar conduits to heritage and civic responsibility. McDuff (2010) identifies creating sacred space as a genuine ministry, and reasons the resulting care for Creation draws Christians closer to God (Box 10.3). LEED is not just about climate, but packages multiple sustainability concerns together, including water conservation and eliminating toxic materials. It can educate business communities and local governments who are uncertain about prioritizing climate, but already schooled in water shortages, and the dangers of asbestos and lead paint.

Box 10.3 Five principles of Christian green building

Mallory McDuff (2010:78–80) identifies five principles for Christian green building:

1 "Promote justice and economic opportunities for church members with green building and energy efficiency."
2 "Create green sacred spaces that serve as models for other churches and for parishioners in their homes."
3 "Ensure green building is not just an addition to the church but permeates the fabric of the church, including worship and Christian education."
4 "Recognize that decision-making about sacred spaces will involve multiple players and therefore the potential for conflict, but also room for reconciliation."
5 "Sacred spaces that care for creation reflect Christians' deepest religious values."

Religious bodies synthesize sustainability with other priorities and ethical norms. Jeremey Kidwell et al. (2018) conducted interviews in Scottish eco-congregations and found primary environmental issues were not the key drivers of their activities. The eco-churches were instead focusing on community building, and "a concept of environmental citizenship which spans multiple scales from local to international." Their keystone values incorporated stewardship and environmental justice. The eco-congregations' approaches to climate change might appear to be "conservative" because they work slowly and carefully to preserve institutional structures and build networks. The congregations are prone to underreporting their achievements, due to a religiously mediated "culture of modesty," making their positive steps even less noticeable. Environmental advocates encouraging religious institutions to go green need to allow them to internally adapt the 4-Cs to this calling.

Issue: religious institutions and national cooperation—Moroccan mosques, Indonesian sermons

Equipping religious institutions with carbon-neutral infrastructure can advance at the national scale. In predominantly Muslim Morocco, the government has committed to supporting the Paris Climate Agreement within the UN Framework Convention on Climate Change. Sunny, coastal Morocco has ideal conditions for efficient solar and wind power generation, yet many remote districts still lack access to inexpensive electricity. Morocco has initiated a program to produce 52% of its energy from renewable sources by 2030. In the process, they plan to reduce energy demand from their 51,000 mosques. In 2016, the village of Tadmanet erected the first Moroccan solar-powered mosque "built from scratch." The photovoltaic panels covering the roof generate enough electricity to serve the mosque, the imam's home, and part of the village. As the hamlet's only public building, the mosque now serves as an educational space, replacing a school lacking artificial lighting. Villagers no longer contribute their own money to pay the mosque's power bill. A green mosque has the potential to power pumps, reducing hand labor in drawing household and irrigation water. Sustainable mosques can teach youth new job skills, and imams can educate the public in the ways green technologies actualize the Islamic values of "respect, restraint, and moderation" (Ceurstemont 2017).

Islamic environmental ethicists, such as Ibrahim Abdul-Matin (2010: 77–78), affirm the efforts of Muslims inventing or advancing sustainable technology. Masoud Amin, an Iranian American engineer, for example, coined the term "smart grid."

National programs can cooperate with religious leaders to curtail cultural practices that release carbon and deplete biodiversity. Indonesia has 15 million ha of peatland, containing an estimated 37% of the earth's peat-based carbon stores. Burning land for clearing has caused uncontrollable fires, and severely damaged Indonesia's remaining rainforests and wetlands. The plumes of smoke pour into cities and towns, causing a choking, toxic haze (Rochmyaningsih 2020). Under natural conditions, peatlands sequester tons of carbon annually by slowly burying undecayed plant material in their anaerobic soils.

Jeanne McKay et al. (2013) trained Indonesian imams in water conservation. The imams then developed sermons for delivery in mosques and Islamic boarding schools. The project found that "raising awareness of the linkages between Islam and conservation rather than on conservation principles alone…," produced greater knowledge concerning ecosystem services and contributions to conservation activities. Adopting this concept, the Indonesian Ulema Council (the country's highest Islamic authority), the Center for Islamic Studies in the National University, and the Peatland Restoration Agency have worked cooperatively to train hundreds of Muslim clerics to advocate for peatland restoration. The imams raise awareness and persistence in villages participating in rewatering and planting trees on burned-over peat. The Ulema Council has also released **fatwahs** (non-legally binding ethical opinions) on environmental issues to guide the populace. Behavioral change can be slow, and villagers are often skeptical about undoing the damage. Yet, Mustangin, an imam in Tanjung Makmur, and other local clerics have been willing to preach that burning is *haram*—forbidden. Mustangin notes that aside from trees, they are destroying "small animals that we can see, and we can't see…. These creatures are all among God's worshippers." Villages with clerics trained by the program do appear to be igniting fewer wildfires (Rochmyaningsih 2020). The strategy is simultaneously precautionary, healing, and restorative, as it intends to both recover degraded habitats and reduce future carbon dioxide releases contributing to the climate change already endangering Indonesia's rich biota and forests.

Issue: Climate ethics—intergenerational, international, and precautionary

Prepared or not, the world's faiths are participants in the internationally framed ethical dialogs concerning climate. Like everyone else, religious communities must consider **epistemology** or how humans acquire the knowledge informing their decision-making. Climate scientists overwhelmingly concur concerning the significant trends, and many are professionally motivated by care for other people and the biosphere (Williston 2019: 46). Understanding science as a source of wisdom concerning how the world works rather than as competition for cultural authority is a critical first step. Religious organizations have a **duty** to the greater human community to base their policies and public statements on the best and most accurate information available.

All the world faiths proscribe injuring the livelihoods or health of "neighbors." Populations already bearing exceptional climate risk include small farmers, urbanites facing elevated heat stress, coastal residents, and indigenous peoples. For the most vulnerable, atmospheric change is potentially lethal. The negligence of the earth's current occupants will cause grave harm to **future generations**; thus, an ethical response

should pursue **intergenerational justice** (Williston 2019: 85–103). The dire apocalypticism of imminent "last days" mutes advocacy for the welfare of grandchildren
and great grandchildren. For most faiths, however, their values normatively promote
self-sacrificing nurturing of the young and assume **future-spanning responsibilities**. Evangelicals Katherine Hayhoe and Andrew Farley (2009), for example, believe
the earth will pass away, yet the timing is the prerogative of an omnipotent God. As
a matter of planetary housekeeping, Christians should address the immediate damages caused by anthropogenic pollution, thereby protecting themselves and their offspring while relieving the current and future suffering of the humans and ecosystems
worldwide.

Proactive religious environmentalism has frequently arisen in response to violations
of **human rights**. **Eco-justice** and **international justice** underpin the most difficult quandaries concerning morally accountable climate action. The Euro-American
industrialized nations have contributed far more than their fair share to greenhouse
gas emissions and are continuing to do so. They have the greatest wealth and technical expertise, and thus the greatest capacity to innovate. A core issue is who bears the
burden of **economic externalities**? Environmental externalities are the impacts and
benefits of extraction, processing, and distribution of natural resources and business and
industrial management not incorporated in the monetary exchanges resulting from the
production and sale of goods and energy. Stakeholders incur externalities involuntarily,
as is the case of Pacific Island nations suffering from accelerated sea-level rise. Orestes
and Conway (2010) identify externalities like changes in agricultural production due to
global warming as free-market failures.

The first principle of climate justice is the **polluter pays** (Williston 2019: 77–79).
Recognizing the production of consumptive resources and releasing energy can be
hazardous, the Torah makes farmers accountable if a dangerous bull injures a neighbor
or their field-clearing fires escape. An ethos based on the Hebrew scriptures will hold
parties who release greenhouse gases to the detriment of others responsible for damages.
Representatives of the developed nations have, however, downplayed historic responsibilities. This introduces the question of whether the faiths of the Global North should
do more to invest in climate solutions? Should they compensate for the past benefits
their members have received from burning fossil fuels?

The second principle of climate justice is the **beneficiary pays** (Williston 2019:
77–79). Religious coda and values from multiple traditions demand fair and honest
dealings in conducting business and discourage taking more than an equitable share.
By inference, the faithful should pay for climate services and rectify the adverse impacts
of energy consumption. The beneficiary pays, however, introduces the issue of how
religious organizations, which in techno-industrial democracies are voluntary associations, can play a constructive role in spheres where national governments manage the
accounting for the international liabilities of their citizenry.

The third principle of climate justice is stakeholders should remedy climate wrongs
based on their **ability to pay** or **capability to act** (Williston 2019: 80–81). Pro-social
religions encourage institutions and individuals to perform charitable acts to relieve
adverse situations, even where they are not personally responsible for any harm. The
Christian parable of the good Samaritan tells of a righteous man who had no family
or ethnic bonds to the injured person he assisted. The principle of ahimsa commends
acts of mercy extended to the poor, disenfranchised, and other species. By inference,
religionists who have the resources or capability should act on behalf of "distant human

others" or other species suffering harm and strive to mitigate climate change, thereby forwarding divine compassion.

Environmental ethicists have invoked the **tragedy of the commons** relative to the atmospheric chemistry (Chapter 4). Pro-social religions demonstrate **moral cosmopolitanism**—a concern for the welfare of distant "others." Yet, the magnitude of atmospheric change suggests that shared local ritual participation is inadequate to address its transboundary origins. Haluza-Delay (2014) proposes that religions with higher degrees of organization and centralization are better able to transcend international borders and assist communities that do not share their beliefs. The concept of ability-to-pay infers the wealthier congregations, and institutions should bear more of the burden for the damages, extending to harms they did not directly cause. As a corollary, capacity-to-act infers faiths with global networks have a greater responsibility to organize across boundaries.

Among the various religious models of relationship to other species, those based in pristine, primal states have the weakness of inadequately addressing the fate of degraded ecosystems. Edenic idealizations often depict God's garden as spatially and temporarily static, remote, and devoid of human intrusion. The Ethiopian church groves, in contrast, bring Eden into the heart of the community, invoking a dynamic interaction with time and terrain, where restoration and redemption are continual. Buddhist service to other sentient beings incorporates maintaining "resources for their everyday use, such as water, trees, and even space" (Dunne and Goleman 2018: 226). Models based in cosmic divine ownership or regency, including Islamic conceptualization of Allah as active within the universe and the Christian creedal tenet "the earth is the Lord's," have more than adequate scope to address climate. Their effectiveness may depend on whether, like the Gaian emphasis on planetary wellness, they can apply an ethos of health and restoration on a whole-earth scale. As Christian climate change skepticism has proven, believing the earth's fate in the hands of the omnipotent, omniscient God protecting the faithful, regardless of their actions, can fuel an **ideology of business as usual**.

The 2015 Paris Climate Agreement and other international accords actualize the **precautionary principle**—the concept that in the face of a known risk, stakeholders should act to anticipate and prevent or minimize its impacts (Williston 2019: 148–150). For religions, this becomes a question of how best to allocate limited resources, including human capital and funds. Religious NGOs, such as the **Red Crescent**, are already feeding and housing climate migrants. If heroic responses to proximate emergencies consume all the effort, however, the frequency and intensity of disasters will unrelentingly magnify. Religious humanitarian NGOs must also weigh **the right to development** against accountability for long term harm. The Moroccan solar mosques are **precautionary** and will help to stem forced migrations while improving village life. Determining the optimal balance among reducing emissions for home congregations, aiding the displaced and stressed, and stimulating public investment in mitigation will remain a challenge for the foreseeable future.

Conclusion: Linking scales, going global

More than any other issue, atmospheric change challenges the efficacy, adaptability, and leadership of religious environmental accountability. Climate action planning must be a community endeavor, beginning at the neighborhood scale and ascending toward global cooperation. As is the case with CFCs (chloroflourocarbons), the actions of one country can change the chemistry of the entire atmosphere. Halting the current process of ever-increasing greenhouse gases requires international participation. Nations, not religions, construct and approve cooperative global-scale plans like the Paris Climate Agreement, resulting from a UN-sponsored meeting. Religious opposition or factional divisions can, however, slow or block constructive political or legislative engagement. Taking on planetary problems requires faiths to reconcile sectarian or regional differences and establish common goals for action.

Actualizing the Buddhist preference for mutually edifying communication, the Fourteenth Dalai Lama of Tibet sponsored a conversation in Dharamsala, India, including scientists and religious specialists trained in other traditions, such as Christian theologians Sallie McFague and Clare Palmer. Buddhism's many philosophical schools, sects, and geographic expressions lack an acknowledged leader; thus, the exiled Dali Lama, who travels widely, often acts as a facilitator in tackling social ethical quandaries and interreligious dialogs. For Buddhists, attention to influencers of human choice and motivation provides a powerful framework for appraising barriers to constructive climate solutions. Buddhist explanations for the mechanisms of change and transformation initiate a three-step process of viewing or understanding the nature of reality: beginning with meditation, which is not merely focusing but learning a particular way of thinking. The second step is seeing and experiencing, followed by undertaking right action. Aside from countering negative habits, like laziness, skepticism, and addictions to fossil fuels, the conversation in Dharamsala called for cultivating spontaneous right action in everyday life. Along with personal simplicity, the conversation backed practical initiatives, including REDD or Reducing Emissions from Deforestation and Forest Degradation. REDD establishes a global mechanism providing financial incentives not to deforest and supports voluntary systems of achieving carbon neutrality for businesses, such as airlines trading carbon off-set credits (Dunne and Goleman 2018: 202–221, 237–263).

Unlike the Roman Catholic Church, Buddhists do not ordinarily call the equivalent of councils of bishops. In response to the Paris Climate Meeting, though, fifteen Buddhist leaders supported by the signatures of thousands of members of the global sangha endorsed and updated a version of *The Time to Act is Now: A Buddhist Statement on Climate Change*, first released in in 2009. Aside from respected teachers like Zen Master Thích Nhất Hạnh, the Supreme Heads of Buddhism in eight countries, and representatives of several Buddhist associations, such as the President of the Buddhist Association of the USA, confirmed their support (One Earth Sangha 2020; Global Buddhist Climate Change Collective 2020). The World Council of Churches (WCC), headquartered in Geneva, Switzerland, similarly has released statements on the environment and climate change, as have other religions and individual denominations. Faiths regularly send emissaries and spokespeople to international conferences advocating for climate action. The United Nations Environmental Program or UNEP has held multi-faith environmental conferences, such as a 2016 meeting in Tehran, where the President of Iran, Hassan Rouhani, addressed the gathering about issues like water resources and climate change from his faith perspective.

A challenge for religious climate engagement is the gap in the middle. Many thoughtful initiatives such as the LEED certification for the Evanston Reconstructionist Synagogue (Chapter 1) or Gloucester Cathedral's solar installation have arisen at the congregational level. Faiths or denominations may bless these projects, yet, not fully integrate the grassroots and bottom-up efforts with the agendas of the upper-level leadership or faith-wide activities. The results of the Jones et al. (2014) survey discussed earlier in this chapter found that nearly two-thirds of US respondents had no or minimal exposure to climate education in a religious context. Many of these respondents likely belong to houses of worship affiliated with denominations or ecumenical organizations like the WCC that have issued environmental or climate statements.

The same study found that political party allegiance was significantly correlated to beliefs about climate. The United Methodist Church, for example, has issued environmental statements and provided education materials on climate, but according to PEW Foundation surveys, its membership is 54% Republican and 35% Democrat. The AME Church is, in contrast, 4% Republican and 92% Democrat—despite its shared theological heritage with the United Methodists (Box 9.1) (Lipka 2016). Both the United Methodists and the AME belong to the WCC. Individual Methodist congregations, however, will display a range of interest in climate activism, from viewing it as a priority ecojustice concern for people of color to dismissing it as undermining the business community. Dependent on donations for their salaries, pastors are often cautious about using their pulpits to address social issues divided along party lines. Most faiths and denominations have limited resources or professional staff available for advising local bodies on climate matters or green building options.

In the case of the Indonesian peat burning, government agencies and university personnel are helping to link local imams and mosques to national programs. In other regions, RENGOs are increasingly filling the gap, and provide the practical experience and training local clergy or lay leadership are ill-equipped to offer. Originally a Christian **parachurch organization** named Faith Power and Light, Interfaith Power, and Light (IPL) began with "mobilizing a religious response to global warming" and energy sustainability as core missions. Founded on the west coast of the United States, IPL has established branches state by state, scaled up to a multi-faith outreach, and acquired enough expertise and capacity to act as a consultant in adapting sustainable technology to religious settings. RENGO's like IPL, A'Rocha, Earthministry, and Faith in Place act as loci for voluntary personal and institutional affiliation, without precipitating intra-denominational battling along partisan, ideological, or socio-economic lines. Interfaith Power and Light's (2020) rubric remains "faithful stewardship of Creation." Although theologians and movements like Deep Ecology have critiqued the stewardship model as un-Biblical, anthropocentric, or too economically moderate, it is one of the most widely accepted forms of environmental **branding** and self-identification among the Abrahamic laity. Other constructions incorporating positive identifiers like Creation Care, Islamic **Green Deen** (*deen* is the Arabic word for religion), and the Bodhisattva Path also inspire innovative best practices.

IPL has expanded its response to legislative and political trends in the national sphere. Building public awareness, IPL initiates petitions and letters elected officials. It sponsors events advocating for clean, sustainable energy and assists in recruiting and organizing participants for public protests such as in the 2018 Climate March in San Francisco, and its affiliate marches around the United States. IPL makes it clear in their holistic mission statements considering all Creation, they intend to simultaneously address protecting the health of ecosystems and "ensure sufficient, sustainable energy for all." RENGOs build communication networks both vertically and laterally, promoting coordinated action at the regional and national levels.

Suggested readings

Dunne, John, and Daniel Goleman, eds. *Ecology, Ethics, and Interdependence: The Dalai Lama in Conversation with Leading Thinkers on Climate Change.* Somerville, MA: Wisdom Publications, 2018.

Orestes, Naomi, and Erik M. Conway. *Merchants of Doubt: How a Handful of Scientists Obscured the Truth on Issues from Tobacco Smoke to Global Warming.* New York: Bloomsbury Press, 2010.

Pope Francis. *The Encyclical Letter Laudato Si': On Care for Our Common Home.* Mahwah, NJ: Paulist Press, 2015.

Stanley, John, David R. Loy, and Gyurme Dorje, eds. *A Buddhist Response to The Climate Emergency.* Sommerville, MA: Wisdom Publications, 2009.

Veldman, Robyn Globus. *The Gospel of Climate Skepticism: Why Evangelical Christians Oppose Action on Climate Change.* Oakland: University of California Press, 2019.

Veldman, Robyn Globus, Andrew Szasz, and Randolph Haluza-Delay. *How the World's Religions Are Responding to Climate Change: Social Scientific Investigations.* London, U.K.: Routledge, 2014.

Williston, Byron. *The Ethics of Climate Change: An Introduction.* Abingdon, U.K.: Routledge, 2019.

11 Models

Conceptual approaches to a planetary future

Key concepts

1 Religious environmental activism has often aligned with other political or social movements like feminism.
2 Most ecofeminists reject the logic of domination and the instrumentalization of nature in western philosophies. Many deconstruct, not just cosmologies, but conceptualizations of the divine portraying God as strictly masculine, or as distant from the living earth.
3 Religiously based social justice movements, like Liberation Theology and Engaged Buddhism, have identified environmental degradation as a critical concern when improving the lives of the economically disadvantaged and socially marginalized.
4 Ecofeminism in the Global South has arisen in diverse religious contexts, including Hinduism and indigenous religions, and often shares agendas with other social justice movements.
5 In recent decades, ecofeminists have intensified examination of colonialism and other historic worldviews contributing to the parallel oppression of women with children, the lower classes, and the racial and sexual "other." Ecowomanism is a synthesis of African American religious thought in dialog with ecofeminism and ecojustice.
6 The fluidity of gender roles and the environmental focus have helped alternative religions like contemporary Paganism to attract members. Many alternative religions and transformative festivals are intentionally counter-structural in the ways they address industrialization and globalization.
7 Catherine Albanese identifies "nature religion" as a "symbolic center" of American religion, continuing from pre-colonial belief systems to the new religions proliferating in the 1960s.
8 Bron Taylor has proposed dark green religions are counter-structural, actively evolving worldwide, and replacing older traditions. Taylor predicts dark green will raise a decentralist earth revolution, dissolve political hegemony, give birth to non-divisive earth nationalism, and mature into terrapolitian earth religion.
9 Bruno LaTour and other postmodernists identify "nature" as "a dichotomous western cultural construct separating people from their environments."
10 Frustrated with science's tendency to turn existence into endless inventories of facts and numbers, religious philosophers are exploring new cosmologies reconnecting the spiritual and scientific, or resacralizing the material. New materialists treat matter not as something that "is," but as "becoming."

Infusing political philosophies

Contemporary religious, environmental models align with or against political philosophies. Further, environmentalism has reoriented religious creeds and praxis. Using ecofeminism, liberation theology, and engaged Buddhism as examples of symbiosis between social-ethical agendas, this chapter examines how religiously based environmentalism has exchanged ideas and ideals with other reform movements. The chapter then explores the issue of whether some religions are darker green than others, and whether new or alternative religions encourage environmental activism to a greater degree than long-established world faiths. The discussion returns to persistent questions opened by Lynn White, Jr., including the anthropocentrism and dualism of western definitions of "nature."

Infusing political philosophies: Feminism and ecofeminism

The 20th century was a period of rebellion against the remaining colonial regimes and rectification of societal inequities based on race, ethnicity, faith, and gender. Campaigns for equal rights or self-governance and environmental caretaking merged in movements like the Canadian "war in the woods." As an example of identity-based discourse, **ecofeminism** both claims religious foundations and creates novel ethical theories (Box 11.1). In conjunction with the Women's Liberation Movement of the 1960s and

---

Box 11.1 Basic tenets of ecofeminism

Christian theologian Rosemary Radford Ruether (2005: 91–92) summarizes the tenets of eco-feminism:

"Ecofeminism sees an interconnection between the domination of women and the domination of nature. This interconnection is typically made on two levels: ideological-cultural and socioeconomic. On the ideological-cultural level women are said to be closer to nature than men, more aligned with body, matter, emotions, and the animal world. On the socio-economic level, women are located in the spheres of reproduction, child raising, food preparation, spinning and weaving, cleaning of clothes and houses, that are devalued in relation to the public sphere of male power and culture....the first level is ideological superstructure for the second.

Many ecofeminist thinkers extend this analysis from gender to class, race and ethnic hierarchies....The male elites are the "master class" who define themselves as owning the dependent classes of people. This ruling class inscribes in systems of law, philosophy, and theology a "master narrative" or "logic of domination" that defines the normative human in terms of this male ruling group.

René Decartes, a major philosopher for early modern European thought, deepened the dualism between mind and body, seeing all bodily reality as mere "dead matter" pushed and pulled by mechanical force. The mind stands outside matter contemplating and controlling it from beyond. In modern liberal thought essential humanity corresponds to rationality and moral will.... Although such views of the self claim to define the generic "human," what is assumed here is the male educated and propertied classes. Dependent people, women, slaves, workers, peasants, and colonized peoples are made invisible. They are de facto lumped with instrumentalized nature."

1970s, women from the Abrahamic faiths were among the first to challenge gendered norms for religious leadership. In 1968, Roman Catholic theologian Mary Daly published *The Church and the Second Sex*, an appraisal of inherently masculine Christian chains of command. Her 1978 book, *Gyn/Ecology: The Metaethics of Radical Feminism*, linked male oppression of women to the mistreatment of nature. During the same period, French environmentalist Francoise d'Eaubonne coined the term Ecological or Ecofeminism when she initiated a women's activist organization, in the belief that "the destruction of the planet is due to the profit motive inherent in male power" (Ruether 2005: 91–92). The feminists of the 1960s rejected the **essentialist** belief of earlier generations that inherited or innate and relatively stable characteristics defined gender. Following post-modern philosophy, they treated gender as a cultural construction, rather than as a simple, physical fact.

In a watershed study released in 1980, environmental historian Carolyn Merchant traced the evolution of Christian interpretation of the human–nature relationship. She documented a conceptual shift from the medieval view of nature as a **moral subject** to the mechanistic model of the Renaissance, where nature becomes a collection of objects, albeit for scientific study. Enlightenment **deism** held a transcendent God constructed the cosmos to operate under the rule of unchangeable physical laws, much like a giant clock. For the deist, the material is mere "stuff." In tandem with a market-oriented culture, this ethically indifferent religious materiality desacralized the universe and living nature, freeing human exploitation from ethical restraints. Merchant argues the earlier organic cosmology centered on the earth as female had assumed the interdependence of humans with the nonhuman environment. The idea of "nature" as separate from humans or God is a western construction encouraging destructive dualisms and the notion that human interests are superior to and independent of those of other species.

Most ecofeminists jettison the **logic of domination** and the **instrumentalization of nature** in western philosophies (Box 11.1). Many **deconstruct**, not just cosmologies, but conceptualizations of the divine portraying God as strictly masculine, or as distant from the living earth. Although the term deconstruction has several meanings, in philosophy, it examines the hierarchies and oppositions or dichotomies inherent in Western thought, such as nature and culture, or mind and body. Theologian Heather Eaton (2005: 74–77) argues that Christian focus on creation *ex nhilo* dwells on the creation of humans, therefore "the earth, although referred to, is not relevant." Christianity has failed to consider the integrated whole as the sum of its parts. In reinterpreting **doctrine**, ecofeminists reject "the monarchial, patriarchal male image of God" on the grounds "it has blinded us to the sacredness of the earth." Their cosmologies preferentially emphasize divine **immanence**. Ecofeminists depict God as a creative and life-sustaining Spirit, intimately, and continually interacting with the earth.

Attentive to each pillar of religious self-conceptualization, Christian Ecofeminism tackles sticky topics like what comprises sin and what is the fate of the planet? According to Eaton (2005: 78–80): "Ecofeminism situates sin within the interlocking oppressions of ethnicity, colonialism, class, gender, and domination of the earth. Sin exists where life cannot thrive." Challenging historical eschatologies, ecofeminists abandon the cultural constructions of the earth as awaiting inevitable, imminent divine wrath. They admonish the faithful to care for the worthy home God has provided.

Actively rewriting creation stories, multiple ecofeminists have adopted the holism of Gaia in addressing climate change. Rosemary Radford Ruether (1992) proposes contemporary scientific understandings of cosmology and earth systems, as articulated in Gaia, can assist in broadening the Christian concept of Creation. Picturing the earth as "the body of God" and the entire of life as dwelling within this body, Sallie McFague (2013: 20–21) envisions a planet-encompassing spirituality, based in **kenosis** or a spiritual "rebirth." Kenosis transforms self-centeredness into a "life of self-emptying love for others," and changes the valuation of the material in ways forwarding ethical environmental-praxis. Referencing Lovelock's self-regulating planet, Anne Primavesi (2009: 87–88) proposes a theology of gift events, with the Creation by God, as the seminal event. For Primavesi, humans "routinely confine the mystery of earth's giving within the closed circle of humanly conceived and contained economics, of human debtors and creditors. We do not see ourselves as belonging within a continuum where members of the earth community gift us with existence...."

A distinctive feature of ecofeminism is the degree to which it has interacted with the arts. Through the 1960s, female artists had difficulty gaining admission to the best training programs, and female art scholars held few competitive academic posts. In response, feminist formal aesthetic criticism has explored the roots of gender-based oppression and humanity's abuse of all living. In the late 20th century, the goddess in many guises and the earth as sacred became common themes. Judy Chicago and her studio team, for example, created *The Dinner Party*, an installation with a table set with ceramic plates and goblets seating spiritual trailblazers and *matersfamilias*, including the Primordial Goddess, the Hindu goddess Kali, Jewish liberator Judith, and African American preacher Sojourner Truth (Chicago 1978). (Multiple photos of the installation appear on the Brooklyn Museum's, New York, website.) Chicago and her contemporaries experimented with performance art, both as street theater and in forests, caves and open fields, often incorporating the themes of embodiment and the goddess personified. In concert with contemporary alternative religion, ecofeminism and its rich aesthetics explore spirituality in greater depth than is usual for the Euro-American religious mainstreams (Box 11.2).

Judy Chicago's corpus of work demonstrates the versatility of the contemporary feminist intersection with environmentalism. In *The Dinner Party*, womanhood is the primary theme, with the organic fonts of life contributing to its essence. The environmental

---

Box 11.2 Ecofeminist spiritualties

Heather Eaton (2005: 86) summarizes ecofeminist spiritualities, they "proliferate in images such as Gaia, Mother Earth, Sophia, Christ(a), Spirit, Goddess, Divine Matrix and Cosmic Egg....A good percentage of ecofeminist spiritualities, as practiced, is an amalgamation: images and practices from one tradition are mixed with another, and interpreted in altogether new ways unrelated to their origins....For most, the ecological dimension of spirituality rests on the presupposition that the earth is sacred, and the immanent presence of the sacred within nature evokes respect for all living things. Interconnectedness, webs of relations, interdependence, mutually enhancing patterns of existence, and the subjectivity of life itself are all terms commonly used to reach beyond the mechanistic, technical, and anthropocentric worldviews. There is a resurgence of non-dualistic spiritualities, with an emphasis on the wisdom traditions from all religions for ecological insights."

concern is implicit. In Chicago's painting, *It's Always Darkest Before Dawn* (2000), a scene dominated by pollution-spewing factories faces an Edenic earth, where Adam and Eve enjoy an intimate encounter by the Tree of Life. Here the environment is an explicit and primary theme, with sexuality as a secondary subject.

Infusing political philosophies: Eco-justice and liberation theology

Paralleling the late 20th-century synthesis of religion with feminism are faith-based movements addressing socio-economic equity. First emerging in Roman Catholicism, **Liberation Theology** has consciously tackled the deficiencies of economic ideologies claiming open markets with little regulation of resource exploitation benefit the disadvantaged by providing jobs. Early leaders like Gustavo Gutiérrez primarily came from the Global South. Initially, the movement did not have a well-defined vision for integrating the environment. Some of its most influential thinkers soon recognized, however, that environmental degradation has a disproportionate impact on the poor. Reproaching Christians for their failure to follow Christ's model of serving the disadvantaged, Brazilian Franciscan Leonardo Boff (1978) proposes the church represents Christ as a sacrament or sign of the sacred in a secular world. Christians thus have a call to relieve social oppression. Boff's (1997) *Cry of the Earth, Cry of the Poor* points to the conjoined fates of the natural environment and the economically marginalized in repressive economies driven by remote international business interests.

Using a whole-earth model, Boff (1997: loc. 180–260) argues the earth is ill, and "the most threatened of nature's creatures today are the poor..." and "living species are likewise threatened." Among the signs of planetary disease are the millions of deaths annually due to hunger, particularly for children under 15. The Latin American theologian finds fault with the modern fetish "that everything must revolve around the idea of progress, and such progress is advancing between two infinites: the infinite of the Earth's resources, and the infinite of the future." Rebuking human exceptionalism, he laments economies striving for "maximum profit with minimum investment in the shortest possible time....," where "human beings are regarded as above things, making use of them for their own enjoyment, never as alongside things, members of a larger planetary and cosmic community." Boff identifies human sin as the root of the malaise. The diagnoses and therapies are ecological and arise from the all-encompassing interface between the material and spiritual he calls the **theosphere**.

Boff's reprimand of the Roman Catholic hierarchy for their failure to protect their flocks and his politicization of ministry did not go unnoticed. Liberation theology inflamed Catholic tensions between conservatives and liberals, and in Boff's case, the conservatives won out. In 1985, a branch of the Vatican charged with maintaining orthodoxy silenced Boff for a year. Boff ultimately left the Franciscans and the priesthood rather than curtail his campaign for environmental justice. Pope Francis, however, weaves the liberation ethos into *Laudato Si'* by borrowing Boff's language and establishing socioeconomic justice for the poor as a benchmark for Catholic environmental care. Boff (2014) has published a book favorably comparing Pope Francis's mission to that of St. Francis of Assisi, thereby cultivating cooperation between moderate Catholics and those in favor of more radical societal change.

Infusing political philosophies: Engaged Buddhism

Also originating in the global South, engaged Buddhism arose in response to the turmoil and suffering caused by civil wars in Asia and the interventions of world powers in countries with large Buddhist populations, as in Vietnam and Tibet. Reflecting on the problems its adherents face, engaged Buddhism often focuses on peacekeeping and human rights, such as freeing Tibet from Chinese rule. The movement bridges traditional Buddhist attention to interdependence, morality, and liberation, in the sense of release from *samsara*, with western modernity's advocacy for democracy and personal freedom. As an initiator of the movement, Thích Nhất Hạnh, a Vietnamese Zen monk, believed social engagement should arise from mindfulness and should "encompass all aspects of life, from family practice to public policy and culture." During the Vietnam War, Hạnh and other like-minded Buddhists advocated a "third way" approach and called for Vietnamese self-determination, even at the risk of Communism suppressing the monasteries (Hunt-Perry and Fine 2000).

Thích Nhất Hạnh and his compatriots modified the oft passive role of Buddhist monasticism relative to secular governance, by organizing actions structured to influence public policy directly. Recognizing the importance of institutional forms to engaged practice, in 1966, Hạnh established the Order of Innerbeing (Tiep Hien Order), which has since spread to multiple countries in the West. The order's charter states its purpose is to actualize Buddhism by "studying, experimenting with, and applying Buddhism in modern life, with a special emphasis on the **bodhisattva ideal**." The bodhisattva relieves the suffering of others, including other sentient beings. Engaged Buddhism has easily accommodated environmentalism and female leadership. The six individuals first ordained in the Order of Inner Being included Sister Chan Khong, who has become an internationally respected speaker on Buddhist practice and values. As Engaged Buddhists, Joanna Macy and Stephanie Kaza have paved the way for green Buddhism in the United States, by countering the political disengagement and social isolation of some strands of western Buddhism. They have creatively adapted Buddhist discourse about the material to address the environmental impacts of consumerism (Hunt-Perry and Fine 2000; Queen 2000).

Issue: Adapting ecofeminism to cultures and economies of the Global South

Ecofeminism has spread globally on a highly diverse religious base. In South and Central America, activists expeditiously accessed the writings of North American and European feminists and initiated their distinctive movement in the 1970s. The advent of Liberation Theology stimulated their revisioning of ethical paradigms, and the two streams of thought have often merged. Having committed to living with the poor, Brazilian Roman Catholic sister Ivone Gebara began to examine theology from the perspective of women's daily lives. For Gebara (1999: 25–50), life cannot be defined solely by abstract theories but is rooted in experiences and networks of relationships, extending to the nonhuman. People do not exist independently and then decide to connect with others. They are "constituted in and by relationships," including those with the earth. Christians need to recognize their interdependence and understand the Trinity "as a way of expressing the dynamics of life as interrelational creativity." This model extends to the biosphere, unfolding in a diversity of biota, changing through the eons via processes of extinction and speciation (Ruether 2005: 113).

Gebara (1999) reasons good and evil reside "in natural life itself," which "exits in a dynamic tension of life and death, creativity and vulnerability." Unfortunately, humans have been able to escape natural restraints and assert their power over other living creatures. Very concerned about exploitive hierarchies, Gebara notes those in charge view themselves as autonomous and innately superior. They promulgate ideologies representing the inequality and inhumanity as "the order of creation" or as divine will (Ruether 2005: 114). This Southern strain of ecofeminism prefers to remain very down to earth, taking on projects like forming rural women's cooperatives. To a greater extent than their US and European counterparts, Latin American ecofeminists and their religious communities have suffered censure, political oppression, and government instigated violence.

Beginning in the 1970s, environmental activist Vandana Shiva brought the degree to which women from rural communities and economically disadvantaged families in India might suffer disproportionately from forest clearing or water contamination to worldwide attention. Trained as a life scientist, Shiva reasons western scientific **epistemology** promotes destructive resources management in assuming male dominance over females and the natural realm. Western modes of development and the Green Revolution have overridden the importance of women in rural societies. In preindustrial subsistence agriculture, women play critical roles in planting, foraging, and tending livestock. Their knowledge and respect for natural cycles support renewable production practices like mulching fields and maintaining sacred forests providing villagers with a ready supply of wood. The international banking system and Northern professional elites have introduced pesticides, HYVs, commercial logging, and massive dams as the solutions to famine and rural poverty. However, these capital-intensive strategies displace rural small farmers, lay bare hillsides, and unravel previously sustainable irrigation networks (Shiva 2016).

With her first book, *Staying Alive: Women, Ecology and Development*, Vandana Shiva (2016) elicited Indian public and international support for the **Chipko Movement** in the Garhwal Himalaya. Chipko began when rural Indian women protected sacred groves and village forests by standing in the way of chainsaw-wielding commercial logging crews. For the women, the loss of the trees was both a spiritual and practical disaster, threatening both their cultural identities and their access to consumptive resources like firewood, fruits, and medicinal plants. Drawing on Hindu cosmology, *Staying Alive* argues western thought forwards a false dichotomy of the masculine as aggressive and active, and the feminine as dormant and passive. In Hinduism, male and female energies are actively and dynamically engaged. Both *Shakti* or activating energy and *Prakriti* or nature are female. Indian popular piety and semiotics thus support the roles of rural women and counter notions that nature is mere dead stuff. Industrialized disturbance of ecosystem function threatens the health and ontological security of women (Fig. 11.1).

For Shiva (2016), recovery of the Feminine Principle discourages violence toward nature. It allows both men and women to "see themselves as active participants in nurturing life in partnership with nature's own vitality." Other Indian environmental activists have, however, critiqued Vanda Shiva's model as ignoring the world negating aspects of Hindu cosmology. They believe Shiva understated Hinduism's role in subordinating women and maintaining the caste system that has socioeconomically immobilized the *Dalits* (untouchables) and indigenous peoples. In more recent publications,

Figure 11.1 In Hinduism, women play significant roles in rituals expressing reciprocity with ecological systems. A devotee performs a puja in the polluted waters of Yamuna river at Kalindi Kunj on the occasion of Chhath Puja, on November 3, 2019 in Noida, India. Toxic industrial foam coats the river's surface. Thousands of devotees celebrating Chhath Puja gathered on the banks of the river, lakes, and canals to pay obeisance to the Sun God on the third day of the festival. Chhath Puja is a major festival of Bihar, which is performed in order to thank Sun for sustaining life on earth.

Photo: Sunil Ghosh/Hindustan Times licensed via Getty Images

Shiva has sidestepped discussion of the "feminine cosmological principle," while honing her exposé of neocolonialism (Ruether 2005: 108).

African eco-feminists both seek to reclaim Traditional religious worldviews and to coordinate environmental action among distinctively African expressions of world religions. Veterinarian and Kenyan women's advocate, Wangari Maathai founded the Kenyan Green Belt Movement in 1977. Recognizing the devastating impacts of deforestation, she first cultivated a tree nursery and then taught other women to build nurseries and transplant healthy seedlings. Not just about timber harvest, the program teaches sustainable farming growing bio-regionally adapted cultivars for local consumption. Green Belt planning situates trees near homes, reducing the need for women to walk long distances for firewood, and adding fresh fruit to family meals. Catholic by upbringing, Maathai encourages the recovery of traditional knowledge and pre-colonial Kenyan values. She has not hesitated to develop a theological frame oriented toward the immanent and challenges of this world, rather than a supernatural realm. Maathai "speaks of God being in herself, in other people and in the earth" (Ruether 2005: 104).

In Zimbabwe, feminist scholar Tumani Mutasa Nyajerka has directly restored Tradionalitst cosmology by invoking the **Mutupo principle** from her Shona heritage. Informed by two traditions, the *Karanga,* where a Great Pool generates all life, and the *Mbire* where the Great Monkey is the progenitor of all biota, each Shona subgroup has totem animal or *Mutupo*, which is also close kin. A Shona begins the day by greeting their *Mutupo*, attends celebrations where each clan dances the part of their *Mutupo*, be it a hippo, crocodile, antelope, or lion, and protects their sacred animal, exempting the species from killing or harvest. Balancing life and death, youth and age, the terrestrial and aquatic, Shona cosmology avoids separating the human from the nonhuman, as "humans, animals, and plants are parts of one extended family" (Ruether 2005: 101).

Issue: Reducing dualism

Eco-feminism has evolved in response to external critiques, internal reflection, and coordination with other philosophies of reform. Desiring to displace anthropocentric world views, some Deep Ecologists have found ecofeminism too focused on contesting **androcentric** (male-centered) forms of human dominance. Ecofeminists have countered that they are willing to share principles like **ecospheric egalitarianism** and embrace an expanded concept of the ecological self. Ecospheric egalitarianism "holds that biota have equal intrinsic value; it denies differential valuation of organisms" (Keller 2008). Ecofeminists will, however, continue the strenuous trek toward gender equality (Estavéz-Saá and Lorenzo-Modia 2018, 2020).

Some feminists have articulated worries that ecofeminism diverts attention away from the unrelenting political oppression of women. Ecofeminists themselves reason that the academic treatises of the 1970s and 1980s, like *Gyn/Ecology* and *The Death of Nature*, still operated with the very dualisms they should reject—"such as woman-nature that worked in opposition to that of men-culture." By the 1990s, theorists like Greta Gaard were exploring bridges to animal liberation and queer studies. The second generation of ecofeminists intensified examination of colonialism and other historic worldviews contributing to the **parallel oppression** of women with children, the lower classes, and the racial and sexual "other." Ecofeminists became warry of an "essentialist and reductionist view of women that conceived them in terms of their reproductive, nurturing, and caring abilities, which naturally connected them to Mother Earth." They believe this stereotype diminishes the power to liberate. The movement has increasingly addressed deeply encultured **racism, speciesism, and maldevelopment** (Estavéz-Saá and Lorenzo-Modia 2018, 2020).

Issue: Expanding identity models via ecowomanism and African Christianity

As a corrective to the oft narrow experiential frame of white feminists, African Americans created **Womanist theology**, to explore the intersection of race and feminism, and address the barriers black women face within churches and the greater society. Novelist Alice Walker coined the term "womanism" in 1982. In *The Color Purple*, her character Shug Avery names "the earth as sacred and herself as an intimate part of divine existence." Theologian Melanie L. Harris defines **Ecowomanism** as a synthesis of African American religious thought, as expressed through womanism, in dialog with ecofeminism and ecojustice. Harris (2017: loc. 370–390) posits the lived experiences, spiritual values, and social activism of African American women are valuable sources of **ecowisdom**, emerging as environmentally rich epistemologies. Ecowomanism draws on Traditional African cosmological visions, where Spirit, humanity, and nature exist in an "interconnected web of life." Harris proposes the virtues of "beneficence, forbearance, practical wisdom, improvisation, forgiveness and justice" provide a powerful ethical rationale for Ecowomanism's focus on **earth justice**. Striving to balance theory and praxis, Ecowomanism pursues deconstructive analysis of environmental failures, while debunking racial myths and stereotypes.

Africans have also been weaving new patterns from a synthesis of Traditional religion, Christianity, women's empowerment, and environmental need. Drawing on both indigenous African religion and Christianity, Zimbabweans harvested their bioregional heritage and the growth of Christian bodies in building the **Association of African Earthkeeping Churches** (AAEC) in the 1990s. Accommodating Shona beliefs that ancestral spirits protect the land and violating them initiates deficient rainfall, the AAEC conduct tree-planting Eucharists, where worshippers petition the spirits for forgiveness for land abuse and deforestation. In addition to taking communion with each other, the participants "seek to reestablish communion with the land." The ceremony terminates with the assembly moving out across the landscape to engage in conservation actions, reestablishing vegetation cover, and caring for watersheds. Women assume active leadership roles at the local level, as well as the national (Daneel 2000; Ruether 2005: 101).

Merging movements: Gender and alternative religion

Although **Wicca** and the western revival of Paganism preceded the ecofeminist movement, ecofeminism and alternative religions have interacted, refining the environmental focus of both streams. In Wicca, women have unencumbered access to leadership roles, and Wiccan covens can be entirely female. Alternative religions have recovered pre-Christian European seasonal celebrations and sacred fires, which they stage outdoors. Today's Pagans may gather for the pre-Christian Celtic festival Beltane, incorporating a ritual Maypole dance. Celebrating Lughnasa (Celtic) and other celestial festivals, they light sacred fires, mirroring the energy of the sun. Favoring woodlands, mountain meadows, and other wilder settings, Pagan and Wiccan celebrations deploy artisanal technology to fashion handcrafted ritual objects and community altars. Four Quarters Interfaith Sanctuary, Maryland, for example, holds an annual Stones Rising festival, where attendees pull ropes, rollers, and wooden frames to add two-ton standing stones to a growing circle. Such rituals distance participants from the anonymity, hierarchy, and the mass production of industrial labor, while encouraging individual expression, interaction with nature, and joy in shared creativity.

As comparative religious scholar Hugh Urban (2015: 157–175) concludes, the fluidity of gender roles and the environmental focus have helped movements like contemporary Paganism to attract members. Starhawk, whose 1979 analysis of the religious oppression of sexual identity in *The Spiral Dance: A Rebirth of the Religion of the Great Goddess* drew many women to Wicca, holds that Wicca and Paganism are natural allies of environmentalism. Paganism views the universe as infused with sacred energy, flowing through the human body, drawing all living organisms into a dynamic, interconnected matrix, thereby rejecting human exceptionalism and dominance over nature. Advocating spirituality engaging the rhythms of nature or the "earth path," Wiccans reclaim magic, ancient Goddess religion, the creative energy of women, and "the immanent life force" connecting humans to the world "as a living being" (Starhawk 2005). Starhawk promotes permaculture as an environmentally sound means of food production and encourages demonstrative political engagement. During the 1980s, the Reclaiming Collective, founded by Starhawk, joined in the nonviolent civil disobedience resisting the proposed Diablo Canyon Nuclear Reactor in California, where they "engaged in ritual magic in an explicitly political context" (Urban 2015). Like other religious, environmental activists, Wiccans must find means for cooperating with allies from diverse political perspectives, which at Diablo Canyon incorporated anarchists and pacifists.

Hardly requiring a cue from ecofeminists, LBGTQ (lesbian, bisexual, gay, transgender, and queer) environmental activists began to form organizations post-*Silent Spring*. In 1979, Harry Hay released a call for "gay brothers" to "renew their oaths against patriarchy/corporatism/racism" and join in forming a "great fairy circle." Drawing on alternative religion with its convergence of streams from diverse fonts such as Buddhism, Sufism, and shamanism, Hay's Radical Fairies formed an intentional community residing in immediate contact with nature on a mountain in Tennessee. Hay and other LBGTQ theorists hold that "queering" environmental models, while escaping heteronormativity and patriarchy, will generate "imaginative, non-dualistic, and egalitarian means of living nondestructively embedded within the planet" (Bauman and Eaton 2017).

Issue: Transformative celebration

Many alternative religions are intentionally **counter-structural** in the ways they address industrialization and globalization. Others, such as Sun Myung Moon's Unification Church, have emerged from capitalist logic, organizational structures, and sales techniques. As Peter Beyer (1998) points out, however, "nature itself is a counter-structural symbol: in as much as more dominant global modernities are characterized by a priority of technical, humanly controlled and artificial constructs, so nature is all that which is not technological artifice...." Beginning in the 1980s, **transformative festivals**, promoting spiritually but detached from any one faith, took shape in the Nevada desert and spread internationally. The best known is the theatrical **Burning Man**, culminating in the ignition of a giant human effigy. Attendees assemble temporary temples constructed of wood and torch them to close the gathering. "Burns" sequence "**rituals of reversal**" where the Burners mock, renovate, and destroy normative symbols and revered icons of the greater culture. Many Burners self-identify as pilgrims, leaving their day-to-day routines to undertake a radical personal reorientation. Ethnographer Lee Gilmore (2010: 125) concludes Burning Man "can facilitate significant reorientations in time and space and spark remarkable life changes." Participants do "experience something beyond the ordinary: they touch for a moment and in their own ways, a sense of something meaningful in their lives that was missing before."

In their redecoration of old automobiles and parodies of industrial aesthetics, Burns explore the meaning of the material. Through its **polyvocality** and striking pillars of flame, Burning Man distances participants from the standardization and possession-centeredness of consumer culture. Paralleling the programming of Findhorn, tamer transformative venues weave spiritual exercises like walking a labyrinth into sustainability education. Permaculture and strawbale building demonstrations populate the schedules. A question concerning these short-term escapes from the humdrum is whether ritual without dogma has an enduring impact on personal actions and worldviews? Gilmore (2010: 125–126) concludes the encounters with the community and the connections attendees forge with others continue to stimulate creative expression after they return home. "Having participated in this alternative, albeit temporary, social model, and having witnessed the mutability of cultural norms, values, and symbols through this experience, some individuals are moved to continue to enact Burning Man's ideals in the default [ordinary] world."

Issue: Nature religion, dark green religion

The late 20th century was an era of greening social organizations from political parties to world faiths, with the outcomes ranging from negligible to highly impactful in terms of improved environmental care. Following the example of Lynn White, Jr., religious scholars began to distinguish some religions or movements as more concerned about nature than others. In 1990, religious historian Catherine Albanese published *Nature Religion in America: From the Algonkian Indians to the New Age,* presenting "**nature religion**" as a "symbolic center" of American religion continuing from pre-colonial belief systems to the new religions proliferating in the 1960s. Albanese's broad tapestry incorporated Puritanism's heirs, the Transcendentalists. Pearson et al. (1998: 1) then defined contemporary animism, Wicca, and Paganism as nature religions, "in the sense that they involve a reorientation towards, and a rescaralizaton of external nature and our own physical embodiment." Peter Beyer (1998) further particularized the concept by defining nature religion as resistant to institutionalization. It avoids legitimizing itself via authorities and organizational structures. Beyer (1998) proposes nature religion emerges via countercultural sects and movements. These share the commonality of attributing "divinity to nature." On the societal level, nature religions take "a critical stand with respect to the dominance and negatively judged effects of the globalized instrumentalized systems." Although Beyer counted Creation-centered Christianity as nature religion, popular usage of the identifier often excludes the world religions.

Around the same time, Paul Wapner (1995) and other political analysts began to separate the reformist "light green" ENGOs (environmental nongovernmental organizations) from the more radical politics of militant **dark green** ENGOs. Wapner distinguishes between activism intending to merely halt damage to the material, such as clear-cutting forests and killing whales, and Greenpeace's strategy for revisioning "public ideas and moral sentiments." In bearing witness, Greenpeace seeks to "dislodge traditional understandings of environmental abuse and substitute new interpretive frames." Founding President Robert Hunter held common understandings and popular mores conditioned social behaviors. Greenpeace's goal has been to reshape this wellspring of collective life, rather than simply block harpoons. By bringing ecological understandings and "the hidden spots of the earth" into view, Greenpeace attempts to dislodge old worldviews and "substitute new interpretive frames." Hanging provocative banners, climbing soot-encrusted smokestacks, and filming protesters chained to ships are intentionally **transformative**.

Bron Taylor (2010: 223–224) has applied the distinction between light and dark green to religion. He dismisses Albanese's definition of nature religion as too broad and limits the focus "to those who consider nature sacred in some way." Taylor's (2010: 94–99) thesis is dark green religions are actively evolving worldwide and replacing older traditions. Radical environmentalists demonstrate dark green religion when they experience "earth's sacred energies" or communicate with trees. Taking a stand against logging by sitting for two years in an old-growth redwood, Julia "Butterfly" Hill reported that the first time she entered the grove, "the spirit of the forest just gripped me." Paul Watson, a founder of Sea Shepherd, declared that humanity should abandon the old religions in favor of a religion "that incorporates all species and establishes nature as sacred and deserving of respect." Taylor (2010: 102) summarizes the core of dark green religion as found "in the belief that everything in the biosphere is interdependent, intrinsically valuable, and sacred."

Bron Taylor (2010: 104–105) extends dark green religion beyond religious organizations like dioceses and temples to individuals feeling an exceptional connection to the environments in which they live, work, and play. The recreationists calling themselves soul surfers, for example, consider their avocation to be a religion. Soul surfing connects them "to nature, to its energies, and its wild creatures." The deep emerald depths roll up to the surface when surfing spirituality campaigns against plastic trash and demurs to nesting sea turtles. Dark green germinates in the Gaia Foundation and its pursuit of an earth community, and in the People's Earth Summit, where traditional healers from southern Africa led an evening ritual. Accepting Beyer's characterization of nature religions as counter-structural, Taylor (2010: 195–199) suggests that rather than producing a new religion with established institutions, dark green religion will mature into **terrapolitian earth religion**. Unlike civic religions spawning combative nationalism and exploitive economies, the varied streams of "earth based spiritualities will build loyalties, affections and identities rooted in the earth." Taylor invokes Daniel Deudney's (1995) concept of a transformative Gaian Earth politics and religion—raising a decentralist earth revolution, dissolving political hegemony, and giving birth to non-divisive earth nationalism.

Taylor (2010: 200–207) recognizes the world religions will resist surrendering their cultural turfs, and many people fear movements like radical environmentalism. He reasons the acceptance of evolutionary theory has already restructured worldviews, and the recent growth and diversification of dark green religion "has been breathtakingly rapid." Social change is ordinarily slow, but paradigm shifts spread quickly among the intelligentsia who play a disproportionate role in setting environmental policies. Once fully recognized, the gravity of the threat will expedite global social change. Taylor (2010) concludes dark green religion can overcome the anticipated societal intransigence.

Bron Taylor's utopian optimism envisions exponential growth for dark green spiritualities, largely outside the current religious establishment. However, Americans participating in many of the environmentally-friendly alternative religions, like New Age, are proportionately more likely to come from the professional class and better-educated backgrounds (Stark 2008). Liberation theologians and development-savvy ecofeminists will, meanwhile, remain wary of religious change with advantaged socioeconomic classes as the vanguard, no matter how intensely hued their verdure. Taylor's confirmation that alternative green spiritualties have spread widely in recent decades does not weigh the simultaneous population expansions of Islam and Evangelical Christianity, particularly in the Global South. Further, some strands of contemporary alternative religions like Paganism are more environmentally oriented than others. Eco-shamanism, for instance, is intentionally dark green. One of Starhawk's agendas has been to raise environmental awareness and counter political disengagement within her religious community.

The concepts of dark green and nature religion depict some religions as more "environmentally correct," thus risk stereotyping the remaining faiths as "disinterested" and thereby unworthy of environmental reform. However, as Bron Taylor asserts, some religious responses to environmental management are far more committed and constructive than others. This differential is evident within major religious lineages as well as among them. Enduring environmental coalitions either have a concrete stake in the outcomes or act as proxies for other people or species who do. As the Dalai Lama's climate conversation recognized, right action cultivated as part of everyday life is superior to the repeated complex ethical decision making generated by on-going systematic failures (Dunne and Goleman 2018). The question becomes: is it more critical to form intensely focused dark green faiths or to energize the rank and file of the world's current spectrum of religions—and why not pursue both routes to greater environmental awareness and action?

Issue: Challenges to the idea of nature

Following the trajectories of Lynn White, Jr. and the early ecofeminists, 21st-century philosophers and historians have continued to examine western philosophical models and religions as sources of environmentally flawed worldviews. Philosopher of science Bruno Latour (2004) goes a step further than Carolyn Merchant and proposes that political ecology should let go of the idea of "nature" entirely. Pursuing the ultimate deconstruction of the concept, Latour (2004) identifies "nature" as "a dichotomous western cultural construct separating people from their environments that should be replaced by a communitarian model encompassing humans and nonhumans." "Nature" is a haphazard hodgepodge of Greek Philosophy, French Cartesianism, and the ideals of American national parks. Latour (2004: 91) concludes neither the **externality of nature** nor the **unity of nature** (mononaturalism) by themselves endanger public life. The idea of "nature" is a barrier to civic environmental action "because of the short-circuits it authorizes when it is utilized to bring about this unity once and for all, without due process, with no discussion, outside of political arenas…" Rather than relying on the politics of identity, Latour (2004: 211) proposes replacing the modernist "mononaturalism" and "multiculturalism" with "**multinaturalism**." Multinaturalism avoids dependence on outside experts claiming the authority of absolute reason and relies on communicative and culturally flexible "diplomats" forwarding experimentation. (Note that Latour is still using the word nature, albeit with a prefix.) (Box 11.3). Latour has not directly addressed dark green religion, while he challenges the efficacy of religions in general, as they are inherently culturally particular and arbitrary.

Box 11.3 Bruno Latour's critiques of multiculturalism and modern Christianity

Bruno Latour (2004: 184) argues that multiculturalism cannot provide a unified political response under a rubric of mononaturalism:

> "If the unified universe of nature had nothing to do with humans, it was still possible to bring peace to *many* disunified cultures by falling back on *the one* nature. At least one question seemed to have been resolved: that of the plurality of inhabited worlds. Yet neither mononaturalism nor multiculturalism can continue to sum up the risky situation in which the collective, as I have defined it, now finds itself. There would be too many indisputable essences on the one hand, too many arbitrary identities on the other.…If it were surrounded by essences and identities, the collective would succumb at once (it would become a society)."

Latour (2017: 210-211) accuses modern Christianity of strangling ethical focus: "Believing themselves to be attached to the Spirit, they have lost the Earth. Believing they are defending religion, they have led everyone to assault the Earth through negligence. Led astray by the supernatural, itself a delayed reaction to the invasion of 'nature,' they are no longer in a position to do their duty by *defending materiality, unjustly accused, against matter, unduly spiritualized*....The fate of Christianity is nevertheless of little importance compared to the loss of meaning imposed on materiality by the move to force it to become matter."

Latour (2017) has published a series of lectures on the new climate regime and "natural religion," supporting Lovelock's Gaia as a **secular figure for nature**. Reasoning Lovelock's original concept captured the fragile and dynamic essence of the biosphere, the French philosopher objects to what he deems monolithic misunderstandings of Lovelock's intent, including the earth as superorganism and the New Age goddess. Latour (2017: 210–212) holds religion did cause the environmental crisis, but not for the reasons Lynn White, Jr. proposed—the Abrahamic faiths reifying nature and assuming God had awarded humanity mastery over all-living. Rather, between the 13th and 18th centuries, Christianity "lost its initial vocation by becoming **Gnostic**, before passing the torch to the superficially irreligious forms of counter-religion." (Gnosticism seeks mystical knowledge while treating the material as imperfect and inherently evil.) As White (1967) claimed, however, Christians have "abandoned all concern for the cosmos in order to devote themselves to the salvation of humans alone..." Most blinding of all was the demotion of the material to mere "stuff" (Box 11.3).

Rejecting the religious apocalypticism feeding climate skepticism where believers **situate** themselves as survivors following the final trumpet's call, Latour (2017: 217–218) defends ecologists who warn of the devastating risk posed by atmospheric change because their realism situates them in the Anthropocene or "during the end time." Like supporters of dark green, he holds effective climate change mitigation must overcome the boundary laden politics of nation-states. Confessing his happy surprise that Pope Francis was "capable of taking up the Canticle of the Creatures again while addressing Earth as 'mother' and 'sister'" in *Ladauto Si'*, Latour (2017: 287–288) compliments the pontiff for "reconnecting ecology to politics... without belittling science in the process." On completing his examination of the encyclical, LaTour asks himself if "the intrusion of Gaia might bring us closer to all the gods?" His ruminations raise the question: Could facing Gaia as vulnerable to human meddling reorient wayward religious materiality?

Issue: New cosmologies, new materialisms

Frustrated with science's tendency to turn existence into endless inventories of facts and numbers, religious philosophers are exploring new cosmologies (or redrafting old ones) reconnecting the spiritual and scientific, or resacralizing the material. Mathematician Brian Swimme and Mary Evelyn Tucker (2011) present the universe, not as a chaotic mass of "stuff," but as a "big story" beginning with the Big Bang, and evolving into the earth "community." Harmonizing religious wisdom with scientific theories of origins, they envision a cosmos infused with consciousness and beauty. Swimme and Tucker believe that understanding the universe as sacred is the foundation of environmental care.

Environmental ethicist Lisa Sideris (2017), however, questions models, like Swimme's and Tucker's, that are **anthropic**—centered on human consciousness and perception.

Sideris observes aspects of the "new cosmology" have consecrated science, making humans the omniscient narrators of the metanarrative of all that exists. Swimme's "universe story" is teleological, with humans as its ultimate intent and meaning. Sideris concurs modernity has generated **amythia**—techno-industrial societies no longer have coherent myths or "big stories." Humans feel homeless. Science has **disenchanted** the planet. Rather than accepting the anthropocentric concept that "we are the universe reflecting on itself," or encouraging "celebrations of wonder and reverence for science over and above nature," Sideris (2017: 169–202) points out Rachel Carson recognized human arrogance as a root of the scientific abuses resulting in DDT and radioactive fallout. Sideris proposes we should cultivate a sense of wonder that "preserves otherness" relative to the world around us, making "it possible to act genuinely for the good of the other or with the other truly in mind."

Theologians like Catherine Keller and Mary-Jane Rubenstein (2017), who investigate the intersections of gender, religion, and cosmology, are exploring "**new materialisms**." These conceptualizations "seek to displace human privilege by attending to the agency of matter itself. Far from being passive or inert, they argue, matter acts, creates, destroys, and transforms—and, thus, is more of a process than a thing." They treat matter not as something that "is," but as "becoming." Keller and Rubenstein posit Christianity was afflicted with "materiaphobia," long before the Reformation. For Christians, God and the truly spiritual have resided outside and away from the material. Hierarchal and dualistic, modern "**toxic materialisms**," also distinguish "spirit and matter, life and nonlife, or sentience and non-sentience." The new materialists view humans as entangled in matter. As Karen Barad (2017) summarizes, "we are of the universe, there is no inside, no outside." Rather than declaring the ontological equity of all "things" as discrete, the new materialists point out that "things" are, in essence, "multiplicities, assemblages, hybrids,… and complexities," that are "interactive-hosts." These ideas introduce the question of whether environmental valuation should be based on roles and process and not in entities, and whether it should conserve relationships rather than "things?"

Conclusion: Old and new philosophies

Since the 1960s, innovative faith-based environmental philosophies have more often organized around movements forwarding liberation and empowerment than around sectarian theologies. Movements such as ecofeminism and engaged Buddhism offer support, stimulate new ideas, and buttress courage. Despite Lynn White's (1967) questionable historiography, several of the conceptual issues he opened weave through contemporary conversations concerning ideal models for environmental engagement. Carolyn Merchant and Bruno Latour disagree with White's conclusion that Latin Christianity laid the foundations for the environmental crisis while proposing that changes in Christian cosmology between the end of the Medieval period and the Enlightenment turned nature into "mere stuff." The new materialists argue that Christianity suffers from materiophobia, rejecting not just the importance of spirits in nature, but of the material itself. This same charge could apply to Buddhism's concept of impermanence. The ecofeminists have explored not just anthropocentrism but androcentrism. Lisa Sideris has challenged the very concept of "the Big Story"—a centerpiece of religion—on the grounds it is anthropocentric.

The leading thinkers about the relationship of culture to the physical and biological environment do not agree, however, concerning religion's environmental efficacy.

Bruno LaTour is skeptical of religion's value and forwards a secularized Gaia. Bron Taylor, in contrast, proposes a massive greening of religion will play a crucial role in bringing humans back into a healthy and respectful relationship with their home planet. Although not all ecofeminists have religious interests, the movement as a whole has infused a constellation of mainstream and alternative religious contexts. Ecofeminism has been internally tolerant of diverse expressions of faith. It's affinities with civil rights, liberation theology, and multiculturalism make it a continuing collaborator in the realm of eco-justice. Models such as ecowomanism have built ramps carrying feminism and multiculturalism beyond their particularities to the realm of global environmental activism.

Suggested readings

Albanese, Catherine. *Nature Religion in America: From the Algonkian Indians to the New Age.* Chicago, IL: University of Chicago Press, 1991.

Bauman, Whitney, Richard Bohannon, and Kevin O'Brien, eds. *Grounding Religion: A Field Guide to the Study of Religion and Ecology.* London, U.K.: Taylor & Francis, 2017.

Boff, Leonardo. *Cry of the Earth, Cry of the Poor.* Maryknoll, NY: Orbis Books, 1997.

Chicago, Judy. *The Dinner Party*, 1978. The Elizabeth A. Sackler Center for Feminist Art of the Brooklyn Museum, New York, has a web page dedicated to the work: www.brooklynmuseum.org/eascfa/dinner_party/home (Sept. 12, 2019).

Eaton, Heather. *Introducing Ecofeminist Theologies.* London, U.K.: T&T Clark, 2005.

Estavéz-Saá, Margarita, and Marie Lorenzo-Modia. "The ethics and aesthetic of eco-caring: Contemporary debates on ecofeminism." *Women's Studies* 47, no. 2 (2018): 123–146.

Harris, Melanie. *Ecowomanism: African American Women and Earth-Honoring Faith.* Maryknoll, NY: Orbis Books, 2017.

Keller, Catherine, and Mary-Jane Rubenstein, eds. *Entangled Worlds: Religion, Science, and New Materialisms.* New York: Fordham University, Press, 2017.

Latour, Bruno. *Facing Gaia: Eight Lectures on the New Climatic Regime.* Cambridge, U.K.: Polity, 2017.

Pearson, Joanne, Richard H. Roberts, and Geoffrey Samuel. *Nature Religion Today: Paganism in the Modern World.* Edinburgh, U.K.: University of Edinburgh Press, 1998.

Queen, Christopher. *Engaged Buddhism in the West.* Sommerville, MA: Wisdom Publications, 2000.

Ruether, Rosemary Radford. *Integrating Ecofeminism, Globalization, and World Religions.* Lanham, MD: Rowman & Littlefield Publishers, 2005.

Shiva, Vandana. *Staying Alive: Women, Ecology and Development.* Berkeley, CA: North Atlantic Books, 2016. (Originally published by ZED Books in 1988).

Sideris, Lisa. *Consecrating Science: Wonder, Knowledge, and the Natural World.* Oakland: University of California Press, 2017.

Swimme, Brian, and Mary Evelyn Tucker. *The Journey of the Universe.* New Haven, CT: Yale University Press, 2011.

Taylor, Bron. *Dark Green Religion: Nature, Spirituality, and the Planetary Future.* Berkeley: University of California Press, 2010.

12 Communalities

Greening and the challenges of modernity

Key concepts

1 Common means of greening religions include mining and reframing tradition, frame bridging, and bricolage.
2 Critics have accused *Laudato Si'* of being anti-modern, particularly in its treatment of science. Supporters argue the Encyclical encourages intense dialog with science, while rejecting the Enlightenment philosophy that science should conquer nature for the benefit of humans.
3 Strategies for tackling modernity and modernisms are recover, reform, and renew.
4 Improving communication between religion and science could enhance religious effectiveness in addressing environmental problems.
5 To understand and absorb environmental science and policy, the world's faiths must link religion to the environment in education at all levels, including cultivating environmental understanding for the general public.

The process of greening

Recent scholarship distinguishes "greening" as a contemporary social process where religions increasingly engage environmental concerns and adopt sustainable practices. In the case of American Christianity, the stewardship movement preceded the publication of *Silent Spring*. Paralleling Rachel Carson's barrage of newspaper columns, the Lutheran theologian Joseph Sittler delivered a series of lectures dedicated to ecologically sensitive cosmology at Yale University in 1959, releasing them as *The Ecology of Faith* in 1961. He published *The Care of the Earth and Other University Sermons* in 1964, three years before White's article in *Science*. Yet, Christian efforts through 1990 were diffuse, and denominational buy-in was limited. Approval of formal environmental statements by major denominations, including Methodists, Lutherans, and Presbyterians, resulted only in scattered and oft short-lived programs for church sustainability (Fowler 1995; Sittler 2000; Ellingson 2016: 12). During the same period, Findhorn, Greenpeace, Gaia, La Causa, and ecofeminism became firmly anchored and vigorously pursued their missions. This chapter summarizes impediments and facilitators of religiously based environmental action. It investigates whether some religious environmental programs are anti-modern. The discussion concludes with the possibilities for engaging modernity, science, and education.

Impeding and facilitating environmental engagement

The multiple cases covered in previous chapters have identified common impediments to environmental engagement, which are not specific to any family of faiths (Box 12.1). The environmentalist critique that religious leaders and institutions have not responded to environmental threats in a timely way sprouts up wherever industrialization has caused human health risks or unrelenting degradation of natural ecosystems. The explanations vary from the accusation that Christianity is anthropocentric to the concern that "funeral" Buddhism is too old fashioned and politically conservative to go green. Religious leaders range from thoroughly baffled to well-informed and, like Pope Francis and the Fourteenth Dali Lama, fully committed. The lack of advanced instruction suitable for clergy, absence of scientific expertise in religious governing bodies, and the separation of the religious and civic spheres generate lags between the public recognition of a specific environmental issue and faith-based response.

One of the trickier barriers to unravel is ideology, as environmentalism is inherently ideological. Ideology can advocate for environmental care or place unregulated economic development on a pedestal. Zionism, for example, has fostered tree planting and recovery of landscapes degraded by over-grazing and erosion. It has blessed the reestablishment of extirpated species in the arid lands of the Levant (Fig. 12.1). At the same time, Zionism's enthusiasm for development has sometimes overridden the practical limitations of tapping aquifers and the water rights of transboundary stakeholders. The Jewish National Fund, however, sponsors water conservation projects and acts as a cooperator with ARAVA Institute with its focus on environmental sustainability and implementing water and energy management as a means of peace keeping. Just as the Reformation nurtured the rising middle and business classes of early modern Europe, today's Protestants weave economic ideologies into their moral fabric. In the past, Protestantism provided ethical justifications for both industrialization and the US national park movement. Today, some Christians defend the corporation-dominated,

---

Box 12.1 Impediments to religious environmental engagement

1   Disappointment with religious leadership
2   Lack of educational programming for religious professionals and laity
3   Dissonance with the logic of appropriateness or theological commitments
4   Conflicts with authority structures
5   Fear that environmentalism is heterodox
6   Conflicts between modernity and tradition
7   Environmental/scientific professional dismissal of religion and religious skepticism blocking science
8   Ontological dissonance among environmental, scientific, and religious discourses
9   Ontological insecurity
10 Uncritical acceptance of economic ideologies
11 Disempowerment of indigenous religions and religious minorities
12 Isolation from civic participation or fear of government interference
13 Competition and misunderstandings among religions and sects
14 Inability or unwillingness to enter coalitions or work with ENGOs (environmental non-governmental organizations)
15 Warfare and civic unrest

Figure 12.1 The Nubian ibex, a Biblical species, in Ein Gedi Nature Reserve. Nearly extirpated from Israel, the ibex is now reproducing well in protected areas.

free-market economy as a holy mission. Ideology, rather than **hermeneutics** (scholarly interpretation of texts), argues climate skepticism is the Biblically correct ethical stance. Ontological and ideological dissonance disrupt solidarity and faith-based participation in environmental planning and management (Box 12.1).

Conversely, multiple forms of religious organization facilitate environmental engagement. In a survey of US RENGOs (religious environmental nongovernmental organizations), sociologist Stephen Ellingson (2016: 91–108) examined the process of religious "greening" and classified the most prevalent forms of innovation. He posits faith communities often resist environmental programming because it conflicts with their "logic of appropriateness, authority structures, and theological commitments." Activism of any kind requires justification. Ellingson found **"mining and reframing tradition"** by recovering relevant myths, scriptures, and iconography is a common form of greening. Generating eco-theology consistent with denominational norms and "restructuring the Jewish dietary codes of Kashruth as Eco-Kashruth" are forms of reframing that validate environmental action as compatible with religious heritage (Box 12.2).

A second pervasive greening technique is what sociologists term **"frame bridging,"** defined as "the linkage of two or more ideologically congruent but structurally unconnected frames." Invoking if-then logic, leaders synthesize well-accepted moral priorities and environmental responses, to overcome fears that greening is heterodox. Roman Catholics worry that biocentrism is a form of nature worship, and thus idolatrous. To counter this resistance, *Laudato Si'* openly bridges mainstream Catholic theology with contemporary environmentalism and links the fate of the impoverished as a keystone ministry, to shifting climates. Among multi-faith RENGOs, frame bridging stretches across traditions by focusing on broadly shared values. The Abrahamic lineages, for

---

Box 12.2 Facilitators of religious environmental engagement

Greening creed, coda, and cult

1 Mining and reframing traditions for environmental models
2 Frame bridging by relating the environment to other ethical concerns
3 Bricolage, or recombining available legitimate concepts, scripts, models, and other cultural artifacts
4 Enhancing ecodimensionality by creatively adapting arts, ritual, piety, and coda

Organizing within the religious community

1 Forwarding environmental education at all levels
2 Programming intentionally
3 Cultivating community
4 Supporting bottom-up decision-making
5 Recognizing the value of traditional knowledge
6 Tackling the interface between modernity, tradition, and materiality

In cooperation with other stakeholders

1 Respecting the heritage and values of other stakeholders
2 Staging astute or transformative critique while sharing the responsibility
3 Opening dialogs with science and technology and drawing other fields like philosophy into the conversations
4 Prioritizing the welfare of distant and non-human "others"
5 Incorporating environmental concerns in humanitarian and service organizations
6 Incorporating environmental concerns in peacekeeping
7 Pursuing shared goals with other movements, such as civil rights
8 Forming coalitions with governments and ENGOs (with due caution)
9 Constructing intra and interreligious networks and RENGOs
10 Pursuing justice for all

---

example, share the ideals of "the sacredness of Creation; stewardship; justice for the poor or the most adversely affected by environmental problems and intergenerational equity" (Ellingson 2016: 91–108).

Religious organizations are most effective (and turn a darker green) when they anchor environmental agendas in the 4-Cs. Ellingson (2016: 108–111) considers **bricolage** in which leaders and community members "recombine already available legitimate concepts, scripts, models and other cultural artifacts they find around them in their institutional environment" to be the least common form of environmental innovation for RENGOs. He may be correct when appraising non-profits, as they acquire the administrative structures of secular advocacy organizations, rather than of congregations. Yet bricolage is very evident in movements like ecofeminism. Sarah Pike's (2017) investigation of eco-activism validates a complex and evocative matrix of religious bricolage within more radical ENGOs. Reframing tradition, frame bridging, and bricolage as means of initiating social change also can strengthen anti-environmental activism. Religious spokespeople forwarding climate skepticism reframe tradition by citing Biblical texts.

As the case histories demonstrate, effective religiously based environmental management often balances hierarchal authority, like whaling chiefs or water temple priesthoods, with bottom-up decision-making by clan representatives or farmers cooperatives.

These organizational structures enhance problem solving and share accountability for resource vitality. In today's techno-industrial societies, religious bodies serve as sturdy platforms for environmental activism when they have firmly established goals for engaging relevant socioeconomic causality, like racism or abuse of industrial labor. Combining forces with other social reform movements, as engaged Buddhism and ecofeminism have done, can creatively synthesize and empower compatible agendas. Models respecting the welfare of others build networks and incorporate religious communities in environmental planning and management (Box 12.2).

Issue: Anti-modernism?

Ellingson's identification of processes like recovering tradition as integral to greening points to a conundrum: Does recovering tradition risk inserting pre-modern values and practices where they conflict with science? Can it initiate unrealistic or ineffective environmental practices? Atmospheric and sea change challenge the very essence of religious environmental models in terms of the models' willingness to deal with not just the goods and evils of modernity but also with its tools. In an address to the American Association for the Advancement of Science (AAAS) meeting in 2019, climatologist Christopher Field argued that the global community has the ability and resources to counter climate change, by prioritizing technological innovation, finance, policy, adaption, and leadership. Field favors monetary incentives for business and policies that would "unleash the creativity…vested in individuals, companies, [and] communities around the world." Field's position is hyper-modern as he argues that given adequate financial infusions, applied science and the energy economy can save the planet, much as technological innovation has eliminated ozone-depleting CFCs (chloroflourocarbons).

R.R. Reno, former theology professor and editor of *First Things* magazine, published an article critizing *Laudato Si'* for its **anti-modernism** in 2015, just after the release of the encyclical. Unlike Bruno LaTour, who was impressed by the encyclical's acceptance of climate science, Reno (2015) holds Pope Francis "expresses strikingly anti-scientific, anti-technological, and anti-progressive sentiments." Reno claims *Laudato Si'* is the most anti-modern Roman Catholic encyclical since the middle of the 19th century. He asserts Pope Francis treats the scientific method as part of the problem because it is "a technique of possession, mastery, and transformation." Francis is equally suspicious of the economic globalization which has brought prosperity to countries like China. Reno fears Francis is reopening the Catholic Church's previous battle with modernity, rather than following the pattern of 20th-century encyclicals that have delivered "necessary criticisms to restore the religious and moral basis for modernity's positive achievements." Reno's critique could be applied to many other religious environmental thinkers including Roman Catholics, such as Thomas Berry and Leonardo Boff, who laid the foundations for *Laudato Si'*, and to multiple religious strategies for sustainability. Findhorn's or Anthroposophy's resistance to commercially oriented agricultural science is tacitly anti-modern.

M. Anthony Mills (2015), an editor of *The New Atlantis*, disagrees with Reno. He proposes that in order to understand Pope Francis's message, the reader has to distinguish between "modernity" and "modernism." Modernity, as a time period, resulted from historic forces and cultural trends. Anti-modernity could mean returning to a past, more ideal era or it "could mean calling for radically different forms of economic production, social organization, knowledge production, or systems of government." Modernism is a constellation of ideologies that interpret modernity. Anti-modernism therefore takes a stand against one of more of these ideologies. Among modernism's more common political forms are progressivism, liberalism, and individualism. "Subjectivism, positivism, and scientism can be considered forms of philosophical modernism; they are examples of the belief that modernity demands a radical break with or repudiation of earlier forms of thought and practice." Mills (2015) concludes Pope Francis targets not science in general but a specific philosophy of science and instrumental rationality forwarded by Francis Bacon and by the Enlightenment. *Laudato Si'* rejects "the idea that modern science aims to conquer nature 'for the relief of man's estate.'"

Mills (2015) argues that Pope Francis believes that "the cult of technological progress" and "the technocratic paradigm" tempt abuse of ecosystems and humans alike. Science becomes an ethical problem when it treats scientific methodology "as the only valid way of knowing." Mills (2015) summarizes:

> Pope Francis notes that modern science needs to be part of addressing our technical challenges. But this would not be a science of the technocratic paradigm that tries to be value-neutral, but one that would "take into account the data generated by other fields of knowledge, including philosophy and social ethics." This is why Pope Francis calls for "an intense dialog" between science and religion, "with their distinctive approaches to understanding reality," so that our knowledge about nature be complemented with moral guidance on how to use it.

Assuming Mills is correct, Pope Francis would probably accept the methods for decelerating atmospheric change as suggested by Christopher Field, a fellow of AAAS. Francis, however, would be very concerned about incentivizing business or restructuring economies without careful ethical examination of any unintended consequences for the socially marginalized and economically disadvantaged.

Many, but certainly not all, scientists agree with Pope Francis about the need for "intense dialog." Most scientific professional societies avoid holding meeting sessions or releasing articles explicating religious thought. AAAS's journal *Science*, however, published Lynn White's 1967 paper. As an organization concerned with policy and public education, the AAAS sponsors the DoSER (Dialog on Science, Ethics, and Religion) program. In 2019, climate scientist Katherine Hayhoe delivered the DoSer year-end holiday lecture "A climate of hope: Scientists and faith communities addressing the climate crisis" with Episcopal Bishop Katherine Jefferts Schori as discussant. DoSER followed with a multi-religious panel on climate at the 2020 national AAAS meeting in Seattle, Washington, and plans for further interactive fora. Scientific societies and scientifically oriented ENGOs have perceived Pope Francis as supportive. The Ecological Society of America, for example, released a public comment stating: "In addition to drawing attention to global change, we are very pleased to see a world leader of his stature advocate strongly for ecological research and education" (Lester 2015). As dual venues remain limited, both the scientific community and green religious organizations could further cooperation by sponsoring additional opportunities for respectful idea exchange.

Issue: Addressing modernity and modernisms

Religions have three possible ways to approach modernity or modernisms: **recover** older values and lifestyles thereby displacing modernity, **reform** by accepting modernity while correcting its obsessions or countering problematic modernisms, or **renew** by imaginatively transforming modernity via anti-structural events and lifestyles. Among the cases in this volume, indigenous religions, popular piety, and faiths with deep commitments to heritage, often make civic headway when they compromise between "recover" and "reform"—drawing on their rich traditions while renovating some aspects of modernity and constraining others. The protest at Standing Rock attempted to recover authority over the Sioux sacred landscape. The camps utilized sacred fire, in a pan-Native American frame, as a unifying symbol of renewable energy. The Sioux understood the implications of the available environmental science and attempted to rebuild the legal foundations for protecting their water supply and sacred ground by filing through the courts. Pre-modern cosmologies, ethical values, and concepts of the sacred offer valuable insights into not just the worth of other species, but the immeasurable importance of human community. Movements such as the native Hawaiian recovery of the island of Kaho'olawe understand that when confronting wicked environmental problems like the impact of global warming and ocean acidification on coral reefs, asking scientists, including co-religionists, to assist opens the door to innovation.

In the United States, progressive Protestantism contributed to the rise of both the conservation and preservation movements in the 19th century and the stewardship movement in the 20th (Chapter 4). Protestantism, which co-evolved with modernity, is, however, more successful in forming coalitions and implementing green programming when it understands its origins, and does not confuse modernity itself, scientism, or the market economy with divinely ordained righteousness. Protestants and other denominations or sects that have accommodated modernity may overemphasize the need to modernize and underestimate the importance of tradition when cooperating with other faiths. Protestant blindspots concerning sacred landscapes, ritual sacrifice, and ritual magic have halted more than one multireligious attempt at environmental team building.

The phoenix-like transformative movements and new religions have been natural companions in their refusal to take the modern commonplace at face value and their belief in renewal. Bron Taylor's deep green discontents partially arise from the failure of the very modernized western religious mainstream to reflect on the encumberments of their own allegiances, such as Protestantism's and liberal Catholicism's roles in forwarding growth-oriented models of international development. Improving incomes and the lives of workers contribute to the common good, while clinging to fossil fuel-driven supply chains and transportation infrastructure is an artefact of 19th-century technological successes. Faiths married to modernity can be adept at reform, yet benefit from investment in renewal and radical revisioning. The process of renewal risks tearing down old structures and then not being able to adequately replace them. Projects like the institutional efforts to reach zero carbon and the Moroccan government's plan for solar mosques (Chapter 10) implement change one careful step at a time and revision global economic and development futures. Naming a wind turbine for a Scandinavian saint and pursuing 'ummah solar are not merely recoveries of tradition or frame bridging; they are statements of community values and religious meaning.

Different forms of religious engagement have different strengths. In the techno-industrial context, dark green and transformative religions as models reject the established, bureaucratized, and staid. Anti-structural religious expression examines material values, exposes cultural duplicity, and experiments with sustainable lifestyles. Burners, however, admire the jarringly novel, while César Chávez tapped the drama and familiarity of shared heritage. Popular piety and heritage recovery have been tools of choice for union organizers, tree planters, water protectors, and other crusaders boosting solidarity to improve the livelihoods of disadvantaged populations. Although prone to default to business as usual, more centralized and institutionalized religions often excel at building educational networks, working with government entities, transcending international and cultural boundaries, and transposing sustainable technologies into the matrix of the commonplace.

Issue: Modernity and religious environmental leadership

An additional issue is whether faiths that have co-evolved with modernity are more likely to sponsor intentional environmental programming in the contemporary sense. The assumption that one faith perspective is more compatible with science or is more up to date than another, however, can become a communication barrier in forming coalitions (Chapter 8). Conversely, pre-modern institutions or community structures accompanied by strong social bonds and a sense of place can forge leadership fulcra.

Among faiths esteeming contemplative paths to right action and lifestyle, monastic communities, with their pre-modern origins, are instilling environmental activism into their missions. Catholic nuns, for example, have formed organizations helping them to share their skills and identities as "green sisters." Often combining eco-activism with other ministries, entrepreneurial "earth sisters" have built organic gardens, opened ecology education centers, held prayer vigils by landfills, and joined bioconservationists in defense of the endangered Lake Patzcuáro salamander. "Going renegade," intrepid nuns wearing work clothes built an open-air chapel in their farm's cornfield, blocking Atlantic Sunrise Pipeline construction crews. They also brought a lawsuit arguing the pipeline conflicted with their religious beliefs. Green nuns can accomplish a great deal with limited funds and resources (Taylor 2007; Griswold 2019).

The medieval origins of monastic orders and rules does not inhibit greening the monastic life or its valuation of the material. In concert with holy work, today's monastic workshops often base their artisanal endeavors in environmentally sound methods and technologies. Roman Catholic Trappist monasteries in Iowa and Idaho, USA, make inexpensive yet handsome caskets and burial urns. For the monks of New Mellery Abbey, Iowa, the handcrafted receptacles are a means for easing the pain friends and relatives feel, and a way to support families experiencing loss. The abbey manages its own forest via sustainable practices ensuring production of slower growing cherry, walnut, and oaks trees over many decades. A monk blesses each casket, which serves as an additional confirmation the family will rejoin the deceased in the afterlife (New Melleray Abbey 2016). The Trappists treat each step in the manufacturing and sales process, from caring for saplings to communicating with purchasers, as an act bringing the love of Christ into the world. They sacralize the relationship with the ecosystems on which humans depend in life and in death.

Issue: Modernisms fighting back

Encounters with modernisms, like the concept of progressive economic development, are not abstract theory. They develop quickly into partisan and legal contests. Extending their moral authority, Buddhist ecology monks in Southeast Asia have increasingly entered the political sphere as a route toward relieving suffering for people and other species damaged by environmental change. Engaged Buddhists never intended to limit their activities to a monastic elite, but have continually reached out to the sangha. They engage government officials over environmental initiatives and related issues like farmers' rights. Phrakhu Sangkom Thanapanyo Khunsuri, an ecology monk, has set up an alternative farming school, thorough his temple in Chonburi, Thailand. Its curriculum mixes reflection with Buddhist models of "sufficient economy." He also undertakes speaking tours throughout the Chang Mai region, speaking to an average audience of around a hundred at each venue (Price 2018).

Experiencing backlash from the government and logging and petroleum companies, the monks have proven themselves resilient in the face of adversity. The Thai government has arrested, defrocked, or harassed some of the more outspoken. Like the indigenous elders resisting international mining companies, monks interfering with corporate land acquisition have fallen to assassins. Scaling up, Buddhist activists have formed the International Network of Engaged Buddhists, hoping to connect Buddhists and non-Buddhists who share the concern for relieving suffering worldwide (Price 2018; Vershuuren and Brown 2019).

Issue: Aligning with scientific priorities

Al Gore's (2006) book and film, *An Inconvenient Truth*, precipitated a flurry of religious publications and educational programming responding to climate in parallel with the international press coverage. As Bratton (2014) concludes, ecotheology has behaved very differently from environmental science or applied ecology. Religious ethicists rushed to take on climate as the highest profile and most universal of concerns, while continuing to give only passing coverage to such vital topics as freshwater availability, marine ecosystemic health, and forest fragmentation—all of which are inextricably connected to atmospheric change.

In Ellingson's (2016) survey, 89% of US RENGOs deemed climate change a priority, and over half (52%) emphasized a simple lifestyle. Other priority topics were land stewardship, water pollution, sustainable food production, air pollution, and recycling. Few RENGOs focused on wilderness, endangered species, or biodiversity. Yet, innovators John Muir and Robert Hunter infused religious values and tactics into the Sierra Club and Greenpeace. Ellingson did not incorporate sub-cultures like soul surfers in his analysis. A potential pattern is eco-spirituality, and alternative religious worldviews are compatible with the missions of preservationist and anti-structural movements. Their adherents experience a satisfying level of spiritual camaraderie and acceptance within superficially secular organizations, like Greenpeace. One of the most internationally successful Christian RENGOs, A'Rocha, began as a hands-on biodiversity conservation organization. The emphasis on solving immediate problems via intensely committed volunteerism has likely strengthened both the counter-cultural ENGOs and A'Rocha.

Among the RENGOs surveyed by Ellingson (2016), a mere 3% reported human population growth as a sphere of engagement. ENGOs like the Sierra Club have also fallen back from the alarmist projections of the "population bomb" circulating in the 1970s and 1980s (Cafaro 2015). Most introductory college and secondary school environmental textbooks dedicate a chapter to the topic. Tackling global population growth requires consilience with other religious agendas such as family values and care for the poor (who in many countries have larger families than the middle classes). Socioeconomic factors and residency as well as religious beliefs inform perceptions of ideal family size, making the topic difficult to address in multicultural contexts. Guided by political pragmatism, climate justice activism avoids tensions by advocating inexpensive, sustainable power for all and drawing public attention to the plight of climate migrants. Buried underneath these trends, however, is a vault filled with inadequately resolved questions concerning who has the right to own which natural resources and who may consume them.

Overall, explicitly religious organizations are more likely to take on the high profile environmental issues with repeated coverage in popular media and those clearly related to personal life styles. Concerns that are recent, highly technical, or ecosystem specific receive less attention. Emerging pollutants, like endocrine disrupters and microplastics, draw only sporadic faith-based consideration. As Bruno Latour has complained, religion can be very particular. Multiple cases of astute environmental action in the previous chapters have rightly confronted immediate threats to local and regional faith communities, such as mountain top mining and lead in house paint and drinking water. Religious environmental action could, however, have a greater impact and take a stronger precautionary stance, if it could enlarge its green repertoire to align more fully with scientific identification of the most pressing concerns.

Issue: Environmental education

To understand and absorb environmental science and policy, the worlds faiths must link religion to the environment in education at all levels, including for the general public. Where religion parallels regional heritage, primary and secondary schools are experimenting with syllabi centered on topics like Eco-Holi. Students, in turn, engage in demonstrative environmental advocacy, such sign-waving youth marching on behalf of India's polluted sacred rivers or students taking to the streets in November 2019, after severe air pollution events caused school shutdowns in New Delhi (McCarthy 2019). Children from faith-based schools have joined walkouts intended to draw attention to adult negligence in defending their futures against climate catastrophe.

The growing separation in many nations between public and religious education complicates cultivating conversations among science, religion, and policy. This division is very much a product of modernity and of liberal democracies and communist states. As organizations intending to network stakeholders and fill societal gaps, all the RENGOs mentioned in this book have invested in education. Faith In Place's "Green Team" training has reached several hundred houses of worship in one metroplex. A'Rocha's various international affiliates have taken their bioregional contexts to heart. Programs range from offering one-day field trips to both state and religious primary schools in British Columbia, to teaching adult agriculturalists to conserve and harvest mangroves in Africa (Fig. 12.2). Often low budget, RENGO public outreach can be quite entrepreneurial, and open to operating within secular assessment standards.

More centralized and institutionalized faiths support formal education at all levels. During his lifetime, Thích Nhất Hạnh built communities conducting regular workshops for laity. He published books, circulated worldwide, attracting readers from beginners to masters. *Laudato Si'* has inspired environmental modules in Catholic curricula from pre-school to Ph.D. level. EdX, which delivers MOOCs (massive open online courses) internationally, has offered a course on *Laudato Si'*. Faith-based higher educational institutions, like Brandeis University, Massachusetts, (Jewish), have developed environmental studies or sciences majors and minors. Among the members of the

Figure 12.2 A'Rocha has developed a simple, easy to maintain aquatic study area for primary school children in southern British Columbia. Under the supervision of a professional educator, interns introduce classes to a scientifically sound curriculum.

US Council for Christian Colleges and Universities, multiple institutions have crafted environmental curricula or installed environmental ethics courses. Faith-based institutions and consortia sponsor faculty training seminars, international trips, and field schools, like AuSable Institute, Michigan.

Universities with non-religious admissions and faculty hiring continue to house seminaries, schools of religion, and other vehicles preparing enrollees for service as religious professionals. Duke University is home to the internationally respected Nichols School of the Environment, an experimental forest, and a Wesleyan divinity school. The multi-faith Forum on Religion and Ecology, founded by religious scholars Mary Evelyn Tucker and John Grim, is based at Yale University. Higher academia can be very compartmentalized, inhibiting interactions among scholarly fields. A few forward-looking universities have established dual degrees combing graduate environmental tracks with religion or adding religious courses to environmental studies. Although multi-faith field programs are less common, Arava Institute, Israel, welcomes Jews, Muslims, Christians, and other faiths, to learn desert ecology, permaculture, and water management at the university level. They incorporate peacekeeping into their dynamic sustainability-oriented curriculum.

Despite an increase in course offerings fusing religion and the environment at universities or their equivalents, one of the biggest lacuna in education is at the level of the local sangha, congregations, and houses of worship. The number of RENGO-based educators and religious professionals committed to environmental outreach, like Phrakhu Sangkom Thanapanyo Khunsuri, is small compared to the number of priests, rabbis, pastors, imams, and religious instructors worldwide. Published manuals, prepared materials, and training for lay educators are becoming increasingly available. Yet, more imaginative programs reaching religious leaders already serving local communities, such as the Indonesian training for Islamic imams in regions afflicted with peat burning (Chapter 10), are badly needed. Further cooperation between scientists and religious leaders could enrich educational endeavors for all age groups and cultural contexts.

Retrospective

Popular environmentalism often expects too much from religion, while failing to recognize its accomplishments and facilitate its presence. Surveys of US public attitudes have frequently found that respondents who self-identify as religious are not, on average, more environmentally aware or protective than those who are not. Conversely, optimists have suggested an eco-religious revival could single-handedly save the planet. Values independent of well-anchored communities and social networks will not overcome complex problems like anthropogenic atmospheric change and loss of biodiversity. At its best, religion inspires, commits, organizes, and serves. Spiritual formation has shaped the character and vision of environmental trailblazers. Understanding the strengths and limitations of religions will aid earthkeepers in welcoming faith-based activists to their causes.

Suggested readings

Ellingson, Stephen. *To Care for Creation: The Emergence of the Religious Environmental Movement.* Chicago, IL: University of Chicago Press, 2016.
Mills, M. Anthony. "Is Pope Francis anti-modern?" *The New Atlantis* 47 (Fall 2015): 45–55.
Taylor, Sarah. *Green Sisters: A Spiritual Ecology.* Cambridge, MA: Harvard University Press, 2007.

References

350 Pacific. "Matagi Mālohi." 350pacific.org (Dec. 12, 2019).

A'Rocha International. "A'Rocha International: Conservation and Hope." aroch.org (Feb. 27, 2019).

Abdul-Matin, Ibrahim. *Green Deen: What Islam Teaches About Protecting the Planet.* San Francisco, CA: Berett-Koehler Publishers, 2010.

Abrahams-Kavunenko, Saskia. *Enlightenment and the Gasping City: Mongolian Buddhism at a Time of Environmental Disarray.* Ithaca, NY: Cornell University Press, 2019.

Adhikari, Jagannath. "Hindu traditions and peasant farming in the Himalayan foothills of Nepal." In *Religion and Sustainable Agriculture: World Spiritual Traditions and Food Ethics*, edited by Todd LeVasseur, Pramond Parajuli, and Norman Wirzba, 121–137. Lexington: University of Kentucky Press, 2016.

African American Episcopal Church. "Climate change statement." *The African American Episcopal Church*, ame-sac.org (Aug. 4, 2019).

Albanese, Catherine. *Nature Religion in America: From the Algonkian Indians to the New Age.* Chicago, IL: University of Chicago Press, 1991.

Albanese, Catherine. *America: Religion and Religions.* Belmont, CA: Wadsworth Publishing, 2013.

Aldrich, M.A. *The Search for Vanishing Beijing: A Guide to China's Capital Through the Ages.* Hong Kong, China: Hong Kong University Press, 2008.

Alley, Kelly. *On the Banks of the Gaṅgā: When Wastewater Meets a Sacred River.* Ann Arbor: University of Michigan Press, 2005.

Altman, Nathaniel. *Sacred Trees.* San Francisco, CA: Sierra Club Books, 1994.

Anwana, E.D., R.A. Cheke, A.M. Martin, L. Obireke, M. Asei, P. Otufu, and D. Otobotekere, "The crocodile is our brother: Sacred lakes of the Niger Delta, implications for conservation management." In *Sacred Natural Sites: Conserving Nature & Culture*, edited by Bas Vershuuren, Robert Wild, Jeffery McNeely, and Gonzolo Oviedo, 129–138. Abingdon, U.K.: Earthscan, Routledge, 2010.

Arias-Arévalo, Paola, Berta, Martin-López, and Erik, Gómez-Baggethun. "Exploring intrinsic, instrumental, and relational values in sustainable management of socio-ecological systems." *Ecology and Society* 22, no. 4 (2017): 43.

Arellano, Juan Estavan. *Enduring Acequias: Wisdom of the Land, Knowledge of the Water.* Albuquerque: University of New Mexico Press, 2014.

Asano, John. "Festivals of Japan: Otaue rice planting festival." *GaijinPot Blog* 2015, gaijinpot.com, (May 8, 2017).

Ashkenazi, Michael. *Matsuri: Festivals of a Japanese Town.* Honolulu: University of Hawai'i Press, 1993.

Baker Electrical and Solar Systems. "Rockefeller Center holiday tree and menorah shine with solar power 2014." bakerelectricsolar.com (July 29, 2017).

Baker, Lynne. "Links between local folklore and conservation of Sclater's monkey (*Cercopithecus sclateris*) in Nigeria." *African Primates* 8 (2013): 17–24.

Baker, Lynne, Adebowale Tanimola, and Oluseun Olubode. "Complexities of local cultural protection in conservation: The case of an endangered African primate and forest groves protected by social taboos." *Oryx* 52, no. 2 (2017): 262–270.

Baker, Lynne, Adebowale Tanimola, Oluseun Olubode, and David Garshelis. "Distribution and abundance of sacred monkeys in Igboland, Southern Nigeria." *American Journal of Primatology* 7 (2009): 574–586.

Baker, Lynne, Oluseun Olubode, Adebowale Tanimola, and David Garshelis. "Role of local culture, religion, and human attitudes in the conservation of sacred populations of a threatened 'pest' species." *Biodiversity Conservation* 23 (2014): 1895–1909.

Balboa, Cristina. *The Paradox of Scale: How NGOs Build, Maintain, and Lose Authority in Environmental Governance.* Cambridge, MA: MIT Press, 2018.

Ballew, Nicholas, Nathan Bacheler, G. Todd, Kellison, and Amy Schueller. "Invasive lionfish reduce native fish abundance on a regional scale." *Scientific Reports* 6 (2016), article no. 32169.

Barad, Karen. "What flashes up: Theological-political-scientific fragments." In *Entangled Worlds: Religion, Science, and New Materialisms*, edited by Catherine Keller and Mary-Jane Rubenstein, loc. 493–2195. New York: Fordham University, Press, 2017.

Barrett, Susan. "'This land is me': Indigenous Australian story-telling and ecological knowledge." *Indigenous Peoples and the Environment* 3 (2013): 29–40.

Bartram, William. *Travels of William Bartram.* New York: Dover Publications, 1955.

Bashwira, Marie-Rose, Jeroen Cuvelier, Dorothea Hilhorst, and Gemma van der Haar. "Not only a man's world: Women's involvement in artisanal mining in eastern DRC." *Resources Policy* 40 (2014): 109–116.

Baugh, Amanda. *God and the Green Divide: Religious Environmentalism in Black and White.* Oakland: University of California Press, 2017.

Bauman, Whitney. "What's left (out) of the Lynn White narrative?" In *Religion and Ecological Crisis: The "Lynn White Thesis" at Fifty*, edited by Todd LeVasseur and Anna Peterson, 165–177. New York: Routledge, 2017.

Bauman, Whitney, and Heather Eaton. "Gender and queer studies." In *Grounding Religion: A Field Guide to the Study of Religion and Ecology*, edited by Whitney Bauman, Richard Bohannon, and Kevin O'Brien, 61–74. London, U.K.: Taylor & Francis, 2017.

Bauman, Whitney, Richard Bohannon, and Kevin O'Brien, eds. *Grounding Religion: A Field Guide to the Study of Religion and Ecology*, London, U.K.: Taylor & Francis, 2017.

Beatley, Timothy. *Planning for Coastal Resilience.* Washington, DC: Island Press, 2009.

Beckwith, Martha. *Hawaiian Mythology.* Honolulu: University of Hawai'i Press, 1970.

Bell, Shannon. *Fighting King Coal: The Challenges of Micromobilization in Appalachia.* Cambridge, MA: MIT Press, 2016.

Berkes, Fikert. *Sacred Ecology.* New York: Routledge, 2018.

Berry, Wendell. *The Unsettling of America: Culture & Agriculture.* Berkeley, CA: Counter Point, 2007.

Beyer, Peter. "Globalization and the religion of nature." In *Religion Today: Paganism in the Modern World*, edited by Pearson Joanne, Richard H. Roberts, and Geoffrey Samuel, 11–21. Edinburgh, U.K.: University of Edinburgh Press, 1998.

Bird, Stephen, and Barry Cunliffe. *The Essential Roman Baths.* London, U.K.: Scala, 2012.

Blackstock, Michael. "A cross-cultural approach for reconciling forest-related conflicts." *BC Journal of Ecosystem Management* 6, no. 2 (2005): 37–55.

Blackstock, Michael. "Blue-ecology: A cross-cultural ecological visions for freshwater." In *Aboriginal Peoples and Forest Lands in Canada*, edited by D.B. Tindall, Ronald Trosper, and Pamela Perreault, 180–204. Vancouver: University of British Columbia Press, 2013.

Bodhi, Bhikkhu. "The voice of the golden goose." In *A Buddhist Response to The Climate Emergency*, edited by John Stanley, David R. Loy, and Gyurme Dorje, 156–174. Sommerville, MA: Wisdom Publications, 2009.

Boff, Leonardo. *Jesus Christ Liberator: A Critical Christology of Our Time.* Maryknoll, NY: Orbis Books, 1978.

Boff, Leonardo. *Cry of the Earth, Cry of the Poor*. Maryknoll, NY: Orbis Books, 1997.

Boff, Leonardo. *Francis of Rome and Francis of Assisi: A New Springtime for the Church*. Marynoll, NY: Orbis Books, 2014.

Bohannon, Richard, ed. *Religion and Environments: A Reader in Religion, Nature and Ecology*. London, U.K.: Bloomsbury Academic, 2014.

Bonotto, Daniel Marcos, and Ene Glória da Silveira. *The Amazon Gold Rush and Environmental Mercury Contamination*. New York: NOVA Science Publishers, 2009.

Boyce, Mark, and Robert Keiter, eds. *The Greater Yellowstone Ecosystem*. New Haven, CT: Yale University Press, 1991.

Bradley, Mark. "Approaches to pollution and propriety." In *Rome, Pollution and Propriety: Dirt, Disease and Hygiene in the Eternal City from Antiquity to Modernity*, edited by Mark Bradley, 11–42. Cambridge, U.K.: Cambridge University Press, 2012.

Bratton, Susan P. "The ecotheology of James Watt." *Environmental Ethics* 5, no. 3 (1983): 28–40.

Bratton, Susan P. "Christian ecotheology and the Old Testament." *Environmental Ethics* 6, no. 3 (1984): 5–19.

Bratton, Susan P. "The original desert solitaire: Early Christian monasticism and wilderness." *Environmental Ethics* 10, no. 2 (1988): 31–53.

Bratton, Susan P. "Loving nature: Eros or agape." *Environmental Ethics* 14, no. 1 (1992): 3–25.

Bratton, Susan P. *Christianity, Wilderness and Wildlife: The Original Desert Solitaire*. Scranton, PA: University of Scranton Press, 2009.

Bratton, Susan P. *The Spirit of the Appalachian Trail: Community, Environment, and Belief on a Long Distance Hiking Path*. Knoxville: University of Tennessee Press, 2012.

Bratton, Susan P. "Tradition as benefit or barrier: The case of U.S. Christian religion in the formation of environmental ethics." In *14th Cary Conference, Linking Ecology and Ethics for a Changing World: Values, Philosophy, and Action*, edited by Riccardo Rozzi, S.TA. Pickett, Clare Palmer, Juan Armesto, and J. Baird Callicott, 71–84. New York: Springer, 2014.

Bratton, Susan P. *Churchscape: Megachurches and the Iconography of the Environment*. Waco, TX: Baylor University Press, 2016.

Bratton, Susan P. "Ecodimensionality as a religious foundation for sustainability." *Sustainability* 10, no. 4 (2018): 1021; doi.org/10.3390/su10041021.

Bratton, Susan P. "Spiritual encounters with nature: Day hiker perceptions of trail experiences in three settings—urban, suburban natural area, and wildland; representing three modes of hiking—goal-directed, nature observation, and meditative." *Worldviews* (2020) 24: 35–57.

Bratton, Susan P., and Shawn Hinz. "Ethical responses to commercial fisheries decline in the Republic of Ireland." *Ethics and the Environment* 7, no. 1 (2002): 54–91.

Brenneman, Walter, Jr., and Mary Brenneman. *Crossing the Circle at the Holy Wells of Ireland*. Charlottesville: University of Virginia Press, 1995.

Buck, Elizabeth. *Paradise Remade: The Politics of Culture and History in Hawai'i*. Philadelphia, PA: Temple University Press, 1993.

Bullard, Robert. *Dumping in Dixie: Race, Class, and Environmental Quality*. Boulder, CO: Westview Press, 1990.

Bunce, Michael, Marta Szulkin, Heather Lerner, Ian Barnes, Beth Shapiro, Alan Cooper, and Richard Holdaway. "Ancient DNA provides new insights into the evolutionary history of New Zealand's extinct giant eagle." *PLoS Biology* 3, no. 1 (2005): e9.

Butler, Sarah. "Comic relief and Fairtrade back ethical gold mining in east Africa." *The Guardian*, Oct. 1, 2017, theguardian.com.

Cafaro, Philip. *How Many is Too Many? The Progressive Argument for Reducing Immigration into the United States*. Chicago, IL: University of Chicago Press, 2015.

Caradonna, Jeremy. *Sustainability: A History*. Oxford, U.K.: Oxford University Press, 2014.

Carmichael, Elizabeth and Chloe Sayer. *The Skeleton Feast: The Day of the Dead in Mexico*. Austin: University of Texas Press, 1992.

Carrasco, David. *Religions of Mesoamerica*. Francisco, CA: HarperCollins, 1990.

Carson, Rachel. *Silent Spring.* New York: Houghton Mifflin, 2002 (originally published 1962).

Casey, Joan, Jason Su, Lucas Henneman, and others. "Improved asthma outcomes observed in the vicinity of coal power plant retirement, retrofit and conversion to natural gas." *Nature Energy* (2020), doi.org/10.1038/s41560-020-0600-2.

Catholic Climate Covenant. "Pope Francis's Encyclical and climate change." *Catholic Climate Covenant,* catholicclimatecovenant.org (28 Jan. 2020).

Center for Environmental Education, North Lucknow. "Water conservation and Eco-Holi Campaign in the Schools of Lucknow." www.paryavaranmitra.in (Oct. 23, 2016).

Cesari, Jocelyne. "Mosque conflicts in European cities: Introduction." *Journal of Ethnic and Migration Studies* 31, no. 6 (2005): 1015–1024.

Ceurstemont, Sandrine. "The mosque that powers a village." *Untold World, BBC News,* Sept. 27, 2017, bbc.com.

Chandran, M.D. and J. Donald Hughes. "The sacred groves of South India: Ecology, traditional communities and religious change." *Social Compass* 44 (1997): 413–427.

Chernela, Janet. "Indigenous knowledge and Amazonian blackwaters of hunger." In *Cultural and Spiritual Values of Biodiversity,* edited by D. Posey. 423–426. London, U.K.: United Nations Environmental Program, 1999.

Chicago, Judy. *The Dinner Party,* 1978. The Elizabeth A. Sackler Center for Feminist Art, of the Brooklyn Museum, New York www.brooklynmuseum.org/eascfa/dinner_party/home (Sept. 12, 2019).

Chirikure, Shadreck. "Metals in society: Iron production and its position in Iron Age communities of Southern Africa." *Journal of Social Archeology* 7, no. 1 (2007): 72–100.

Christian Farmers Federation of Ontario. "Issues." christianfarmers.org (Aug. 28, 2017).

Christopher, John. *London's Historic Railway Stations Through Time.* Stroud, U.K.: Amberly, 2015.

Clark, Emma. *The Art of the Islamic Garden.* Marlborough, U.K.: The Crowood Press, 2010.

Colopy, Cheryl. *Dirty, Sacred Rivers: Confronting South Asia's Water Crisis.* Oxford, U.K.: Oxford University Press, 2012.

Cope, Phil. *Holy Wells of Scotland.* Brigend, U.K.: Serend Press, 2015.

Coté, Charlotte. *Spirits of Our Whaling Ancestors: Revitalizing Makah and Nuu-chah-nulth Traditions.* Seattle: University of Washington Press, 2010.

Crane, Peter. *Ginkgo: The Tree that Time Forgot.* New Haven, CT: Yale University Press, 2015.

Crew, Phyllis. *Calvinist Preaching and Iconoclasm in the Netherlands 1544–1569.* Cambridge, U.K.: Cambridge University Press, 1978.

CSAM, Communities and Small Scale Mining Division, The World Bank. *Mining Together: Large Scale Mining Meets Artisanal Mining.* Washington, DC: World Bank, 2009.

Daly, Mary. *Gyn/Ecology: The Metaphysics of Radical Feminism.* Boston, MA: Beacon Press, 1978.

Daneel, Marthinus. "Earthkeeping churches are African churches." In *Christianity and Ecology: Seeking the Well-Being of Earth and Humans,* edited by Dieter Hessel and Rosemary Radford Ruether, 531–552. Cambridge, MA: Harvard University Press, 2000.

Darlington, Susan. *The Ordination of a Tree: The Thai Buddhist Environmental Movement.* Albany: State University of New York Press, 2012.

Davidson, Helen. "Pacific islanders blockade Newcastle coal port to protest rising sea levels." *The Guardian,* Oct. 17, 2019, theguardian.com.

Deil, Ulrich, Heike Culmsee, and Mohamed Berraine. "Sacred groves in Morocco: Vegetation mosaics & biological values." In *African Sacred Groves: Ecological Dynamics & Social Change,* edited by Michael Sheridan and Celia Nyamweru, 87–102. Athens, OH: Ohio University Press, 2008.

Deland, Derek. "The Flint water crisis and NSF's role in protecting public health." Presentation. Environmental Seminar Series, Baylor University, Waco, Texas, Jan. 22, 2020.

Deudney, Daniel. "In search of Gaian politics: Earth's religion's challenge to modern western civilization." In *Ecological Resistance Movements: The Global Emergence of Radical Popular Environmentalism,* edited by Bron Taylor, 282–299. Albany: State University of New York Press, 1995.

Diamond, Jared. "Evolution, consequences and future of plant and animal domestication." *Nature* 418 (2002): 700–707.

DNA Correspondent. "Take a pledge to celebrate eco-Holi." *DNA Indore*, Feb. 15, 2014, dnaindia. com (Oct. 23, 2016).

Douglas, Mary. *Purity and Danger: An Analysis of Concepts of Pollution and Taboo*. Abingdon, U.K.: Routledge, 2003.

Doyle, Cathal, and Jill Cariño. *Making Free, Prior & Informed Consent a Reality, Indigenous Peoples and the Extractive Sector*. London, U.K.: Middlesex University School of Law and the Ecumenical Council for Corporate Responsibility, www.piplinks.org/makingfpicareality, 2013.

Duke University. "Contamination in North Dakota linked to fracking spills: Metals, salts and radioactivity in brine-laden wastewater years later." *Science Daily*, April 27, 2016, www.sciencedaily. com/releases/2016.04/16042715617.htm.

Dulap, Riley, and Peter Jacques. "Climate change denial books and conservative think tanks: Exploring the connection." *American Behavioral Scientist* 57, no. 6 (2013): 699–731.

Duncan, Richard P., Alison Boyer, and Tim Blackburn. "Magnitude and variation of prehistoric bird extinctions in the Pacific." *Proceedings of the National Academy of Science* 110, no. 16 (2013): 6436–6441.

Dunne, John, and Daniel Goleman, eds. *Ecology, Ethics, and Interdependence: The Dalai Lama in Conversation with Leading Thinkers on Climate Change*. Somerville, MA: Wisdom Publications, 2018.

Durham and Northumberland Counties. "Lady's Well, Holystone, Harbottle, No. N1209." *Keys to the Past*, http://www.keystothepast.info/Pages/pgDetail.aspx?PRN=N1209 (13 June 2016).

Dürr, Eveline. "'Tidy Kiwis/dirty Asians': Cultural pollution and migration in Auckland, New Zealand." In *Urban Pollution: Cultural Meanings, Social Practices*, edited by Eveline Dürr and Rivke Jaffe, 30–56. New York: Berghahn Books, 2010.

East, May. "Current thinking on sustainable human habitat: the Findhorn Ecovillage case." *Ecocycles* 4, no. 1 (2018): 68–72.

Eaton, Heather. *Introducing Ecofeminist Theologies*. London, U.K.: T&T Clark, 2005.

Eco-Peace Middleast. *Voices from the Field- Water and Energy- Working Together For More Security* (video), Lage.Bericht//Middle East//EcoPeace - Water and Energy: Working Together For More Security, youtube.com/watch?time_continue=274&v=nrV1QqfvkOM&feature=emb_title, Feb. 17, 2017.

Eisenberg, Ronald. *JPS Guide to Jewish Traditions*. Philadelphia, PA: Jewish Publication Society, 2004.

Elias, Derek, Soimart Rungmansee, and Irwin Cruz. "The knowledge that saved the sea gypsies." *A World of Science* 3, no. 2 (2005): 20–23, unseco.org.

Elizondo, Virgil. *Guadalupe: Mother of the New Creation*. Maryknoll, NY: Orbis Books, 1997.

Ellingson, Stephen. *To Care for Creation: The Emergence of the Religious Environmental Movement*. Chicago, IL: University of Chicago Press, 2016.

Ellwood, Robert. *Japanese Religion*. New York: Routledge, 2008.

Emery, Amanda. "Muslim community donates $10,000 to aid children in Flint's water crisis." *MLIVE*, March 4, 2016, mlive.com.

Energy Transfer Partners. *Dakota Access Pipeline Facts*. daplpipelinefacts.com (22 Dec. 2016).

Erbentraut, Joseph. "Here's what you should know about the Dakota Pipeline protest." *Huffington Post*, Nov. 2, 2016, huffpost.com.

Estavéz-Saá, Margarita, and Marie Lorenzo-Modia. "The ethics and aesthetic of eco-caring: Contemporary debates on ecofeminism." *Women's Studies* 47, no. 2 (2018): 123–146.

Estavéz-Saá, Margarita, and Marie Lorenzo-Modia, eds. *The Ethics and Aesthetics of Eco-Caring: Contemporary Debates on Ecofeminism*. Abingdon, U.K.: Routledge, 2020.

Estes, Nick, and Jaskiran Dhillon, eds. *Standing with Standing Rock: Voices from the #NoDAPL Movement*. Minneapolis: University of Minnesota Press, 2019.

Fernández-Morera, Dario. *The Myth of the Andalusian Paradise: Muslims, Christians and Jews Under Islamic Rule in Spain*. Wilmington, DE: Intercollegiate Study Books, 2016.

Field, Christopher. "Climate change 2019: Finding the accelerator pedal." American Association for the Advancement of Science Annual Meeting, Washington, DC, 2019.

Findhorn Community. *The Findhorn Garden Story*. Forres, U.K.: Findhorn Press, 2008.

Finney, Carolyn. *Black Faces/White Spaces: Reimagining the Relationship of African Americans to the Great Outdoors*. Chapel Hill: University of North Carolina Press, 2014.

Forster, Peter, and Marijke Wilhelmus. "The role of individuals in community change with the Findhorn intentional community." *Contemporary Justice Review* 8, no. 4 (2005): 367–379.

Fowler, Robert Booth. *The Greening of Protestant Thought*. Chapel Hill: University of North Carolina Press, 1995.

Gao, Yufung, and Susan Park. "Elephant ivory trade in China: Trends and drivers." *Biological Conservation* 180 (2014): 23–30.

Garlick, Jennifer, Basil Keane, and Tracey Borgfelt, eds. *Te Taiao: Māori and the Natural World*. Auckland, N.Z.: David Bateman, 2010.

Gebara, Ivone. *Longing for Running Water: Ecofeminism and Liberation*. Minneapolis, MN: Fortress Press, 1999.

Gemmell, Neil, Michael Schwartz, and Bruce Robertson. "Moa were many." *The Royal Society Biology Letters B Supplement* (2004) S430–S432.

Gigliotti, Simone. *The Train Journey: Transit, Captivity, and Witnessing in the Holocaust*. New York: Berghahn Books, 2009.

Gilio-Whitaker, Dina. *As Long and Grass Grows: The Indigenous Fight for Environmental Justice from Colonization to Standing Rock*. Boston, MA: Beacon Press, 2019.

Gilmore, Lee. *Theater in a Crowded Fire: Ritual and Spirituality at Burning Man*. Berkeley: University of California Press, 2010.

Glave, Dianne. *Rooted in the Earth: Reclaiming the African American Environmental Heritage*. Chicago, IL: Lawrence Hill Books, 2010.

Glave, Dianne, and Mark Stoll, eds. *To Love the Wind and Rain: African Americans and Environmental History*. Pittsburgh, PA: University of Pittsburgh Press, 2006.

Global Buddhist Climate Change Collective. "Buddhist Climate Change Statement to World Leaders 2015." Global Buddhist Climate Change Collective, gbccc.org (June 27, 2020).

Gloucester Cathedral. *Gloucester Cathedral*. gloucestercathedral.org.uk (21 June 2019).

Goodell, Jeff. *The Water Will Come: Rising Seas, Sinking Cities, and the Remaking of the Civilized World*. New York: Little Brown, 2017.

Gordenker, Alice. "Sake barrels at shrines." *The Japan Times News*, October 16, 2007, japantimes. co.jp.

Gordon-McCutchan, R.C. *The Taos Indians and the Battle for Blue Lake*. Santa Fe, NM: Red Crane Books, 1991.

Gore, A. *An Inconvenient Truth: The Planetary Emergency of Global Warming and What We Can Do About It*. New York: Rodale Books, 2006.

Gorringe, Timothy. *A Theology of the Built Environment: Justice, Empowerment, and Redemption*. Cambridge, U.K.: Cambridge University Press, 2002.

Gottlieb, Roger. *A Greener Faith: Religious Environmentalism and Our Planet's Future*. Oxford, U.K.: Oxford University Press, 2009.

Green Muslims of Washington, D,C. "Welcome *Sha'ban*: O Allah bless us in *Rajab* and *Sha'ban* and enable us to reach Ramadan." greenramadan.com (Oct. 21, 2016).

Grim, John, and Mary Evelyn Tucker. *Ecology and Religion*. Washington, DC: Island Press, 2014.

Griswold, Eliza. "Radical encounters: Climate change and religious conflict in Africa." In *Confronting Religious Violence: A Counternarrative*, edited by Richard Burridge and Jonathan Sacks, 77–91. Waco, TX: Baylor University Press, 2018.

Griswold, Eliza. "The renegade nuns who took on a pipeline." *The New Yorker*, April 10, 2019, newyorker.com.

Grumet, Robert, ed. *Voices from the Delaware Big House Ceremony*. Norman: University of Oklahoma Press, 2001.

Guha, Ramachandra. *How Much Should a Person Consume? Environmentalism in India and the United States*. Berkeley: University of California Press, 2006.

Guthrie, R. Dale. *The Nature of Paleolithic Art*. Chicago, IL: University of Chicago Press, 2005.

Haberman, David. *River of Love in an Age of Pollution: The Yamuna River of Northern India*. Berkeley: University of California Press, 2006.

Halpern, Benjamin, and Tundi Agardy. "Ecosystem based approaches to marine conservation and management." In *Marine Community Ecology and Conservation*, edited by Mark Bertness, John Bruno, Brian Silliman, and John Stachowicz, 477–493. Sunderland, MA: Sinauer, 2014.

Haluza-Delay, Randolf. "Religion and climate change: varieties in viewpoints and practices." *WIREs Climate Change* 5 (2014): 261–279.

Hampton, O.W. *Culture of Stone: Sacred and Profane Uses of Stone Among the Dani*. College Station: Texas A&M Press, 1999.

Hardacre, Helen. *Shinto: A History*. Oxford, U.K.: Oxford University Press, 2017.

Hardin, Garrett. "The tragedy of the commons." *Science* 162 (1968): 1243–1248.

Hargrove, Eugene, ed. *Religion and Environmental Crisis*. Athens: University of Georgia Press, 1986.

Harkin, Michael, and David Lewis, eds. *Native Americans and the Environment: Perspectives on the Ecological Indian*. Lincoln: University of Nebraska Press, 2007.

Harris, Melanie. *Ecowomanism: African American Women and Earth-Honoring Faith*. Maryknoll, NY: Orbis Books, 2017.

Harris, Peter. *Kingfisher's Fire: A Story of Hope for God's Earth*. Oxford, U.K.: Monarch Books, 2008.

Harrison, Peter. "Protestantism and the making of modern science." In *Protestantism after 500 Years*, edited by Thomas Howard and Mark Noll. Oxford, U.K.: Oxford University Press, 2016, doi: 10.1093/acprof:oso/9780190264789.001.0001.

Harrison, Robert. *Forests: The Shadow of Civilization*. Chicago, IL: University of Chicago Press, 1992.

Hartman, Laura. *The Christian Consumer: Living Faithfully in a Fragile World*. Oxford, U.K.: Oxford University Press, 2011.

Harvey, Graham. *Animism: Respecting the Living World*. New York: Columbia University Press, 2006.

Hayhoe, Katherine, and Andrew Farley. *A Climate for Change: Global Warming Facts for Faith Based Decisions*. New York: Faith Words, 2009.

Hellmund, Paul, and Daniel Smith. *Designing Greenways*. Washington, DC: Island Press, 2006.

Hendrix, Cullen, and Idean Salehyan. "Climate change, rainfall and social conflict in Africa." *Journal of Peace Research* 49, no. 1 (2012): 35–50.

Herbert, Eugenia. *Iron, Gender and Power: Rituals of Transformation in African Society*. Bloomington: Indiana University Press, 1993.

Heschel, Abraham. *The Sabbath: Its Meaning for Modern Man*. New York: Farrar, Strauss and Giroux, 1951.

Hillel, Daniel. *Out of the Earth: Civilization and the Life of the Soil*. Berkeley: University of California Press, 1991.

Hilson, Gavin. "'A load too heavy': Critical reflections on the child labor problem in Africa's small-scale mining sector." *Children and Youth Services Review* 30 (2008): 1233–1245.

Hinz, Shawn, and Susan P. Bratton. "Religion and fisheries decline in traditional Irish fishing communities with a comparison to the Pacific Northwest region USA." *Ecotheology* 8 (2000): 114–131.

Hirsch, Susan, and E. Franklin Dukes. *Mountaintop Mining in Appalachia: Understanding Stakeholders and Change in Environmental Conflict*. Athens: Ohio University Press, 2014.

Ho, Elaine, Chih Woon, and Kamalini Ramdas. *Changing Landscapes of Singapore: Old Tensions, New Discoveries*. Singapore: National University of Singapore Press, 2013.

Horton, Tim. *Turning the Tide: Saving the Chesapeake Bay*. Washington, DC: Island Press, 2003.

Houtman, Dick, and Birgit Meyer. *Things: Religion and the Question of Materiality*. New York: Fordham University Press, 2012.

Hunt-Perry, Patricia, and Lyn Fine. "All Buddhism is engaged: Thích Nhất Hạnh and the Order of Innerbeing." In *Engaged Buddhism in the West*, edited by Christopher Queen, 34–66. Sommerville, MA: Wisdom Publications, 2000.

Hussain, Farhat. *The Cordoba Mosque*. London, U.K.: Farhat A. Hussain, 2014.

Inhabitant. "World's first solar powered Menorah lights up Woodstock, NY." *Inhabitant*, Dec. 21, 2011, https://inhabitat.com/nyc/worlds-first-solar-powered-menorah-lights-up-woodstock-ny/#popup-940756.

Interfaith Partners for the Chesapeake. *Interfaith Partners for the Chesapeake.* interfaithchesapeake.org (March 14, 2019).

International Wire. "Some stunning new numbers from the Treasury Department show just how much money ISIS makes selling oil." Lanham, MD: *International Wire,* CBS Broadcasting, Inc., Dec. 11, 2015, internationalwire.org.

Interfaith Power and Light. "A religious response to global warming." Interfaith Power and Light, interfaithpowerandlight.org (Sept. 15, 2020).

Itam, Talal, trans. *Qur'an in English.* Plano, TX: Clear Quran, 2018.

Jackson, Jean. *The Fish People: Linguistic Exogamy and Tukanoan Identity in Northwest Amazonian.* Cambridge, U.K.: Cambridge University Press, 1983.

Jacobsen, Eric. *Sidewalks in the Kingdom: The New Urbanism and the Christian Faith.* Grand Rapids, MI: Brazos Press, 2003.

Jain, Pankaj. "Dharma for the earth, water, and agriculture: Perspectives from the Swadhyaya." In *Religion and Sustainable Agriculture: World Spiritual Traditions and Food Ethics,* edited by Todd LeVasseur, Pramond Parajuli, and Norman Wirzba, 139–152. Lexington: University of Kentucky Press, 2016.

James, P., J. Hart, R. Banay, and F. Laden. "Exposure to greenness and mortality in a nationwide prospective cohort study of women." *Environmental Health Perspectives* 124, no. 9 (2016): 1344–1352.

James, Van. *Ancient Sites of Hawai'i.* Honolulu, HI: Mutual Publishing, 1995.

Jaubert, Jacques, Sophie Verheyden, Dominique Genty, and others. "Early Neanderthal constructions deep in Bruniquel Cave in southwestern France." *Nature* 534 (2016): 111–114.

Jenkins, Willis, Mary Evelyn Tucker, and John Grim, eds. *The Routledge Handbook of Religion and Ecology.* New York: Routledge, 2016.

Johnson, Russell, and Kerry Moran. *Tibet's Sacred Mountain: The Extraordinary Pilgrimage to Mount Kailas.* Rochester, VT: Park Street Press, 1989.

Jones, Robert P., Daniel Cox, and Juhem Navarro-Rivera. *Believers, Sympathizers & Skeptics: Why Americans are Conflicted about Climate Change, Environmental Policy and Science.* Washington, DC: Public Religion Research Institute, 2014.

Judson, Katherine. *Myths and Legends of the Pacific Northwest.* Chicago: A.C. McClurg & Co., 1910.

Kadampa Meditation Center of Baltimore. "World Peace Garden." https://meditationinmaryland. org/about-us/cafe-shop-gardens/ (March 12, 2019).

Kaho'olawe Island Reserve Commission. *Kaho'olawe Island Reserve FY17 Year in Review.* Honolulu: Kaho'olawe Island Reserve Commission. www.kahoolawe.hawaii.gov (May 14, 2018).

Kaltner, John. *Introducing the Qur'an: For Today's Reader.* Minneapolis, MN: Fortress Press, 2011.

Kaufman, Alexander. "Thailand's Moral Rice Revolution: Cultivating a collective ecological consciousness." In *Religion and Sustainable Agriculture: World Spiritual Traditions and Food Ethics,* edited by Todd LeVasseur, Pramond Parajuli, and Norman Wirzba, 173–193. Lexington: University of Kentucky Press, 2016.

Kaza, Stephanie. *Green Buddhism: Practice and Compassionate Action in Uncertain Times.* Boulder, CO: Shambhala Press, 2019.

Keegan, Marcia. *The Taos Pueblo and Its Sacred BlueLake.* Santa Fe, NM: Clear Light Publishers, 1991.

Keller, Catherine, and Mary-Jane Rubenstein. "Introduction: Tangled Matters." In *Entangled Worlds: Religion, Science, and New Materialisms,* edited by Catherine Keller and Mary-Jane Rubenstein, 56–490. New York: Fordham University, Press, 2017.

Keller, David. "Deep Ecology." In *Encyclopedia of Environmental Ethics and Philosophy,* Vol. 1, edited by J. Baird Callicott and Robert Frodeman, 206–210. New York: Macmillan, 2008.

Keller, Robert. *American Indians and National Parks.* Tucson: University of Arizona Press, 1999.

Kent, Eliza. *Sacred Groves and Local Gods: Religion and Environmentalism in South India.* Oxford, U.K.: Oxford University Press, 2013.

Khan, A. *Plants, Gardens and the Qur'an.* Karachi, Pakistan: Jasmina, 2001.

Kidwell, Jeremy, Franlin Ginn, Micheal Northcott, Elizabeth Bomberg, and Alice Hague. "Christian climate care: Slow change, modesty and eco-theology." *Geo: Geography and Environment* (2018): doi 10.1002/geo2.59.

Kinsley, David. *Ecology and Religion: Ecological Spirituality in Cross-Cultural Perspective*. New York: Pearson, 1994.

Kirch, Patrick. *A Shark Going Inland is My Chief: The Island Civilization of Ancient Hawai'i*. Berkeley: University of California Press, 2012.

Knight, Catherine. *New Zealand's Rivers: An Environmental History*. Canterbury, N.Z.: University of Canterbury Press, 2016.

Krasny, Marianne, and Keith Tidball. *Civic Ecology: Adaptation and Transformation from the Ground Up*. Cambridge, MA: MIT Press, 2015.

Kraybill, Donald. *The Riddle of Amish Culture*. Baltimore, MD: Johns Hopkins University Press, 2001.

Krech, Shepard, III, ed. *Indians, Animals and the Fur Trade: A Critique of Keepers of the Game*. Athens: University of George Press, 1981.

Krech, Shepard, III. *The Ecological Indian: Myth and History*. New York: Norton, 1999.

Krech, Shepard, III. "Animism and reincarnation: Lynn White in Indian Country." In *Religion and Ecological Crisis: The "Lynn White Thesis" at Fifty*, edited by Todd LeVasseur and Anna Peterson, 27–88. New York: Routledge, 2017.

Krieger, Barbara. *The Dead Sea and the Jordan River*. Bloomington: Indiana University Press, 2016.

Lansing, J. Stephen. *Priests and Programmers: Technologies of Power in the Engineered Landscape of Bali*. Princeton, NJ: Princeton University Press, 2007.

Lansing, J. Stephen, and James Kremer. "Emergent properties of Balinese water temple networks: Co-adaptation on a rugged fitness landscape." *American Anthropologist* 95, no. 1 (1993): 97–114.

Lansing, J. Stephen, Stefan Thurner, N. Chung, Aurélie Coudurier-Curveur, and others. "Adaptive self-organization of Bali's ancient rice terraces." *PNAS* 114, no. 25(2017): doi. 10.1073/pnas.1605369114.

Latour, Bruno. *Politics of Nature: How to Bring the Sciences into Democracy*. Cambridge, MA: Harvard University Press, 2004.

Latour, Bruno. *Facing Gaia: Eight Lectures on the New Climatic Regime*. Cambridge, U.K.: Polity, 2017.

Lauer, Nancy, Jennifer Harkness, and Avner Vengosh. "Brine spills associated with unconventional oil development in North Dakota." *Environmental Science & Technology* 50, no. 10 (2016): 5389–5397, doi: 10.1021/acs.est.5b06349.

Laughland, Oliver. "'Evil economics': William Barber condemns proposed plastics facility in Cancer Alley." *The Guardian*, Oct. 24, 2019, theguardian.com.

Lawson, Steven. *Running for Freedom: Civil Rights and Black Politics in America Since 1941*. New York: Wiley-Blackwell, 2014.

Layzer, Judith. *Natural Experiments: Ecosystem-Based Management and the Environment*. Cambridge, MA: MIT Press, 2008.

Lennon, Jack. "Pollution, religion and society in the Roman world." In *Rome, Pollution and Propriety: Dirt, Disease and Hygiene in the Eternal City from Antiquity to Modernity*, edited by Mark Bradley, 45–58. Cambridge, U.K.: Cambridge University Press, 2012.

Leopold, Aldo. *A Sand County Almanac and Sketches Here and There*. New York: Oxford University Press, 1949.

Lester, Lisa. "Ecological Society of America responds to Pope Francis's *Encyclical Laudato Si': On Care for our Common Home*." Ecological Society of America, June 29, 2015, http://www.esa.org/esa/ecological-society-of-america-responds-to-pope-francis-encyclical-laudato-si-on-care-for-our-common-home/.

Leung, Rebecca. "Sea gypsies saw signs in the waves." *CBS News*, March 18, 2005, cbsnews.com.

LeVasseur, Todd. *Religious Agrarianism and the Return of Place: From Values to Practice in Sustainable Agriculture*. Albany: State University of New York Press, 2017.

LeVasseur, Todd, Pramond Parajuli, and Norman Wirzba, eds. *Religion and Sustainable Agriculture: World Spiritual Traditions and Food Ethics*. Lexington: University of Kentucky Press, 2016.

Lewis, John, and Stephen Sheppard. "First Nations' spiritual conceptions of forests and forest management." In *Aboriginal Peoples and Forest Lands in Canada*, edited by D.B. Tindall, Ronald Trosper, and Pamela Perreault, 205–223. Vancouver: University of British Columbia Press, 2013.

Lipka, Michael. "U.S. religious groups and their political leanings." Pew Research Center, Feb. 23, 2016, pewresearch.org.

Lotze, Heike K., and Loren Mcclenachan. "Marine historical ecology: Informing the future by learning from the past." In *Marine Community Ecology and Conservation*, edited by Mark Bertness, John Bruno, Brian R. Silliman, and John Stachowicz, 165–200. Sunderland, MA: Sinauer, 2014.

Louden, James, Michael Howells, and Augustin Fuentes. "The importance of integrative anthropology: A preliminary investigation employing primatological and cultural anthropological data collection methods in assessing human-monkey co-existence in Bali, Indonesia." *Ecological and Environmental Anthropology* 2, no. 1 (2006): 1–13.

Lovelock, James. *The Vanishing Face of Gaia: A Final Warning.* New York: Basic Books, 2009.

Lowe, David, Cassandra Atherton, and Alyson Miller, eds. *The Unfinished Atomic Bomb: Shadows and Reflections.* London, U.K.: Lexington Books, 2018.

Lowe, Kevin. *Baptized with the Soil: Christian Agrarians and the Crusade for Rural America.* Oxford, U.K.: Oxford University Press, 2016.

Lowery, Richard. *Sabbath and Jubilee.* St. Louis, MO: Chalice Press, 2000.

Lujala, Paivi, and Siri Aas Rustad, eds. *High-Value Natural Resources and Post-Conflict Peacebuilding.* Tokyo, Japan: University of Toyko, 2012.

Luther College. *Luther College, Decorah, Iowa.* luther.edu (17 June 2019).

Lüthi, Damaris. "Private cleanliness, public mess: Purity, pollution and space in Kottar, South India." In *Urban Pollution: Cultural Meanings, Social Practices*, edited by Eveline Dürr and Rivke Jaffe, 57–85. New York: Berghahn Books, 2010.

Mabee, Holly, D.B. Tindall, George Hoberg, and J.P. Gladu. "Co-management of forest lands: The case of Clayoquot Sounds and Gwaii Haanas." In *Aboriginal Peoples and Forest Lands in Canada*, edited by D.B. Tindall, Ronald Trosper, and Pamela Perreault, 242–259. Vancouver: University of British Columbia Press, 2013.

MacDonald, James M., and Robert Hoppe. "Large family farms continue to dominate U.S. agricultural production." *America's Diverse Family Farms*, United States Department of Agriculture Economic Research Service, www.ers.usda.gov (22 Sept. 2017).

Magnusson, Warren, and Karena Shaw, eds. *A Political Space: Reading the Global Through Clayoquot Sound.* Minneapolis: University of Minnesota Press, 2003.

Maguire, Lynn, and James Justus. "Why intrinsic value is a poor basis for conservation decisions." *Bioscience* 58 (2008): 910–911.

Mallarach, Josep-Maria, and Thymio Papayannis. "Sacred natural sites in technologically developed countries: Reflections from the experience of the Delos Initiative." In *Sacred Natural Sites: Conserving Nature & Culture*, edited by Bas Vershuuren, Robert Wild, Jeffery McNeely, and Gonzolo Oviedo, 198–208. Abingdon, U.K.: Earthscan, Routledge, 2010.

Mallet, Victor. *River of Life, River of Death: The Ganges and India's Future.* Oxford, U.K.: Oxford University Press, 2017.

Martin, Calvin. *Keepers of the Game, Indian-Animal Relationships and the Fur Trade.* Berkeley: University of California Press, 1982.

Martin, Paul. *Twilight of the Mammoths: Ice Age Extinctions and the Rewilding of America.* Berkley: University of California Press, 2005.

Matthews, Washington. "The Mountain Chant: A Navaho ceremony." *Fifth Annual Report to the Bureau of [American] Ethnology.* Washington: Smithsonian Institution, 1884.

Mayhew, Elizabeth. "British advisor speaks on climate change." *Liberty News,* March 10, 2009. www.liberty.edu/alumni/alumni-news/?MID=16533.

McKanan, Dan. *Eco-Alchemy: Anthroposophy and the History and Future of Environmentalism.* Oakland: University of California Press, 2018.

McCarthy, Emer. "'My right to breathe': Indian students protest against pollution." *Reuters News Agency,* Nov. 17, 2019, reuters.com.

McDuff, Mallory. *Natural Saints: How People of Faith are Working to Save God's Earth.* Oxford, U.K.: Oxford University Press, 2010.

McFague, Sallie. *Blessed are the Consumers: Climate Change and the Practice of Restraint*. Minneapolis, MN: Fortress Press, 2013.

McGregor, Davianna Pōmaika'i. *Nā Kua'āinka: Living Hawaiian Culture*. Honolulu: University of Hawai'i Press, 2007.

McKay, Jeanne, Fachruddin Mangunjaya, Yoan Dinata, Stuart Harrop, and Fazulan Khalid. "Practice what you preach: A faith-based approach to conservation in Indonesia." *Flora and Fauna International* 48, no. 1 (2013): 23–29.

Meawad, Stephen. "The wholeness of living ecologically: The development of Coptic Orthodox Politeia and its contributions to ecological ethics." Session A18-123, *American Academy of Religion Annual Meeting, Boston*, Nov. 18, 2017.

Medina, Daniel. "'Water Is Life': A look inside the Dakota Access Pipeline Protesters' Camp." *NBC News* Dec. 3, 2106a, nbcnews.com.

Medina, Daniel. "Governor orders pipeline protesters to leave, citing winter weather." *NBC News*, Nov.28, 2016b, nbcnews.com.

Medina, Daniel, and Chiara Sottile. "Reprieve for Native Tribes as Army denies Dakota Pipeline permit." *NBC News*, Dec. 4, 2016, nbcnews.com.

Meffe, Gary, Larry Nielsen, Richard Knight, and Dennis Schoenborn. *Ecosystem Management: Adaptive, Community Based Management*. Washington, DC: Island Press, 2002.

Mehyar, Munqeth, Nader Al Khateeb, Gidon Bromberg, and Elizabeth Koch-Ya' ari. "Transboundary cooperation in the Lower Jordan River Basin." In *Water and Post-Conflict Peacebuilding*, edited by E. Weinthal, J. Troell, and M. Nakayama, 265–270. Abingdon, U.K.: Routledge, 2014.

Meier, Albert, Susan P. Bratton, and David Duffy, "Biodiversity in the herbaceous layer and salamanders in Appalachian primary forests." In *Eastern Old Growth Forest: Prospects for Rediscovery and Recovery*, edited by Mary Davis, 49–64. Washington, DC: Island Press, 1996.

Meltzer, Graham. *Findhorn Reflections: A Very Personal Take on Life Inside the Famous Spiritual Community and Ecovillage*. Findhorn, U.K.: Graham Meltzer, 2015.

Merchant, Carolyn, *The Death of Nature: Women, Ecology, and the Scientific Revolution*. San Francisco, CA: Harper and Row, 1980.

Mills, M. Anthony. "Is Pope Francis anti-modern?" *The New Atlantis* (Fall 2015) 47: 45–55.

Mitchell, Garrett. "Arizonans march against Dakota Access Pipeline." *The Republic* (Phoenix, AZ), Nov. 26, 2016, azcentral.com.

Moloney, Anastasia. "The poorest in Guatemala bear brunt of climate change, research says." Thomson Reuters Foundation, reuters.com (Feb. 23, 2020).

Mompó, Maite. *Rainbow Warriors: Legendary Stories from Greenpeace Ships*. Oxford, U.K.: New Internationalist, 2014.

Mooney, James. *History, Myths and Sacred Formulas of the Cherokees*. Asheville, NC: Historical Images, 1992.

Morito, Bruce. "A modern albatross for the ecological approach." *Environmental Values* 12, no. 3 (2003): 317–336.

Mortada, Hisham. *Traditional Islamic Principles of Built Environments*. London, U.K.: RoutledgeCurzon, 2003.

Mosissa, Dereje, and Birhanu Abraha. "A review of conservation of biodiversity in sacred natural sites in Ethiopia: The role of the Ethiopian Orthodox Tewahedo Church." *Plant Science & Research* 5, no. 1 (2018): 1–9.

Mozingo, Louise. *Pastoral Capitalism: A History of Suburban Corporate Landscapes*. Cambridge, MA: MIT Press, 2011.

Muckle, Robert. *The First Nations of British Columbia: An Anthropological Overview*. Vancouver: University of British Columbia Press, 2014.

Muir, John. *My First Summer in the Sierra*. New York: Modern Library, 2003.

Murray, Grant, and Andrew Agyare. "Religion and perceptions of community-based conservation in Ghana, West Africa." *PLoS One*, (2018) doi.org/101371/journal.pone.0195498.

Muzaini, Hamzah. "Heritage landscapes and nation-building in Singapore." In *Changing Landscapes of Singapore: Old Tensions, New Discoveries*, edited by Elaine Ho, Chih Woon, and Kamalini Ramdas, 25–42. Singapore: National University of Singapore Press, 2013.

Mypower. "Let there be light." Mypower, June 2016, mypowercom (22 June 2019).

Naess, Arne. *Ecology, Community and Lifestyle: Outline of an Ecosophy*. New York: Cambridge University Press, 1989.

Nagendra, Harini. *Nature in the City: Bengaluru in the Past, Present and Future*. New Dehli, India: Oxford University Press, 2016.

Naidoo, Robin, L. Chris Weaver, Richard W. Diggle, Greenwell Matongo, Greg Stuart-Hill, and Chris Thouless. "Complementary benefits of tourism and hunting to communal conservancies in Namibia." *Conservation Biology* 30 (2015): 628–638.

Nash, James. *Loving Nature: Ecological Integrity and Christian Responsibility*. Nashville, TN: Abingdon Press, 1991.

Nash, Roderick. *Wilderness and the American Mind*. New Haven, CT: Yale University Press, 1967.

Nasr, Seyyed Hossein. *Religion and the Order of Nature*. Oxford, U.K.: Oxford University Press, 1996.

National Trust. "Lady's Well Holystone, Cragside, Record ID 10024/MNA124666," *National Trust*, https://heritagerecords.nationaltrust.org.uk/HBSMR/ (June 13, 2016).

NCN News Staff. "Michigan church responds to water crisis." *News Church of the Nazarene*, Feb. 6, 2019, Nazarene.org.

Negru, John. *Bodhisattva 4.0: A Primer for Engaged Buddhists*. Ottawa, Canada: Sumeru Press, 2019.

Nelson, Richard. *Make Prayers to the Raven: A Koyukon View of the Northern Forest*. Chicago, IL: University of Chicago Press, 1985.

Nesbitt, Eleanor. "'Deg Tegh Fateh!' Metal as material and metaphor in Sikh tradition." In *Soulless Matter, Seats of Energy: Metals, Gems and Minerals in South Asian Traditions*, edited by Fabrizio M. Ferrari, and Thomas W.P. Dähnhardt, 174–197. Sheffield, U.K.: Equinox, 2016.

New Melleray Abbey. "TrappistCaskets." New Melleray Abbey, trappistcasket.com (Oct. 14, 2016).

Nishikawa, Jun. "The choice of development paradigms in Japan after the 3/11 Fukushima nuclear disaster." In *This Precious Life: Buddhist Tsunami Relief and Anti-Nuclear Activism in Post 3/11 Japan*, edited by Jonathan Watts, loc.1324–1682. Yokahama, Japan: International Buddhist Exchange Center, 2012.

Norenzayan, Ara, and Azim Shariff. "The origin and evolution of religious prosociality." *Science* 322 (2008): 58–62.

Norenzayan, Ara, Azim Shariff, Will Gervis, and others. "The cultural evolution of prosocial religions." *Behavioral and Brain Sciences* 39 (2014): 1–65.

Norgaard, Kari. *Living in Denial: Climate Change, Emotions and Everyday Life*. Cambridge, MA: MIT Press, 2011.

Northcott, Michael. *A Moral Climate: The Ethics of Global Warming*. Maryknoll, NY: Orbis Press, 2007.

Northcott, Michael. *A Political Theology of Climate Change*. Grands Rapids, MI: William B Eerdmans Publishing, 2013.

Norton, Bryan. "Biodiversity and environmental values: In search of a universal earth ethic." *Biodiversity and Conservation* 9 (2000): 1029–1044.

Novak, Barbara. *Nature and Culture: American Landscape and Painting, 1825-1875*. Oxford, U.K.: Oxford University Press, 2007.

O'Faircheallaigh, Ciaran. "Negotiating cultural heritage? Aboriginal–mining company agreements in Australia." *Development and Change* 39 (2008): 25–51.

One Earth Sangha. "*The Time to Act is Now: A Buddhist Declaration on Climate Change*." One Earth Sangha, onearthsangha.org (June 27, 2020).

Orestes, Naomi, and Erik Conway. *Merchants of Doubt: How a Handful of Scientists Obscured the Truth on Issues from Tobacco Smoke to Global Warming*. New York: Bloomsbury Press, 2010.

Orlowska, Izabela, and Peter Keppei. "Ethiopian church forests: A socio-religious conservation model under change." *Journal of Eastern African Studies* 12 (2018): 674–695.

Orsi, Robert. "Everyday miracles: The study of lived religion." In *Lived Religion in America: Toward a History of Practice*, edited by David D. Hall, 3–21. Princeton, NJ: Princeton University Press, 1997.

Oster, Lily. "Decolonizing the sacred." *Sacred Matters: Religious Currents in Culture*, Feb. 3, 2017, sacredmattersmagazine.com/decolonizing-the-sacred/.

Özdemir, Ibrahim. "Toward and understanding of environmental ethics from a Qur'anic perspective." In *Islam and Ecology*, edited by Richard Folta, Frederick Denny, and Azizan Baharuddin, 3–37. Cambridge, MA: Harvard University Press, 2003.

Pacific Rim Institute. *The Pacific Rim Institute*. www.pacificriminstitute.org (March 4, 2019).

Pagels, Elaine. *The Origin of Satan*. New York: Random House, 1995.

Patton, Kimberly Christine. *The Sea can Wash Away All Evils: Modern Marine Pollution and the Ancient Cathartic Ocean*. New York: Columbia University Press, 2007.

Pearson, Joanne, Richard H. Roberts, and Geoffrey Samuel. *Nature Religion Today: Paganism in the Modern World*. Edinburgh, U.K.: University of Edinburgh Press, 1998.

Pearson, Lynn. *Victorian and Edwardian British Industrial Architecture*. Ramsbury, U.K.: Crowood Press, 2016.

Pelly, David. *Sacred Hunt: A Portrait of the Relationship between the Seal and the Inuit*. Seattle: University of Washington Press, 2001.

Perez, Ines. "Climate change and rising food prices heightened Arab Spring." *Scientific American*, March 4, 2013, scientificamerican.com.

Pew Research Center for Religion in Public Life. *The Future of World Religions: Population Growth Projections, 2010-2050*. Boston, MA: Pew-Templeton Global Religious Futures Project, 2015.

Pike, Sarah. *For the Wild: Ritual and Commitment in Radical Eco-Activism*. Oakland: University of California Press, 2017.

Pilkey, Orin, Linda Pilkey-Jarvis, and Keith Pilkey. *Retreat from the Rising Sea: Hard Choices in an Age of Climate Change*. New York: Columbia University Press, 2016.

Pons, Diego, Matthew Taylor, Daniel Griffin, Edwin Castellanos, and Kevin Anchukaitis. "On the production of climate information in the high mountain forests of Guatemala." *Annals of the American Association of Geographers* 107, no. 2 (2017): 323–335.

Pope Francis. *The Encyclical Letter Laudato Si': On Care for Our Common Home*. Mahwah, NJ: Paulist Press, 2015.

Price, Kelly. "Ecology monks in Thailand seek to end environmental suffering." Pulitzer Center, pulitzercenter.org (Aug. 13, 2018).

Prideaux, Gavin, John Long, Linda Ayliffe, John Hellstrom, Brad Pillans, and others. "An arid-adapted middle Pleistocene vertebrate fauna from south-central Australia." *Nature* 445 (2007): 422–425.

Primavesi, Anne, *Gaia and Climate Change: A Theology of Gift Events*. London, U.K.: Routledge, 2009.

Pukui, Mary Kawena, *Hawai'i Island Legends: Pele, Pīkoi, and Others*. Honolulu, HI: Kamehameha Schools, 2010.

Pyne, Stephen. *World Fire: The Culture of Fire on Earth*. New York: Henry Holt and Company, 1995.

Qingxi, Lou. *Traditional Architectural Culture of China*. Beijing, China: Chinese Travel and Tourism Press, 2008.

Queen, Christopher. *Engaged Buddhism in the West*. Sommerville, MA: Wisdom Publications, 2000.

Rackham, Oliver. "Greek landscape: Profane and sacred." In *Human Development in Sacred Landscapes*, edited by Lutz Käppel and Vassiliki Pothou, 35–49. Göttingen, Germany: V&R Unipress, 2015.

Raheb, Mitri. "Creating public space: Observations from the Palestinian context." In *Religious Plurality and the Public Space: Joint Christin-Muslim Theological Reflections*, edited by Simeon Sinn, Mouhanad Khorchide, and Dina el Omari, 119–132. Leipzig, Germany: Evangelische Verlagsanstalt, 2015.

Rapport, Roy. "The obvious aspects of ritual." In *Ecology, Meaning and Religion*, edited by Roy Rapport, 173–321. Richmond, CA: North Atlantic Books, 1979.

Rattue, James. *The Living Stream: Holy Wells in Historical Context*. Woodbridge, U.K.: Boydell Press, 1995.

Reed, A.W. *Māori Myths and Legends*. Auckland, N.Z.: Penguin, 2011.

Regan, James. "Pacific protesters in canoes, kayaks target Australian coal port." *Reuters*, un. mobile,reuters.com (Oct. 17, 2019).

Reichel-Dolmatoff, Gerardo. *Rainforest Shamans: Essays on the Tukano Indians of the Northwest Amazon*. Foxhole, U.K.: Green Books, 1997.

Reilly, Mollie. "New Jersey town to pay millions after denying mosque permit." *Huffpost*, huffpost. com (May 30, 2017).

Reimann, Lena, Athanasios Vafeidis, Sally Brown, Jochen Hinkel, and S.J. Tol. "UNESCO World heritage at risk from coastal flooding and erosion due to sea-level rise." *Nature Communications* 9 (Oct. 16, 2018), article 4161.

Reno, R.R. "The return of Catholic anti-modernism." *First Things*, firstthings.com (June 18, 2015).

Richards, J. Stuart. *Death in the Mines: Disasters and Rescues in the Anthracite Coal Fields of Pennsylvania.* Charleston, SC: The History Press, 2006.

Rio Tinto Corporation. *Argyle Diamonds, Sustainable Development Report 2014.* Rio Tinto Corporation, riotinto.com (11 Dec. 2018a).

Rio Tinto Corporation. *Beauty with Integrity.* Rio Tinto Corporation, riotinto.com (14 Dec. 2018b).

Robb, Carol. *Wind, Sun, Biblical Ethics and Climate Change.* London, U.K.: Taylor & Francis, 2010.

Rochmyaningsih, Dyna. "The Muslim clerics preaching for Indonesia's peat." *Future Planet*, BBC, bbc.com (Mar. 11, 2020).

Rockefeller Center. "Rockefeller Center Christmas Tree." *Tishman Speyer Properties, LP*, rockefeller-center.com (July 29, 2017).

Rodríguez, Sylvia. *Acequia: Water Sharing, Sanctity, and Place.* Santa Fe, NM: School for Advanced Research Resident Scholar Book, 2006.

Rogers, Elizabeth Barlow. *Landscape Design: A Cultural and Architectural History.* New York: Harry N. Abrams, 2001.

Roman Catholic Bishops of the Columbia River Region. *An International Pastoral Letter: The Columbia River Watershed: Caring for Creation and the Common Good*, wacatholics.org/_ui/img/files/crplp.pdf (Jan. 8, 2001).

Rotherham, Ian. *Roman Baths in Britain.* Stroud, U.K.: Amberly Publishing, 2012.

Ruddiman, William. *Plows, Plagues, and Petroleum: How Humans Took Control of Climate.* Princeton, NJ: Princeton University Press, 2005.

Ruelle, Morgan, Karim Aly Kassam, and Zemede Asfaw. "Human ecology of sacred space: Church forests in the highlands of northwestern Ethiopia." *Environmental Conservation* 45, no. 3 (2018): 291–300.

Ruether, Rosemary Radford. *Gaia and God: An Ecofeminist Theology of Earth Healing.* San Francisco, CA: Harper San Francisco, 1992.

Ruether, Rosemary Radford. *Integrating Ecofeminism, Globalization, and World Religions.* Lanham, MD: Rowman & Littlefield Publishers, 2005.

Ruse, Michael. *The Gaia Hypothesis: Science on a Pagan Planet.* Chicago, IL: University of Chicago Press, 2013.

San Diego Union Tribune. "Beijingers re-enact a Qing Dynasty ritual for the Spring Festival," *The San Diego Union-Tribune*, sandiegotribune.com (Feb. 6, 2016).

Sanford, A. Whitney. *Growing Stories from India: Religion and the Fate of Agriculture.* Bowling Green, KY: University Press of Kentucky, 2012.

Sanford, A. Whitney. "Gandhi's agrarian legacy: Practicing, food, justice and sustainability in India." In *Religion and Sustainable Agriculture: World Spiritual Traditions and Food Ethics*, edited by Todd LeVasseur, Pramond Parajuli, and Norman Wirzba, 153–172. Lexington: University of Kentucky Press, 2016.

Schaeffer, Francis. *Pollution and the Death of Man.* Wheaton, IL: Tyndall House, 1970.

Schillaci, Michael, Gregory Engel, Agustin Fuentes, Aida Rompis, Arta Putra, I. Nengah Wandia, James Bailey, B.G. Brogdon, and Lisa Jones-Engel. "The Not-So-Sacred Monkeys of Bali: A Radiographic Study of Human-Primate Commensalism." In *Indonesian Primates, Developments in Primatology: Progress and Prospects*, edited by S. Gursky-Doyen and J. Supriatna, 249–256. New York, NY: Springer Science, 2010.

Schjonberg, Mary. "'Winter Count' brings indigenous storytelling method to the Gospel: Niobrara Convocation combines Episcopal, Sioux traditions." *Episcopal News Service*, episcopaldigitalnetwork.com (June 25, 2012).

Schramm, James Martin. "We rise: Climate Justice Week." *Luther College, Decorah, Iowa*, April 30, 2019, luther.edu (June 17, 2019).

Shaltout, Mohamed, and Anders Omstedt. "Sea-level change and projected future flooding along the Egyptian Mediterranean coast." *Oceanologia* 57, no. 4 (2015): 293–207.

Shariff, Azim, and Ara Norenzayan. "God is watching you: Priming god concepts increases prosocial behavior in an anonymous economic game." *Psychological Science* 18 (2007): 803–809.

Sharp, P.M., and B.H. Hahn. "Origins of HIV and the AIDS pandemic." *Cold Spring Harbor Perspectives in Medicine* 1, no. 1 (2011): a006841, doi:10.1101/cshperspect.a006841.

Sheldrake, Philip. *Spaces for the Sacred: Place Memory, and Identity.* Baltimore, MD: Johns Hopkins University Press, 2001.

Sheridan, Michael, and Celia Nyamweru. *African Sacred Groves: Ecological Dynamics & Social Change.* Athens, OH: Ohio University Press, 2018.

Shiva, Vandana, *Staying Alive: Women Ecology and Development.* Berkeley, CA: North Atlantic Books, 2016.

Shorthand, Edward. *Māori Religion and Mythology.* Auckland, N.Z.: Paphos Publishers, 2015.

Shu, Wang, and Lan Peijin. *Lamasery of Harmony and Peace.* Beijing, China: Foreign Languages Press, 2002.

Sideris, Lisa. *Consecrating Science: Wonder, Knowledge, and the Natural World.* Oakland: University of California Press, 2017.

Sidky, H. *The Origins of Shamanism, Spirit, Beliefs, and Religiosity: A Cognitive Anthropological Perspective.* Lanham, MD: Lexington Books, 2017.

Silver, Harris. "The Rockefeller Center Christmas tree: Not as green as it looks." *The Huffington Post*, Huffpost.com/entry/Rockefeller-center-christmas-tree_b_1125549 (Dec. 12, 2011).

Sinn, Simeon, Mouhamad Khorchide, and Dina el Omari, eds. *Religious Plurality and the Public Space: Joint Christin-Muslim Theological Reflections.* Leipzig, Germany: Evangelische Verlagsanstalt, 2016.

Sittler, Joseph. *Evocations of Grace: The Writings of Joseph Sittler on Ecology, Theology, and Ethics.* Grand Rapids, MI: Wm. B. Eerdmans, 2000.

Sliva, Julia, and Alfons Mosimane. "Conservation-based rural development in Namibia: A mixed-methods assessment of economic benefits." *Journal of Environment & Development* 22 no. 1, (2012): 25–50.

Smelcer, John, ed. *The Raven & The Totem: Alaska Native Myths and Legends.* Kirksville, MO: Naciketas Press, 2015.

Snyder, Gary. *Mountains and Rivers Without End.* Berkeley, CA: Counterpoint, 1996.

Sorrell, Roger. *St Francis of Assisi and Nature: Tradition and Innovation in Western Christianity.* Oxford, U.K.: Oxford University Press, 1988.

Sosis, Richard, and Bradley J. Ruffle. "Religious ritual and cooperation: Testing for a relationship on Israeli religious and secular Kibbutzim." *Current Anthropology* 44 (2003): 713–722.

Spiro, Amy. "Synagogues taking the LEED on greening." *The Jewish Week: Connecting the World to Jewish News, Culture, and Opinion*, thejewishweek.com (Aug. 15, 2011).

St. James Church. *Illustrated Guide to St. James's Church Piccadilly.* London, U.K.: St. James's Church, 1966.

St. James Church. *St. James Church Piccadilly London*, sjp.org.uk (June 13, 2019).

St. Olaf's College. "Carbon." *Facilities Department, St. Olaf's College*, wp.stolaf.edu/faciltiesdepartment/ energyand utilities/carbon (Feb. 8, 2020).

Standing Rock Sioux Tribe. "Memorandum in support of motion for preliminary injunction," attached to "Motion for Preliminary Injunction Request for Expedited Hearing," Case No. 1:16-cv-1534-JEB, filed in The United States District Court for the District of Columbia, Aug. 4, 2016.

Stanley, John, David Loy, and Gyurme Dorje, eds. *A Buddhist Response to The Climate Emergency.* Sommerville, MA: Wisdom Publications, 2009.

Starhawk (Miriam Simos). *The Spiral Dance: A Rebirth of the Religion of the Great Goddess.* New York: Harper, 1979.

Starhawk (Miriam Simos). *The Earth Path: Grounding Your Spirit in the Rhythms of Nature*. New York: HarperOne, 2005.

Stark, Rodney. *What Americans Really Believe*. Waco, TX: Baylor University Press, 2008.

Steadman, David. *Extinction & Biogeography of Tropical Pacific Birds*. Chicago, IL: University of Chicago Press. 2006.

Stevenson, Marc. "Aboriginal peoples and traditional knowledge: A course correction for sustainable forestry." In *Aboriginal Peoples and Forest Lands in Canada*, edited by D.B. Tindall, Ronald Trosper, and Pamela Perreault, 114–128. Vancouver: University of British Columbia Press, 2013.

Stewart, Hilary. *Cedar*. Seattle, WA: University of Washington Press, 1984.

Stoll, Mark. *Inherit the Holy Mountain: Religion and the Rise of American Environmentalism*. Oxford U.K.: Oxford University Press, 2015.

Stranahan, Susan. *Susquehanna, River of Dreams*. Baltimore, MD: Johns Hopkins University Press, 1995.

Straughan, Baird, and Tom Pollack. *The Broader Movement: Nonprofit Environmental and Conservation Organizations, 1989–2005*. Washington, DC: The Urban Institute, 2008.

Stuart, Tristam. *The Bloodless Revolution: Radical Vegetarians and the Discovery of India*. New York: Harper Collins, 2012.

Stuart-Fox, David. *Pura Busakih: Temples, Religion and Society in Bali*. Leiden, Netherlands: KITLV Press, 2003.

Summerson, John. *Architecture in Britain, 1530–1830*, Vol. 3. New Haven, CT: Yale University Press, 1993.

Swanton, John. *Haida Texts and Myths*. Washington, DC: U.S. Bureau of Ethnography, Smithsonian Institution, Bulletin 29, 1905.

Swimme, Brian, and Mary Evelyn Tucker. *The Journey of the Universe*. New Haven, CT: Yale University Press, 2011.

Swinomish Indian Tribal Community. *Swinomish Climate Change Initiative: Climate Adapatation Action Plan*. Anacortes, WA: Swinomish Tribal Community, Swinomish-nsn.gov, 2010.

Takeda, Louise. *Islands' Spirit's Rising: Reclaiming the Forests of Haida Gwaii*. Vancouver: University of British Columbia Press, 2015.

Tal, Alon. *Pollution in a Promised Land: An Environmental History of Israel*. Berkeley: University of California Press, 2002.

Tan, Tian. *The Temple of Heaven: The World Cultural Heritage in Beijing*. Beijing, China: Beijing Arts and Photography Publishing House, 2008.

Tauger, Mark. *Agriculture in World History*. New York: Routledge, 2011.

Taylor, Bron. "Exploring religion, nature, and culture: Introducing the *Journal for the Study of Religion, Nature, and Culture*." *Journal for the Study of Religion, Nature, and Culture* 1, no. 1 (2007): 5–24.

Taylor, Bron. *Dark Green Religion: Nature, Spirituality, and the Planetary Future*. Berkeley: University of California Press, 2010.

Taylor, Joseph E. III. *Making Salmon: An Environmental History of the Northwest Fisheries Crisis*. Seattle: University of Washington, Press, 1999.

Taylor, Sarah. *Green Sisters: A Spiritual Ecology*. Cambridge, MA: Harvard University Press, 2007.

Thirgood, J.V. *Man and the Mediterranean Forest: A History of Resource Depletion*. New York: Academic Press, 1981.

Thomas, Keith. *Man and the Natural World: A History of the Modern Sensibility*. New York: Pantheon Books, 1983.

Thomas, Peter, and Robert McAlpine. *Fire in the Forest*. Cambridge, U.K.: Cambridge University Press, 2010.

Thompson, Andrew. *Sacred Mountains: A Christian Ethical Approach to Mountaintop Removal*. Lexington: University of Kentucky Press, 2015.

Tilahun, Abiyou, Hailu Terefe, and Teshome Soromessa. "The contribution of Ethiopian Orthodox Tewahido Church in forest management and its best practices to be scaled up in North Shewa Zone of Amhara Region, Ethiopia." *Agriculture, Forestry and Fisheries* 4, no. 3 (2015): 123–137.

Tooker, E., ed. *Native North American Spirituality of the Eastern Woodlands*. Mahwah, NJ: Paulist Press, 1979.

Tortajada, Cecilia, Yugal Joshi, and Asit Biswas. *The Singapore Water Story: Sustainable Development in an Urban City-State*. London, U.K.: Routledge, 2013.

Tulku, Ringu. (2009) "The bodhisattva path at a time of crisis." In *A Buddhist Response to The Climate Emergency*, edited by John Stanley, David R. Loy, and Gyurme Dorje, 126–139. Sommerville, MA: Wisdom Publications, 2009.

UNESCO. "My Son Sanctuary." *UNESCO World Heritage List*, whc.unesco.org (Jan. 1, 2020).

Urban, Hugh, *New Age, Neopagan, & New Religious Movements: Alternative Spirituality in Contemporary America*. Berkeley: University of California Press, 2015.

U.S. Court of Appeals for the Ninth Circuit, No. 17-71636, LULAC v. Wheeler, filed August 9, 2018.

U.S. Green Building Council. "Baylor University." *Projects*, usgbc.org (March 15, 2020).

U.S. Government, Pub. L. 95-341, Aug. 11, 1978, 92 Stat. 469.

U.S. National Park Service. "National Christmas Tree." *President's Park (White House)*, nps.com (July 29, 2017).

Vecsey, Christopher. *Handbook of American Indian Religious Freedom*. Hertford, NC: Crossroads Press, 1991.

Veldman, Robyn Globus. *The Gospel of Climate Skepticism: Why Evangelical Christians Oppose Action on Climate Change*. Oakland: University of California Press, 2019.

Veldman, Robyn Globus, Andrew Szasz, and Randolph Haluza-Delay. *How the World's Religions Are Responding to Climate Change: Social Scientific Investigations*. London, U.K.: Routledge, 2014.

Vershuuren, Bas, and Steve Brown, eds. *Cultural and Spiritual Significance of Nature in Protected Areas: Governance, Management, and Policy*. Abingdon, U.K.: Routledge, 2019.

Vershuuren, Bas, Robert Wild, Jeffery A. McNeely, and Gonzolo Oviedo, eds. *Sacred Natural Sites: Conserving Nature & Culture*. Abingdon, U.K.: Earthscan, Routledge, 2010.

Walbert, David. *Garden Spot: Lancaster County, the Old Order Amish, and the Selling of Rural America*. Oxford, U.K.: Oxford University Press, 2002.

Walker, Alice. *The Color Purple*. New York: Harcourt Brace Janovitch, 1982.

Walker, David. "Railroading independence: Pulpit Rock and the work of Mormon observation." *John Whitmer Historical Association Journal* 37, no. 1 (2017): 29–50.

Walsham, Alexandra. *The Reformation of the Landscape: Religion, Identity, & Memory in Early Modern Britain & Ireland*. Oxford, U.K.: Oxford University Press, 2011.

Walters, K. and Lisa, Portmess. *Religious Vegetarianism: From Hesiod to the Dalai Lama*. Albany: State University of New York Press, 2001.

Wandel, Lee. *Voracious Idols and Violent Hands: Iconoclasm in Reformation Zurich, Strasbourg, and Basel*. Cambridge, U.K.: Cambridge University Press, 1995.

Wapner, Paul. "In defense of banner hangers: The dark green politics of Greenpeace." In *Ecological Resistance Movements: The Global Emergence of Radical Popular Environmentalism*, edited by Bron Taylor, 300–314. Albany: State University of New York Press, 1995.

Watson, Bruce. *Light: A Radiant History from Creation to the Quantum Age*. New York: Bloomsbury Press, 2016.

Watt, Alan. *Farm Workers and the Churches: The Movement in California and Texas*. College Station, TX: Texas A&M University Press, 2010.

Watts, Jonathan, ed. *This Precious Life: Buddhist Tsunami Relief and Anti-Nuclear Activism in Post 3/11 Japan*. Yokohama, Japan: International Buddhist Exchange Center, 2012.

Weber, Max. *The Protestant Ethic and the Spirit of Capitalism*. New York: Routledge, 2001.

West, Esme, ed. *Gloucester Cathedral, Faith, Art, and Architecture: 1000 Years*. London, U.K.: SCALA, 2011.

West, Michael, and Suzanna, Smith. "Diamonds are not forever: Indigenous communities grapple with the end of mining boom." *Australian Broadcasting Corporation News*, June 28, 2017, abc.net.au.

Wethe, David, and Ryan, Sachetta. "Oklahoma shuts more oil fracking waste wells as quake upgraded." *Bloomberg Markets*, Sept. 7, 2016, bloomberg.com.

Weyler, Rex. *Greenpeace: How A Group of Ecologists, Journalists and Visionaries Changed the World.* Richmond, Canada: Raincoast Books, 2004.

White, Lynn, Jr. "The historic roots of our ecological crisis." *Science* 1955 (1967): 1203–1207.

Williston, Byron. *The Ethics of Climate Change: An Introduction.* Abingdon, U.K.: Routledge, 2019.

Willoya, William, and Vinson Brown. *Warriors of the Rainbow: Strange and Prophetic Dreams of the Indian Peoples.* Healdsburg, CA: Naturegraph, 1962.

Wilson, Lynette. "Peaceful, prayerful, nonviolent standoff solidarity with the Standing Rock Sioux." *Episcopal News Service*, Nov. 5, 2016, episcopaldigitalnetwork.com.

Wirzba, Norman. *Food & Faith: A Theology of Eating.* Cambridge, U.K.: Cambridge University Press, 2011.

Witt, Joseph D. *Religion and Resistance in Appalachia: Faith and the Fight Against Mountaintop Removal Coal Mining.* Lexington: University of Kentucky Press, 2016.

Wolf, Aaron. *The Spirit of Dialogue: Lessons from Faith Traditions in Transforming Conflict.* Washington, DC: Island Press, 2017.

World Health Organization. *Artisanal and Small Scale Gold Mining and Health.* Geneva, Switzerland: World Health Organization, 2016.

World Health Organization. *Ebola virus disease: Fact sheet No. 103.* who.int/mediacentre/factsheets/fs103/en/, 2014.

Worthy, T.H. and R.N. Holdaway. *The Lost World of the Moa: Prehistoric Life of New Zealand.* Bloomington: Indiana University Press, 2002.

Yasuda, Yumiko, Julianne Schillinger, Patrick Huntjens, Charlotte Alofs, and Rens de Man. *Transboundary Water Cooperation Over the Lower Part of the Jordan River Basin: Legal Political Economy Analysis of Current and Future Potential Coorperation.* The Hague, Netherlands: The Hague Institute for Global Justice, 2017.

Zaleha, Bernard, and Andrew Szasz. "Keep Christianity brown! Climate denial on the Christian Right in the United States." In *How the World's Religions are Responding to Climate Change: Social Scientific Investigations*, edited by Robyn Globus Veldman, Andrew Szasz, and Randolph Haluza-Delay, 208–228. London, U.K.: Routledge, 2014.

Zamore, Mary, ed. *The Sacred Table: Creating a Jewish Food Ethic.* New York: Central Conference of Reform Rabbis, 2011.

Zelko, Frank. *Making it a Green Peace: The Rise of Countercultural Environmentalism.* Oxford, U.K.: Oxford University Press, 2013.

Index